PURANA PURUSHA

YOGIRAJ SRI SHAMA CHURN LAHIREE

Dr. Ashoke Kumar Chatterjee D. Litt.

Translator **Joyati Kapur**

(Translated from the Bengali original into English)

Publisher :
Alok Chatterjee
YOGIRAJ PUBLICATION
26A/9, S. B. Neogi Garden Lane
Kolkata-700 036, India
Fax : 91-33-2577-5986
E-mail : yogiraj@cal2.vsnl.net.in

1st Edition - January, 2000
2nd Edition - July, 2001
3rd Edition - May, 2004

ISBN 81-87563-01-X

Price : Rs.400/-

Printer :
Royal Halftone Co.
4, Sarkar Bye Lane,
Kolkata - 700 007

Composer :
Neha Commercial Designeers Pvt. Ltd.
161/1, M. G. Road,
Bangur Building
3rd floor, Room No. 75
Kolkata - 700 007

— TASMAI SRI GURUVE NAMAH

CONTENTS

FOREWORD

Purāṇá Púrusha is the *Gītā* of *Satyáyuga*. This is significant because of the loftiness of thought inherent in the book. Initially, it is certainly not possible for mortals like us to decipher it's intrinsic implication. But of course if we delve deep into it and make a studious effort to glean the latent meaning then surely we should be able to succeed. Again the question may arise, how sure can we be of succeeding to comprehend the depth of thought inherent in it? This is possible only by the Grace of the *Sadgurú*. Who is this *Sadgurú*? Dear reader, I wish to impress upon you that *Sadgurú* is none other than God Himself. Thus there is only one *Sadgurú*. His Grace is showered only if we are sincere and diligent in our efforts.

Gītā universally is regarded as a scripture. It was narrated by Bhagavan Krishna and composed by Krishna-Dvaipayana-Vyasadeva. Vyasadeva was born in a black island i.e. *Kútastha*. *Kútastha* is Krishna. Therefore this infers that Vyasadeva is none other than the partial manifestation of Bhagavan Krishna. When the *Gītā* was composed i.e. in the end of *Dvāpárayuga*, how many understood it's real significance then? But as we note today, it has attained a worldwide eminence.

The incarnations *(avatāras)* of God are not His full-fledged manifestations, but only partial. God makes His Advent only at the juncture of two *yugas* when humanity suffers a religious decadence. However, there may be an exception to this rule when according to His discretion, He may mark His Readvent within a short span. He wholly manifests Himself in the Form of a Human Being to enable us mortals to come closer to Him, to enable us divulge all our afflictions and joys to Him and also in order to impart His teachings to us. If He appears in any other Form, it would never be possible for us to be close to Him. Being born as a Mortal, He does not break His own rule i.e. He has to abide by the mortal afflictions, sorrows, etc. This rigorous discipline on His part is intended for our upliftment and knowledge. We notice that at the end of *Trétāyuga* (in *Satyayuga* His Advent was not necessary, because then each and everyone were engaged in *Kriyāyoga Brahma-sādhana*) and the beginning of *Dvāparáyuga*, when 25% of people deviated from *yógasādhana*, He made His Advent as Bhagavan Ramachandra. Again at the juncture of *Dvāparáyuga* and *Káliyuga* when the deviation was augmented to 50%, He appeared as Bhagavan Krishna. Again during the last phase of *Káliyuga* when almost every individual had deviated from the *Sanātána* path, God appeared as Sri Shama Churn Lahiree and revived this *Sanātána Kriyāyoga* amongst the masses.

Now comes the crux of the matter. It has been stated that God arrives only at the juncture of two *yugas* when there is a religious decline. However, there may be an extremely rare exception to this rule. In accordance to His discretion He may reappear. But why should this occur? That is because the occasion may necessitate His arrival. He had referred to this in a subtle innuendo :— ***Hum phir jāgeṅge*** — I shall appear again. As we go through the book, we will note that Shama Churn Lahiree had informed about His Departure to His wife Kashimani Devi six months in advance and had asked her to retain His Mortal Frame in the *padmâsana* posture or to place this under the ground of the same room after His Departure, for He would mark His Readvent. For reasons best known to Him, Kashimani Devi completely forgot this, hence His Mortal Frame was cremated.

Hence, the question is why did He decide to make His Readvent ? The reasons are :—

1. To compile all His *sādhana* realisations recounted in His

twenty-six confidential diaries in the form of a revived scripture.

When God Himself made His Advent at the end of *Trétāyuga* in the Form of Bhagavan Ramachandra, then He Himself did not compose *Rāmāyana*, it was composed by another manifestation of Him, Valmiki. Again at the end of *Dvāpárayuga* when God marked His Readvent in the Form of Bhagavan Krishna then He did not compose *Mahābharata* and *Gītā* Himself, this task was accomplished by Krishna-Dvaipayana-Vyasadeva, His alternate manifestation. Likewise, when God made His Readvent at the end of *Káliyuga* in the Form of Shama Churn, *Purāná Púrusha* the scripture manifested in the same manner.

2. The mammoth significance of the scripture in this age was foreseen, for His principal aim was to re-establish His Own ideals and give declining *Kriyāyoga* a push. Thus in this manner at the transition of each *yuga* in accordance with it's respective necessity, God establishes His Own ideals.

3. The world has already entered into *Satyáyuga* after His Departure, but the influence of *Káliyuga* still persists. The golden influence of *Satyáyuga* will attain it's full bloom within a short period. He decided to usher humanity into the golden efflorescence of *Satyáyuga* and depart. Thus from this point of time, the full-fledged Advent of God is certainly not necessary till the end of that era which lasts for about 50,000 years.

4. To issue summons to mankind :— "Arise, awake, you have enjoyed enough, suffered enough, known enough. The goal of your human existence should be solely one i.e. to seek salvation. Drown yourself totally in this *Kriyāyoga sādhana* for if not in this birth, within the successive few births you will inevitably attain salvation." He advises us to be childlike. Just as a child is innocent, surrenders himself totally to his mother

and diligently obeys her command, similarly we should possess this childlike attribute and surrendering ourselves wholly obey the *Sadgurú's* command.

My *Gurúdeva* has advised us to reorient our lives by constantly ruminating, contemplating, cogitating, communing, reminiscing and discussing on Yogiraj. In other words, we should make endeavours for our whole entity to be pervaded by Yogiraj, the Almighty. This is his only message to mankind.

Nothing pains my *Gurúdeva* more than the non-practice of *Kriyā* on our part, for his mission is to emancipate us. He will be happy if his objective is fulfilled. No wealth, sycophancy, opulence and murmuring pleasantries will ever appease him. Only the practice of *Kriyāyoga sādhana* on our part can propitiate him.

'*Purāná Púrusha*' is a composite scriptural work by my Revered Gurudeva Yogacharya Dr. Ashoke Kumar Chatterjee intended to be a biography. But in course of time as *Kriyāyoga* gradually spreads it's tentacles throughout the world, it will bind man towards it and make him realise that this *Kriyāyoga* is the sole and exclusive religion i.e. *Sanātaná Dhárma* - that was, that is and that will be. God is One, therefore it is imperative that religion also has to be one. This scripture is aimed at delineating the domestic life, life of *sādhana, sādhana* realizations and the ideals and precepts of Yogiraj Sri Shama Churn Lahiree. From this we can deduce that to enter the spiritual path we do not need to be a renunciate, we can simultaneously practise *sādhana* and maintain a domestic existence. We hereby observe that Yogiraj has beautifully juxtaposed His family life alongwith His life of *sādhana*.

Sanātaná Kriyāyoga has been revived by Yogiraj and is exclusively and absolutely based on science and rationality. There is no scope of emotion here, I repeat, no emotion at all. My Revered *Gurúdeva* has often stated that he has detailed all the facts about

Yogiraj from the Latter's twenty-six diaries. Apparently to all of us, this seems to be the truth but have we made assays regarding this? No. We have heard him mentioning this several times, but we have declined to ponder about the actual truth. Had anyone of us been assigned this task of compiling the biography of Yogiraj with the help of twenty-six diaries, would we have been able to accomplish this mammoth feat? Never. The author has meticulously detailed each and every fact about the life of Yogiraj — the product being ***'Purāṇá Púrusha'***, a scripture for the future generation. Why we would never be able to accomplish this noble feat is simple. Who else can write about the biography of Bhagavan Krishna-Shama Churn?

Moreover ***'Kriyāyoga*** and ***Advaitabād'*** another book of his, is an annotation of one hundred of the several quotations of Yogiraj and his last and final book ***'Who is this Shama Churn'*** will reveal to the discerning reader the truth which has since long been concealed.

Let us go back to where we began. ***'Purāṇá Púrusha'*** has been compared with the *Gītā*. Should not we weigh the magnitude of such a comparison? We must pause and contemplate thus; who else in this world can be the composer of this? Need I say more? I leave it for the reader to ascertain.

The ennobling experience of translating this scripture has chastened me, my life having attained a wholly new significance. I bow at the Lotus Feet of my Revered *Gurúdeva* and am grateful for the blessings showered upon me and pray to him to bless soul-seekers, so that in the future they can completely realise the total concept of Yogiraj from ***'Purāṇá Púrusha'***, ***'Kriyāyoga*** and ***Advaitabād'*** and ***'Who is this Shama Churn'***. I would prefer the reader to know that it is he only who has penned all my thoughts while translating the book.

I am indebted to my *Gurúdeva* who has showered his infinite grace on me for the marvellous realisations I have experienced while working on the translation. These realisations have immensely assisted me in humbly assessing the subtle nuances of the scripture.

Here I wish to note that apart from showering his infinite grace, he has been gracious and kind to be physically present from time to time (finding time off from his domestic, official, epistolary routine, counselling devotees and practising *sādhana*) to guide me verbatim et litteratim and with meticulous detail so that no fact or theory is distorted as it may prove harmful for the future generation.

It is indeed a misfortune that today due to religious groupism, sectarianism, unrest and bartering, the true *Kriyāyoga* as has been revived by Yogiraj is on the verge of extinction. Whatever is being imparted under the guise of *Kriyāyoga* from some corners is basically a sham. Since *Kriyāyoga* is absolutely scientific, this imposture has proved detrimental to quite a number of innocent and devout people who are actually unaware of it's exactness, thereby being deprived. However, it can be vouched that this book will serve as a guide to the reader seeking *Kriyāyoga* which has been revived by Yogiraj Himself.

Yogiraj and *Kriyāyoga* are inextricable. He is the embodiment of *Kriyāyoga*. Yogiraj and *Kriyāyoga* are eternal. He is complementary to *Kriyāyoga*. *Kriyāyoga* is the science of the path by which a human being can gradually and steadily progress towards attaining oneness; merging with Yogiraj and becoming Yogiraj Himself. In other words the attainment of salvation exclusively and wholly infers Yogiraj.

Since He is the Absolute, He has conferred an exalted position to *Kriyābans* (ones initiated into *Kriyāyoga* and practising it) by terming them as *yogis* and *devátās*. Throughout this *sāstrá*

'Purāṇá Púrusha', the reader will come across these appellations. Because Yogiraj is the Fountain-Head of *Kriyāyoga*, it is imperative that all sincere, austere, devout and industrious *Kriyābāns* will finally merge in that Fountain-Head, thus Yogiraj has conferred the appellation *'yogis'* to them. But in actuality what is the true concept of *'yogi'? Yogi* is One, thus *Yogi* is Absolute *Brahma*. A *Kriyābān* or *devátā* is an aspirant *yogi* in his path of *sādhana*. *Devátā* infers one who dwells in void. The root of void is *Brahma* so all deities merge in Absolute Void *Brahma*. An aspirant *yogi* can at the most attain merging; but after he has attained this he becomes One and Absolute, thereby losing his entity and merging with *Brahma*. But after he has attained this state of mergence, he can neither express this state of merging or express the fact that he has merging with the Absolute become a *yogi* or God himself. His realisation ends at the precise moment he attains the state of Godhood or till he himself metamorphoses into a *yogi*. Only Yogiraj having the Divine Prerogative to attain the post attainment state of merging has recounted this and thus declared the Omnific Words — 'I Am God' in His diary which the reader will glean from Chapter-IX.

Dear reader, I fervently pray to Him for enlightenment to dawn upon you — that Shama Churn is Indefinable, Unquestionable, Non-answerable, Incomparable, Non-debatable, Unconfinable, Indivisible. He can be defined as; questionable to; answerable to, compared with; debated for and against; confined within; divided by; none other than Shama Churn Himself. He is Unquestionable for He is Univocal. He is the Only and Eternal Truth. This was, is and will be the Absolute Knowledge. So no matter how hard various factions try to establish their credentials in Shama Churn's name, they will die a natural death, for pretentiousness in the name of the Primordial and Absolute cannot exist for long.

Soul and Yogiraj are inextricable. Therefore Yogiraj and Soul are Omnipresent. Thus this Omnipresence exists within all of us. In this regard a pithy saying of my *Gurúdeva* may be recalled that this book will be beneficial for soul-lovers in whose lives the influence of *Satyáyuga* has commenced.

I wish to make six pertinent points to the reader. The first is that it is absolutely imperative for the reader to keep in mind that this book is not a run-of-the-mill biography. Spiritual and philosophical connotations given in this book are unique. They have been harmoniously represented and blended. In this context I would request the foreign reader to kindly note that since English is an ever-growing language, new words have been coined in this book because of it's intrinsic philosophical concept, which he may not be acquainted with and as this book is based on *yóga* realisations, the repetitiveness in style is but inevitable.

The second is that it has been extremely difficult to exactly translate these connotations expounded in the original Bengali book (first published in July 1981) into English. The principal reason for this is that any Indian language is afferent especially in the *yóga* concept. But we have been absolutely faithful and established a close harmony with the original, so that the reader can lose himself in the spiritual nuances of Yogiraj. However, certain Indian words on *yóga* have been retained (for which a Glossary has been provided) so that they do not lose their essence and significance.

The pedantic style adopted at times should be excused, for it has been used to explain the concept of Yogiraj. The discerning reader will surely envisage that since Yogiraj is God Himself and not Mahapurusha or Avatara, it will certainly not be proper to ascribe phrases or words in common usage to Him, be it in the noun, verb, adjectival or adverbial forms. Therefore, it follows suit that the Absolute need solely be explained in a language coined to be rigorously absolute.

Paying due attention to the foreign reader's desire to pronounce these words in the Indian way, we have scrupulously followed the accents in Monier Williams's Sanskrit-English Dictionary.

The third is that epithets like *'visualisation', realisation', 'visualise'. 'envisage', 'envision', 'perceive', 'realise'* etc. used to delineate Shama Churn's progress in the path of *sādhana* or that of a *yogi's* are not sensory, they are suprasensory, hence should be regarded as transcendental.

Fourthly, the name 'Shama Churn Lahiree' has been spelt in accordance with the spelling He has used in several places in His signature.

Fifthly, Shama Churn is God Almighty. But Shama Churn has been referred to by the pronoun 'He', 'Him', 'His' etc. It is the inevitable truth that God cannot be ascribed by any pronouns but to avoid erroneous grammatical monotony and effect correct grammatical uniformity and a lucidity in comprehension to the reader, the pronouns have been used. God cannot be specified by any particular gender as God is Omnigender, Omnineutral, all genders evolve from Him, thus He is free from genders.

Finally, it has taken ten years of laborious endeavours to translate the book. The English version is replete with subtle copious details to facilitate the foreign reader to grasp the yoga-essence, which was not necessary in the Bengali original. Therefore the book is greater in volume than the Bengali book and is invaluable. All inclusions in the translation have been done in the author's presence with his due approval.

As Shama Churn is Absolute and Almighty we cannot describe Him to be Ambidextrous. In this regard Shama Churn declared thus— "I have no hands and feet. I only am the Orbed Indivisible Infinity. My Effulgence pervades the whole creation". In *Sanātána Dhárma*, the word 'ambidextrous' has been applied to Arjuna, not to God.

I conclude here by humbly bowing at the Lotus Feet of My *Gurúdeva* and pray to him to kindly bless all the translations of this book, so that the future generation reveres it universally as a scripture and affirm it to be the be-all and end-all of their lives.

Joyati Kapur

N.B.

(1) The intrinsic significance of '*Purānā Púrusha*' has been expatiated from Pages 236 - 239 of Chapter-IX. (See Gl. also)

(2) Expatiation of the term "Yogiraj" :—

Unison with God through *yóga* bears an equivalence with the term "*Yogeśvara*". First let us consider what is designated to be *yóga*? Regarding this Rishi Patanjala has thus exposed — ***"Niścintya yóga ucyate"***. The thought-free state is *yóga*. When does the mind attain freedom from thoughts? When *Prâṇá* ceases, in other words on the cessation of *Prâṇá*-dynamism when confluence with the still *Prâṇá* is effected, this state is designated to be *yóga*. In this state—mind, thoughts etc. are all absent. In short, the still state is *yóga*. Conversely union of the two is also termed as *yóga*. This also is an analogous statement, that is causation of mergence of dynamic *Prâṇá* with still *Prâṇá*. Dynamic *Prâṇá* originates from still *Prâṇá*, hence the total creation. Later when vibratory *Prâṇá* attains confluence with *Prâṇá* in statice then nothingness prevails. This state of nothingness is *yóga*.

Now let us consider what the appellation *Īśvara* infers. *Ī*=power of observation latent in the eyes; *śva*=breathing motion; *ra*=heat essence latent in the navel. The action of inhalation and exhalation is controlled by the heat essence, in other words, continually executing the breathlike arrow or *Prâṇâyāma*, the soul power which emanates is *Īśvara* only. When the incessant breathing motion which externally continues through the medium of the heat essence is with fortitude oriented internally and through this medium of internal orientation of the breathing motion, the state of *Īśvara* evdves. Only a *yogi* and none other can achieve this still state. The one who perpetually exists in the sublimely static *Brahma*, He only is *Yogeśvara*. For this reason *Mahādevá* or Krishna is termed *Yogeśvara*. Shama Churn also would abide in perpetuity in the same state "*Niścalam Brahma Ucyate*". The eternal static state is assigned as *Brahma*. Shama Churn Himself is Static thus He has made the emphatic solemn assertion,

"I only am Amorphous *Brahma*". He Himself being Amorphous, Static *Brahma*, He is *Yogeśvara* or Yogiraj. 'Raj' denotes principal or pivotal and Supreme, thus the term Yogiraj signifies One Who is Supreme amongst *yógis*, in other words He Himself is the Origin or the Fountain-Head and the ultimate mergence and destination of all *yógis*. This implies eventually after practising *yógasādhana* austerely when *yógis* attain mergence with the Sublime Statice, that *Brahma* only is Yogiraj Himself. Thus *Yogeśvara* and Yogiraj are inseparable.

INTRODUCTION

Late Gopinath Kaviraj, the most eminent and great scholar, and many other illustrious persons expressed their desire that I should write a full length biography of my Departed grandfather, Yogiraj Shama Churn Lahiree Mahasaya. The reason why they were so eager to get me to write such a biography lies in the fact that I possess twenty-six diaries of my grandfather, which were written by Him and that I constantly remained with my father and was his affectionate son, thereby having access to relevant information regarding my grandfather.

Most of the saints and sages who adorned the mythological period were all family men. In the midst of their family preoccupations, they practised *sādhana* and the direct realisations which they attained cannot be noticed in thousands of years. But though the great Lahiree Mahasaya passed His whole life as a family man serving the government, drawing pension and eventually engaging Himself as a private tutor, He practised *sādhana* and through the medium of self-realisation, introspection and divine sound made a quest for the spiritual world, which it is doubtful, has been ever achieved by anyone else in this age. It is doubtless that in the path of *yóga*, after the Great Soul Kabirdas, the only Sādhaka with direct self-realization is none other than the Great Lahiree Mahasaya. Many, specially the devotees of the Great Lahiree Mahasaya were under the notion that the Great Kavirdas himself was born again in this world in a noble Brahmin family in the name of Shama Churn Lahiree. Though there has not been any direct proof of this Re-Advent, yet a comparision of the sayings of the Great Kabirdas with that of the Sublime Lahiree Mahasaya obtained from His direct realisations in His own diaries justify the strength and fairness of such a belief. The Great Kabirdas was a householder till he breathed his last, and the Great Lahiree Mahasaya also was the same. Kabirdas used to chant — ***Rimi jhimi rimi jhimi cādariyā bini re*** (let me weave my sheets in harmony with the melodious rhythmical sound of a weaving shuttle). Having been reared up in the family of a weaver, he took up weaving as his profession but always would remain in *sādhanā's parābāsthā* (i.e. a state of being totally merged in the Absolute —a state which is achieved only by a *yogi* through his constant *yóga* practice). Lahiree Mahasaya also remained in the same state. By perpetually abiding in this state, He too used to perform His daily tasks at ease. This was a remarkably wonderful state. Keeping that state in view, Bhagavan Krishna says — ***Tasmād sarveshu kāleshu yógayukta bhavārjuna. Yukta āsit madparaḥ*** etc. (for that reason and for all times, oh! Arjuna, be at one with *yóga;* be united with Me accordingly). From amongst those who were fortunate to be associated with Shama Churn and find shelter at His Holy Feet, I have heard that He achieved the similar state. Though I am His grandson, being born direct in His sacred family lineage, I was unfortunate not to see Him, because I was born nine years after His Sublime Departure. It is not known to me whether there was any relationship with Him in any of my previous births, but I do presume that a spiritual relationship did exist. Whom I have not seen, or ever enjoyed the company of, or had any direct acquaintance with, why I felt such intense love, reverence and devotion towards Him is known to the Omniscient only.

All have been repeatedly reminding me to write a full biography of the great Lahiree Mahasaya, but it is a pity that not being a litterateur, I do not know how to write it. Many have written His biography before, which also appeared in the monthly magazines now and then but they are almost like hearsay. But I depend wholly on His Lotus Feet.

Vísva karichey pūjā, tabu mor mone haye
Āmi nā karile pūjā, pūjā taba nāhi haye
Āmār īśvara tumi, Prabhu tumi, dāsá āmi
Āmi nā karile pūjā, pūjā taba rahe bāki.

The world is adoring Thee,
Yet this is the voice of my say,
Adoration to Thee remains absent,
If homage to Thee I do not pay,
Thou art my God, oh my Master
I am Thy humble servant only
Worship to Thee remains due
If I do not offer it solely.

If I do not chant the *Gītā* everyday before His Holy Image, it seems He is displeased with me. Through His grace, such has been the relationship between us that He is as dear to me as I am to Him. Thus discussing Him will not entail an unauthorized move on my part and I find it necessary to discuss something. I believe that He will excuse His dear grandson.

I realised that it would be impossible for me to write a full biography of my grandfather, firstly because I am not in the habit of writing and secondly, I do not have any time at all. A few hours are spent practising *sādhanā*. Three hours in the evening are spent in recitation and explanation of religious scriptures and in the singing of devotional songs such as *bhajans* (hymns) and *kirtans* (carols). Each day I have to reply to some letters. Besides these I have got to attend to the visitors frequenting my place, hold conversations and discourses with them. After the publication of His short biography, in the two books namely "Autobiography of a Yogi" by Paramahamsa Yogananda and "Bharater Sadhaka" by Sri Shankar Nath Roy, people from all over the world visit me and engage themselves in various types of discussions.

With the intention of writing a biography of my grandfather, I came to Calcutta in November 1979 and spent eighteen days living incognito at Ashoke Kumar Chatterjee's fourth floor residence 'Santineer' at Baranagar. I brought with me twenty-six diaries of my grandfather written by Him from Kashi alongwith other essential relevant records and books whatever I had in my custody and asked Ashoke to author the biography. Toiling day and night in this old age, in addition to those diaries and records, further facts and figures that I knew about my grandfather was briefed to Ashoke who wrote them down. Moreover, whatever I had learnt from the verbal communications with father, mother, grandmother and my two aunts (father's own sisters) and many of the old disciples of my grandfather and as much as could be remembered, I made him jot down. Ashoke has arranged these facts and figures sequentially and laboriously written it in the form of a biography. Thereafter, Dr. Shibnarayan Ghoshal Sastri, Professor of Visva Bharati University, has looked into the grammatical aspect of the book. Both of them are very near and dear to me, so it is my firm belief that they have succeeded in performing their respective assignments quite faithfully and diligently.

The *yógasādhana* grandfather acquired from His *Gurú* is really an invaluable one and in accordance to his command, what my grandfather imparted to mankind is based on direct realisations and not on conjecture. There is no scope for erudition here. Even if anyone is deaf or dumb, he can undoubtedly enter the spiritual realm and through the medium of direct realisation, perceive, hear and comprehend about the God-essence. The path of *sādhana* which our sages had showed thousands of years ago has in course of time almost become obsolescent. Few techniques of *sādhana* have been retained in the form of mystic syllables, but due to the onslaught of time, technique of *Kriyā* became extinct and only the mystic syllables remained. The actions of *sādhana* being extinct, those mystic syllables became almost lifeless and therefore ineffective, but none paid heed to this. At present the so-called *Gurús* whisper those ineffective mystic syllables into the ears of their disciples, considering initiation to be complete. The action and reaction of those mystic syllables are unfamiliar to the *Gurús* and do not produce any benefit either to the *Gurú* or to the disciples. A knowledge of those mystic syllables enables one to carry on the profession of a *Gurú* from generation to generation or adorn the post of *Mohanta* (abbot), because the common people who are simple can easily be befooled. Noticing this unscrupulous and businesslike attitude towards religion in our country, the Great Soul Kabir has with intense grief expressed :—

Kān phukne kā gurú āur hai,
Behad kā gurú āur;
Behad kā gurú yo mile,
Panhucā deowe thour.

The idea of the above verse may be represented as follows :—

The *Gurús* who cast spells in the ears are of one kind and the boundless *Gurús* are of another kind, the one who acquires a boundless *Gurú* is brought to his exact destination.

Thour means *Dhāma* which in the real sense, is "Ultimate Abode'. It is this *Dhāma* or 'Ultimate Abode', that has been spoken about in the *Gītā* by *Bhagavān* Himself — ***Yadgatvā na nivortante taddhāma paramaṃ máma.*** It implies that abode is My Supreme Abode where after once entering, there is no return. Excepting the perfectly self-realised *sādhaka* can there be anyone else to interpret the profound significance of these words, such as *máma* i.e. my, mine; *Dhāma* i.e. abode, in the manner Lahiree Mahasaya has done? The battle in *Mahābhārata* concluded on the eighteenth day, but the battle between materialistic desires and cessation of these desires has been infinitely continuing and will never end in the many births to come. Then what is the means to settle this conflict? By following the path of *sādhana* or *Karmayóga* (i.e. union with Supreme *Brahma* through a specified course of action) a cessation of the conflict can be caused and this was learnt by Lahiree Mahasaya from His *Gurú* and imparted to the world. This conflict between material attachment and material detachment is continuing within everyone. If the victory of material attachment occurs, it denotes that the highly valuable human life is rendered fruitless, while if material detachment wins, then human life becomes fruitful. Material desires imply a great deal of demands, but the cessation of these desires implies contentment with the barest minimum. Thus it is noticed that Duryadhana (a character in *Mahābhārata*) would not part with even the smallest space of land available on a needle tip to the Pandavas, whilst on the contrary, Yudhisthira was contented if he was given five small villages for five brothers. This reveals that one side is replete with material attachment and the other side is devoid of material attachment.

Unless and until one can be free from attachments in all respects in this manner, one cannot attain success in this *sādhana*. One may say "I am above all attachments", but by merely expressing these orally one cannot be really detached. How can one be detached? For this, it must first be understood, from where does attachment originate? In every living being, *Prâná* is present in a still manner. When this still *Prâná* attains dynamism, the mind originates and this is known as the restless mind of a living being. A living being considers this kinetic mind to be the mind. From this kinetic mind arises the propensity for material attachment. Then, to be devoid of attachment one must make one's existing restless mind mindless. The means and the technique of *sādhana* by which mindlessness can be achieved or the essence of mind eliminated have been clearly stipluated in the *Gītā* and in the *yóga p*hilosophy of *Pātañjala*. But in the present age, the person to delineate that technique of *sādhana* is rare. Many learned men or theologians have rendered explanations or annotations to the scriptural texts. There are innumerable scholastic and philosophical explanations but none have rendered explanations derived from realisations through *sādhana*. The great *yogis* and *Mahāpurushas* who had attained direct realisations through *sādhana* have not purposely perhaps uttered even a hint about the most inner spiritual significance attached to those scriptural texts, because they knew that what was entirely dependent on *sādhana* or direct self-realisation, could not be comprehended by anyone at all even if it was orally expressed or explained through writings. For example, without tasting sugar, can one learn about its taste by merely listening to it's description? However, in course of time, this scientific technique of *sādhana*, resulted in it's becoming extinct. Lahiree Mahasaya's *Gurúdeva* (whom He used to address as *Bābāji* and in His own self-written diaries, mention of *Bābāji* only has been made and we do not get any other reference about His *Gurú* other than this) yogically took Him to Ranikhet and initiated Him into *Kriyāyóga*. This fact clearly reveals that the relationship of *Gurú* and disciple must have existed with Him from His previous birth. After initiation, when Lahiree Mahasaya was in Kashi, a spiritual communication prevailed with His *Gurú* and this is evident from His diaries. This scientifically oriented technique of *sādhana* which was on the verge of extinction was restored to the world by Lahiree Mahasaya after rederiving it from His *Gurú, Bābāji*.

It is commonly noticed that most people practise *Haṭhayóga*. While practising *āsanás*, they think that they are practising *yóga*. The practice of *Haṭhayóga* imparts physical benefits no doubt, but it does not provide any lead in the finding of the soul within the body nor does it make the mind still. Again, one cannot enter the spiritual realm if the mind is not made still. For this the practice of *Rājayóga* is essential. Until self-realisation, permanent settlement or visualisation of *Kūtastha*-consciousness occurs, till then human life cannot be complete.

Bhruvormadhye prâṇamāveśya samyak, sa taṃ paraṃ purushamupaiti divyam. — If the mind and *Prâṇá* are placed between the eyebrows completely, the Supreme Being can be realized and the supreme state attained.

For this is required, an assemblage of *Rājayóga*, *Hathayóga* and *Layayóga*. *Rājayóga* enables the mind to become still, *Layayóga* enables self-realisation and *Haṭhayóga* is necessary to eliminate the exhaustion arising from the practice of *Rājayóga* and *Layayóga*. *Haṭhayóga* assists in activating the benumbed body caused by a prolonged sitting session in the same *āsaná*. We search for God in Heaven, in the Milky Sea, in places of pilgrimage, in temples, churches and mosques, but are unaware of the fact that He is constantly prevalent in our body, between the eyebrows and yet the interest to seek Him does not awaken. In this body the Consecrated is existent between the eyebrows and the sages have stipulated directly how to perceive Him and have denoted the path of *sādhana* technique. But with the progress of time, this technique of *sādhana* became obsolescent, chiefly because it depended entirely on the austerities of *sādhana*. For such *sādhana,* a considerable period of time and patience are required which nobody feels inclined to do. The main reason for this is, in the present age many *Gurús* preach that by touching the head, one falls into *samādhi,* the mind attains stillness etc. Thus, who is willing to waste time? But a bit of contemplation regarding this will enable everyone to understand, that to achieve the One for which renouncement of all sorts of earthly pleasures is necessary, can He be so easily attained? It has to be admitted by all that in the body-temple, God exists between the eyebrows as the Soul. Without searching for such a Truth we frantically run about. We have been hearing about the Three Deities— *Brahmā*, *Víshnu* and *Śivá*. But the

One who controls them from behind is never perceptible nor will ever be perceptible. Yet quest for Him or for that Truth provides life's happiness. We Indians, followers of the Vedic faith pay our homage to the Holy Triad. But the One who controls them from behind is never perceptible nor will ever be perceptible. Yet quest for Him or for that Truth provides life's happiness. We Indians, followers of the Vedic faith pay our homage to the Holy Triad. But people in other parts of the world are unaware of the names of the Three Deities. Yet none disregards the creation, preservation and dissolution or the three attributes, *sattva*, *rájas* and *támas*, because are these three attributes non-existent anywhere? The respective functions of the three attributes have been explained as idols in accordance with the philosophical essence. These forms can be visualised if the mind is made still in any manner, it surely is a state of the mind's stillness and a few hints pertaining to this can be obtained, but all these are illusory. Because if these images were real as well as eternal, then if the mind of any person of any country or of any religious follower was made still, he also could visualise these forms. But this is not possible. They visualise only those facts they are conscious of or have an idea about. But if the mind is made still between the eyebrows, Soul or *Kūṭastha-Brahma* can be visualised and is possible to be visualised by each and every *sādhaka* of the world. There is no difference here. The Infinite Soul is beyond our reach but the Soul or *Kūṭastha-Brahma* is well within our reach. It is He who is prevalent in every living being, then why do we fail to find this Supreme Truth? Why does the mind attain kineticism? Because of the vibration of *Prâṇá*, the mind becomes restless, this dynamism of *Prâná* is called the mind. If *Prâṇá* is made still, the mind becomes still. Again, if the mind is made still then *Prâṇá* becomes non-vibratory. Vibratory *Prâṇá* is slightly grosser than the mind. We can arrest *Prâṇá* for a while if we wish to, but it is very difficult to arrest the mind. So *Prâṇáyāma* is the best way to make *Prâṇá* passive. Just as Ganges is the most sacred of all the rivers, *Gāyatrí* is the greatest of all the *mántras*, *praṇáva* is the best of all the mystic syllables and Kashi the holiest of all the pilgrimages, so also *Prâṇâyāma* is the best technique amongst all the techniques of *sādhana*, which has been approved by all scriptures. There are various kinds of *Prâṇâyāmas*. Among them, the greatest one is the *sushumná*-oriented *Prâṇâyāma*. In the form of vital *Prâṇá*-air, this *Prâná* communes within the body. Being located at five different places in the body, they have individually been named as *prâṇá, apâṇá, samāná, udāna* and *vyāna*. If these five airs maintain an equilibrium in the body, the mind remains still but an aberration in the equilibrium for any reason will cause it to become restless. Likewise if wind, bile and phlegm remain in a balanced manner in the body, there is no disease. If due to some reason, there is an aberration, then disease occurs as a result of that reason. As for example, exposure to cold gives rise to phlegm etc. The technique by which the five airs can be equipoised within the body through *sādhana* has been imparted by Lahiree Mahasaya to us. *Prâṇâyāma* stills the *apâṇá* and *Prâṇá* airs, *nábhikriyā* stills the *samāná* air, *mahámudrā* stills *udāna* and *vyāna* airs. If these five airs are thus stilled, the mind becomes still and this tranquillity of the mind enables self-realisation. *Yónimudrā* produces soul-realisation. The accesses of all the sensory perceptions have to be closed forcefully, the mind has to be wound up from all material aspects and placed between the eyebrows and the path of *sādhana* practised as has been instructed by the *Gurú*, after which the incognizible soul will be visualised and the *sādhaka* attains success. ***Rathe ca vāmanaṃ dṛishṭā punarjanma na vidyate*** — which means that by beholding V*āmanadeva* (incarnation of *Víshṇu*) in the body chariot, a *yogi* can make his birth successful. One who visualises this *Púrusha* (Supreme Being) never undergoes rebirth and gains eternal release. He is that *Púrusha* described in the

Purushôttama Yóga chapter of *Gītā* whose realisation will make a *sādhaka* fulfil his life. Kabirdas has immaculately expressed thus :—

Marte marte jag marā, marnā nā jānā koye,
Aisā marnā koi na marā, jo phir nā marnā hoye.
Marnā haye duye bhāntikā, jo marnā jānā koye,
Rāmaduāre jo mare phirnā marnā hoye.

The verse implies that the death-flow is continuous, but also none undergoes such a death which will not be repeated. Death is of two kinds in this world. One is common death which is constantly occurring, another is uncommon death which occurs at *Rāmaduār* or at Rama's door. Common people consider this to be the facade of a Rama temple. Lahiree Mahasaya has explained what this *Rāmaduār* is in actuality. This *Rāmaduār* implies the place between the eyebrows or *Kúṭastha*. The one who fixes *Prâṇá* and mind and departs from this earthly abode while visualising the Supreme Being, is never reborn again. This is an extremely practical *sādhana* and is not an incidental remark. This is possible only for him who maintains this practice throughout his life. This is the aim and result of *Kriyāyóga sādhana*. I assert this truth with firmness because I myself witnessed such an uncommon death — that of my father's. It is not an incidental remark nor a hearsay, but has been observed with my own eyes. Others also noticed it. What an unique death ! He magnetized the entire *Prâṇá*-air completely between the eyebrows, placed his mind there and departed. At this moment, the place between the eyebrows was quivering immensely which was indescribable. It seemed as though a marble was forcing it's way out from within. Just at the moment of his death, father bore a placid countenance, a calm body and it seemed as though his whole body assumed the reddish hue of a fresh rose.

Prayāṇakāle manasācalena bhaktyā yukto yógabalena caiba, Bhrubormadhye prâṇámāveśya samyak sa taṃparaṃ púrush-amupaiti divyam.

In other words, at the time of death if through the medium of *yóga*, the mind and *Prâṇá* are placed on *Kúṭastha* between the eyebrows with devotion, the Supreme Being can be realised and the supreme state attained.

It was a wonderful sight, as though *Mahádeva* Himself was lying there. While *Kúṭastha* was quivering, Bansidhar Kshettry, a disciple of my grandfather told me... "Look, Satya Babu, compare it with the eighth chapter of *Gītā*, it only is the *Rāmaduār*, it only is the permanent settlement of *Brahma*." This state cannot be achieved with a few days' effort, to attain this permanence an entire life's *yógasādhana* is required. So the *Gītā* says — ***Svádharme nidhanaṃ śreyaḥ paradhárma bhayāvahaḥ***. *Svádharma* means soul-religion or else by practising this soul-religion-*Kriyāyóga*, if one dies it is better than dying in *paradhárma* or the bodily disposition or the disposition of the senses which is terrifying because then the cycle of birth and death is inevitable.

In recent times, none other than Lahiree Mahasaya has shown the manner by which one can enter the spiritual kingdom.

Many have invented several fanciful and imaginary stories about His *Gurú Bābāji Mahárājá* and perhaps the reason for this could be to increase their dignity. During the lifetime of my grandfather, some had expressed their keen desire to see *Bābāji Mahárājá*. Among then was Taraknath Sanyal, son of Lahiree Mahasaya's brother-in-law. I had heard from Taraknath Babu, that Lahiree Mahasaya had stated *Bābāji Mahárājá* would not appear, but however He would try. He had tried but *Bābāji Mahárājá* did not appear. Taraknath Babu was a devout and advanced *Kriyābān*. [1]

Rampadarath was another devoted and progressive *Kriyābān*. I heard from him that my father after completing *Kriyāyóga sādhana* for fourteen hours in one sitting, *Bābāji Mahárājá* granted

1. One who practises *Kriyāyoga*.

his holy vision to him. Then my grandfather was alive. He was astonished to find *Bābāji Mahārājá* in his subtle body and asked "Why have you appeared at this time suddenly?"

Bābāji Mahārājá replied— " Tinkari was sincerely remembering me."

After this my grandfather forbade my father, not to trouble *Bābāji* in this way. When I heard all these incidents from Rampadarath, my father was alive. I asked my father whether all these were true, to which he replied—"Who said so?" After I mentioned Rampadarath's name to him, he avoided answering my question and was disappointed. Father was very grave and reserved by nature and used to incomparably conceal himself. At present I know about four *Bābājis*. Besides them, how many more *Bābājis* exist, I cannot tell. Many say—"I am just returning after meeting *Bābāji*." Again it is they who express their eagerness to obtain *Kriyāyóga sādhanā* from me. I tell them — "When you have personally met *Bābāji Mahārajā*, then instead of obtaining *Kriyāyóga sādhanā* from him, why have you come to me?" In this manner, a few people in order to establish themselves, are belittling the name of Krishnalike *Mahāpurusha Bābāji Mahārājá*..

The immortal, scientific, facile *yógasādhanā* that Lahiree Mahasaya has imparted to us, if practised even a little conscientiously, will bring immense welfare to the person concerned. God has made a similar statement in *Gītā* — ***Svalpamapyasya dhármasya trāyate mahato bhayād***. It brings deliverance from mental, physical and financial distress. The important aspect of Lahiree Mahasaya's life was that He after attaining this marvellous *sādhanā* was not the only One to be graced by it, there were others who were graced by His propitioussness and derived eternal peace and emancipation. This I have seen with my own eyes. Lahiree Mahasaya being devoid of selfishness imparted this glorious *yógasādhanā* to future mankind. It is beyond doubt and comparision that the scientifically oriented *Kriyāyóga sādhanā* which He imparted to the world comprises both knowledge and science. Being beyond selfishness He has imparted to us all what He practised in *sādhanā*, i.e. direct realisation, intra-visualisation, intra-audition etc. which in Kabirdas's language is :—

Likhālikhikā bāt nahi,
Dekhādekhi ki bāt,
Dulhā dulhin mil gaye,
Fiki pari barāt.

The literal meaning of the above verse is :— It is not a matter to be penned down but one of direct realisation. The marriage procession has been cited as an example. It constitutes the groom's party, music, lights etc, but when the groom and bride meet the others belonging to the marriage party return to their respective locations. Or else when a *sādhaka* is capable of being united with the Primordial Female Energy and Primordial Male Energy or with the soul of a living being or the Infinite Soul, then only can he arrive at *Kriyā's* transcendental state. The departure of the marriage party after the bride and groom meet is akin to the insignificance of the process by which we attain mergence immediately after we attain mergence. This is a self-realisable state. Many explanations have been rendered to the *Gītā*. All of them are either scholastic or intellectual or philosophical but a self-realised explanation has been conferred by Lahiree Mahasaya only or by His devoted *sādhakas*. He is at the root of this. *Gītā's Srī Bhagavānubāca* as denoted by Him means that realisation occurs through *Kūṭastha*. This indeed is an excellent explanation. Bhagavan Krishna personally advised Arjuna on the chariot during the battle of *Mahābhārata* which ended on the eighteenth day but the conflict in the body-chariot between material attachment and material detachment will not end even in eighteen births. Krishna has left His Mortal Frame, but the Krishna within the Krishna is Omnipresent in each and every body-chariot and will eternally be so because He is imperishable. Since He is present, we can realise everything and He imparts advice being seated in the body-chariot. Bhagavan has said — "Dear Arjuna, I will not remain, neither will you." Then what will remain? ***Īśvarā sarvabhūtānāṃ hṛiddeśearjuna tishṭhati.*** Addressing Arjuna, He addressed the whole of mankind thus —"Dear humanity, take recourse to that God in Whose propitiousness you will attain eternal peace and immortal abode." Lahiree Mahasaya has shown us the scientifically oriented *sādhanā* by which we can take shelter in the God within us and the manner by which the mind can be prepared. This is Lahiree Mahasaya's bestowal to the world. Maintaining a complete family existence, being a true householder, the ideal which He set for mankind by arriving at the pinnacle of *sādhanā* cannot be found in thousands of years. Countless religious mendicants, *saṃnyāsins*, self-renouncers and householders were most blessed to have found shelter in Him. I have heard from those who had seen Him that if any unknown person met Him, He would immediately bow in regard. This one *slóka* is enough to cause discernment about His Esse.

Brahmānandaṃ paramasukhadaṃ kevalaṃ jñānamūrtiṃ,
Dvandātītaṃ gaganasadṛiśaṃ tatvamasyādilakshyam.
Ekaṃ nityaṃ vimalamacalaṃ sarvadhīsākshībhutam,
Bhāvātitaṃ triguṇarahitaṃ sadgurúṃ taṃ namāmi.

The English rendition of the *slóka* is as follows :—

"You are the Bliss of *Brahma,* Divine Joy, Image of Knowledge, beyond conflicts, Sky-Semblant, perceptible beyond all essences. You are One, Eternal, Pure, Static, You only are present in all the elements as a Witness, are beyond all thoughts and emotions, beyond all the three attributes; You are the real *Gurú*, I pay my obeisance to You."

This *slóka* mirrors the Vividities and Glory of His Esse. The essence of His advice is :-

"Practise *Kriyā* and remain in *Kriyā's* transcendental state." He was not in favour of altering the normal attire or of ostentatious display, nor of formation of any factions or groups. He used to remark that hyacinths breed in an unused pond.

It is found that with the creation of the universe, innumerable creatures have been created by God. All the creatures are born with the gift of swimming. If any animal falls into water, it can easily reach the slope by swimming. God was compassionate towards them but was unfavourable towards man, His highest creation, for they were not gifted with the art of swimming. Why is this so? There surely must be an objective for this. He told mankind that they should learn swimming to traverse any stretch, because man is born with conscience and intelligence. For instance, a mother laboriously cooks for her child, sets the table for him and if it is not possible for the child to eat himself, even feeds him, but the child has to swallow the food himself. This function cannot be performed by any other person but has to be performed by the self. Just as when one consumes rice, the other's appetite will not be appeased, similarly the *Prâṇá*-action-*sādhanā* has to be practised by the self only and not by anyone in lieu of the self.

A book of this stature cannot be written only with a command of knowledge, language or with possessing the writing faculty. For this is required *sādhanā*-derived realisation. Although Ashoke Kumar Chatterjee is not a writer, yet I have asked him to write this book because being an advanced *Kriyābān*, he can deeply delve into the complete subject-matter. Eventually, I have been satisfied going through the whole book. Aged *Kriyābān* Subodh Chandra Mukhopadhyay and another *Kriyābān* Prabir Kumar Dutta have rendered financial assistance at the time of publication of the

Bengali first edition of this book and Ashoke Kumar Sen has rendered active assistance in many ways, I tender my heartiest blessings to all these *Kriyābāns*. It would not have been possible for me to accomplish this noble task at the ripe age of seventy-seven years if He had not showered His grace.

Sri Satya Charan Lahiri

(1905 – 1987)

PREFACE

The hallowed womb of Mother India is the producer of many gems. Innumerable exalted *yogis* by being born on the soil of India have sanctified the motherland and gratfifed countless men by showing them the path of righteousness. The life-notes of those great souls resonate till today. Their immensely precious biographies have enriched the literature and storehouse of knowledge of the motherland. Great souls existed in the past, exist in the present and will exist in the future. As and when society proceeds, the great souls show the path of light to mankind. In this manner, to introduce the right path for the right age, Yogiraj Shama Churn Lahiree Mahasaya descended. In spite of the biographies of many great saints having been written, is it necessary to compose a biography of this Sublime Soul? This Soul like any common man by maintaining an unostentatious family life or by maintaining an existence befitting a complete householder; by meticulously performing all the responsibilities worthy of a householder and by mounting the highest pinnacle of spiritual life, has set an illustrious example to mankind for which humanity is ever grateful and indebted to Him. It is true that before, many have composed short biographies of this Sublime Yogi, but none have till date composed His complete biography. Therefore in accordance with the command of revered Satya Charan Lahiri *Mahāśaya*, the youngest grandson of this Sublime Household-Yogi, I have been encouraged to write the biography of this Apogean Esse. But he has repeatedly cautioned me to sequentially arrange true facts and essences, never to include any wrong facts or essences, or imaginary, baseless tales produced by the writer, which have been noticed in previous biographies.

Many erudites and *Kriyābāns* have for a long time been requesting the revered Satya Charan Lahiri *Mahāśaya* to compose a complete and factual biography of Yogiraj Shama Churn during his lifetime, because in his absence the correct facts may become extinct. But due to old age and lack of time he could not accomplish this. Therefore he advised me, who was like a son to him, to compose this biography. I humbly appealed to him as to how it would be possible for me to compose the biography of this Sublime *yogi*? It was a high hope indeed! Just as a small blade of grass cannot assess the gigantic banyan tree, similarly I felt that while writing the biography of this Noble Yogi, I might lose its exactness and authenticity.

The venerable Sri Satya Charan Lahiri *Mahāśaya* assuring me made a remarkable statement. He said, "Why do you worry, commence the task, for then He Himself Whose biography it is will compose it. Forsake the attitude 'I am doing' for then you will notice that He Himself will complete the task."

Thus I derived mental strength by remembering his message of assurance and engaged myself with the task of writing, my only hope being the Lotus Feet of the Sublime Yogi. Just as a cripple by the grace of *Śrī Mādhava* is capable of climbing a high mountain, similarly by the grace of this Great Yogi, I have been able to venture discussing His biography. Many a time I sat with pen in hand, words failing me, but cogitating on Him through *Kriyā* the pen started writing. In this manner day after day, month after month elapsed amounting to fourteen months.

It is comparatively easier to compose the biographies of politicians, socialists, poets, authors and other great personalities, because in almost every aspect, their lives bear external manifestations. But in the spiritual world, the lives of *yogis* are exactly the reverse, external manifestations are almost absent there. The biographies of the aforesaid intellectuals are dependent on facts, but the biographies of noble *yogis* are dependent on essences beyond the senses. Therefore it is very difficult to compose their biographies. As and when it necessitates *yogis* exhibit miracles, but the ideals they establish or the path of *sādhana* which they introduce to mankind for the attainment of salvation is more secret than secretive, the path which if followed by man can enable him to arrive at his ultimate and highest objective and this facet is regarded to be the greatest one in their biographies. Because even after their departure, their established ideals in the path of *sādhana* keep on continuing for many centuries. Therefore in this book, I have to the best of my ability attempted to elucidate the scientific essence of *sādhana* and it's ideals, as revived by Yogiraj.

The conception of common man is that the more a *yogi* exhibits magnificent miracles, the more greater he is. But our conception is that all *yogis* are capable of exhibiting many miracles. Judging *yogis* by this yardstick is belittling them. It is not the appropriate yardstick to understand conversant *yogis*. Instead, the *yogi* who without renouncing anything, in a short while has mounted the highest peak of *sādhanā* by practising the facile and simple *yógasādhanā* is regarded to be the ideal *yogi*. His ideals are extremely acceptable to humanity.

Man is bound by social norms, material attachment is dear to him. From the spiritual viewpoint, the domestic existence amongst the fourfold existence of life has been regarded to be the greatest. So man desires to practise *sādhanā* by remaining within the orbit of the family. This path is an easy one because it is inherent. The *Máhatmās* who maintain a family existence like householders enlighten the household people through the currents and cross-currents of daily life about the path to spirituality; their ideals are ascertained by householders as the beacon of life. From this aspect, the ideals of this Sublime Yogi are undoubtedly lovable and acceptable to householders. These same ideals were followed by the ancient sages long ago.

The revered Sri Satya Charan Lahiri *Máhaśaya* by presenting all facts from the twenty-six self-written diaries of Yogiraj, by imparting many familiar details and exact incidents in the life of Yogiraj has enriched this book. In short, without his active assistance it would have been impossible to obtain accurate information about the life of Yogiraj. Therefore I remember him with reverence for this contribution.

In order to present accurate and correct facts, ideals and essences of *sādhana* pertaining to the life of Yogiraj, explanations of the *śāstrás* (scriptures) made by Yogiraj hundred years ago have been obtained; His self-written twenty-six diaries have been specially discussed and taken as a basis; the letters written by Him to His various devotees have been secured; information from widely dispersed devotees of this Great Yogi pertaining to His life's incidents, counsel and *sādhana* essences have been derived and from the grandson of Yogiraj, Sri Satya Charan Lahiri *Mahāśaya*, their family history and ideals have all been acquired and assembled in this book. I therefore acknowledge my gratitude to all those past *sādhakas* and to those who have furnished old letters providing relevant information material. I also extend my gratefulness to Dr. Shibnarayan Ghoshal Shastri, Subodh Chandra Mukherjee, Prabir Dutta, Ashok Kumar Sen and all such magnanimous men who have rendered active assistance in various ways for this biography. I offer my prayer to the Holy Feet of the Great Yogi for the material and spiritual welfare of these benevolent and devout men.

The essences from the self-written diaries of Yogiraj and facts from His letters to His devotees have been directly incorporated without any amendment or alteration. They have been retained exactly in bold letters and His realisations are included so that those facts do not lose their significance and the statements are not distorted in any manner in the future. The direct statements of almost all great *yogis* are rarely available to future *sādhakas* because due to the onslaught of time they assume a distorted shape. I hope that by this, the future devoted *sādhakas* will derive benefit.

Incidentally, all the maxims from different *śāstras* in the book and their various explanations which have been conferred are all explanations rendered by Yogiraj or explanations in accordance with His ideals.

Many a time many words have been oft repeated to elucidate the realizations and the *sādhana* essences of great *yogis*; there was no alternative other than this. ***Gurú kṛipāhi kevalam.*** The *Gurú's* grace is absolute.

Dr. Ashoke Kumar Chatterjee

PURNA PURUSHA

Y
O
G
I
R
A
J

SRI SHAMA CHURN LAHIREE

Chapter 1

THE SUBLIME ADVENT

"Shama Churn, come here."

The voice echoed in the mountain and reverberated in the ears of Shama Churn. Shama Churn was amazed.

Who might call Him by name in this mountainous region enveloped by forests ! How was it possible for the summoner to know His name!! Shama Churn cast His glance upon a placid *Saṃnyāsin*, standing on the mountain summit and calling Him by name.

Is it a coincidence? Shama Churn proceeded spellbound vacillating on account of doubt. Having arrived at the mountain peak, He noticed a *Saṃnyāsin* beckoning Him with a gentle smile. He possessed a fatherly affection in his eyes. The elated *Saṃnyāsin* accorded him a warm welcome with the same spirit of happiness a father feels when his son returns home from a long sojourn.

"How strange Shama Churn, can't you recognize me? Can you recollect having come here before? Can't you recognize this tiger skin, this ascetic's bowl also? Have you forgotten everything?"

Shama Churn failed to remember any of them and said — "I have never come here before."

"Listen Shama Churn, all these are the play of illusion. It is this illusion which has made You forget all these things. Saying this the *Saṃnyāsin* lightly touched Shama Churn. The whole universe evanesced from Shama Churn. He succeeded now in recollecting the events of His previous birth.

With tearful eyes, Shama Churn prostrated at the feet of the *Saṃnyāsin* for He now retrieved the nearest one of all His births and rebirths.

Since ages vexed householders have prayed to their respective deities, thus — "O God, show us such a path that will enable us to practise *sādhanā* by remaining within the family. Barring family life, we cannot practise *sādhanā*. O *Bhagavān* send such a guide who being a family man himself, can show the true path to householders." Before this, man had gained a great deal of experience. They had observed that the one who had come to introduce the path to them were either family renouncers or though maintaining a family existence were dependant on others for their subsistence. But in this age, there is a dearth of such a guide who remains in domesticity and does not abandon them. Perhaps their God has after such a long time heard their prayers. Therefore today householders are ecstatic. The domestic women by producing an ululatory sound of joy and the men by chanting Vedic *mantras* befitting the Auspicious Moment invoked and prayed for that Sublime Effulgence from Heaven Who assuming the Form of a Divine Child descended on this earthly abode at village Ghurni beside the town of Krishnagar, District Nadia, West Bengal, India. That Divine Child taking a solemn oath stated — " I will remain amidst you, will remain like you. I will not be like those ones who willingly abandon the domestic existence, yet show you the path. Just as you exist by bearing all the miseries, pains, poverty, sorrows, afflictions, I also will do the same. God has bestowed hands, feet and intellect to all, with the help of these just as you make your own earnings and execute your life, I will also do the same. Or else, by remaining exactly like you in this earthly ambit, I will show you that path by which you can practise *sādhanā*."

At the hour of 7 Danda 30 Pal (08 hours 27 minutes, 47 seconds IST) on the morning of Tuesday, the seventh day of the dark fortnight and 16th Aswin of the Bengali year 1235 (30th September 1828 A.D.), this Divine Child caused His Descent at village Ghurni, His parents being Gourmohan Lahiri (Sarkar) and Muktakeshi Devi, second wife of Gourmohan. By his first wife, Gourmohan had two sons, Chandrakanta and Saradaprasad and a daughter, Swarnomoyee. His first wife expired in the course of a pilgrimage. Then Gourmohan married for the second time. Five years after the Advent of Shama Churn, Muktakeshi Devi gave birth to a daughter named Sulakshana. Thus Gourmohan had three sons and two daughters.

The town of Shantipur was about to be immersed by the influx of *sādhanā* and the district of Nadia was already flooded. Nadia district herself being drowned with the flood of *sādhanā*, influenced others to be drowned also. In this sacred soil of India had arrived a Divine Child Who would portray to men, vexed and tormented with the pangs of earthly existence, the path of *sādhanā*. The district of Nadia which was benefitted by the dust of the feet of many great souls and blessed by memories of innumerable *paṇḍitás*, gave shelter in her lap to this Sublime Soul. The air of Nadia smacked of the spirit of festivity, the dust from the earth by rising upwards; the trees by swaying; the birds by singing dulcet notes; the bees by flitting from one flower to another were all felicitating this Divine Child. The neighbouring housewives assembled in the Lahiri house to have a glimpse of that fair-complexioned, handsome Divine Child. It was a cause for joy and celebration in the village of Ghurni. Gourmohan treated everyone to sweets. For the well-being of the new arrival, he implored everyone's blessings.

Gourmohan was a virtuous, devout and religious person. He used to engage himself performing *pūjā*, reading the *śāstrás* and discussing religious facts. He was also an earnest devotee of *yógasādhanā*. He had sincere regard for all gods and goddesses. Muktakeshi Devi too used to daily worship the household deity, *Śivá* with sincere devotion. Before worshipping *Śivá*, she would not even accept breakfast. Whenever any beggar arrived, she would part with whatever she had. Muktakeshi Devi was extremely compassionate, charitable and good-natured. Therefore she commanded respect from all the neighbouring women. A Divine Child is born only to such parents. God has also declared :—

Śucīnāṃ śrīmataṁ gehe yógabhrashṭoabhijāyate
Athavā yogināmeva kule bhavati dhīmatām
Etaddhi durlabhataraṃ loke janma yadīdṛiśam — *Gītā 6/41-42*

A person who has not been able to pursue his *yógasādhanā* due to his untimely demise is born in a holy and noble household or in the family of realized *yogis*. Such births are scarce.

Certain moments arrive when the country becomes replete with knowledge, glory and cultural heritage. The nineteenth century was such a moment for India. The effulgent sun of India was at it's acme then. In this period, just as many great souls were born in the spiritual path, likewise in the spheres of politics, sociology etc., India had become replete. People would earn money then, but not by sacrificing the principles of *dhárma* as is prevalent now. People then would abide by *dhárma* and it's precepts. A long period of Mughal rule and later British rule did disrupt India's *Sanātána Dhárma* partially. Irrespective of being wealthy or poor everyone belonging to the *Sanātána* faith was temptingly weaned away and forcibly converted into Islam or Christianity. It was necessary at this point of time for great souls in all aspects to be born. Therefore it can be observed that in the nineteenth century, the whole of India produced great men in the spheres of religion, politics, sociology etc. In the realm of religion, the contributions of Nadia and Kashi are immensely great.

The Dear Child of Muktakeshi Devi grew up gradually. He was affectionately named Shama Churn by everyone. In those days there was a general practice of naming children after gods and goddesses. It would serve the purpose of calling the children as well as remembering God. Sometimes Muktakeshi Devi would lull the Child to sleep or sometimes take Him to the *Śivá* temple, place Him beside her and worship *Śivá* with rapt attention. The Child would also keeping His eyes closed, be seated like *Śivá*. Again she would sometimes accomplish her tasks by making the Child sit on the sandy banks of the river. The Child would smear sand all over His body and assuming the posture of *Śivá*, sit down with eyes closed. Childish impudence was rarely found in this Divine Child. Instead, He could be seen wandering in the realm of thoughts stoically, as though He wanted to establish an union with the Infinite. By observing the attitude and behaviour of this Child, many guessed that He was not an ordinary Child.

Śivá was the household deity of the Lahiri family. The temple of the deity was adjacent to the house. One day Muktakeshi Devi was absorbed in deep meditation of *Śivá* with the Child seated beside her. The Child also was sitting with closed eyes emulating His mother. Suddenly a handsome, large-built *Saṃnyāsin* with matted hair appeared before the temple and addressed Muktakeshi Devi as 'Mother'. She became unnerved and lifted the Child on her lap.

The *Saṃnyāsin* said — " Mother don't be afraid. I am a *Saṃnyāsin*, there's nothing to be afraid of me."

Still Muktakeshi Devi stood overwhelmed with fear.

The *Saṃnyāsin* stated — " That Son of yours is not an ordinary human Child; it is I who have sent Him to this earth, to show the esoteric path of *sādhanā* to countless people, distressed with the worries and woes of family life. This Child Himself will maintain a family existence and attract others to practise *yógasādhanā*. Mother, you have nothing to fear. I shall constantly keep a watch upon Him like a shadow." After this the *Saṃnyāsin* departed with gentle steps.

Chapter 2

EDUCATION AND FAMILY LIFE

Gourmohan's forefathers were all religious minded. They used to undertake pilgrimages every now and then. But in those days undertaking pilgrimages was not as easy as it is at present. The railways were not introduced in India then and therefore one had to go on a pilgrimage either by foot or by boat; for this reason the fear of robbers persisted. It is heard that Gourmohan's father undertook pilgrimages to Kashi several times. As a result, Kashi was familiar to Gourmohan. His pecuniary position was not stringent. Though he was the Zamindar of Ghurni, yet he decided to settle at Kashi with his family. The exact reason why he decided to settle at Kashi was unknown. But probably a few reasons might have led him to settle there. As far as it can be learnt, the first reason was that when Shama Churn was five years old his second wife, Muktakeshi Devi expired. Perhaps because of this he developed an apathy towards family life. It is not exactly known whether Muktakeshi Devi had expired in Ghurni or at Kashi. The second reason was that his religious feelings being strong and Kashi being familiar to him since before, he decided to settle there. The third reason as much as can be learnt is that the Lahiri family had suffered a reversal of fortune. Their house being situated on the banks of the river Kharey was destroyed by a devastating flood alongwith a great number of landed properties. Many have expressed their opinion that Gourmohan settled at Kashi in quest of fortune. But this cause is not the correct one. Because normally in this type of misfortune one does not desert his ancestral land. This is not applicable to Gourmohan specially when he possessed real estate. In this state he could have rebuilt his house. Thus between the first two reasons cited, any one of the reasons intensified his religious leanings and Kashi being familiar to him from before, he settled there. Whatever the reason, he went to Kashi with his sons and daughters by a long water route. There his eldest son, Chandrakanta had purchased a house in advance at Simon Chauhatta, an area of Madanpura. Everyone then started residing in this house.

Alongwith his landed property the temple of his household deity dissolved into the river bed because of that flood. Probably in 1840, a local devotee retrieved the idol of the reigning deity *Śivá* from the river-bed and reinstated it in a newly built temple. As the idol had been retrieved from the water, it was named *'Jaleśvara'*. This area is now renowned as Shibtala of Ghurni, which has now become public property.

A lack of supervision of his estate because of Gourmohan's long period of stay at Kashi resulted in him losing control over it.

When Shama Churn completed five years of age, Gourmohan began to consider about the education of his son. Being a scholar himself, he would appreciate the value of education. In those days, most of the orthodox families inclined to *Sanātána Dhárma* would not approve of an English education. Their conception was that English was the language of untouchables. Probably Gourmohan thought that due to the decadent state of his real estate, an income-oriented education would be the most suitable for his son. In those days people with an English education could easily acquire jobs. Thus he had no conservatism for languages. For whatever reason it might be, to keep in accordance with the spirit of the age he admitted his son to 'Joynarayan English School' at Garureswar locality established by Raja Joynarayan Ghosal of Bhukailash.[1]

---

1. This school is probably one of Varanasi's oldest school. At present it is situated at Sadanand Market on the main road, amidst Ramapura and Rewari talabs.

After this at the age of twelve, Shama Churn was admitted to an English medium school which was a branch of Government Sanskrit College. Later, this Government English school was converted into a college and He had studied here for a period of eight years till 1848. Then he was twenty years old. Though it is not precisely known as to how long He had pursued His academic education, enough information has been culled regarding His receiving higher education. Because at a later date He undertook the responsibility of teaching innumerable students. From this it can be deduced that He was highly educated. Besides English, Bengali, Hindi and Urdu, He learnt Persian also. In addition to this He studied Sanskrit, the *Vedas*, *Upanisháds* and other scriptural texts from His teacher, a Maharashtrian *paṇḍitá* named Nagvatta who was well versed in the scriptures.

Shama Churn married in 1846 at the age of eighteen while He was a college student. Amongst the Bengalees like Gourmohan who settled in Kashi, *paṇḍitá* Vacaspati Devnarayan Sanyal *Mahâśaya* of Belur in Howrah District of West Bengal was one of them. He was a devout Brahmin and in Kashi's erudite circles, he was quite renowned. He had a cordial relationship with Gourmohan. It can be heard that the great Tailangaswamy would accept alms only from the house of Devnarayan. Vacaspati *Mahâśaya* lived in the ward of Khalishpura near Gourmohan's residence. For this reason, he would occasionally come to Gourmohan's house and discuss the *śāstrás* with him. Vacaspati *Mahâśaya* was a widower. He reared his three sons and only daughter Kashimani, on his own. Kashimani used to visit Gourmohan's residence alongwith her father and play there. The womenflok of the house would jokingly ask her —"Whom will you marry?" The child used to then point at the handsome Shama Churn. Gourmohan gave marriage to his son, Shama Churn with this nine year old Kashimâni.

Shama Churn possessed a good health. He practised a few physical exercises and was an expert swimmer. He was industrious and grave by nature. He never used to waste time gossiping with those of the same age. He never committed any unjust action and had a keen sense of judgment in all respects. If food was not served to Him, He would never ask for it.

In 1851, at almost twenty three years of age, He was appointed clerk in the Public Works Department, Military Engineering Works at Gazipur. At that time, the function of this department was to despatch provisions to the army and construct roads. Later, He had to work at different locations like Mirzapur, Buxar, Katua, Gorakhpur, Danapur, Ranikhet, Kashi etc. on transfer. At the end of His service period, He was promoted to the post of barrack master (now known as S.D.O.).

During His service at Gazipur, His salary was not enough. For this reason, He earned an extra amount by teaching Hindi and Urdu to a few English army officers, retained this small income for His personal expenditure and sent His salary to Kashi for household expenditure. In 1852, the Gazipur office being shifted to Kashi, He arrived here on transfer. On 31st May of that year, His father departed for His Heavenly Abode. After His father's demise, a family dispute ensued with His brothers. Peace loving and religious-minded Shama Churn always avoided discord, specially when He had descended on this earth for imparting a particular path to humanity since it was predestined, which though was not to be effected by Him then, the propensity for such actions would naturally pull Him towards peace. The Soul Whose mission was to bestow the message of peace could never remain in a non-peaceful environment. But He would have to establish the ideals of a householder in all aspects. To impart education to the masses, the illustrious maxim "Practise what you preach", should first be observed in one's life. Therefore family strifes existent in common households, struck Him also. This holds good because He had vowed that He would maintain a family existence meticulously, only after which He would confer His precept to humanity. He spent a short while amidst this family discord that had plagued Him after which He rented a portion of a two-storeyed house in Simon Chauhatta and resided there with His family. The subsistence of His family then depended upon His inadequate salary and small income from private tuitions. His family was being maintained on this unsubstantial income. This also is another aspect of educating the masses, or else He demonstrated to mankind that despite financial stringency, one can gradually construct one's life and advance towards *sādhanā*. This is uncommon in the life of a mortal. What ordinary men cannot perform, this Sublime Soul has easily initiated it in His Own Esse first. Otherwise why should the common man accept the ideals of this Sublime Soul? Bhagavān Krishna has advised Arjuna :-

Yadyadācarati śreshṭhastattadevetaro janaḥ
Sa yad pramāṇāḥ kurute lokastadanuvartate. — (*Gītā* 3/21)

That is, common people perform whatever the great men perform, what the great men determine as responsibility is abided by the common man.

* * * * * * *

In the year 1863, a long period after His marriage, His eldest son, Tinkari Lahiri *Mahāśaya* was born in this rented house on the holy bathday of *Bhagavān Jagannāth*. Kashimani Devi was an extremely quiet, compassionate and accomplished housewife. Despite the acute financial stringency, she managed the household affairs with supreme patience. By virtue of her judiciousness and sound domestic management, she saved from her husband's petty income from which Yogiraj purchased a house at Garureswar in 1864 and thereafter started residing there. Here on the day of the Car Festival in 1865, their youngest son, Dukari Lahiri *Mahāśaya* was born. In this very house their eldest daughter Harimati, second daughter Harikamini and the youngest daughter Harimohini were born respectively in 1868, 1870 and 1873. Shama Churn effected His mortal existence in this house.

Kashimani Devi never spent time idly. Early in the morning she would herself grant alms to any beggar who would come. She believed that beggars did not approach the house of the unfortunate. So her anxiety knew no bounds the day beggars would arrive late. She herself would perform all the household chores as the income of her husband was limited. Guests and newcomers would frequent her house. She would cook herself and would serve all to their entire satisfaction. In those days womenfolk had a false notion that the women who indulged in education would become fallen women in their next birth. Therefore Kashimani Devi was averse to education. But Shama Churn Himself had a liking for education. So He taught His wife Himself a few subjects. At a later date it was noticed that Kashimani Devi would read all the *śāstrás* herself. This pious lady acquired longevity by practising *yógasādhanā* in which she was initiated by her husband. She arrived at the acme of *sādhana*. Kashimani Devi consciously departed for her Heavenly Abode in 1930, (Bengali year 1337, 11th Chaitra) at the age of ninety-four.

Shama Churn was assiduous and industrious. He inspired social welfare services. It was through His endeavours and the co-operation of the then notable persons of Kashi like Ramkāli Chowdhury, Girish Chandra Dey, Kashinath Biswas etc. that the Bangalitola High School was established. Despite working for the whole day at office, performing the functions of a private tutor and executing household responsibilities, He would remain engaged in various types of social welfare. Due to His industrious nature and firm determination, the austere practice of *yógasādhanā* in His *sādhana* life could not tire Him. By existing within the family precincts, He set an example for mankind that practice of *sādhanā* with strong determination can result in spiritual attainment. The *Upanishads* have similarly stated — *Nāyamātmā Balahīnena Lavyaḥ* (*Muṇḍakopanishád* 3/2/3). Realisation of the soul can be attained only by spirited men and an example of this is the philosophy of the Esse of Shama Churn.

After the Bangalitola High School was established, Shama Churn became it's Founder-Secretary and remained so throughout His life. He desired that everyone should receive education and become well-established in life. He undertook all sorts of endeavours for the development of the school. He was observant as to whether the pupils were receiving proper education and the properties of the school were being properly maintained. He would pay surprise visits to the school to observe whether the teachers were discharging their duties perfectly. One day late at night, He had gone to school suddenly and found that the nightguard of the school was sleeping instead of performing his duty. The following day He fined him one anna as punishment.

In those days female education was not in vogue. But He advocated the necessity of female education. So He set up a girls' school with the assistance of some eminent persons. But the guardians abstained from sending their daugthers to school, therefore the school closed down.

His Highness the *Mahárājā* of Nepal appointed Him tutor on 24th March 1864, for the fourth prince, Narendra Krishna Sha alias Khala. Her Highness, the Queen of Nepal again appointed Him for the same job on 4th March, 1866. From this it can be observed that He was engaged as a private tutor for a long period of time in the Royal Family of Nepal. Apart from this, it can further be noticed that on April 5, 1867, He was appointed as a private tutor for the son of Harashankar Prasad Singh, the then affluent businessman of Kashi on a monthly fee of rupees five.

Rammohan Dey, the famous lawyer of Kashi was Lahiree Mahasaya's most affectionate. They were five brothers and one sister Manmohini, who lost their father at a tender age. Shama Churn Lahiree Mahasaya dispensed with a lot of favours regarding their education and path of progress. Later Rammohan earned a substantial sum from the legal profession. The Grace of a Sublime Soul has a far reaching effect. Rammohan's son Taramohan also became a reputed lawyer of Kashi. His son-in-law, Dr. S. C. Dev became the Head of Department of English at Allahabad University and was a renowned litterateur and philosopher. All the brothers and sister were initiated into *Kriyāyoga* by Shama Churn. They used to comment — "The love and affection which we have obtained from the *Gurú* cannot be obtained from our parents."

Chapter 3

INITIATION AND SADHANA

Many supernatural events occur beyond the range of human knowledge, how many keep account of that! The decree of fate is directed in various ways. Man's attention is towards the production of results. They are blessed by tasting the consequences of action. Smouldering fire after emitting smoke now gets the opportunity to burn brightly. Which is primary, acceptance or relinquishment? Without acceptance, relinquishment is not possible. To impart something to somebody, the imparter first has to accept. Shama Churn descended on the earth with a noble vow. He had pledged to householders that He would show them a marvellous, skilful facile path of *yóga*, thus the path for emancipating innumerable men would first have to be achieved by Him. Whatever action has been ordained by providence for man, has to be performed by him. None have the capacity to violate it. Now providence pulled Shama Churn towards the path He was destined to take.

On 23rd November 1868, Shama Churn received the order for His transfer to Ranikhet. Here He was promoted to the post of Head-clerk and His salary gained an increase to some extent. Leaving behind His wife, sons and daughters at Kashi and relinquishing the domestic comforts and pleasures, He set out for distant Ranikhet on November 27, 1868. In those days, there being no rail service, He availed Himself of the means of transport like ekka (a small one-horse carriage) or other forms of transport in vogue then. He reached Ranikhet a few days later and resumed His duty. Ranikhet is situated in the Himalayas in northern India and it's height is 5980 feet. It is fifty miles from Kathgodam and unlike now Ranikhet was not a populated place. It was surrounded by forests, was without habitation and towards the north the snow-laden mountain peaks stood majestically penetrating the sky. Ranikhet characterized by her natural splendour reminds anyone of *Mahādevá* engrossed in deep meditation. Arriving here even an irreligious person will become inclined towards religion. The natural beauty here has an infinite strangeness. Hermitages are located in some places and for *Śiválike* hermits Ranikhet is a wandering ground. In this solitude, they are absorbed in meditation of the infinite soul. The soul-sacred Himalayas are being paid intrinsic homage by the Indians from times immemorial. This is renowned throughout the world. It is the firm belief of the devotees that *Mahādevá*, the reigning deity of all the other gods, abides here. The Himalayas resemble the image of a trance-engrossed sage.

Roads were to be constructed for the army; provisions to be supplied for them and barracks to be built. To serve this purpose, a new office was opened here. Since properly constructed houses were not present then, Shama Churn lived in a tent. He did not have much work in office. Supervision and replying to some letters constituted His course of work for the day. As a result, He had ample time to savour the natural beauty of the place.

One day Shama Churn, accompanied by armed guards and orderlies was proceeding along the solitary hilly path carrying official cash with Him. Suddenly, He heard someone calling Him by name. Shama Churn cast His glance at the mountain top and found a *Saṃnyāsin* calling Him. The *Saṃnyāsin* hastily came down and stood before Shama Churn. The *Saṃnyāsin* had a shapely robust built, long arms reaching down to the knees, a calm and placid gaze and a gentle smile on his lips. Shama Churn thought that the *Saṃnyāsin* was the leader of a gang of robbers and that his men were hiding somewhere nearby, so He alongwith His men became cautious.

The *Saṃnyāsin* said, " Shama Churn, do not be afraid. I knew that you would come by this path. I have been awaiting you. Complete your office task quickly and come to my hermitage. I shall wait for you." Saying this the *Saṃnyāsin* pointed out his abode on the hill and departed.

Shama Churn completed His official task as early as He could and returned to His tent. He pondered whether He should visit the *Saṃnyāsin* or not. Again He mused as to how the *Saṃnyāsin* knew His name. It was known to Shama Churn that in this solitary region of the Himalayas many good saints did reside. Therefore naturally the religious-minded Shama Churn's desire to meet that *Saṃnyāsin* became intense and thus He set out.

Walking on the acclivity and declivity of a mountain path easily tires a man belonging to the plains. Shama Churn alone took the narrow path along the mountain-side leading to the peak. In this celestially beautiful region, hermitage of the trance-engrossed *Śivá*, many great *yogis* are engrossed in deep meditation. From times immemorial, people have been frequenting this place with a desire to acquire a holy view of these great *yogis*.

Having travelled a long distance, Shama Churn became exhausted and wondered whether He should proceed further. For if He did not return to His tent before evening, then there would be danger as the place was infested with wild animals. Gradually, the sun was making arrangements for setting behind the mountains for the day. Shama Churn seated Himself on a rock and took rest. There was no one around, moreover, it was not expected for anyone to be around. Winter had just set in. The place was surrounded by dense forests and Shama Churn proceeded through this jungle path. Sometimes doubts plagued His mind as to whether He came to the wrong path. Ahead lay the majestic expansive splendour of the Himalayas. As far as was visible, the mountains undulatingly mingled with the horizon. It seemed as though gods resided in this Himalayan forest. These Himalayas are the region for the religious austerities of great souls and saints. Beneath, a slender stream flowed down between two rows of mountains washing the feet of the Himalayas. It seemed as though it brought on this earthly abode, the water with which the feet of *Śivá* had been washed. The waterfalls rushing towards the lap of the River Ganges beneath, plunged into it. The incessant warbling sound of the water could be heard in the air as though Dryad was imperceptibly playing a musical instrument. In the path of the river's current, innumerable rocks with their heads held high listened to this sound with a stunned silence. The pines and chir (another variant of coniferous trees) stood like guards with their bayonets raised and commanded the entire mountain range. Amidst it's sylvan-azure, the steep, mountainous path-strip beckoned the spiritually inclined traveller Shama Churn, to an unknown domain.

Suddenly He heard the same familiar voice calling Him — "Shama Churn come here." He noticed the same *Saṃnyāsin* standing on the mountain peak, beckoning Him. With a vacillating doubtful mind, Shama Churn gaspingly reached the pinnacle being driven there by an unknown attachment. He noticed that the *Saṃnyāsin* observing Him was smiling mildly. It appeared as though the son returned home from a long sojourn and stood before the father whose placid eyes were drenched with affection. With a stunned steadfast gaze, Shama Churn looked at the *Saṃnyāsin*, bowed down and offered His obeisance to him.

The *Saṃnyāsin* asked — "Shama Churn, can't You recognize me? Can You recollect Your having come here before?" Pointing out to the tiger skin, ascetic's bowl etc. in the cave, the *Saṃnyāsin* again told Him — "Can't You recognize these also?"

Shama Churn replied — "I have never come here before; I cannot recognize them, they must belong to somebody else."

The *Saṃnyāsin* stated — "Listen Shama Churn, all these are the play of illusion. She has caused You to forget everything." The *Saṃnyāsin* touched Shama Churn gently. An electric current traversed throughout His body. This caused Him to recollect His previous life of *sādhanā*. He understood that this great *Saṃnyāsin* was His *Gurú* in His previous birth.

The *Saṃnyāsin* continued, "You practised *sādhanā* in Your previous birth here. This tiger-skin, ascetic's bowl all belonged to You. I have preserved them with utmost care. Your life ended here while practising *sādhanā*. After that You were born as Gourmohan's son in the village of Ghurni. Since then I have been observing all Your aspects. I have arranged for Your transfer in this hilly region to impart initiation into *yóga* to You. I have been waiting for You here since last forty years."

Residing at Kashi the place of great pilgrimages, Shama Churn had noticed many sages from childhood. He had an immense practical knowledge about sages. Apart from this by virtue of His sharp intellect, power of judgment and scholasticism, His emotional impulses were controlled. Thus as long as He did not dispel the doubts regarding the practicality of the *Saṃnyāsin*'s statements made to Him in course of their various discussions, till then Shama Churn did not agree to take initiation in *yóga*.

After this the great *Saṃnyāsin* initiated Him into *Kriyāyoga*. Shama Churn attained the state of non-dynamism and became engrossed in *samādhi*. By this time the sun had set behind the mountains. Gradually the evening stars silently adorned the infinite expanse akin to the platter of worship. A sublime tranquillity pervaded the whole universe. Nature also became a motionless *yogin* (female *yogi*) absorbed in deep meditation like Shama Churn. The surrounding mountains bathing in moonlight assumed the effulgent form of *Śivá*. It appeared as though the moon-god worshipped the *dhyāna*-rapt, placid, *Śivá*-beauteous. Endless manifestations of that ever-beauteous *Śivá* illumined the entire surface of the earth.

Gradually the faint light of dawn appeared in the sky. The stars still shone weary of a wakeful night. The moon concealed her existence behind the hills in the western sky. The mist as white as vapour extended till the horizon. The silent veil of thin mist slowly evanescing, the dim lustre of dawn appeared in the east. The stars disappeared with a reverence mingled with awe and submission. The lotus resplendence of morning blossomed in the east. This is the majestic splendour of the Supreme Being's creation.

The chorus of *Saṃnyāsins* present chanting the glory of *Śivá* arose, the material sound reverberating in the hills resounded within the innermost recesses of Shama Churn producing a gladdening resonance in Him.

Śivá, reigning deity of the gods emerged from His *dhyāna*. Shama Churn stood up. The sky assumed a splendid blue form. The cool caress of the breeze was felt everywhere. Melodious chirpings from tree branches were sounded. Shama Churn proceeded to return to His tent, His mind being replete with the spiritual ecstasy of a supreme gain.

His place of initiation was fifteen miles away from Ranikhet in the Dunagiri or Drongiri hills of the Dwarahat mountain range.

A golden era of *yóga* culture in India commenced the very moment Shama Churn's initiation into *yóga* occurred and this initiation roused His latent spiritual faculties and powers. This recognition of yogic wealth paved the way not only for His Own salvation but also for that of millions of people. Alongwith His initiation, the fate of future mankind was brightened. That the innumerable men of the world would receive initiation in this path of *sādhanā*; that many *sādhakas* hoping to acquire *sādhanā* would again take shelter in Him, that the knowledge of *Gītā* be preached in every Indian house again; that the ancient *yóga* practice introduced by sages be easily acquired by humanity; all these possibilities of future action germinated alongwith His initiation. Therefore His day of initiation opened the doors of *sādhana* to this world.

From then onwards Shama Churn would daily complete His official duties early, visit His *Gurú*, engage Himself in the austere practice of *sādhanā* in the manner introduced by His *Gurú*. After a few days of His *sādhana* practice, the yogic wealth of previous births; many unsavoured spiritual ecstasies; the abstruse essence et al manifested in His Divine Vision. He became thoroughly rapt in *sādhanā* and developed an ardent devotion for His *Gurú*. In life's path the entity who was unknown to Him even a couple of days before, now, he only unravelling a new world for Shama Churn became His very Own. It seemed selfless love and pure affection of someone very own gushed forth. *Bābāji* now became Shama Churn's exclusive own.

Shama Churn would address His *Gurú* as *Bābāji*. This is why at a later date His innumerable devotees and disciples termed His *Gurú* as *Bābāji*. Intense absorption in *sādhanā* made the self-oblivious Shama Churn grow apathetical towards His earthly existence, wife, sons, daughters etc., this engrossment was so profound that He no longer was willing to forsake His *Gurú's* proximity. In His previous Advent, Shama Churn by dwelling in this cave practised austere *sādhanā*. As a result, in His present Advent by observing the practice of intense *sādhanā* for a few days only, He reached the highest pinnacle of it's realm developing a stoicism towards His home and family. Just at that time, *Bābāji* informed that he would have to leave the cave within a few days and go elsewhere because this habitat was gradually becoming crowded rendering it unfit for *sādhanā*-oriented habitation, specially when the task for which

Bābāji was inhabiting the cave for so long was accomplished. *Bābāji* in an elaborate manner explained to Shama Churn the means adopted to bring Him here. Another clerk was supposed to have been transferred in this mountainous region, but due to the influence of *Bābāji's* power, Shama Churn was placed in his stead by the authorities. *Bābāji* further stated — "The task for which You were brought here is over. Now You will have to return to the place You belong. There You have to perform many activities." But Shama Churn did not return to His place. As predestined He had again acquired His beloved *Gurúdeva*, therefore He remarked that by remaining in close proximity to His *Gurú*, He would pass the rest of His life in austere *yógasādhanā*.

Bābāji replied —"That can't be Shama Churn. You will have to remain in the family ambit as a complete householder and practise austere *sādhanā* by which You can establish an illustrious ideal. Many are awaiting You. You will have to show the path of salvation to all those honest householders. You cannot forget that You have made a vow to them. Family men desire to practise *sādhanā* remaining within the family, but they are plagued by problems and possess little time. Therefore You will have to show them this *yógasādhanā* which is facile, simple, unostentatious and effective. It is because of this You have descended on this earthly abode, You cannot forget this."

Shama Churn made a humble prayer to *Bābāji* as to how He would engage Himself in austere *sādhanā* amidst the vortex of life's activities. This seemed impossible for Him as He would get no time.

Bābāji again said — "That is not correct, return to Your family life and You will find that there is enough time. In due course You will be transferred to Kashi and there cooked meals will be served to You. You Yourself by maintaining a family existence will attain spiritual fulfilment, for only then Your ideals will be acceptable to family men. Also bear in mind that the material world cannot be renounced. None has ever been able to do so. Wherever man resides, the material world stays with him. Besides this, it is the men belonging to the family precincts who have made this world so beautiful and endowed it with so much wealth and prosperity. The world would not have been so beautiful without the contribution of these men. If there had been no family existence, the creation of the Absolute would have waned. Everybody is born in this family existence. *Sādhanā* is not for renouncers only. As for example, the container from which I drink water is also a contribution of the non-renouncer." *Bābāji* continued sympathetically — "Family men today are not finding any means to make the quest for God. By remaining within the family ambit You will show them the true path. You have nothing to be perturbed about, return to Your family life. You can meet me from time to time and whenever You desire You can see me. Let a *sādhanā*-oriented householder be established in this manner." After this *Bābāji* pointed out to a few men present there and said — "You will have to initiate them. I have kept them waiting for You so long."

Shama Churn replied — "You being present, why should they take initiation from Me?"

Bābāji answered — "They are not indebted to me, this relationship exists with You and therefore You have to initiate them." *Bābāji* taught Shama Churn the manner of imparting initiation. After this those awaiting received initiation. Then *Bābāji* sent Shama Churn into the family realm. Because at a later date, Shama Churn would have to perform all these for educating the masses and showing them the path of salvation. Winter had set in Ranikhet. In accordance with the instructions of His *Gurú Bābāji*, Shama Churn applied for a transfer from Ranikhet on 17th December 1868 to the authorities on the ground that His health was failing due to the perpetually cold climate of the mountainous region. He attached a medical certificate alongwith His application for transfer which was granted within a few days.

Just as a river bearing an abundant source of water descends the plains from the mountains, similarly Shama Churn entered the family existence by fully realizing all the essences of *Kriyāyógasādhanā*. On the eve of departure from His *Gurú*, many extraordinary, spiritually fulfilled *sādhakas* met Him and bade farewell. Just as an old father adorns his young son in military attire, inspires him before sending him to the battlefield, similary *Bābāji Mahārājá* adorned Shama Churn with the esoteric essence of *yógasādhanā* before sending Him to the field of worldly action where the superficial aspect of the material world could not affect Him in the least.

In due course, the transfer order of Shama Churn arrived. This time He had to resume His duties at the Mirzapur office in Uttar Pradesh. Well equipped with yogic resources, Shama Churn departed from His *Gurú* with tearfiul eyes for Mirzapur on 15th January 1869. On the eve of His departure, the Omniphile Shama Churn humbly kept a prayer to His *Gurú* that He be able to preach this *sādhanā* to all irrespective of caste and creed. *Bābāji* gave his consent to this.

On His way to Mirzapur, Shama Churn stayed at Moradabad for a few days. A strange incident occurred there at that time. One day a discussion on religion was in progress with His friends. One of them remarked — "Nowadays, no such *sādhu* invested with extramundane power exists." None of them were aware of the spiritualdom Shama Churn had entered.

Shama Churn remarked — "This is not correct. Such a *Mahāpurusha* does exist. If you are eager to see such a *Mahāpurusha*, I can bring him here through *yóga*-power."

Curiosity of His friends increased. They repeatedly kept on requesting Shama Churn. In order to pay due respect to the *Mahápurusha*, Shama Churn agreed — "Well, give me a solitary room and close all it's doors and windows."

Shama Churn recalled the assurance of His *Gurú* and having full faith in it, entered the room, sat in a yogic posture offering a fervent prayer at His *Gurú's* feet. In a short while a brilliant cumulative effulgence emanated slowly assuming the form of *Bābāji Mahárājá*. *Bābāji's* seat was placed from before. Seating himself there, *Bābāji* in a grave tone stated — "Shama Churn, I was promise-bound to You to answer Your call, therefore I have come. But it has been improper of You to call me for mere fun."

Being reproached, Shama Churn kept silent and understood that this had been an unjust behaviour on His part. In a firm voice, *Bābāji* continued — "In the future, whenever You remember me, You will not be able to meet me. Whenever You have the necessity I shall come on my own accord."

Begging apology Shama Churn said — "My objective was to instil faith in the mind of the unfaithfuls." With bowed head He appealed — "When you have kindly appeared I pray to you to gratify all by showing your presence."

Bābāji accorded His prayer and asked Shama Churn to open the door. The friends who had been waiting outside entered the room, viewed him, paid him obeisance and were blessed.

Chapter 4

IN THE PATH OF SADHANA

After being transferred to a few places Shama Churn was posted at Danapur office. While staying here, He engrossed Himself in austere *sādhanā*. At this time He maintained such a secrecy that none knew about His *sādhanā*. *Gurú*-imparted-*yógasādhanā* became His mainstay. By the grace of *Bābāji Mahārājá*, He entered the domain of spirituality by which He easily ascended the gradual steps of *yógasādhanā*. After completing His daily official task, He engaged Himself in deep *sādhanā* in seclusion. During this period He made exemplary progress in *yógasādhana*. The taciturn yet affable Shama Churn was industrious. He would never advocate idleness. It is for this reason the austere practice of *yógasādhanā* could not deter Him.

From this period onwards, Shama Churn would constantly remain absorbed in self-introspection and a stoical attitude towards all aspects could be thus noticed. Because of this His boss would affectionately call this Bengali gentleman, Paglababu (self-absorbed gentleman).

One day Shama Churn found His boss much depressed and asking him the reason for this, learnt that the boss's wife was suffering from such a serious illness that her life was endangered. The boss was extremely anxious because he did not receive any news for a few days.

Compassion was aroused in the mind of Omniphile Shama Churn. His benevolence brought about it's outpourings. He assured His boss that He would in a short while bring the news of his wife.

The boss had been residing in India for a long time. He had heard many tales of supernatural powers of the Indian *yogis*, yet credence refused to come easily in an incredulous mind. So he gazed helplessly at Shama Churn.

Shama Churn entered a solitary room of the office and absorbed Himself in *dhyāna*. After some time He came out from the room, informed His boss that his wife was improving and that her letter was on it's way. He also apprised him the contents of the letter.

Would the cynical boss have faith in this? After a few days the letter duly arrived and noting a similarity in the contents as stated by Shama Churn, he was astounded.

After a few months, his wife arrived at Danapur from England. Many a time, English women would frequent the offices of their husbands. One day she came to her husband's office alongwith him. Suddenly seeing Shama Churn she recognized Him and was amazed. She told her husband that during her illness, this Sublime Soul had appeared by her bedside and it was by His grace that she was freed from her afflictions.

Hearing about the extra-mundane powers of Paglababu, the boss was extremely elated.

A few days later Shama Churn was transferred to Kashi and started residing with His wife, sons and daughters at His Garureswar residence. Earlier Shama Churn used to be away from home on account of His distant posting. He would come home occasionally and live with His family. Impeccable wife Kashimani Devi, would manage all the household affairs herself. Though her husband was living with the family He was apathetical towards family affairs. He would hand over the entire amount of His salary to His wife Kashimani Devi. The dedicated wife would never trouble her husband with domestic demands. She would cook herself, send her sons to school, make payments to respective recipients and look after all other domestic aspects. Shama Churn would remain stoical in every respect. He executed His official duties after which he would engage Himself in austere practice of *yóga*. Devoted Kashimani Devi never created any opposition in the way of His *sādhanā*, instead she would keep a strict vigil so that He did not have to face any difficulties in *sādhanā*. By mounting the gradual steps of abstruse *yógasādhanā*, Shama Churn caused immense spiritual and yogic wealth to be showered upon Himself.

From this time He commenced imparting initiation in society. A florist would sell flowers at the entrance of Kedareswar temple. He was the first disciple in society to receive initiation from Shama Churn. When flowers bloom, bees swarm in search of honey. Similary people seeking salvation gradually swarmed to Him. Though He preferred to remain unobtrusive, His renown as a Yogic Preceptor gradually effloresced.

Husband's immensity of progress in His *yógasādhanā* was unknown to Kashimani Devi. One midnight on awaking from her sleep she could not find her husband, so she lit a lamp and searching for Him found Him seated in *Padmâsana* in levitation in a corner of the room. By observing this extra-mundane yogic wealth of her husband, tears streamed down Kashimani Devi. She begged pardon with folded hands because many a time unknowingly she had been wrongful towards Him. After sometime when Shama Churn reverted from the transcendental state, Kashimani Devi begged apology and prayed for yogic initiation. The following day she was initiated into *yóga*. Her father was a renowned *paṇḍitá* and because of this, since childhood she had the habit of worshipping idols. After initiation she practised *yógasādhanā* also. Idol-worship was never practised by Shama Churn. He would ask people to abide by their respective faiths, would impart afflatus to them and advise them to practise *yógasādhanā*. He would remark that the basis of religion is *yóga*. Self-realisation is not possible without *yógasādhanā*. Again without self-realisation, soul-consciousness is not possible and without soul-consciousness, salvation cannot be attained.

Gradually the number of His devotees were increasing. From cobbler Bhagawan Das, tanner Giridhari, constable Vinda Haluai and hawkers to eminent personalities, many kings and the like obtained His grace. Preferring to remain unobtrusive, He never delivered any speeches in a congregation. If any devotee appealed for this, He would remark —"Is it necessary to inform people when the sun rises by beating drums? He who has vision can definitely perceive. Similarly the propagation of soul-religion is unnecessary. When one feels it is necessary or when one has a strong yearning, he will make the endeavour on his own accord. Propagation is necessary where there is an absence of the real essence." He never established any *maṭhas*, missions, *āśramas* or religious establishments. He would attach more importance to householders than to renouncers.

There are a few *sādhakas* in whom an extraordinariness can be noticed in their way of life and their path of *sādhanā*. They never flow in life's tide. The *Mahātmās* who are a class apart from the rest in their path are designated as *Mahāpurushas*, uniqueness in the part of *yóga* hence concealed, was brought to the fore by Shama Churn.

Vacaspati Devnarayan *Mahāśaya*, aged father-in-law of Shama Churn was a devout, renowned *paṇḍitá*. Being attracted by the remarkable yogic attainment of Shama Churn, he also obtained initiation from Him. Since then he never addressed Him as 'son-in-law'.

Affectionately he used to call Him **YOGIRAJ**. From then, Shama Churn gradually came to be known as **YOGIRAJ**. A renowned devotee of Yogiraj, *paṇḍitá* Panchanan Bhattacharya *Mahāśaya* of Deoghar used to address Him as **KASHI BABA**. At present followers of Yogiraj address Him as **BARABABA**.

His old father-in-law, Vacaspati Devnarayan left this earthly abode nearly a centenarian. When the father of Kashimani Devi was at his death-bed, she had a strong desire that Yogiraj visit him and pay obeisance to him. She expressed this desire to Him, but Yogiraj kept silent and smiled. Before death, Yogiraj met His father-in-law but not paying obeisance to him hurt Kashimani Devi.

Yogiraj retired from service in September 1880. His monthly pension was fixed at rupees twenty nine four annas and six pies (an obsolete Indian coin). Being difficult to maintain His family with that paltry sum, He engaged Himself as a private tutor for teaching the scriptures to Pravunarayan Singh, son of Iswari Narayan Singh, the King of Kashi. His tuition fee was fixed at the rate of thirty rupees per month. Everyday the King's boat would come to take Yogiraj to the Ramnagar palace on the other side of the Ganges. During the monsoons when the Ganges would swell up, arrangements would be made for His stay at the palace. The King was extremely pleased with Shama Churn being well-versed with all the scriptures especially *Vedãnta* philosophy and was eager to learn more about Him. Yogiraj always maintained a strict privacy about Himself. Girish Chandra De, a classmate and friend of Yogiraj was a top-ranking official in the Royal Estate of Kashi and hence he had an intimacy with the King. One day, in the course of conversation with the King, Girish Babu said —"Shama Churn is not an ordinary man, He is a Yogi in all repleteness."

The King replied —"By having a *dárśana* of Him and hearing about His scriptural knowledge, I had guessed likewise. Now I believe what you have said." After this, the king and the prince were blessed to have Yogiraj as their *Gurú.*

* * * * * *

Shama Churn had three daughters Harimati, Harikamini and Harimohini. Kashimani Devi grew very anxious regarding the marriage of the eldest daughter, Harimati. The wedding had been arranged, but where was the money for the marriage? Kashimani Devi brought this to the notice of her husband.

Yogiraj stated — "There is no point in worrying. Let Him think, who thinks for all. In due time *Áṅgada*[1] will bring everything."

After a few days, the King of Kashi, sent a few gold coins in a beautiful pouch woven with golden thread to Yogiraj through a messenger for the purpose of His daughter's marriage. By this the authenticity of God's infallible declaration has been proved —

> ***Ananyaścintayanto māṃye janāḥparyupāsate,***
> ***teshāṃnityābhiyuktānāṃ***
> ***yogakshemaṃbahāmyaham.*** (*Gītā* 9/22)

—which means I undertake all earthly and unearthly responsibilities of one who prays to Me (*Ātman*, the soul) in a thought-free state.

The eldest daughter of Yogiraj was married to Ramcharan Maitra[2] of Latakhola village in the district of Dhaka. Later His second daughter, Harikamini was married to Gangadas Chowdhury of Varanga village in Pabna District now Bangladesh and His youngest daughter, Harimohini was married to Ramamoy Bhattacharjee of Kadakuli in Bishnupur, West Bengal.

Normally, Yogiraj would not be affected by any illness. He was the true possessor of sound health. Once during summer, He was attacked with piles but they disappeared after a minor treatment.

Yogiraj would attire Himself in a dhoti, waistcoat and panjabi. He would wear canvas shoes outside and wooden sandals at home.

---

1. A devotional character in *Rāmāyana*.
2. Ramcharan Maitra expired on 12.2.1884.

Those shoes are still preserved in His house at Kashi.[1] He never took any breakfast. In the morning, He would take tiffin with a little amount of ghee and sugar. For lunch He would take rice with vegetables. He was a strict vegetarian. He would drink great quantities of milk. While smoking the hookah everyday after dinner, He would amuse His family members. He was five feet and four inches in height. His arms were long reaching down to the knees. The lower position of His body was milk-white in complexion; the middle rosy and the upper peaches and cream. His presence was so magnetic that those who were unacquainted with Him would bow down their heads in respect and make room for Him to pass when they met Him. At the primary stage He would practise *yógasădhană* throughout the night and at the concluding stage He would practise *sădhană* in the early morning. After this in the morning He would take a holy dip in the Ganges and resume *sădhană*. Normally He would not meet anyone in the mornings.

Matru, one of the devotees of Yogiraj had a small tailoring shop at Kashi. Almost every evening he would come to Yogiraj and listen to His sermons. As he was poor, he was unable to serve Yogiraj but he had a strong desire to do so. So Matru would bring two rolls of betel everyday for Yogiraj, Who also would enjoy taking the betel roll after lunch and dinner. Matru took a vow that he would treat Yogiraj to betel rolls throughout his life in this manner. Matru was alive for a long time, even after the Departure of Yogiraj. Till the last days of his life, he would daily bring two rolls of betel, place it on the sandals of Yogiraj and offer prayers there with folded hands. Tears would roll down the cheeks of the self-absorbed Matru then.

---

1. Also, a tooth of Yogiraj has been preserved at 52 Bigha, Deoghar, Bihar in the house of *paṇḍitá* Panchanan Bhattacharya.

Chapter 5

RAPT IN YOGA

Yogiraj visualised the immanence of *Nārāyaṇá* (*Ātman*) in all living beings and in all elements. When any devotee or any person would come to have a *dárśana* of Him and offer homage to Him, He would reciprocate, but obeisance by touching His feet was not preferred by Him.

It has not yet been known whether anyone who has attained salvation has penned his daily *sādhanā* experience in his diary. Twenty-six such diaries have been penned down by Yogiraj only, which is still carefully preserved. He wrote those diaries in Hindi language but in Bengali script. The purpose of writing them was to enable one to understand His gradual progress in *sādhanā*. That He had mounted the pinnacle of *sādhanā* can be deduced from His diaries even today. In one part of His diary He has recounted — ***Mai kuch nāhi ohi sūryahi jo kuch haye bilkul Mālik uha choḍāy dūsar kuch nāhi uskā rupá nicey likhā dekha*** — It infers — I am nothing, that *Ātmasūrya* (Soul-Sun) is everything and the Absolute. Nothing exists except that *Ātmasūrya*. His form is sketched below.

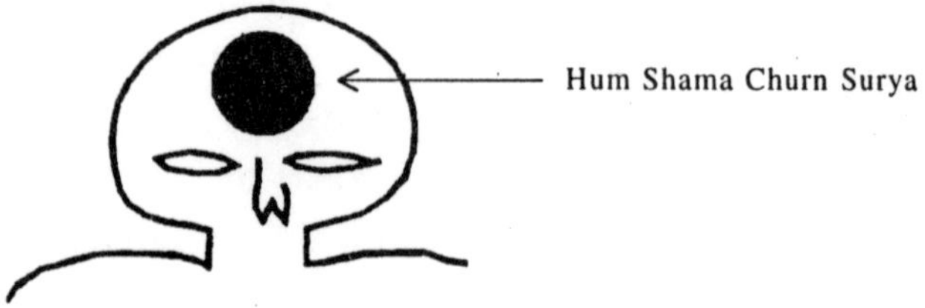

After this He has delineated a human form and inscribed on it's forehead, ***Hum Shama Churn Sūrya.*** — I only am the *Ātmasūrya* Shama Churn.

In another place He has written :—***"Ohi sūrya usikā jyot samet Ohi Mahāpurusha Brahma haye — baḍā ānand — āb baḍā majā huyā, ab bilkul svāsā bhitar caltā haye iske barābar ānand koi dusrā bāt nahi isikā nām Cidānanda — ehi Brahma — etteroj bād āj janam safal."***

The significance is — The effulgent *Ātmasūrya* is *Mahāpurusha* (Great-Soul) *Brahma*. Now there is an intense ecstasy and the breath is wholly internally oriented. This type of ecstasy cannot be derived from anything else. He is called *Cidānanda* (the Supreme Being conceived as a source of spiritual consciousness and delight of bliss), He is *Brahma*. After a long period today, My Descent has been fulfilled.

In other words by practising *Prâṇákarma* when the breathing motion being totally arrested becomes *Sushumná*-oriented, only then is this state gained. Thus He remarked that the ecstasy in this state cannot be derived from anything else other than this. By attaining permanence in this eternal bliss, He expressed that after several days now His descent has been fulfilled or else complete conversance about *Brahma* occurred in Him.

He has further stated that — ***Āpnāhi svárūpá Nārāyaṇkā dekhā. Mahādevá o Pārvatī ādmi kā rūpá dekhā, Pārvatī hame cumā diyā*** — implying "I visualised *Nārāyaṇá* akin to Me. I saw *Mahādevá* and Goddess *Pārvatī* in the human form. She gave Me a motherly kiss." Establishing Himself in non-duality, He realized *Nārāyaṇá* and Himself to be inseparable.

Amidst many such writings, only a few exact quotations have been quoted here. From these it can be inferred that He had mounted the highest pinnacle of *sādhanā*.

Commenting on one of His devotees, constable Binda Haluai, Yogiraj would comment — "Binda Haluai is floating on the sea of eternal bliss."

After His retirement, an expansive role of this Great Preceptor began. Though being a possessor of unlimited yogic wealth by the *Gurú's* grace, this Great Yogi maintained a domestic existence and preached *yógasādhanā* to householders mainly. All castes of Hindus, from Brahmins to Sudras; Muslims, Christians; from kings to beggars, all had received His grace. Balananda Brahmachari of Deoghar, Bhaskarananda Saraswati of Kashi, Saidasbaba,[1] a follower of Nanak, alongwith many *saṃnyāsins* were blessed by coming into close proximity with Him.

Iswarinarayan Sigh, the King of Kashi would sometimes visit Tailanga Swami and Bhaskarananda Sarasvati. Once having eulogised about this household Noble Yogi to Bhaskarananda, the latter expresed his desire to meet Him. Being a *saṃnyāsin*, he opined that it would be improper to visit a householder, therefore he asked the King to request this household Yogi to come to him. At first Yogiraj did not agree to this. Eventually, Yogiraj agreed after

1. The great *yogi* Saibaba of Shirdi, Maharashtra, appeared probably after 1850 A.D. and departed on 18th October, 1919 A.D. From his biography, it can be noticed that he was a follower of Kabir. The fact whether he had come to Kashi is also not known. But it had been written in Lahiree Mahasaya's diary that He had initiated Saidasbaba, a follower of Nanak into *Kriyāyoga*. It is known that Saibaba of Shirdi would never disclose the name of his *Gurú* but would refer to his pseudonym, 'Venkush'. Hindus, Muslims, Christians and people belonging to all classes of society took shelter in him. Many similarities can be noticed between them in the principles of religion and technique of *sādhanā*. It cannot be ascertained whether Saidasbaba of Shirdi was truly a follower of Kabir. On the other hand during Lahiree Mahasaya's lifetime, Saidasbaba of Shirdi's name finds mention, and not any other Saibaba. The place from where Shirdi's Saibaba hailed is also not exactly known. Probably in 1872 A.D. he had suddenly come to the village of Shirdi. It has been noted in his biography that he belonged to the Kabir sect, but how far it is true, cannot be definitely stated, because Saibaba would keep everything secret. Perhaps it is for this reason, Shirdi's Saidasbaba might have obtained *Kriyāyoga* initiation from Lahiree Mahasaya and maybe he belonged to the Nanak sect instead of the Kabir sect.

repeated entreaties and the King of Kashi brought Him to Bhaskarananda in his own chariot. A rendezvous ensued between two noble souls. Bhaskarananda learnt a great deal about the *sādhanā* technique of Yogiraj and requested Him to impart His *sādhanā* technique to him.

Gopal Chandra Bandopadhyaya, an eminent homoeopath of Kashi alongwith one of his friends would visit *Mahātmā* Tailanga Swami. Bandopadhyay *Mahāśaya* was the disciple of Yogiraj. One day both friends requested Yogiraj to meet Tailanga Swamiji. In Kashi then, Swamiji had a wide renown. He earned the reputation of a living *Śivá*. The silent Swamiji would sit at his *āśrama* at Panchaganga Ghat. He would be surrounded by devotees. Seeing the dhoti-panjabi clad Shama Churṅ alongwith Bandopadhyaya *Mahāśaya*, Swamiji stood up, proceeded quickly towards Him and accorded Him a warm embrace. After they paid homage to each other, they stood in silence for a few minutes. On observing the union of two noble souls, tears of devotion rolled down Bandopadhyaya *Mahāśaya*. After this, they left for their respective destinations.

The devotees present there were not familiar with Yogiraj. They had never seen Swamiji tender a loving embrace. On asking out of curiosity, the silent Swamiji wrote down his reply on a slate — "For attaining that 'One', the ascetics have to abandon even their loin cloth, but this Mahatma, by remaining within the family precincts has attained that 'One'."

One of the devotees amidst those present there had come the next day to pay *dárśana* to Yogiraj out of curiosity and mentioned about the written remarks of Swamiji to Gopalbabu.

Through this perception of *Mahātmā* Tailanga Swamiji, Shama Churn, one of India's greatest household Yogis became highly renowned within a short while. Surpassing the limits of Kashi, abode of *Śivá*, the supreme spiritual activities of Yogiraj started spreading from one part of India to the other. Irrespective of caste, religion, sect, people from all strata of life started arriving in teeming numbers. He as a Redeemer delivered graces to all generously.

He desired that everyone should progress in the spiritual path by maintaining a family existence. If anyone expressed their desire to take *saṃnyās*, He would refrain them from doing so, send them back home and remark — "The life of a *saṃnyāsi* is austere. If any error is committed by a householder, he can be forgiven, but a *saṃnyāsi* has no reprieve. The garb of a *saṃnyāsi* is the external manifestation of spirituality; but non-desirous of self-revelation the quiet household *sādhaka's* unostentatious *sādhanā* has no external manifestation." Nevertheless, many of His disciples were anchorites also. Since He would impart *Sanātána Dhárma's* intensely esoteric *Kriyāyoga* initiation to men of all castes, different types of criticisms were raised. With a gentle smile He would reply to His critic — "I see ignobility in nobility, again nobility in ignobility. Fortunately, I have entered the true path. When I see humanity within a human and if he wishes to be enlightened, then it is My responsibility to enlighten him."

Kashi's famous monotheist Swami Bisuddhananda Saraswati who used to bear a staff, previously a householder Maharashtrian Brahmin also was blessed by the grace of Yogiraj. He used to stay in Bishuddhananda *maṭha* near Ahalyabai Ghat in Kashi. Before his demise, Bishuddanandaji was suffering from various physical ailments. Because of his indisposition, Tinkari Lahiri *Mahāśaya*, son of Yogiraj would visit him often. At that time he was being neglectfully looked after. Therefore one day he lamented to Tinkari Lahiri *Mahāśaya* — "Now I find that domestic existence is better." In this manner, Bisuddhanandaji placed domestic existence on a high pedestal.

Sir Gurudas Banerjee and Kalikrishna Tagore alongwith Surendranath Ganguli, a distinguished lawyer of Chinsurah Court and devotee of Yogiraj came to Kashi and stayed at Kakina estate Thakurbari of Rangpur. It was later learnt through Surendranath Ganguli that the first two obtained *Kriyāyoga* initiation from Yogiraj then.

Both the brother of the King of Udaipur and a leucoderma patient from there obtained initiation from Him. At a later date it has been noticed that this patient was cured of the disease and attained a high state in *sādhanā*.

Another Shyama Charan Lahiri of Serampore in Hooghly district, was an eminent person. He was initiated by Yogiraj on 15th October, 1888. During the lifetime of Yogiraj, the aforesaid Shyama Charan Lahiri expired. This being published in newspapers, many devotees mistook the incident and sent enquiring letters to the Abode of Yogiraj.

Chapter 6

RESEMBLANCE TO INDIAN SAGES

In Indian culture (culture here does not signify it's traditional concept but the spiritual upliftment resulting in attainment of the state of equilibrium in everything mundane and extra-mundane), a marvellous union between scriptural injunctions and yogic codes have taken place. In accordance with the four stages of life, Indians by maintaining an existence as directed by *śāstrás* achieved yogic attainment and by doing this was able to conquer death. When the body became decrepit, they by easily discarding it like worn-out clothes, assumed a new frame through yogic technique. This sequence can be noticed till the time of the great poet Kalidasa and that information can be derived from his comment ***Yogenānte tanutyajām***. i.e., (changing the body by yogic process).

Yogiraj has rendered spiritually yogic interpretations to *Vedānta, Upanisháds, Gītā* and various other religious texts. These interpretations are a rare asset. These are incomprehensible to ordinary man but are specially meant for *sādhakas*. It is not known to us whether this type of *sādhana's* esoteric and spiritual yogic interpretations particularly of the *Gītā*, have been rendered before. Previously, *Gītā* would normally be discussed amongst the coterie of *paṇḍitás*. These discussions were not prevalent amongst ordinary people. Yogiraj has advised mankind to accept the *Gītā* as a guide to the spiritual path. That for India, *Gītā* is equivalent to *Prâṇá* was His connaisance. Thus He printed more than thousand copies of the *Gītā* and distributed them amongst His devotees. Everyday He would explain the *Gītā* to His devotees and make them understand. Being attracted by His remarkable explanations of the *Gītā*, many devotees would come to Him. In the past many *Mahātmās* had interpreted the *Gītā* in various ways. Some through the doctrine of dualism, some through the doctrine of non-dualism and some through the doctrine of dualism and monism have explained the *Gītā*. Some have noticed the importance of consciousness, some the importance of devotion and some the importance of action within it. But very few scholars have realized the *Gītā* to be a complete *yógaśāstrá*. All eighteen chapters of the *Gītā* pertain to *yóga*, for instance *Vishādayoga, Sāṃkhyayoga, Karmayoga, Bhaktiyoga* etc. Apart from this it can be noticed that at the end of each Chapter of *Gītā* — ***Iti śrīmadbhagavadgītāsūpanishadsu brahmavidyāyāṃ yógaśāstre śrīkṛishṇārjuna saṃbāde*** etc. has been written which means the *Gītā* is a *yógaśāstrá* which is *Brahma*-knowledge. Just as the paths of action, devotion and knowledge are important for attaining salvation, similarly the path of *yóga* is another important path. In the ancient period, the path of *yóga* was extremely favourable to the sages. Facts about *yóga* have been expounded throughout the *Gītā*. The essence of *yóga* has been scientifically discussed here. It is not merely a scripture for discussion, it designates the action of *sādhanā* in the spiritual path and it's technique. God has advised Arjuna to be a *yogi*, because none excepting a *yogi*, can realise the *Gītā* properly. *Gītā* is a *śāstrá* of *sādhanā* and realisation. Thus in whatever path *sādhanā* is practised be it *karma, bhakti* or *jñāna* etc. all are *yóga*. *Sādhanā* cannot be practised without *yóga*. *Yóga* means union. To bring about an union of the soul of a living being with that of the infinite soul is *yóga*. All *sādhakas* have the same orientation i.e. to bring about an union between the soul of the living being and the infinite soul.

Alongwith the *Gītā* a few other scriptural interpretations of Yogiraj can be obtained.[1] When He used to make spiritual

---

1. *Yogiraj has rendered yogic interpretations to the following twenty six scriptures : — (i) Gītā (ii) Vedānta Dárśanam (iii) Goutam Sūtra (iv) Ashtābakra Saṃhita (v) Sāmkhya Dárśanam (vi) Omkāra Gītā (vii) Gurū Gītā (viii) Tejabindú Upanishád (ix) Dhyānabindú Upanishád (x) Amṛítabindú Upanishád (xi) Abināśi Kabir Gītā (xii) Kabir (the Hindi couplet of Kabir) (xiii) Mīmāṃsārtha Saṃgraha*

interpretations of other scriptural texts, His devotees Panchanan Bhattacharya, Prasaddas Goswami and Mahendranath Sanyal would write it down. Afterwards they published the scriptures in their respective names. Yogiraj forbade the publication of the scriptures in His name. In His diary, a remarkable interpretation of *Vaiśeshika Dárśanam* in accordance with the yogic scriptures can be noticed.

His explanation of *Gītā* was excellent, for example *Sri Bhagavān Ubāc* as has been mentioned in the *Gītā*. Those before and after Him have explained it as "God said". But Yogiraj has conferred a spiritual connotation to this — "Realisation occurs through *Kűṭastha*". It is completely a new percipient annotation. *Kűṭastha* is everything. Because God has remarked —

Dwāvimou pűrushou loke ksharaścākhara evaca,
Kshara sarbāṇi bhūtāni kűṭasthokshara ucyate. (*Gītā* 15/16)

The verse means that two types of Primordial Energy are reputed to exist in this world; one is perishable, the other imperishable. Between these two, all elements are perishable and the *Kűṭastha*-consciousness is termed as imperishable.

None have before described what *Kűṭastha* is. Needless to say, it is not describable, it is made comprehensible through *sādhana*-derived realisation. Only the *yogis* are aware about it. The word *Kűṭ* infers the anvil or the iron block on which the ironsmith or goldsmith by hammering iron or gold into shape produces various types of objects, but the anvil remains as usual. It does not undergo any change, it remains unaffected. Similarly the whole universe is existent by taking recourse to *Kűṭastha*. Everything is undergoing a change, but *Kűṭastha* does not undergo any metamorphosis and is

---

(xiv) Nirālambopanishád (xv) Cáraka (xvi) Caṇḍī (xvii) Liṅgapurāṇa (xviii) Tantrasār (xix) Yantrasār (xx) Japaji (the main text by Gurú Nanak) (xxi) Vaiśeshika Dárśanam (xxii) Pātañjala Yogasūtra (xxiii) Mánusaṃhitā or Mánu Rahasya (xiv) Pāṇiniya Sikshā (xxv) Taittrīya Upanishad (xxvi) Abadhut Gītā).

imperishable. Thus what we call the Third Eye, the vision which occurs when one is in communion with the Infinite; the Eye of Wisdom is *Kūṭastha*. After attaining permanence in *Kūṭastha*, the whole universe becomes known to him, everything becomes manifest and realisation occurs. It is the origin of everything and is the place of manifestation of the spiritual world. By achieving permanence here, a *yogi* asks questions to his own self and receives the answers to it. All questions automatically arise in him and are solved also. For instance, just as a binocular is used to locate quite distant objects, similarly by attaining permanence in *Kūṭastha*, the whole universe can be visualised. Arjuna is the heat essence and it is through this that questions occur in the inner realm of a *yogi* and answers evolve through the medium of *Kūṭastha*. Since it is exclusively realised by *yogis*, *Gītā* is a scripture on realisation. Therefore Yogiraj has elucidated that "Realisation occurs through *Kūṭastha*". By becoming an adept in *Prâṇâyāma*, a *yogi* through *Yónimudrā* can perceive in the *Ājñācakrá* an encompassing golden lustre, the middle of it being black in colour and within this black colour a dot which resembles a star. Later by assuming the effulgence of the manifestation of a million suns it makes the *yogi* lose his own entity. This is the *Sudarśaná Cakrá*, by visualising this all the accumulated sins of a *yogi* are severed and seized, therefore He is Hari. He causes the seizure of all the accumulated sins. *Sudarśaná* signifies beauty. Since the middle of it is black in colour, He is Krishna and within this a static star is present which is truth and reality. He only is *Tāraknāth*. By attaining permanence in *Kūṭastha*, a *yogi* acquires true knowledge. Since it is sky-semblant, it is known as Cavern of the Union with the Absolute Void. If permanence is achieved in the aforesaid Cavern a *yogi* becomes conversant with all the essences of religion. Addressing *Kūṭastha*, Yudhisthira has noted —***Dhármasyatattvaṃ nihitaṃ guhāyām*** (*Mahābhārata Vanaparba, Bak-jakha Saṃbād*). This *Kūṭastha* only is imperishable or in other words is reputed to be the indestructible Primordial Energy. By the visualisation of *Sudarśaná Cakrá* or else *Kűṭastha*, the negative feelings or the devilish propensities in a *yogi* are annihilated. Then a *yogi* is capable to proceed in the path of renunciation. Observing this Tulsidasa has quoted :—

Jagu pekhan tumha dekhnihāre,
Bidhi Hari Śambhu nācāo nihāre.
Tneu na jānhni marmu tumhārā,
Auru tumhahi ko jānnihārā.

(*Rāmacaritmānasá Ayodhyā Kāṇḍa*)

The above verse implies that the world is visible and You are the Viewer; You are the Controller of the three deities (*Brahmā*, *Víshṇu* and *Mahêśvara*). When they also are not aware of Your inner significance, then how is it possible for others to know You?

Tulsidasa cites that this world is perceivable and You are the Perceiver. You are controlling *Brahmā*, *Víshṇu* and *Mahêśvara* or else the three attributes of *Sattva* (the primal quality of virtuousness and knowledge about reality), *Rájas* (the second quality characterized by activeness and spiritendness) and *Támas* (the third lowest quality marked by ignorance and vice) which are the three deities. *Brahmā* is the Creator and hence symbolises the *Rájas* attribute, *Mahêśvara* is the Destroyer, hence personifies the attribute of *Támas* and *Víshṇu*, the Controller is the *Sattva* attribute. You only are the Controller of these three attributes, because they are located within the body and are controlled by *Prâṇá* energy. If *Prâṇá* is absent, the aforementioned three attributes are also absent. Their existence depends upon the existence of *Prâṇá*. Therefore Tulsidasa states that *Kűṭastha* controls these three attributes.Thus, O *Ātmârāma*, (one delighted in soul-knowledge) You prevail amidst these three deities in the form of *Kűṭastha*-consciousness, therefore they also are incapable of knowing You wholly. Then, in what manner can the senses know you? You are prevalent in the form of *Ātmârāma* or *Kūṭastha*-consciousness in all beings. Therefore Yogiraj has remarked — ***Nijarūpá bindi sabhonse haye*** — implying the self-like dot is existent in everyone —

Again, *Mahātmā* Kabir observing *Kūṭastha* has stated —

Marte marte jag marā,
marnā nā jāne koye.
Ayayesā marnā koi nā marā,
yo phir nā marnā hoye.
Marnā hyāye dui bnhāti kā,
yo marnā jāne koye.
Rāmaduyāre yo mare,
phir nā marnā hoye.

This verse signifies that the people of the world keep on dying but none know how to die in an actual manner. None die such a death so as not to die again. Death is of two types. One is an ordinary death and the other a supernal death. One who dies at *Rāmadvār*, does not have to die again, because there is no birth, for if birth occurs death is inevitable.

What is *Rāmadvār*? Has *Mahātmā* Kabir asked man to die at the gates of a *Rāma* temple? If anyone accepts death at such a temple gate, will rebirth not occur then? *Mahātmā* Kabir has not stipulated this. The dot in the middle of *Kūṭastha* is termed as Cavern of the Union with the Absolute Void. Those who have progressed a little farther in the path of *sādhanā*, can perceive this. This dot is *Ātmârāma* or *Rāmadvā*r (gate of the *Rāma* temple), He is Soul-*Nārāyaṇá* and being the Destroyer of all sorrows is the Annihilator of all adversities. The one who leaves this earthly abode by visualising that dotlike *Rāmadvā*r is a *Mahātmā*, such a *Mahātmā* is never reborn. Thus *Mahātmā* Kabir aggrievingly notes as to how many people are there who can die by visualising the *Rāmadvār* like

Kűṭastha. The one who dies likewise is freed from the cycle of births and rebirths. Yogiraj has stated —

Jānā jānā sab koi kahate,
Jānāko nahi jānā haye;
Jānā uhnikā jnāhāse,
Phir lout nahi ānā haye.
Jiski lāgi lagan isse,
Ohi wayākif haye oos gharse.

This verse implies that everybody talks about leaving this world, but nobody is aware of what this departure is, departure takes place only from where there is no ṛeturn. Only He, by Whose grace I am alive is conversant about that state.

With a view to this, God has cited —

Prayāṇkāle mansācalena
bhaktyā yukto yógabalena caiba.
Bhrubormadhye prâṇáṃāveśya samyak
sa taṃ paraṃ púrushamupaiti divyam.
Sarbadvārāṇi saṃjamya mano hṛidi ṇirudhya ca
Murdhyanyādhyāyatmanaḥ prâṇámāsthito yógadhāraṇām.
Omityekāksharaṃ brahma byāharasmāmánusmaran,
Yaḥ prayāti tyajan dehaṃ sa yāti paramāṃ gatim.

— (*Gītā* 8/10, 12, 13)

This infers that at the time of departure, one who in a still mind united with devotion places *Prâṇá* between the eyebrows through *yogic* process and remembers Me can attain that Divine Infinite Soullike Primordial Energy; by controlling all the avenues of the senses or by not accepting material objects through the senses; by stilling the mind supportlessly; by placing *Prâṇá* completely between the eyebrows and by practising *Ómkāra Kriyā* of the Imperishable One; one who recalls Me, *Kűṭastha* and departs, attains eternal salvation. Therefore Yogiraj has stated — ***Marṇe wakt yo jaysā bhāowe soi woysā hoye. Āp sad cittānanda haye, āprūpá haye*** — signifiying whatever one thinks at the time of death, he becomes that in his next birth. In reality you are True, Blissfully Conscious and the Intrinsic True Form.

The *Ṛig Veda* states — ***Jyotishmantaṃ ketumantaṃ tricakraṃ sukhaṃ rathaṃ sushadaṃ bhūribāraṃ.****(Ṛig Veda 7/4, 29) Kūṭastha Brahma* has three *cakrás*, the first is the effulgent *cakrá*, the second the dark *cakrá* and within this is the starlike *cakrá*. By remaining in these three *cakrás*, one can remain in *Brahma* in an excellent manner. Mounting this three *cakrá*like chariot and proceeding is abiding in *Brahma*. After visualising *Ātmasūrya* (Soul-Sun) many a time millions of suns evolve and then everything becomes pervaded by *Brahma*. ***Guhāyadi kabiṇā biśāṃ nakshatra śabasāṃ*** (*Ṛig Veda* 7/8/25). This denotes that by attaining permanence in the starlike cave within *Kūṭastha*, a *yogi* gains the capacity to speak about supernatural facts and then he constantly views that effulgence of *Brahma* as a star. This is *Tāraknāth*. ***Aksharaṃ bindu jyoti manve abismahe. Parasūryeti śā saha paramgujhya.*** (*Ṛig Veda* 7/8/25). The effulgence of the starlike dot within the imperishable *Kūṭastha* is essence of *Brahma* and it is imperative that constant oblation should be offered to Him only. Later the merging with *Nārāyaṇá* the Supreme Master within the extensive Sun is extremely esoteric. Yogiraj has quoted — ***Kriyār dvārāy cákshu unmilan haye — tāhātei boliāche — cákshuunmilitaṃ yena tasmai śrīgurabe namaḥ.*** This implies that through *Kriyā* practice, the Third Eye is opened, Third Eye is the *Gurú* to Whom obeisance is paid.

In all living beings a spiritually perceived *aṇu* or an *aṇu* replete with consciousness is prevalent. It is subtlest of the subtle. The manifestation of the effulgent sphere from that conscious *aṇu* is *Kūṭastha*.

Yogiraj has recounted His realisations everyday in His diary and it is here while describing *Kūṭastha* He has noted — ***Bhulonā bhulonā tāre se ghana sṛishti saṃhāre, sarbadā āche sanmukhe dekhonā dekhonā tāre. Sadā smaraṇa kara ómkārer tāre.*** The inference of this is, never forget *Kūṭastha* Who is present in all states from creation to destruction in the form of a deep black colour. He is constantly present, observe Him, perpetually remember Him through *Ómkāra Kriyā*. Therefore Yogiraj would remark that if you desire to know about the *Gītā*, then enter your own body. temple. *Gītā* cannot be comprehended outside the body. As an example, God stated in the first sloka of *Gītā* — ***Dhármakshetre kurukshetre...*** Here God has stipulated about two fields, one is the field of spirituality and the other, field of action. Though God has mentioned two fields in actuality there is only one field, the body field, because it is by the medium of this body field that spirituality and actions are executed. Thus barring the body, spirituality and action cannot be accomplished. The testimony of the fact that this body is the field lies in God's dictum in the *Gītā*. — ***Idaṃ śarīraṃ Kaunteya kshetramityabhidhīyate*** — (*Gītā* 13/2). This implies — *O Kaunteya*, this body is termed to be a field. Therefore in order to completely understand *Gītā* the inner realm of the body-temple needs to be entered, for only then the underlying significance of *Gītā* can be discerned. For Indians *Gītā* is *Prâṇá*, therefore *Gītā* is worshipped by Indians as God. *Gītā* is totally a *yógasāstrá* and spiritual text. If *Gītā* is understood in this manner, then what the actual acme of human life is, can be attained. What benefit can be derived through reading by rote? *Gītā* knowledge depends upon *sādhana* of *Prâṇákarma*. *Kuru* signifies material attachment i.e. the faculty which induces one to perform bondage-oriented actions and *Pāṇḍava* signifies material detachment i.e. the faculty which weans one from performing bondage-oriented actions. The conflict between these two has been infinitely continuing within a human being. Therefore the battle cited in *Gītā* also is continuing infinitely. *Mahātmā* Ramprosad also has observed likewise :—

Pravṛitti nivṛitti jāyā,
Nivṛittire saṅge nibi.
Vivek nāme tāri byātā,
Tattvakathā tāre śunābi.

He speaks about two facets of a wife. Wife here implies the Female Primordial Energy. One facet is material attachment and the other is material detachment. It is advisable to make material detachment a lifelong companion. Spiritual essence should be delivered to conscience, product of material detachment.

* * * * * *

It has been written in the *Kāśīkhaṇḍa* of *Skandápurāṇá* that one who leaves this world at Kashi, the supreme place of pilgrimage and abode of *Śivá*, does not undergo rebirth. Having faith in this belief, a devotee in his old age started residing at Kashi. He was highly educated and earned a lot of money in his life. He was staying alone in a rented house. He used to come often and listen to interpretations of the *Gītā* by Yogiraj. He was quite older than Yogiraj. One day after the explanations were over, he rose up and paid obeisance to Yogiraj. Yogiraj told him — "You are older than Me, do not pay obeisance to Me."

The old man replied — "Till today, I have heard and read many types of interpretations of the *Gītā* but I have not heard of an interpretation of this nature. My eyes have opened. From today, I am Your devotee."

One day, Yogiraj was sitting encircled by devotees and a reputed *paṇḍitá* was explaining the *Kāśīkhaṇḍa*. The belief that rebirth does not occur while dying at Kashi was being explained but due to the use of some sceptical words, the old devotee arose and with folded hands entreated — "Do not make such remarks, I am counting the days of my departure in this abode of *Śivá*. If you comment likewise, I will lose faith."

That old devotee, due to age had become very ill. He could not move around as before. The landlady of his house, an old woman one day came to Yogiraj and said — "If that gentleman defecates and urinates in bed, then who will tend him?" The old lady was facing difficulties since the old man was not leaving the house.

Yogiraj rejoined — "What can I do? He does not stay with me."

The old lady replied — "He used to come regularly to You for listening to interpretations, therefore it is You Who should make some arrangements.'"

Yogiraj displeasingly stated — "You do not have to bother, He will look after Whose responsibility it is."

News arrived that the devotee was critical. He was desirous to have a *dárśana* of Yogiraj before his death.

Yogiraj went to see him. Immediately on arriving there, the old devotee said — "Kindly place Your feet on my head."

Yogiraj with a gentle smile made the observation — "How can you say this, instead you should bless Me before you die."

The old man wholeheartedly blessed Yogiraj with raised hands. After this he gradually expired, in consciousness.

Though being replete with *Brahma*-consciousness Himself, He would pay respect to elders in this manner and execute social responsibilities of a householder.

Yogiraj used to say that it is imperative for everyone to still the mind. If the mind cannot be stilled, *sādhana* cannot be practised, the worldly actions also cannot be accomplished in an immaculate manner. A person becomes inhuman because *Prâṇá* is dynamic and the mind is kinetic. Since the breathing motion is external, the mind is externally oriented. When the breathing motion becomes internal through *yóga* action, the mind becomes internally oriented and still. Through the still mind, the subtlest of the subtle eternal existence of God can be ascertained. Therefore He would advise everyone to practise *Sahajákarma* of *Rājayoga* in the *Gītā*. Especially He would ask all young in age to practise this action, for then their lives would become fulfilled.He would specially endear them towards *Kriyāyoga*. Because He would remark if this *yóga* action is acquired at a young age, then a long period of time for practising *sādhana* can be obtained and ultimate success in the spiritual path in this life itself can be derived. He would cite — Whether you practise *sādhana* or not, it is absolutely imperative to keep the mind under control rather than be controlled by the mind. Everything pivots around the mind. Without *yoga*-action the mind cannot be kept under self-control. If one does not possess the mind to practise *sādhana* even then this action should be practised by all, because the mind is controlled through this action. In ancient times, the sages also would practise this action. Yogiraj has revived that path introduced by sages for family men.

What is this *Sahájakarma*? Regarding this God in the *Gītā* has remarked — ***Sahajáṃ karma kaunteya sadoshmapi na tyajed.*** (*Gītā* 18/48), meaning O Kaunteya, do not abandon this *Sahajákarma*, even if it is fraught with faults. Generally in India, *sahajá* means easy but it does not imply so here. *Sahajá* implies that which has been derived from birth, for which no action or endeavours had to be made. Immediately after birth, a living being's inhalation and exhalation commences through both the nostrils known as *Iḍā* and *Piṅgalá*. A living being is alive as long as breathing continues. This breathing is a lifelong companion. Addressing this, Meerabai has stated— ***Mere janam maraṇke***

sathī, tnuhe nā biśro din rāti. This signifies that man should never forget the breathing which is his companion from birth to death. Meerabai forbids to abandon this breathing motion of *Sahajákarma* or *Prâṇákarma* or soul-action or *Prâṇâyāma*. If this *Prâṇákarma* due to lack of practice has faults initially, then also it should not be abandoned. By constant practice, these faults will be eliminated, that is what God has stated.

Yogiraj would never advise anyone to abandon family existence. Instead He would ask them to practise *yógasādhanā* by remaining within the family precincts. He would stipulate to mankind that by remaining within the family only *yógasādhanā* should be practised. Through the medium of this scripturally approved *yógasādhanā* the concentration of the *citta* [1] is achieved. By this the mind becomes purified gradually. In this purified mind, love, affection, peace and devotion towards God will arrive. Then by being one with universal consciousness, malice and envy will cease and an ordinary man will be transformed into a great man. *Prâṇá* is everything. He is Supreme. Only by uniting with the Supreme, man attains greatness. By executing a domestic existence uninterruptedly and by practising austere *yógasādhanā*, Yogiraj expounded the necessity of the practice of *Kriyāyoga* and sowed the seeds of *yógasādhanā* by instilling inspiration in *Kriyāyoga sādhana* amidst ordinary people.

Taraknath Sanyal, son of Rajchandra Sanyal brother-in-law of Yogiraj, was a highly educated youth. Once he was affected by a chronic stomach infection. Even after prolonged treatment when his affliction was not allayed he eventually left for Kanpur, for a change in climate and started residing at his father's intimate friend's house.

1. *Mánas* and *Cittá* are words used in the Indian language. These two words have been used often in this book. The word *cittá* has a much more subtler plane than *mánas*. The English equivalent for *mánas* is mind but *cittá* has no English equivalent though lexically mind has been used, therefore we have been compelled to retain mind for both the words.

While staying at Kanpur, a local resident told Taraknath — "Medicines cannot cure you of this disease. If you can obtain the grace of a *Mahātmā*, then your affliction will be immediately alleviated." He further continued — "Such a *Mahātmā* exists in Gorakhpur. Immediately go there and try to obtain his grace."

While Taraknath was making arrangements for going to Gorakhpur, his father's friend hearing everything replied — "A Mahātma exists in your family, and you are going elsewhere in search of a *Mahātmā*?"

Taraknath enquired — "Where is the *Mahātmā* in my family? I have not heard of any *Mahātmā*."

His father's friend answered — "Don't you know your uncle (husband of Rajchandra's sister) Shama Churn Lahiree Mahasaya? He only is the Mahātmā. Try to obtain His grace, for this will be beneficial for you."

Taraknath returned to Kashi. He visited his uncle with his father.

When Yogiraj heard everything He administered a herbal medicine to Taraknath. Using this medicine he was completely cured. After this he was initiated into *Kriyāyoga* and became absorbed in *sādhanā*. Since he stopped making endeavours to earn a living, his uncle commanded him to decrease his *sādhanā*. He said — "*Sādhanā* has to be practised and at the same time you have to earn your livelihood. It is improper to depend upon someone for your subsistence. You should maintain your family yourself."

Later this Taraknath became Head of the Department of English but despite this was able to arrive at the highest state of *sādhanā*.

From this incident it can be deduced how secretive Yogiraj would keep Himself.

Iswari Narayan Singh, the king of Kashi had become old. He

was taken ill due to old age and was awaiting death. The palace was located on the opposite side of the Ganges in Ramnagar. It is believed that one who expires on this opposite side of Kashi in Vyaskashi is born as a donkey in his next birth. Due to this dread, the Royal family had built a palace in Kashi proper. Thus when any Royal member was about to face death he would be brought to the palace at Kashi. Similarly Iswari Narayan also was brought here to tide over the gnawing fear of the aforesaid belief. One day through a messenger he informed his Guru that before death he was desirous of seeing Him. If only once He would be clement enough to grant him this prayer.

Hearing everything, Yogiraj replied —"I do not much go anywhere these days, let's see."

The king passed away. Taraknath Sanyal son of His brother-in - law asked Him after a few days — "The King was highly desirous of having Your *dárśana* but You did not grant him."

With a gentle smile Yogiraj replied — "I no longer visit any place in this body; the King has obtained My *dárśana*, you need not worry!"

Hearing this, those present looked at each other in surprise.

Dr. Gobardhan Dutta, one of the devotees of Yogiraj was employed as a doctor in the Navy. He had to travel many countries by sea. Whenever the ship would return to Calcutta port, he would then go to Kashi and have a *dárśana* of his Gurudeva. Once, he had come to Kashi likewise, paid obeisance to Yogiraj and sat down beside Him.

Yogiraj affectionately told him — "Why do you take the trouble for coming from so far? This involves both labour and expenditure."

In a humble tone Gobardhan replied — "I work in the Navy and thus travel to many places by sea. When the ship arrives at Calcutta port, I hasten to have a *dárśana* of You. Since I stay in the ship, I cannot maintain any sanctity or practise *sādhanā* regularly. Kindly bless this base mortal that on remembering You, I can get a *dárśana* of You."

Yogiraj nodded smiling gently.

It has been later heard from Gobardhan that while on board the ship whenever he would recall his Gurudeva, He would appear before him. Towards the end of his life. Gobardhan became a resident of Kashi and was able to reach the highest state of *sādhanā*.

A little distance away from the house of Yogiraj, Bhairav would stay. He would shave Yogiraj regularly and perform other household chores. Since he was slightly demented, none would any longer shave or have their hair cut by him, everyone was afraid to do so. But Yogiraj never abandoned him.

One day Yogiraj was going upstairs for lunch after coming out of the parlour downstairs. At that time Bhairav also was going up ahead of Yogiraj with a pitcher of water. Seeing Yogiraj, he stood at one side and when Yogiraj came near him, he chanted "Hara Hara Mahadeva" and poured the water on His head. Yogiraj did not utter a word, just smiled gently, went up and changed His clothes.

Amarananda Brahmachari, a devotee of Yogiraj would reside at His home. He was extremely angered by this but did not express it. Like every day, that day also Yogiraj went for a promenade on the banks of the river Ganges. Then Amarananada bound Bhairav to a pillar and beat him. The latter started crying aloud. Hearing his cries, Kashimani Devi rushed out and reprimanded Brahmachari thus — "The One on Whose head the water was poured did not utter a word. Why are you beating by binding him? He is not sane, he has not done anything knowingly."

Rammohan De, while appearing for his Law Examination had

vowed that if he succeeded, he would bathe *Mahādeva* of Garureswar and Yogiraj with milk. Having passed the aforesaid examination, he bathed *Mahādeva* of Garureswar with milk and arriving at the house of Yogiraj said — "I shall bathe You with milk during Your bath."

Yogiraj asked him the reason for this and Rammohan mentioned about his vow to Him.

Yogiraj remarked — "You have bathed the *Mahādeva* of Garureswar, that will do. There is no need to bathe Me."

Rammohan again prayed to Yogiraj in supplication — "I had vowed, please fulfil my wish. I shall later bathe You with water."

Eventually, Yogiraj fulfilled his prayer.

Yogiraj would often practise *Kriyāsādhana* throughout the night and go for a holy dip in the Ganges at Ranamahal Ghat in the morning. His great devotee, Krishnaram would accompany Him. While Yogiraj would go for the dip, He would be in a thoroughly rapt state and totter like a drunkard. On the roadside, there was a betel leaf shop. Seeing Yogiraj in this drunken state, the shopkeeper would make fun and comment — "Today, He is drunk again. Look at this Bengali Gentleman, He is intoxicated having drunk such a lot in the morning."

It can be noticed at a later date that the shopkeeper selling betel leaves became His ardent devotee and advanced a great deal in the path of *sādhana*.

* * * * * *

Yogiraj would never worship idols or visit the temples of gods and goddesses. He would remain perpetually engrossed in the soul. Only on Sundays He would visit Batuk Bhairava of *Kashi*. One day a devotee enquired — "You are replete with *Brahma*-consciousness, why do You pay a visit to Batuk Bhairava?"

Yogiraj replied in a grave tone — "Why will you go if I do not?"

Yogiraj surrounded by devotees was imparting advice. One devotee asked Him — "What is *śāstrá* (scripture)?"

Listen, *śāstrás* are infinite. But generally *śāstrás* signify the *Vedas* and in accordance with the *Vedas, Smṛiti-Purāṇás* are also known as *śāstrás*. For what is unknown, the *śāstrás* make that known. Again for what exists yet is unknown, *śāstrás* only can apprise us. To learn about those unknown facts there are some scriptural injunctions, in other words *sādhana*. The *Vedas* have both the chapters on action and knowledge. In accordance with the rules of the chapter on action, people by practising action attain heavenliness. But the chapter on knowledge is different, a living being achieves salvation through it. But entry into the chapter on knowledge is not possible without the chapter on action. Therefore the *Vedas* are the guide for all paths. Without *Vedic* knowledge or true knowledge, a living being cannot attain salvation. Those who do not perform good actions or even performing violate the rules of the *śāstrás*, cannot achieve happiness, divine grace or salvation. But *śāstrás* are endless, their prescripts are also endless. Therefore where is the certainty that everyone will abide by all the *śāstrás*? There are innumerable rules and taboos in the *śāstrás* and they are so much in opposition with each other that it is impossible to be followed by everyone. Again all the rules are not applicable for all. A profound knowledge of the *śāstrás* is required for outlining the apt prescripts to respective people. Again a mere knowledge of the *śāstrás* will not suffice; a great deal of memory power is necessary to understand which rule is proper for which person. But all do not possess this. The conceptual knowledge and memory power should be such that the essential element of all *śāstrás*, *Brahma*, can be known. This can be derived by a *sādhaka's* austere *sādhanā*. He has to be soul-rapt. Thus by reading the *śāstrás* efferently, no fruits are attained. Therefore the discussion of various *śāstrás* has been forbidden. One who is well-versed in the *śāstrás* but does not involve himself in soul-engrossment or soul-realization, or is not soul-illumined, his reading and explanation of the *śāstrás* is an unworthy labour. But one who is inexperienced about the *śāstrás*, yet is soul-illumined, his labour is fruitful.

There are innumerable *śāstrás,* facts worth knowing about are also endless, but one life-span is short. Therefore the substance of all *śāstrás* has to be accepted.

Śāstrás refer to the *Vedas* and the *Vedas* mean knowledge. Knowledge is eternally pure. Just as the temporary shade for the shining sun is cloud, similarly the temporary shade for knowledge is ignorance. Just as the sun becomes perceptible when the cloud disappears, similarly when ignorance is removed, knowledge reveals itself. Thus there is no deviation from what is the truth. Similarly though we are unaware about it, the soul which is the truth does not deviate from the normal state, it constantly remains the same. But why does visualisation of this unchanging soul not occur? The shade for the sun is the cloud and ignorance is the shade for true knowledge. When the cloud disappears the sun becomes visible, similarly when ignorance is removed, the soul, an embodiment of true knowledge manifests itself. Therefore it is true that before we knew the soul, it existed like the shining sun. Endeavours assist in removal of the shade of ignorance merely. To attain that knowledge, it is imperative to practise *sādhana* as prescribed by *śāstrás*. What is that *śāstrá*? *Śāstrá* implies that which controls or commands. Who controls or commands this body? ***Vāyurdhātā śarīrinām*** — The senses, mind, intelligence all function through the power of air. Amongst the airs, *Prâṇá* air is the principal one. Therefore *Prâṇá* air is the controller of the body or is *śāstrá*. The word *śāstrá* needs to be broken into two syllables. *Śā* + *astrá*, *śā* = breath and *astrá* = weapon. *Śāstrá* is the breathing-weapon. One who by wielding this breathing-weapon has attained dexterity or become proficient in *Prâṇâyāma* is considered to be well-versed in *śāstrás*. The *Vedas, Purāṇás, Upanisháds* etc. are also known as *śāstrás*. Because by wielding the breathing-weapon in this manner those who have become *śāstrá*-conversant, these *ṛishis* have recounted their realizations, which are acknowledged as *Vedas, Purāṇás, Upanisháds*, the *śāstrás*. Therefore these are authentic. By taking shelter in this breathing-*śāstrá*, the entire dynamism comes under it's control. Then becoming aware of the Male and Female Primordial Energy, diversity is eliminated and the cycle of birth and death is ceased. If this *Prâṇá*-oblation-*śāstrá* practice can be executed, soul-attainment occurs and the long sought prayer through the continuum of births of reverting to the ultimate destination is granted. Because of this only it is ascribed as —

Rājavidyā rājagujhyaṃ pavitramidamuttamam,
Pratyakshābagamaṃ dhármyaṃ susukhaṃ kartumvyayam.

(*Gītā* 9/2)

This soul-knowledge is the greatest compared to all other knowledge, immensely esoteric and purer than pure. There is nothing else purer than this. This soul-knowledge is directly and distinctly comprehensible and is approved by *śāstrás*. Being scientific, it can be practised blissfully and in comfort, for this reason it is indestructible, in other words this *sādhana* never perishes.

Prâṇá-air being dynamic makes the mind restless and material enjoyment occurs with the help of that mind. When the air becomes still, the mind merges in *Prâṇá* and becomes one, only then *Brahma* is visualised. When the air becomes still through *Prâṇâyāma*, a direct perception occurs. *Sādhanā* of this *Prâṇá*-air is only worth knowing. Since this air is the controller of everything, the rules or regulations pertaining to it's *Kriyā* is the scriptural injunction. *Kriyā* of this *Prâṇá* air is known as knowledge of *Brahma*. Through the medium of this *Kriyā* from *Mūlâdhāra cakrá* to *Sahasrâra cakrá*, when an universal consciousness is achieved, Vedic knowledge arises. Sequentially *Iḍā*, *Piṅgalā* and *Sushumná* are the three *Vedas*. When Vedic knowledge is complete, knowledge beyond the *Vedas* is attained or settlement derived in *Sahasrâra*. Therefore God has directed Arjuna — ***Traiguṇyavishayā vedā nistraiguṇyo vabārjuṇa***. (*Gītā* 2/45). The *Vedas* represent three attributes, but you should be free from all the attributes. Through this Vedic injunction that is through this soul-knowledge-*Kriyā* of *Prâṇá* air, an attributeless state or passive state is achieved. This Vedic injunction is the *Kriyā* of six *cakrás*. Just as what is worth knowing is learnt through *sādhana* of *Prâṇá*-air, this is knowledge and knowledge is no longer required after this, so also by practising *Prâṇâyāma-Kriyā* through six *cakrás*, a special type of settlement is achieved, that is the attributeless state in other words *Sattva*, *Rájas* and *Támas* or *Iḍā*, *Piṅgalá* and *Sushumá* or *Brahmā*, *Víshṇu* and *Mahêsa* are all absent. Then no type of *Kriyā* is necessary because the one who will perform the action is non-existent. This is known as the state beyond action. A *yógi* has to arrive at this state. Practising *Kriyā* is *Karmayoga* or study of the *Vedas*. While practising this action, soul-visualisation is attained and then the attraction or the pull of the *sādhaka* towards the soul is *Bhaktiyoga* and subsequently settling in the transcendental state of *Kriyā* or in the state beyond action is *Jñānayoga,* in other words it being the end of knowledge or *Vedas*, is *Vedãnta*. *Karmayoga*, *Bhaktiyoga* and *Jñãnayoga* are not independent *yógas*, they are a *yogi's* gradual progress in *yogasãdhanã*. Devotion does not dawn barring the exact action; barring devotion, knowledge cannot be achieved and barring knowledge salvation cannot be attained. Therefore these are inextricably linked; neither of them are independent *yógas*, but common man opines *Karmayoga*, *Bhaktiyoga* and *Jñãnayoga* to be independent *yógas*.

If the mind is placed on material objects instead of within the six *cakrás*, then it is a violation of the scriptural injunction. For this reason it has been forbidden to violate the scriptural injunction at first.

Yaḥ śãstrábidhimudsṛijya bartate kãmakãrataḥ.
Na sa siddhimbãpnoti na sukhaṃ na parãṃ gatim. (*Gītã* 16/23)

This infers that the person who forsakes the scriptural injunctions and is inclined to self-desired actions, cannot attain success, peace and salvation. Thus from whom can the substance of the *śãstrás* be obtained?

Mahitvã caturo vedãn sarvaśãstrãṇi caiba hi.
Sãrastu yogibhiḥ pītastakramaśnati paṇḍitãḥ. — (*Jñãnasankalinī Tántra*)

By churning the four *Vedas* and all *śãstrás*, the *yogis* have devoured their substance and the remaining unsubstantial part has been drunk by so-called popular *paṇḍitás*. Therefore Yogiraj has *quoted* —**"General people drink milk and consume it's condensed form, but the milk scrapings are consumed by children or *sãdhakas*."** (Here *sãdhakas* are considered to be children). If *Prâṇá* achieves settlement in *Sahasrâra*, *Kriyã* or action ends there. It is for this reason *Kriyã* of six *cakrás* is the chapter on action in *Vedas* and settlement in *Sahasrâra* is the chapter on knowledge. In knowledge only conclusion comes. But in the end, neither knowledge nor ignorance are present, because where there is knowledge, there is ignorance. Just as if there is day, there is night;

or if there is happiness, there is misery also. On the completion of action, action ceases. Then the self being absent, knowledge and ignorance are also absent. When the one who will know is not present, then who will derive that knowledge? In this state there is neither happiness nor unhappiness, neither emancipation nor bondage. Then by constantly remaining in *Brahma*, he becomes apathetical towards the world, or is as good as dead. In the state beyond action, the entire universe becomes pervaded by *Brahma* and this is the non-dual state. Present mind has originated from the dynamic state of *Prâṇá* but there is no vibration in still *Prâṇá*. Thus Yogiraj has remarked — ***"If breath is constantly shuffled, there is a cessation of breathing or stillness occurs. This stillness is called yóga. A living being is habitually restless, thus there is no alternative other than the still state — stillness is achieved by Prâṇâyāma. A hand-fan moves when pulled, if the mind desires it is pulled but if mind does not desire then there is no inclination to pull it, when mind becomes still, unnecessary desires are not existent and not performing unnecessary actions is known as the cessation of desires."*** When dynamism of *Prâṇá* is removed or when there is the state beyond actions, then the present kinetic mind merges in still *Prâṇá* and everything becomes *Brahma*. Then since mind, intellect, knowledge are all absent, an attributeless state is achieved. This type of *Brahma*-conversant *yogi* merges in the non-dual Supreme Being, then scriptural and material knowledge lose their significance for him and he exists only in *Brahma*. This *Brahma*-replete *yogi* cannot any longer be regarded to be *Brahma*-conversant because attaining confluence in *Brahma* becomes B*rahma* himself, thus connoting him to be *Brahma*-conversant then does not conform to rationality.

If anyone states he has attained salvation, then this would infer that he has not attained salvation because he possesses hunger, thirst alongwith body consciousness and knowledge. But for one who has actually attained salvation; hunger, thirst, body consciousness and knowledge are all absent. His knowledge, anger, envy and attachment are all exterminated. Then he is neither knowledgeable nor ignorant. The consciousness for knowing whether he has achieved salvation or not is also non-existent then. He becomes intensely rapt. It is a marvellous state. In this state all existence dissolves. But who by knowledge understands that he has achieved salvation; in reality he has not; because whatever has to be known is within the ambit of not knowing. Yogiraj directs — **"The one who is emancipated in *Kriyā's* transcendental state is also emancipated in it's pre-transcendental state because he never returns to duality, he sees *Brahma* in everything and remains united in *Brahma* effortlessly. If this is not so, it will be man's non-pursuit for spiritual attainment."**

After this special settlement is attained the vibration of *Prâṇá* and mind disappear and becoming tranquil is engrossed in the soul. This action has first to be practised in the *Iḍa* and *Piṅgalá*, because it is perceptible then. Later the action takes place in *Sushumná*, then the pure *Sattva* attribute emerges. *Yogis* pull air through *Prâṇâyāma* and draw attention towards *Kūṭastha*, for it is then that they can comprehend what should be performed.

Ye tvakkharamnirddeśyambyaktaṃ paryupāsate.
Sarvatragamacintyanca kūṭasthamacalaṃ dhrubam..
Saṃniyamyendriyagrāmaṃ sarvatra samabudhayaḥ.
Te prāpnubanti māmeba sarvabhūtahite ratāḥ.. (*Gītā* 12/3,4)

This implies that if all those persons having an equability in intelligence control all the senses completely and worship the inexplicable, amorphous, all-pervasive, inconceivable, tranquil, thus constant and indestructible *Kūṭastha* or those who worship the Omnipresent Imperishable *Kūṭastha* above *Ājñācakrá*, they by being the benefactor of all created beings, can attain Me.

A *yogi* has positively to release three obstructions — the

obstruction of tongue, the obstruction of *Anāhata cakrá* and that of *Mūlâdhāra cakrá* that is the obstructions of *Brahmā*, *Víshṇu* and *Rudra* respectively. He who has succeeded in releasing these three obstructions, is *Tríbhaṅgamurāri* (an appellation of Krishna standing crosslegged as He pipes His flute). That is a state. This state of a *yogi* has been allegorically described through the medium of Krishna's image of piping His flute standing. The *śāstrás* have noted thus —

Vidyate hṛidayagranthiśchidyante sarvasaṃśayāḥ.
Khīyante cāsya karmāṇi tasmin dṛishte parābare..
(***Mundakopanishád*** 2/2/8 and *Śrīmad-Bhāgavata* 1/2/21)

This denotes that when obstruction of *Anāhata cakrá* is released through the medium of *Ómkāra Kriyā*, all doubts of a *yogi* are severed and with the attainment of true knowledge, he being rapt solely in soul-visualisation, all types of actions are eliminated or actions are absent then. It is now that by achieving the state beyond actions or *Kriyā's* transcendental state, a *yogi* only perceives soul-*Nārāyaṇá*. Thus, since everything becomes one, it is a self-existent state and then there is neither bondage nor salvation, because there is none to express the state of salvation. This is the fearless state for due to absence of duality, fear is non-existent. By merging there the cycle of birth and rebirth is arrested, this state is the place of origin. An allegorical representation of the *Kriyā* of releasing obstruction of *Anāhata cakrá* is slaying of the demon by Goddess Durga as is depicted in Her idol worshipped during Durga Puja festival.

Yogiraj would further express — As long as the bestial proclivities are controlled, till then man cannot discover the supernatural power within *Prâṇá*, mind and intellect. The means by which this supernatural power can be manifested has been discussed in the *śāstrás* by sages in many places and they have explained it through the medium of idols of different deities and illustrations. If

Prâṇá, mind and intellect are directed towards providence, then faith, devotion and knowledge are attained. The more *Prâṇá*, mind and intellect attain excellence through *yóga*, devotion and cultivation of knowledge, the more God-orientation results. If this *Prâṇá* power cannot be driven towards providential wealth, then it is this *Prâṇá* which will pose as the greatest impediment for uniting with God.

Bandhurātmātmanastasya yenātmaibātmanā jitaḥ.
Anātmanastu śatrutve bartetātmaiva śatrubad. — (*Gītā* 6/6)

This implies that for one who has controlled the mind or has been able to still it in *Ājñā cakrá* at the occiput through *Ātmakarma*, the soul is his intimate companion. The person who has been capable of stilling the dynamic *Prâṇá* in *Ājñā cakrá* is the truly continent one (*Ūrdhváretā*). '*Retā*' means semen, thus ***Śukradhāturvabed Prâṇá. (Jñānasaṇkalinī tántra).*** The semen is grossly represented as *Prâṇá's* energy. The one who can still the vibratory motion of *Prâṇá* through *Prâṇákarma* and place it in *Ājñā cakrá* is the continent person. Since emission of seminal fluid occurs, the person who perforce abstains from copulation and restrains his sensual appetites would not be the continent person, because his kinetic mind has not been checked. The one who has been unable to keep *Prâṇá* above in this manner has been incapable of controlling the senses, thus his dynamic *Prâṇá* or the present kinetic mind act as an enemy for it instigates the performance of evil actions. The power of dynamic *Prâṇá* is vibration. Because of vibration, senses are existent and the mind is perpetually oriented materially. Just as *Prâṇá* motion is incessant, material attachment of the senses is equally incessant. Therefore the first endeavour of a *yogi* should be to prevent *Prâṇá* from being vibrated. (In *Tántrayóga śāstrá*, the philosophy of vibration is a special branch of study. There a scientific and *yogic* explanation of vibration's form, action etc. has been rendered). The learning or dexterity by which *Prâṇá* is prevented from vibrating and is oriented providentially has been ascribed by sages to be *yóga* knowledge. ***Tasmād yógāya yujyasva yóga karma sukauśalam*** (*Gītā* 2/50) implying — be appointed in the *yóga* action, it is extremely skilful. The dexterity of *Prâṇákriyā* is *yóga* because ***Samatvaṃ yóga uccate*** (*Gītā* 2/48), implying that an equability is termed to be *yóga*. It's main facet is *Prâṇáyama* or *Prâṇákarma* or soul-action or passive action. That is the *śāstrás*. ***Asaṇgaśastreṇa dṛirena chittvā*** (*Gītā* 15/3) — it is only (*Prâṇákarma*) which is free from all the senses. It's practice is the study of the *śāstrás*. If it can be exercised firmly, all types of senses should be severed. Thus by acquiring this human body, the field of action, (*Prâṇákarma*) should never be neglected. ***Karmaṇyebādhi-kāraste mā phaleshu kadācana*** (*Gītā* 2/47). You should be the authority of this passive action, but not of the consequence of action. Therefore God has stated —***Tasmāduttishṭha kaunteya yuddhāya kṛitaniścayaḥ***. (*Gītā*- 2/37) —"O *Kaunteya*, arise confident of your success in the battlefield and wage the battle of *sādhana*. Because ***svalpamapyasya dhármasya trāyate mahato bhayād*** (*Gītā* 2/40) meaning even if a little of this passive action of *yóga* (*Prâṇákarma*) is practised, there is a release from the greatest Fear. In a living being, the Fear of Death is imperative, this *Prâṇákarma* emancipates man from death. Regarding this, Yogiraj has Himself recounted the spiritual counsel in His diary — ***Kévala recaka o pūraka āur barāoye siddhi de — lāge āur samādh — recaka pūraka binā jayse bandhākup, prâṇá vāyú ko bal le āoe mánas niścal hoye jāye — āur barāoye — róga na rahe — pāp jalāoe nirmal kare — jñāna hoye timir nāśe***. This signifies that in *Prâṇâyāma* the three actions of *recaka*, *pūraka* and *kumbhaka* are prevalent. Yogiraj here asks to increase the actions of *recaka* and *pūraka* for then *Prâṇá* will become still, the state of *samādhi* will arrive and salvation achieved. There is no necessity for practising *kumbhaka* separately. The *Prâṇâyāma* barring *recaka* and *pūraka* or if the *Prâṇâyāma* occurring through the medium of internal inhalation and exhalation of breath does not occur, it is as fruitless as an empty well. If the *Prâṇá* air can be inhaled and exhaled internally with vigour then the mind becomes static. Increase this action for then there will be no diseases, the accumulated sins of all births will be burnt off, purity and knowledge will be achieved and ignorance exterminated.

He has recorded about His direct realisation regarding this state thus — ***Ṡvāsā ekdam se band huyā, barā majā. Ābkī majāki bāt kuch kahā najāye*** — implying after breathing completely stopped there was an immense ecstasy. This ecstasy is indescribable because there is no means by which it can be stated, it is self-realisable.

*   *   *   *   *   *

Surendranath Bandopadhyaya of Serampore, one of the devotees of Yogiraj used to work in Rawalpindi. While returning home, he halted in the middle of his journey at Kashi. He had a strong desire to have a *dárśana* of his Gurudeva. He looked visibly exhausted due to this long journey. He presented himself before Yogiraj and paid obeisance to Him with devotion. Yogiraj in a grave tone enquired — "Why have you come here? Go home immediately."

Surendranath was hurt by this statement of his Gurudeva. He could not understand what his offence was. Why was Yogiraj so merciless towards him? The corner of his eyes became tearful.

In an affectionate tone Yogiraj then said — "Go Suren and have your bath, have lunch with whatever has been cooked. After this hurry home in whatever train is available."

Suren did not have the courage to ask the reason for this. Spellbound, he executed all these commands.

Yogiraj called Matru and told him — "Go with Suren and see

him off in the train."

Suren arrived at Serampore Railway station. Proceeding a few steps, he saw his younger brother awaiting him.

— "You have come so late, brother! I had sent a telegram two days before and since then I am awaiting your arrival in each train."

— "Why, what has happened? I have not received any telegram."

— "Mother's condition is serious."

Suren hastened home.

— "Suren, have you come? I am awaiting you, my son. The time has arrived." The affectionate mother raised her hands towards Suren. He embraced his mother. Then gradually the lamp of her life was extinguished.

Tears streamed down Suren's cheeks. Now he remembered why his Gurudeva was so merciless then.

Haripada Bandopadhyaya of Dadhimukha village in Bankura district, was travelling to the adjacent village on account of work. It was a three to four mile journey. Therefore instead of taking a circuitous route, he made use of the jungle path. The forest was dense with sal (shorea-robusta), teak and mahua trees with a narrow path in the middle. There was no sign of any habitation. The fragrance of wild flowers and chirping of birds were being wafted by the breeze. Haripada proceeded, rapt in Godly thoughts. Fear could not touch him. Suddenly he became startled, seeing the messenger of Death before him. A man-eating tiger wagging it's tail, was slowly advancing towards him. It seemed as though it's prey was within it's reach, there was no cause for haste. Haripada could understand that death was inevitable, for the forerunner of death had already arrived. There was none here who could save him. Only his compassionate Gurudeva could save him. It seemed as though someone was saying from within him — "Gurudeva, please save me, Gurudeva please save me." Haripada and his slayer were facing each other now. Suddenly Haripada could hear as if someone was driving the beast away. After this the man-eater disappeared into the dense forest wagging it's tail. Tears of love flowed down Haripada's cheeks.

A few days after this incident, Haripada came to Kashi. Lying prostrate in obeisance at the Lotus Feet of Yogiraj, he said — "You have saved my life in this instance."

— "Because you were extremely scared." Yogiraj gave a little smile. The devotees present there exchanged glances, not understanding the incident.

Later all of them had heard about the incident from Haripada Babu.

Yogiraj the Salvator being All Pervasive, in this manner would save His devotees in distress. The innumerable ways He would render welfare to all cannot be accounted for.

On that day, like other days, Yogiraj was imparting advice to many devotees who were listening. It was about how man could be kind to all beings. He explained — There is everything within this body. This body is composed by five elements. The five elements that exist within the body are the same as the five external elements — earth, water, fire, air and space. The location of the five elements within the body are the essence of earth in *Mūlâdhāra cakrá*, the essence of water in *Svâdhishṭhāna cakrá*, the essence of fire in *Maṇipūra cakrá*, the essence of air in *Anāhata cakrá*, the essence of space in *Viśuddha cakrá* respectively and above it is beyond the essences. Knowing these five elements within the body the external extensive five elements can be comprehended. But if attempts are made to learn about the external extensive five elements at first, it will not be possible, for then that person will lose himself. Thus by knowing all the five elements within the body, the internal and external all fuse into one. Duality is non-existent then. *Prâṇá*-God prevalent in the five elements can then be realised and settlement in *Kū́ṭastha* occurs. Just as distant objects can be brought near with the help of binoculars, so also through the medium of *Kū́ṭastha*-binocular the *yógi* becomes conscious of the extra-intra facet of the entire universe. Everyone can attain this through endeavour. Since *Prâṇá* is dynamic, settlement in *Kū́ṭastha* does not occur. When *Prâṇá* becomes still through *Prâṇákarma* i.e. journeying through the path of six *cakrás*, settlement in *Kū́ṭastha* is achieved, then everything becomes lucid to a *yogi*. An inner sky within the Eye of *Kū́ṭastha* can be observed. It is not a visible sky, it is the sky within the sky which is the infinite void. It is so crystalline that no impediment exists there. Since it lacks impediments the distant-near relationship is absent. Everything from the small to the smallest and from the big to the biggest can be noticed. What a mustard seed at hand looks will look the same even if it is thousands of miles away. There is no light and darkness, yet everything can be perceived, it is self-manifested. The objects on the opposite of a lofty mountain alongwith the smallest object millions of miles away can be noticed easily, as in the case of a telescope which enables distant objects to be brought near. By visualising that infinite void, a *yogi* derives knowledge regarding the past and present. That crystalline imperishable Absolute Void *Brahma* is constantly static and present inextricably in all the elements. If He is absent, everything else is absent. This whole Creation has originated from Him and merges there. Therefore on 3rd June, Yogiraj had detailed facts about His *sādhana* derived experience thus — ***Śūnyáke bhitar yo śūnyá haye so alakh haye — soi bindi soi sū́rya. Śūnyáke bhitar yo śūnyá haye uskā ādi nahi. Lekan uha śūnyáse iha ṣūnyákā bheḍ haye. Sabuj śūnyá ananta ohi Brahma. Sū́raj usime laya ho jātā haye. Ab barā majā bhitar se uṭhtā haye bhitar jātā haye. Ab agam sthā-***

nme gaye yāne sthir. Abhi bahut dūra gagan panthme jānā haye. Ānkh bandh karke bāharkā cija mālum hotā haye — implying that the void within the present void or the void from which the present void has originated is imperceptible, it is the dot and the *Ātmasūrya*. The void within the void or the infinite void has no beginning thus no end, but that crystalline infinite void is different from the present void (i.e. the sky) because the distant-near relationship exists in the present void and is the last of the five elements, but that infinite void lacks the distant-near relationship; the past, present and future, the five elements and is beyond the essences. The existence of the present void depends upon the existence of the infinite void. That crystalline void is evergreen and infinite, that is *Brahma. Ātmasūrya* also merges in that infinite void, because the sources of origin and merging for everything is that infinite, amorphous, ageless, immortal, infinite void. Now I am feeling extremely ecstatic and this ecstasy is arising and travelling within. I have reached that inaccessible place where none else other than a *yogi* can reach i.e. I have arrived at the sublime still state. Now I have to travel a long distance in the path of that infinite void meaning I have to attain that state of merging. Even if I close my eyes now, I can visualise and realise all that is external. It's superficial representation is the black geode worshipped as the symbol of *Nārāyaṇá*. Just as the gigantic rocks under the water remain static even if there is a torrential current, similarly the perishable names and forms of God are torrential, but it's root Void-*Kūṭastha-Brahma* remains static and unchangeable. If the perishable form and name is unheeded, only then the conversance about the infinite voidlike eternal, omniscient and ever-blissful state can be achieved. Just as the soul cannot be apprehended to have a form, similarly name and form also cannot be apprehended to be a part of that crystalline void. Therefore Yogiraj advised everyone — ***Ei śarīre ye Kūṭastha āchen tānhāke ye gurúr upadeśe nā dekhe se andha. Yeman kabutarer pālak uḍte uḍte āste āsṭe ghurte ghurte paḍe temni vāyú kramaśa rukte rukte sūkshma***

haye abaśeshe śūnyer madhye diyā anek diner par gamanāgaman karite pāre— inferring the one who fails to visualise *Kūṭastha* which is within this body in accordance with his *Gurú's* advice, is blind. Just as a pigeon's feather flutters in the air and gradually and steadily falls in a winding manner because of its lightness so also *Prâṇá* air by being gradually arrested becomes subtle, light and eventually, travelling within the void becomes possible after many days.

Yogiraj had unlimited mercy for His devotees who had surrendered to Him. He would be perpetually alert to save them.

Abhaya, the wife of a famous lawyer in Calcutta was the devotee of Yogiraj. This couple lost a few children one after the other, for this they were intensely aggrieved. One day, Abhaya prayed at the Lotus Feet of Yogiraj her Guru, to bless her with a child who would remain alive in sound health.

The Great Yogi with a placid countenance was seated wandering in one of the realm of thoughts. He seemed to be freed from all bondages like a soaring bird. He did not keep track of who came and went and of the various conversations of different people.

Abhaya thought that perhaps Gurudeva could not hear what she said. She offered a fervent prayer again.

Gradually the Great Yogi returned to His normal senses.

Abhaya repeated her prayer at His Lotus Feet, i.e. she wholeheartedly wanted a child who would remain alive.

Yogiraj in a pacific tone stated — "Listen Abhaya, you will have a daughter and she will remain alive. But can you follow an instruction ? See that there is no mistake."

A faint ray of hope arose in Abhaya's mind. She thought that if her *Brahma*-conversant Guru was merciful then even the impossible would be made possible. Overwhelmed with emotion Abhaya said

—"I shall do whatever You instruct."

Yogiraj Who was affectionate towards the devoted said — "The daughter will be born in the early hours of the night. Keep a lamp burning in the room where you will give birth sometime before sunrise. But you must be careful that the lamp remains aflame."

In due time, Abhaya gave birth to a daughter. The lamp was kept burning in accordance with the instructions of the Guru. But in the latter part of the night both the fatigued mother and midwife fell asleep. The oil of the lamp now was almost exhausted and the flame of the lamp was on the verge of becoming extinct.

At that time an incident occurred in the puerperal room. Suddenly the door opened noisily. The sleeping mother awoke from her sleep, and with an amazed gaze saw her compassionate Gurudeva the Salvator, the be-all and end-all to His devotees, Incarnate of mercy and Sublime Yogi Shama Churn standing at the door.

Casting a benign look, He pointed at the dying flame and instructed — "Look Abhaya, the lamp is about to burn out, pour oil immediately."

The weakened Abhaya arose and poured oil in the lamp. By this time the compassionate countenance of her Gurudeva disappeared.

Remembering about the grace of her Guru, tears of love rolled down Abhaya's cheeks.

Later when Abhaya had informed her Gurudeva about this, Yogiraj smiled gently and replied — "The habit of all of you is to neglect your responsibility. Never be remiss."

The fact that Yogiraj had arranged for the birth of children to many childless couples in this manner, can be ascertained from His diary. Regarding this matter, on 8th February (year not mentioned)

He wrote — ***"Shyamlalko putra honekā upāy batlāyā."*** "I have stipulated the means by which Shyamlal can have a son.'

Yogiraj had two sagelike sons, Tinkari Lahiry and Dukari Lahiry and three daughters Harimati, Harikamini and Harimohini. Harikamini, the sixteen year old married second daughter, had come to her father's house. Suddenly she was afflicted with an attack of Asiatic cholera. Kashimani Devi requested Yogiraj to make some arrangements to save the daughter, He being present how could she die?

Yogiraj remained unperturbed as though nothing had happened. Kashimani Devi repeatedly kept on entreating Yogiraj to save the daughter by any means. The Great Yogi without speaking a word gave the root of *Apâmārg*[1] and two and half peppercorns and instructed — "Grind these two together and feed her."

Kashimani Devi thought since her daughter was married, it would be better to administer medicine to her according to the doctor's advice. If not, then if something untoward happened they would be reprimanded by the daughter's family of in-laws. Therefore without giving the medicine as instructed by Yogiraj, she started administering the doctor's medicine to her daughter. But the daughter expired the next day.

On that evening, like other evenings, Yogiraj was explaining the *Gītā* and His most worthy devotee *paṇḍitá* Panchanan Bhattacharya *Mahā́śaya* was reading the *slókas* of *Gītā*. Many devotees were listening. At this moment, loud wails from the room above could be heard. This perturbed everyone present.

When asked the reason for this, Yogiraj replied — "The second daughter has expired, therefore everyone is crying. Perhaps the

1. A creeping plant whose root is used as medicine.

relatives and neighbours who will take her to the burning ghat have come."

Bhattacharya *Mahāśaya* closed the *Gītā* and said — "Let the explanation be stopped for today."

Yogiraj solemnly expressed — "Let them do their task, you perform your task."

All the devotees present stated — "That steadiness of mind required for listening to the interpretations of the *Gītā* is not there. Let it be discontinued for today."

Yogiraj was nonchalant, as though nothing had happened. In a calm tone He said — "Alright, stop reading then."

The next day, Rajchandra Sanyal *Mahāśaya*, brother-in-law of Yogiraj came and asked Him — "Does the misery that occurs to an ordinary person with the loss of a dear one, occur to You?"

Yogiraj smiling gently replied — "Everyone feels the misery but there is little difference in the case of a knowledgeable person. If marble is struck on the firm ground it leaps up and retreats, but if struck on a soft clayey ground, the marble gets embedded in it. Similarly misery cannot render blows to a knowledgeable person. Blows do afflict him but it cannot create any impact on him. An ignorant person laments when afflicted."

By maintaining a family existence like a lotus leaf which remains undrenched though aquatic, this Noble Household Yogi easily remained unaffected by all sorrows and afflictions. This is exactly what God in the *Gītā* has expressed —

Yaṃ hi na byathayanteyte púrushaṃ púrusharshava,
Samadukshḥasukhaṃ dhīraṃ soamṛitatvāya kalpate.

(*Gītā* 2/15)

This implies that the person who considers happiness and

misery to be equal is sedate; is not pained by sorrows and can achieve immortality and eternal bliss.

* * * * * *

Yogiraj would daily go for a promenade in the evening at Ranamahal Ghat on the banks of the Ganges. His devotee Krishnaram's habitat was here. After strolling for a while, Yogiraj would sit on Krishnaram's verandah and make various discussions of the *Gītā*. After this, He would return home before dusk and sitting in His parlour would impart advice to His devotees. At nine in the evening, His devotees would depart. While He would sit in the parlour and give advice to the devotees in this manner, it would be noticed that occasionally He would accept obeisance paid to Him by placing His folded hands on His forehead. Why He would sometimes return the obeisance and to whom He would return, baffled the devotees present. None had the courage also to ask Him. Gradually, curiosity developed amongst them. One day, while He suddenly accepted the obeisance, immediately a devotee arose, went outside and saw another devotee lying prostrate in obeisance on the verandah and Yogiraj was returning this obeisance. This could not be noticed from inside the room. Thus, whenever anyone paid obeisance to Him from outside in this manner, He would return it. It was such that, if anyone paid obeisance to Him from afar also, Yogiraj could be seen returning it. The near and distant, the internal and external all were lucid to Him. He would see oneness amidst everything.

Both Priyanath Karar and his intimate friend Ram were favourite disciples of Yogiraj. The two friends had come to Kashi. They would regularly pay a *dársana* to their Guru and listen to His advice. Thus they were spending their days happily.

Suddenly one day Ram was attacked by a bout of Asiatic cholera. The place was an alien one and Priyanath became extremely anxious. Not being able to decide what action to take, he rushed to his Gurudeva.

Hearing everything, Yogiraj in accordance with the social norms replied — "Get him treated by a good doctor."

Priyanath brought two specialists but the affliction kept on increasing. Eventually the specialists losing hope stated that the patient's end had come and there was no other way by which he could be saved.

The helpless Priyanath again rushed to his Gurudeva. He informed Yogiraj about the terminal stage of his friend and felt that by now he had expired. Tears streamed down the eyes of the griefstricken Priyanath.

The tranquil, devotee-loving, sublime Yogi leaving His seat rose up. Taking a bottle, He poured some castor oil in it from the lamp and commanded—"Go and immediately make the patient drink this."

Priyanath pondered as to whom would this be administered. Perhaps Ram had expired by then. Again he thought his Guru is *Brahma*-conversant. His words can never be untrue.

Priyanath reached the patient in haste, he saw that the patient did not have any sign of life in him. Still taking recourse to his faith, he slightly opened Ram's mouth and poured a few drops of castor oil within. There were many others present there. A miraculous episode occurred in everyone's presence. Gradually the lifeless body stirred and breathing resumed. The patient revived again.

This Priyanath Karar *Mahāśaya* at a later date attained fame in the name of Swami Yukteswar Giri.[1]

---

1. Priyanath Karar *Mahāśaya* obtained initiation on 19th August, 1883, from Yogiraj and this had been noted in the Latter's diary.

This Noble Yogi would constantly dwell in the extra-sensory realm. A Himalayan serene tranquillity would perpetually prevail in Him. He disliked futile religious discussions with people who did not practise *sādhana*. Rather He assigned a greater importance on *yama* (control); *niyam* (rule); *āsanā* (sitting posture); *Prâṇâyāma* (*Prâṇá- action*); *pratyāhāra* (withdrawal of senses); *dhāraṇā* (realization); *dhyāna* (soul-engrossment) and *samādhi* (trance); the esoteric eight steps of action of the scripturally stipulated *yoga-sādhana*. His direct yogic realization was marvellous. Depending on those *yóga*-derived realisations, He would impart religious advice and confer interpretations to the spiritual texts. None of His expressions were underlied with emotion. The counsel given to His devotees was His direct yogic realisation. Therefore His advice would create an impression on the minds of men. His descriptions were lifelike. He would ask man to derive direct realisation through *Kriyā* and gradually become one with the infinite soul. This is the highest wealth in a man's life. Without *dhyāna*, realisation and *samādhi*, one cannot enter the domain of the spiritual kingdom's subtlest of the subtle essence of the infinite soul. This is His fundamental statement. He would say — *Prâṇá* is the origin of all power. By practising *Prâṇásādhanā*, all *sādhanās* can be performed. This *Prâṇá* has three states. In the beginning and end He is still, in the middle dynamic. Being still in the beginning and end comprises one state and the middle being dynamic is another state, thus *Prâṇá* basically has two states. ***Abyaktādīni bhūtāni byaktamadhyāni Bhārata***. (*Gītā* 2/28) — this implies that all elements initially are inexpressible; expressible in the middle when they attain shape and finally after merging inexpressible again. Dynamic *Prâṇá* is the Primordial Energy. The vibratory *Prâṇá* is a living being's present existence. The entire universe has manifested itself from this dynamic *Prâṇá*. All actions emanate from this vibratory *Prâṇá* but still *Prâṇá* is the place of origin for dynamic *Prâṇá*. Neither does the passive *Prâṇá* perform anything nor does He actuate any action. He is a constant spectator only. Still *Prâṇá* actuates when He becomes dynamic. Dynamic *Prâṇá* is the Female Primordial Energy and still *Prâṇá* is the Male Primordial Energy. This dynamism is the living being and the stillness is *Śivá*. This dynamism is bondage and stillness is emancipation. Thus the pull or motion towards *Prâṇá*'s vibratory state is bondage and the pull or motion towards stillness is salvation. The *śāstrás* have similarly noted thus ***Niścalaṃ Brahma ucyate*** —the static or still state is *Brahma*. That is the state of immortality, because in this sublimely still state there is neither birth nor death. It is constantly eternal, for there is none before Him, He is all pervasive. This is the state of Buddha, since it is beyond knowledge for knowledge also cannot reach there. It is ever emancipated, for bondage is absent here. This state is state beyond action or is the transcendental state of *Kriyā* because all types of actions are non-existent there. Due to the extermination of dynamism, no type of action can exist here. The contracted state of *Prâṇá* is *Śivá* and expansive state is the living being. Therefore it is imperative for a *sādhaka* to completely cease dynamism through *sādhana* and attain stillness. When a living being by terminating dynamism achieves the sublimely still Absolute *Prâṇá*, he himself only will become *Śivá* then.[1] Everyone is the Ambrosial son. None is base or noble. Though Yogiraj Himself was seated in the exalted rank of Preceptor, He would always disregard this exalted position and would advise all to think likewise. He stipulated the requisites of *yógasādhana* to be a healthy and sound human body, alongwith immense mental strength and a noble intention. One who possesses this wealth can easily practise *yógasādhana*. No impediment can act as a deterrent. None is sinful or sinless. Everyone is equal. Since everyone is the son of God, everyone has the right to practise

---

1. According to the Buddhist philosophy, this is the attainment of Sublime Stillness, *Nirvāṇa*.

sādhana. Irrespective of sex or class all have the right to practise this *yógasādhana*. It is not meant for any particular class of society. Yogiraj would state that placing the mind on *Kūṭastha,* sin is absent, not placing tantamounts to sin. *Kūṭastha* is God, He is the Supreme *Brahma*. Whether you maintain a domestic existence or renounce the world, wherever you are, *Prâṇá* exists within your body; meaning God is within you. If He is absent, you are non-existent. As long as *Prâṇá* is alive in your body, you are alive. What is the necessity for renouncing the world when you have to search for Him in your body? Rather, the domestic existence is a favourable domain for *sādhana*. By remaining here everything can be achieved. The one who by maintaining a family life practises *sādhana* of *Prâṇá*-God within the body is a heroic *sādhaka*. On realisation of *Prâṇá*-God within the body, the ubiquitous God-essence can be compehended. To practise *sādhana* of *Prâṇá*-God, it is necessary for *Prâṇá* to exist in the body. *Prâṇá* Himself is required for the attainment of *Prâṇá*. Barring *Prâṇá*, *Prâṇá* cannot be attained. *Prâṇá* should be worshipped or tended with the help of *Prâṇá*.[1] It is not possible to worship or nurse *Prâṇá* with any material objects. Whatever exists is *Prâṇá*-replete. There is nothing excepting *Prâṇá*. He only is *Brahmā, Víshṇu* and *Mahêśa*; He is the embodiment of goddesses *Durgā, Kālī* and *Jagaddhātṛi*. Therefore the sages giving a clarion call have noted thus—

Prâṇohi Bhagavānīśaḥ Prâṇo Víshṇu pitāmaha,
Prâṇena dhāryate lokaḥ sarvaṃ Prâṇámayaṃ jagad.

This denotes that *Prâṇá* is the father, mother, son and intimate one. The sages have similarly noted — ***Pitā ha bai Prâṇáḥ, mātā ha bai Prâṇáḥ, putra ha bai Prâṇáḥ, ācārya ha bai Prâṇáḥ*** (*Upanishád*). *Prâṇá* originates from *Prâṇá*, again settles in *Prâṇá*,

1. An elaborate discussion pertaining to this fact has been made in the author's book '*Prâṇámayaṃ* Jagad.'

Prâṇá is *dhárma* [1] (religion), because everything is held by *Prâṇá*. *Prâṇá* is action, for without *Prâṇá* no action can be accomplished. *Prâṇá* is the living being because since *Prâṇá* is vibratory, a living being remains alive. *Prâṇá* is *Śivá*, for He only is the Destroyer. *Prâṇá* is *Víshṇu*,[2] because He is the Protector. *Prâṇá* is *Durgā*, for by dwelling in this body-fort He annihilates all adversities. *Prâṇá* is the Primordial Energy, since He is the only one to dwell in the body-abode. He is all pervasive within and without this body. He is Omnipercipient. Therefore from man to insects, winged creatures, the animate or inanimate beings, for all, *Prâṇá* is the only worship and religion. All gods and goddesses worship this *Prâṇá*. From *Muslims, Hindus, Christians*, etc; from human beings to all types of creatures; all worship this *Prâṇá* without any discrimination. If *Prâṇá* is non-existent in the body, then nothing remains. The senses, organs, mind, intellect, pride etc. all exist upon the existence of *Prâṇá*. Therefore all should love the Universal *Prâṇá*, thereby love towards all living beings will emanate. He is the origin of love, He is the Master of all, therefore He is the Controller of the Universe, thus love Him. All should nurse *Prâṇá* by practising *Prâṇá's* breathing-like incessant action of *Prâṇákarma*. It is now that *Prâṇá* can be attained. You are *Prâṇá*. That *Prâṇá* has confined your 'present you', again it is He who will release your 'present you'. It is beyond the power of anyone other than *Prâṇá* to cause salvation. *Prâṇá* is the Master of bondage and the Emancipator. Therefore Yogiraj would emphasize that *Prâṇá* exists within this body, but how many make the quest for Him?

By restraining the externally oriented breathing motion which is like external *Prâṇâyāma*, if the internally oriented internal

---

1. *Dhárma* has originated from the Sanskrit conjugation *dhṛi*. *Dhṛi* means to hold.

2. *Vísh* — to be thoroughly rapt or to have perseity. One who by permeating all substances exists, is *Víshṇu*.

Prâṇâyāma be practised in substantial amounts all types of desires are eliminated, the state of knowledge is attained or rebirth does not occur; and if one dies in this state he will be free from rebirth, for he attains the state of salvation.

Prâṇâya namo yasya sarvamidaṃ baśe yo bhūto sarvasyeśvaro yasmin sarvaṃ pratishṭhitaṃ. Namaste Prâṇákrandāya namaste stanayitnabe. Vidyute barshate aushadhi yad Prâṇá ṛitābāsate abhikrandabyoshadhe Prâṇo mṛityú Prâṇáṃ devā upāsate Prâṇohi satyabādin suttam loka ādabad. Prâṇo birāṭ, Prâṇo deshṭṛi Prâṇáṃ sarva upāsate Prâṇoha sūryaścandramā Prâṇámāha prajāpatiṃ Prâṇâpānou brīhi yābānatvāna Prâṇá ucyate, yābad Prâṇá āhitā Apâno brīhirucyate, Apânati Prâṇati púrusho garve antarā yadātvaṃ Prâṇá jinvasathe sajāyate punaṃ Prâṇámāha mātarīśvanāṃ bātoha Prâṇá ucyate. Prâṇoha bhūtaṃ bhavanca Prâṇe sarvaṃ pratishṭhitaṃ. Prâṇá māsad paṛyāvṛito namadanyo vabishyasi. Apāṃ gavamiva jīváse Prâṇávadhnāmitvāmayī. (*Atharvaveda* 11/23/1/3)

The verse signifies that obeisance is being paid to *Prâṇá*-air within the body, that is paying obeisance to Him through His medium only by *Ómkāra Kriyā*. The whole Creation is under *Prâṇá* control, if He is non-existent, everything else is non-existent. Through *Prâṇá* all the external and internal actions are accomplished. It is imperative to nurse *Prâṇá*, the Ruler of the Universe, i.e. one should practise *Kriyā*. *Prâṇá* is God for whatever is being manifested. To serve this *Prâṇá*-God, there is nothing else other than *Prâṇá* Himself. The deceleration of *Prâṇá's* rhythm thus increasing the inherent stillness is referred to as *Prâṇâyāma*,. therefore all sensible people should regularly serve *Prâṇá* i.e. practise *Kriyā*. Everything is stationed in *Prâṇá* and this body contains Him. By having faith in the precept of *Gurú*, it is imperative for everyone to practise *Prâṇákarma* which is a supremely infallible remedy. Attainment of oneness is the main objective of *śāstrás* and the foremost is *Prâṇâyāma*. An aberration of *Prâṇá* air results in death. *Prâṇá* has irradiance yet manifestation occurs through *Kūṭastha* effulgence. He only is heat, water, the Sustainer and the personified Female Energy worshipped in the *Vedas*, in Whose manifestation the internal and external are revealed. To remember God is also action of *Prâṇá*. Cessation of *Prâṇá* results in the imaging of extensivity and the authority of visualising this state is *Prâṇá*. Everyone worships *Prâṇá*, some attentively and some inattentively. The Soul-Sun and Soul-Moon can be perceived through this *Prâṇá*. Within *Prâṇá* and *Apâná* airs, the Primordial Energy exists, that *Prâṇá* appears and disappears and the name of that *Prâṇá* is *Mātarīśvā*, i.e. Mother-Goddess. Everything has been and will be accomplished through that *Prâṇá* air and everything is settled in *Prâṇá*. Excepting *Prâṇâyāma* everything is untrue because by not habiting in truth, everything becomes untrue. Thus *Ātmakarma* is the doctrine of all *śāstrás* and should be practised. ***Sarvamoṃkārāṃ ebeda óm sarvaṃ Gāyatrī ca trāyate ca*** (*Chāndogopanishád* 5/4) — This body is *Ómkāra*, realising this is realising totality, *Kriyā* is *Gāyatrī*, the personified Female Energy worshipped in the *Vedas* and by practising *Kriyā* salvation is attained. ***Ye agnivarṇāṃ śuvāṃ soukhyāṃ kīrtayasanti ye dvijā tāṃ tābayati Durgā ninābeba sindhu duritātyagni.*** (*Ṛigveda* 7/8/14)—denoting that the *Kriyābān* (one who practises *Kriyā*) who regularly visualises *Kūṭastha*, through *yónimudrā* is aided by Goddess *Durgā*, the Empress of the *Kūṭastha*like fort to traverse the worldly sea. By keeping on traversing the worldly sea in the *Kriyā*like boat, the kinetic mind is stilled and the transcendental state of *Kriyā* being achieved, all sins present are destroyed — ***Kriyā kariyā kriyār parābasthāye thākā*** i.e. remaining in *Kriyā's* transcendental state by practising *Kriyā*. This sentence explains the totality.

The deeds in the previous birth are known as providence and the present deeds executed are regarded as human effort. Thus to annihilate the afflictions caused by providence and human efforts, *Kriyābāns* should perpetually concentrate in *Kriyā* in accordance with the advice of their *Gurú*. By practising 1728 or 20,736 *Prâṇâyāmas* all desires are fulfilled and the state of settlement in *Kūṭastha* is assigned to be the state of Goddess *Lakshmī*. The peaceful state can be derived in this manner; practising *Kriyā*, positively brings fulfilment. *Prâṇá* is *Vísvakarmā*, who nurtures creation. The dark sphere within *Kūṭastha* is *deva*. By practising *Ómkāra Kriyā*, settlement occurs on the left core of *Anāhata cakrá* and this is termed to be *Vāmadevá*. *Kūṭastha*-God Who exists within the six seasons (this classification of six seasons pertains to the Orient) prevalent in the six *cakrás* of this body is the Supreme and the Gleaner of whatever that emanates from dynamic *Prâṇá*. This *Kūṭastha* is *Rāma* because He holds the *Iḍā-Piṅgalá* like bow. Since He seizes both material attachment and material detachment, He is *Hari*. Again due to the deerlike transcendental ecstatic vision *Kūṭastha* is synonymous with the internal chanting of *Hari's* name which *yogis* realize. *Hari* seizes all the elements, He is named the Captor of all elements. Since He is ever-constant, He is eternal. He is Possessor and Relinquisher of the Divine wealth — hunger, thirst, birth, death, happiness and misery; thus He is God. On 28th October, 1874, Yogiraj had penned — ***Óm jyotrūpá — ehi jyot śarirme byāpak ho jāyegā tab sab dekhegā āur bolnekā tabiyat na cāhenepar*** — this *Ómkāra*like *Ātmajyoti* (Soul-Effulgence) after extending throughout the body or after the body becomes replete with the *Ómkāra*like *Ātmajyoti* (this body comprises the three worlds of Heaven, earth and the nether world) everything can be visualised and everything can be expressed even with the desire being absent. Aiming this Arjuna has said —

Dyābāpṛithibyoridamantaraṃ hi
Byāptaṃ tvayaikena diśaśca sarvāḥ
Dṛistvādvutaṃ rūpamugraṃ tabedaṃ
Lokatrayaṃ prabyathitaṃ mahātman.. (*Gītā* 11/20)

This denotes—*O Mahātman*, (the great *Prâṇá*) in between Heaven and earth (middle region), that means in between the *Mūlâdhāra* and *Sahasrâra* and in all directions, Your (Soul's) fiery resplendence has become all pervasive. This signifies that the upper, lower, right and left positions of the body have become replete by Your (Soul's) effulgence, visualising this wonderfully intense, fiery, terrifying form, the three worlds become extremely petrified. This infers that the three regions of the body, upper, lower and middle becoming astounded makes the mind terror-stricken.

* * * * * *

Yogiraj was averse to the promulgation of His tenets to the insincere. He never wanted anybody to take a photograph of Him. Once His devotees had decided to take a snap of Him and thereby invited Gangadhar De, a skilled photographer and devotee of Yogiraj. After this they prayed for His consent. Yogiraj remarked — "There is no need to take a photograph. If a photograph is taken; then in the future all will abandon *sādhanā* and start worshipping the photograph."

But the devotees were dogged in their determination. Repeatedly entreating Yogiraj, He finally agreed. All devotees alongwith Gangadhar Babu were elated and made arrangements for the photograph to be taken. By going near the camera, Yogiraj in a childish manner started enquiring about it's various mechanisms. Gangadhar Babu being inspired, started explaining about the different parts of the camera.

Eventually at the time of taking the photograph, Gangadhar Babu was faced with an acute problem. In the viewfinder, the Image of Yogiraj was not being reflected. He thought that there must be some defect in the camera. But on examination, it was found that the images of others were being reflected on the viewfinder. It was now that Gangadhar Babu understood the actual matter. He saw that Yogiraj was smiling mildly. Gangadhar Babu prayed with folded hands now — "Kindly have mercy, otherwise the photograph cannot be taken and the desire of devotees cannot be fulfilled."

Yogiraj now gently said — "Take the snap."

It was now noticed that the Image of Yogiraj was being reflected on the viewfinder.

The photograph which millions of His devotees possess today is the one which Gangadhar De had snapped on that day. Excepting this, no other snap of Yogiraj had been taken. But it is a strange fact that His photograph does not exist in any shop. Probably because He was averse to His Own propaganda, this secrecy has been maintained. Any person seeing His photograph is magnetized by the perfect yogic alignment of His Physical Bearing. Focussing on His gaze makes anyone realise that His gaze is the Intra-Vision making an universal afferent scrutiny. The eyes are settled in the *Śāmbhavī Mudrā*. But it is indeed unfortunate that various photographs of Yogiraj are being noticed which have no semblance to the original.

Even by mounting the highest pinnacle of *sādhanā* and attaining the state of resemblance to the life of ancient Indian sages, He would constantly maintain a simple existence. His attire was extremely ordinary. The reticent and soft-spoken Shama Churn would never reveal the yogic power unnecessarily. It has been noticed that He had showered yogic grace either under the guise of Divine Abstruse Causations or for the purpose of intensifying the faiths of devotees desirous of salvation. Though He remained established as the Origin of spiritual power, Yogiraj would regard Himself as insignificant. He would likewise advise His devotees —

If one does not consider himself to be small, one cannot enter the realm of the self. Many a time He would tell His devotees — "I am not the Guru, I do not maintain a barrier between Guru and disciple."

At this time, Yogiraj replete with spiritual power executed the role of a Salvator for the benefit of mankind. Not only this, just by paying Him a *dárśana*, many underwent a spiritual transformation. Quite a number of sadhus and *saṃnyāsins* would be seated at His Lotus Feet till late in the night and would derive substantial knowledge of abstruse *yógasādhanā*. Again all of them would leave at dawn. In this manner, He would spend innumerable sleepless nights, but was never noticed to be exhausted on account of this. With an ever-cheerful countenance He would constantly strive to fulfil the desires of devotees. On observing Him then, He seemed to be a condensed Image of compassion. Being devoid of the discrimination between the high and the low, it has been noticed many a time that this Sublime Yogi would Himself arrange for devotees who were destined to come under His Divine Presence and shower spontaneous mercy on them.

Jaipal Bhagat, the milkman had a milk and curd shop a little distance away from the residence of Yogiraj. He would sell milk and curd throughout the day and observe the entry and exit of the assemblage at the place of Maharajji. Many were blessed by obtaining His grace. Jaipal had an intense devotion towards Yogiraj. He would ponder that he being an ordinary man, would Yogiraj be merciful towards him? Jaipal could not say anything due to lack of courage. One day, he was walking along the road. Suddenly noticing Maharajji advancing towards him he paid obeisance to Him with modest devotion and stood aside. Maharajji returned his obeisance and smiling mildly remarked — "Jaipal, come tomorrow, I shall give you initiation."

Jaipal paid a reverential obeisance and said — "Glory to Maharajji." Being overwhelmed with ecstasy, Jaipal contemplated — "Maharajji has mercifully offered His grace to me, but can I abide by His advice?"

The next day arriving in the due time, Jaipal obtained initiation.

At a later date it can be noticed that from that small milk and curd shop, Jaipal had acquired immense wealth. The devoted Jaipal though he was steeped in the wealth and happiness of family life, subsequently handed over everything he possessed to his sons and would perpetually remain engaged in *dhyāna* in a hut on the banks of the river *Jāhṇabī* (the Ganges). He was able to reach quite a high level of *sādhanā*.

Hitlal Sarkar was an employee of a brick-field in a remote village by the banks of the river Bhagirathi in West Bengal. He would run his family expenses on a paltry income. But the inclination to render assistance to others was inherent in him. If any needy or distressed person had any requirement he would immediately grant him so according to his ability, without considering about the difficulties he and his family would have to face. Hitlal performed all the activities of a domestic existence but at times his mind used to wander. Hitlal would quietly sit on the banks of the river Ganges for hours together. Though he would accomplish all his tasks nothing seemed right to him. An indefinable yearning was plaguing Hitlal. It seemed as though this life remained incomplete.

Like other days, that day also Hitlal had gone to his place of work. He was supervising everything. Suddenly a thought-wave struck him. For no reason, his mind became extremely disturbed, he thought that there was no benefit accruing from his stay there, he had to go somewhere immediately. He executed this thought into action at once. Leaving his factory premises, Hitlal started walking.

It seemed as though he was pulled by an unknown power intensely attracting him. He was unaware of where to go and what to do. Hitlal proceeded spellbound. After a little while he arrived at a Railway Station and saw a train standing. He boarded the train and reached Howrah Station. The unmindful Hitlal went to the ticket counter and said — "Give me a ticket."

The man at the counter asked him — "Where will you go?"

Hitlal replied — "This is all the money I have, give me a ticket with that."

The aged man at the counter understood that this gentleman must have been mentally agonized for some reason. Therefore he asked him — "Have you ever been to Kashi?"

Hitlal replied — "I have never gone to Kashi."

The ticket-man gently smiling said — "Then go to Kashi, for this money will suffice. You will obtain peace by the grace of *Vísvanāth.*"

Hitlal knew that there was a Bengali locality named *Bāngālitolā* in Kashi, where many Bengalees resided. Alighting at Kashi Station, he proceeded towards Bangalitola enquiring about it's location. Hitlal was proceeding along a narrow lane. The exhausted and famished Hitlal was unaware as to where he would go. He was proceeding as he had to proceed. He suddenly saw a placid looking gentleman come out of a house and beckon him — "Hey there, come here."

Hitlal was astounded and proceeded. Approaching the person, he said — "You don't know me, neither do I know You. Then why did You call me?"

The gentleman tenderly smiled and replied — "We'll talk later about that, you are tired and hungry. First have your bath, then lunch and take rest."

Hitlal contemplated as to how this gentleman knew about his suffering.

Due arrangements were made for Hitlal's bath, lunch and rest. After his rest was over, conversing with other people Hitlal learnt that this gentleman was the Mahatma Yogiraj Shama Churn Lahiree. Before this, he had merely heard His name.

It was now that Yogiraj called Hitlal to His own room and remarked — "The time for your initiation has arrived, therefore it is Me Who has brought you here."

Hitlal sprawled at the Lotus Feet of Yogiraj. Obtaining the grace of the Great Yogi, he was blessed.

Chandramohan De, a neighbour of Yogiraj was a young man who had passed his medical examination and returned home. One day, Chandramohan came and paid obeisance to Yogiraj and prayed for His blessing. He blessed him and enquired him about the many facets of modern medical treatment. Chandramohan was a new doctor and his enthusiasm was endless. He explained various aspects of the developments in medical science. Yogiraj desired to know what the definition of death was in medical science.

Chandramohan explained what the definition of death was.

Jocularly and administering a gentle smile Yogiraj said — "Examine Me and see Chandramohan, whether I am alive or dead?"

Chandramohan examined and was amazed. There was no sign of life in the body. The heart beat was also static. Chandramohan was speechless.

Suddenly Yogiraj banteringly stated — "Chandramohan, you should then give Me a Death Certificate."

Chandramohan was even more nonplussed. He started thinking what to reply. Abruptly an idea flashed across Chandramohan's mind. He said — "I would have given You a Death Certificate, but You are still talking . A dead person is unable to talk."

Yogiraj laughed and remarked — "You are right. But remember, much remains to be learnt beyond your modern medical science where the latter cannot reach. But *yogis* can easily attain the quest for that knowledge."

This incident became a memorable one in Chandramohan's life. Later, though he had become an established medical practitioner he had advanced immensely in the spiritual path.

Yogiraj desired that everyone should maintain a family existence, earn their livelihood and within the family precincts practise *yóga* action and achieve self-attainment. He Himself had established that ideal. He Himself maintained an ordinary, spartan, unostentatious existence, was employed in a transferable service, executed a self-earned livelihood and amidst this practising *sādhana* gradually, He reached it's highest pinnacle and set an illustrious example for householders. It is not known whether anyone else has been able to establish such an ideal. Yogiraj would never accept any pleas for the non-practice of *sādhana,* i.e. despite staying within the family precincts failing to find the time He would state that for anyone truly desirous of practising *sādhana,* it would be possible to do so even by residing in the domestic ambit. He would never support executing one's existence depending upon others. He knew that the modern earning man suffered an inequality of income in an economically backward society. Therefore He did not approve of the rigorousness of ancient *yóga.* He advocated the convenience of a *sādhana*-oriented *yogi* who could practise *sādhana* secretly in his own house. Yogiraj simplified the rigorous techniques of *yóga* as introduced by sages for the use of common man and by unfolding the closed doors of *yóga* made it's path accessible to ordinary man. That it was impossible for modern man devoid of fortitude to practise the ancient austere *yógasādhanā* was not unknown to Him. Therefore, by eliminating it's ancient complexities He transformed it into a direct result-oriented, facile, unostentatious and simple *yógasādhanā* for the common man. Before this reviviscence of *yógasādhanā* by Yogiraj, the ancient Indian austere *yógasādhanā* was apparent to ordinary men as impossible. He bestowed welfare to humanity by making this austere *yógsādhanā* accessible to the common man. Mankind will never forget this noble benefaction of Yogiraj. This benefaction of His has uplifted man to the higher level of quest for the self. Today *yógasādhanā* is no longer difficult for householders. Our ancient sages were all beings who achieved yogic attainment and salvation. They also remained within the family precincts and by maintaining a conjugal existence in accordance with the regulations of the four stages of life had performed all functions by remaining united in *yóga*. This is the pattern of Indian tradition.

Household-Yogi Shama Churn would state that it would be extremely difficult for men of the present age to practise *sādhana* only in the path of emotion-oriented devotion. There would be a dearth of such devoted persons in a society ridden with problems or in the modern, faithless, abundantly luxurious society, therefore He drew men towards the facile, simple, unostentatious *yógasādhanā* and made an avowal that this facile *yógasādhanā* which was befitting the age was as infallible as the science of mathematics. Irrespective of caste, religion or sect, any man can practise this *sādhana*. Shama Churn, the Omniphile imparted social welfare in this manner.

In those days, the system of racial discrimination was very acute. Yogiraj belonged to a high-ranking Brahmin family. To disregard the custom of racial discrimination, was an extremely difficult task in those days. Society was not sparing in taking punitive measures towards such a person. Despite this it can be observed that Yogiraj disregarded the system of racial discrimination in the sphere of *sădhana*.

Ramprasad Jaiswal, a practising lawyer, belonged to an echelon of society which should have been regarded with equality. From amongst the devotees of Yogiraj who would listen to His advice most of them were Brahmins. Ramprasad also would sit beside them daily and hear the advice. The Brahmins present were dissatisfied with this demeanour of Ramprasad and one day expressed their dissatisfaction. But Jaiswal without raising any objections remained silent with devotion.

After a few moments, Yogiraj beckoned Jaiswal and told him — "Come and sit where I am sitting." Saying this He moved a little away from His Own seat.

Jaiswal started feeling immensely diffident. How was it possible for him to sit on the place of his Guru Maharaja!

Amongst the disciples present, Rai Bahadur Girish Prasanna Lahiri[1] who had expressed a great deal of dissent regarding this, was now extremely ashamed by this command of Yogiraj and prayed forgiveness from Him and made Jaiswal sit beside him.

Without maintaining any racial discrimination, in this manner Yogiraj would impart equal respect to everyone who practised *sădhana*.

Kashi, the domain of *Sivá* encircled by the river Ganges in the form of a crescent moon, has been drawing Indians towards the spiritual path from the Vedic age. This *Sivá* domain had borne the Indian tradition and maintained it's motion uninterruptedly till today. From kings and feudal princes to sages, monks and the poor

1. He was the zamindar of Kashimpur in Rajshahi district (now Bangladesh) and obtained initation from Yogiraj on 18th April, 1882.

all pay their homage to this Abode of *Sivá* and pour their earnest prayers at the feet of *Vísvanāth*. Everyone who visits this place is on an equal footing.

The then king of Kashmir had come to Kashi, the Abode of *Sivá*. He had previously heard about the Householder-Yogi. The king sent an officer to Yogiraj to learn about the time and manner by which he could meet Him.

When the officer came and made a humble representation of the king's wish, Yogiraj replied, "After nine in the night, when there isn't anybody, the king can then come along. If necessary he can be accompanied by a trustworthy person. But the king has to keep the fact of his coming here a secret."

The king arrived in due time. After paying obeisance to Yogiraj, the king had discussions with Him and was delighted. The king asked Yogriaj the reason for this secrecy.

Yogiraj stated — "You are a king and many know you. If you come publicly, there will be an uproar. It is for this reason I had instructed for secrecy to be maintained."

The king was extremely gladdened and later received initiation from Yogiraj.

The then kings of Nepal and Burdwan met Yogiraj likewise secretly and obtaining His grace were blessed.

Yogiraj had in His appointed path of *sādhana* indicated a few steps of it's practice. By practising *sādhana,* a *sādhaka* can achieve the higher to the highest steps alongwith the relative states of realisation in *sādhana*. He had Himself placed respect on this system imposed by Him throughout His life and instructed this to be followed by future *sādhakas*. None can ever have any means to violate this system.

One day a devotee with folded hands appealed to Yogiraj — "Kindly make an immaculate arrangement while present that from whom I should learn the progessive steps of *sādhana* in Your absence."

Yogiraj replied — "So many notable ideals have fallen prey to the onslaught of time. When your time will arrive, even if you are in the Sahara Desert, you will surely obtain *sādhana*."

Yogiraj never insisted anyone to become an apostate. This was another speciality of the *sādhana* technique revived by Him. He would say — There is no impediment to practise the *yógasādhanā* for men belonging to any religion or for those adhering to any doctrine. All types of Hindus belonging to the faiths of *Śākta, Śaiva, Vaishṇavá, Saúrya, Gáṇapatya* and Muslims, Christians all can practise the *yógasādhanā*, which is free from impediments. Yogiraj would term it to be *Ātmasādhana*. The same soul prevails in all living beings. Therefore there is no impediment for practising *Ātmasādhana*. The religion which one has faith in, the devotion which one has towards particular deities, the tutelary deity which one possesses will all remain the same. Proceed by depending upon your own respective faiths. Therefore it can be noticed that all types of Hindus, Muslims, Christians and people belonging to different other religions and castes desirous of salvation and the quest for truth, all had taken refuge at His Lotus Feet. Abdul Gafur Khan, a poor Muslim devotee, after attaining initiation from Him attained quite a high state in *yógasādhanā*.

Yogiraj Himself by imparting *yóga* to many devotees caused their progress in the path of self-advancement. The exact number of people whom He initiated cannot be correctly known. Amongst them at a later date, the ones who became famous as *yogis* were His two sagelike sons, Tinkari Lahiri and Dukari Lahiri and others like Panchanan Bhattacharya, Swami Pranabananda Giri, Swami Yukteswar

Giri, Bhupendranath Sanyal, Swami Keshabananda, SwamiKevalananda, Bisuddhananada Sarasvati, Kashinath Sastri, Nagendranath Bhaduri, Prasaddas Goswami,[1] Kailashchandra Bandopadhyay, Ramgopal Mazumdar, Mahendranath Sanyal[2], Ramdayal Mazumdar, Harinarayan Paladhi etc. Apart from them, it is heard that Bhaskarananda Saraswati, Balananda Brahmachari though maintaining their respective paths of *sādhana* exercised the *yógasādhanā* imposed by Yogiraj as well. The then King of Kashi alongwith his sons; the then kings of Nepal, Kashmir and Burdwan, Kalikrishna Tagore, Sir Gurudas Bandopadhyay etc. all the men belonging to the highest echelons of society obtained *yógasādhanā* from Yogiraj. Not only this, the people belonging to the lower strata of society also were blessed by obtaining the path of salvation from Him. Yogiraj would state that the greatest *āśrama* is the household existence because all the other *āśramas* are dependent upon it. Among the four stages of human life, i.e. celibacy, domesticity, recluseness and asceticism, the first, third and fourth are nurtured by the second. The household existence, therefore is the greatest.

It can further be noticed that at a later date Kaji Najrul Islam and Netaji Subhas Chandra Bose obtained this noble *Kriyāyoga* initiation[3] from Barodacharan Mazumdar *Mahāśaya*[4] disciple of Panchanan Bhattacharya *Mahāśaya,* and Headmaster of Lalgola High School. Sitaramdas Omkarnath acquired this *yogic* initiation from Ramdayal Mazumdar *Mahāśaya*. This *yóga* had made their lives splendid and successful in all respects.The principal secret key of their lives was this noble *yóga*. Through this key each of them

---

1. Prasaddas Goswami obtained initiation from Yogiraj on 23.12.1883.
2. Mahendranath Sanyal obtained initiation from Yogiraj on 18.10.1888
3. Netaji Subhas Chandra Bose obtained initiation on 12th June, Monday, 1939.
4. It is learnt that saint Aurobindo had made a remark about this Barodababu thus — "The greatest *yogi* of modern Bengal."

were able to open the gates of their innermost temples. This imparted an exalted and supreme excellence to their lives. They had discovered their inherent deities through this *yógakarma* and because of this were capable of dedicating their lives for the welfare of mankind. In the present age most of the people do not practise this *yógakarma*, as a result their sensory faculties remain unrefined and because they are attracted by the superficial glamour of religion there is a great deal of injustice in the nation today. Therefore Yogiraj would state — practising this *yógasādhana*, a man's life becomes beautiful and sublime. One becomes aware of soul-excellence and it is then that he becomes a true gentleman. But how can the main door of the inherent temple be opened? Yogiraj has expressed — ***Ulaṭ pavanakā ṭhokar māre khole darwājā.*** This implies that the breath-like air which has become externally oriented from above has to be made internally oriented and through the technique of *ṭhokar kriyā* can unfold the main gate of the inherent temple. Again He has written — ***Óm jorse dhakkā denese tab darwājā khulegā*** — meaning if a forceful impact is made on the *Anāhata cakrá* through *Ómkāra Kriyā* only then the gate of the temple of *Anāhata cakrá* opens. He has further written thus — ***Óm jeyādā jorse hṛidayme ṭhokar mārnese āpse āp nesā hoye o ṭhahar jeyādā hoye***. Through the medium of *Ómkāra Kriyā*, when the *Anāhata cakrá* is struck forcefully, a spontaneous deep engrossment occurs and a state of being staid is augmented. He has repeated in His diary — ***Jorse Ómme ṭhokar mārnese jeyādā sthir hotā haye***. This implies that if the *ṭhokar kriyā*like *Ómkāra Kriyā* is forcefully practised, the obstruction of the *Anāhata cakrá* is released and it is only then that the abstruse access opens and ignorance is thereby exterminated. By practising this *ṭhokar kriyā*, automatically a deep engrossment will arise and there will be settlement in the still state for a prolonged period. By achieving this state the mind becomes aggrieved by other's misery. Therefore He chanted —

Dukh dusrekā dekh kar dayā kar hṛiday,
Tabi pāyege caitanyarūpá jas candroday.
Āpne sāmarth košiš karo homat niṭhur,
Parmātmā santushṭ huyese mánas hota madhur,
Tarjāo āp amarpada onhā karo bāsā,
Calo rāha Sadgúrukā karo ohi upadešā.

This particular verse is being rendered in prose because justice cannot be done to the latent meanings as has been expounded here by Yogiraj. Thus it can well be understood that if this verse is translated as verse, the essence will be lost.

"Have compassion for those in misery i.e. for the ones whose *Prâná* is dynamic. When settlement is attained at *Kúṭastha*, visualisation of the effulgence of the Soul-Moon occurs which is equivalent to the effulgence of millions of Soul-Moons after which one will gain renown. Make ardent efforts with the capacity you possess to settle at *Kúṭastha* and do not deviate from this path. The Supreme Divinity is appeased with the settlement at *Kúṭastha* for then the mind will become blissful. Strive to settle in the immortal state of *Kúṭastha* abiding by the *Sadgurú's* instructions meticulously."

Yogiraj would remark — All images pertain to that One. A latent oneness prevails in various images. Discrimination of this oneness is inconceivable. This type of visualising images, listening to advice, emotionally contemplating on God and various types of customs are merely the external features of the spiritual path. Ultimately the base for non-duality has to be attained. The zenith of knowledge and complete success depends upon the settlement in non-duality, where there is no discrimination between the devotee and God. An inexpressible soul entity prevails there in the form of self-manifestation.

Primarily Divine visualisation and hearing the Divine sound are not so difficult. But the actual God visualisation is an abstruse affair.

Passing through several tests and practising austere *sādhanā*, when one is uplifted on the true base of *sādhanā* then the actual God visualisation can be attained. A *yogi* proceeding from the living being state to the *Śivá* state attains the Supreme *Śivá*like soul-visualisation and is gratified. But in the present age men have become faithless and disrespectful, thus such types of visualisation are difficult. In the present, men are only argumentative and cynical. Simple faith in modern times is extremely rare. Therefore objects which can be easily acquired have become unattainable. But *yóga* initiation is exclusively based upon scientific educational steps. For instance, just as two plus two equals four, similarly in accordance with *yógakarma's* practice and realisation, the gradual steps of ecstasy are unfolded one by one. If in the world man posseses any essence termed *Ātmadhárma*, then it is this *yógadhárma,* the essence of which has been mentioned in *yóga* philosophy and after the decadence of the Indus Valley civilization in the past quite a great deal of gross testimony to this truth has been found. Till the present time, a direct and indirect relationship of the *yóga* essence can be noticed amidst the people of all the countries and races of the world. God descends in the form of *Gurú* and controls the devotee, imparts advice etc. when it is necessary for the devotee. This *Gurú* is the *Sadgurú* (the real *Gurú*). Once the *Sadgurú* is acquired, the anguish due to the dearth of a *Gurú* is no longer felt.

If the one who seeks truth is ridden with faithlessness and cynicism, then the path for the manifestation of God's merciful powers ceases. It is easy to obtain God's grace through emotion, but to retain it through the strength of own *sādhana* and realisation and to cause a revelation of self-power by observing God's grace is extremely difficult.

By knowledge we mean, common knowledge, but science infers neither bookish knowledge nor syllogism nor emotion or imagination. That knowledge is the direct visualisation, direct realisation or in other words what is special type of knowledge is science. This is known as soul-knowledge. A visible object implies knowledge. Thus the true significance of the word visualisation is knowledge. The object which is infinitely pervasive in the universe, visualising that unchangeable object is soul-visualisation or *Brahma*-visualisation. He is the Infinite Soul, but is realizable. He exists in every living being homogenously. Therefore the authors of the *śāstrás* have proclaimed ***Ātmā ha bai gurúrekaḥ***[1]. This implies that the soul is *Gurú*.

Impermanent or temporary devotion is not devotion. Permanent devotion is necessary. When the differences in devotion, devotee and God are eliminated then the state of permanent devotion evolves. The state in which the conversant one, that which has to be known and knowledge all fuse into one that is the state of science. It is termed to be true devotion or knowledge. As long as the mind wanders externally, till then knowledge and devotion remain concealed. If the mind can be internally drawn then by God's grace it can enter the path of *Brahma*. Then the impediment is dispelled and becoming soul-oriented, the form of *dhárma*-essence is revealed — ***Dhármasya tattvaṃ nihitaṃ guhāyāṃ, guhāyāṃ nihitaṃ Brahma śāśvatam.***[2] — the actual essence of religion is latent within the cave. What is latent within that cave is the eternal *Brahma*. Is this cave any mountainous cave? If that had been so, then all would have gone there and learnt about the religious essence. It is not so. It is prevalent in the form of *Kúṭastha* in all human bodies. It is also known as Cavern of the Union with Absolute Void. If the mind can be emplaced within the dot-like cave in the middle of *Kúṭastha*, the conscious *Aṇu* becomes evident, then

1. *Kulārṇavatántra.*

2. *Mahábhārata* Vanaparba, Bak-Yaksha *Saṃbād.*

the true essence and esotericism of religion are disclosed. It is possible only through *Prânákarma* and all *yogis* visualise this *Kuṭastha*. Therefore Yogiraj has recounted on 29th March (year not mentioned) — ***Antarved khulā yāne bhitar bhitar śvāsā calnekā rāh milā mánas dhyāna śabd yehī asal haye — isiko yogilog gahar kahate haye.*** — implying that the path for entering the innermost region has opened, or I acquired a state of the internal flow (in the path of *Sushumná*) of breath. By reaching this state, cogitation, *dhyāna* and *Ómkāra* sound which can be heard are real and are termed by *yogis* to be the cavern. ***Esā sab bindi caltā dekhā bicme safed yonike wahi baḍā cnād choṭā jab tab rahe to uskā tārā kahate haye oahi chidra haye*** — signifying I could see a white dot travelling within the triangular place of origin, it is known as the moon when it appears to be large and when small is termed to be a star. That is the perforation; entry must be made through this perforation. This essence is not the faith or philosophical mystery. One who is constantly rapt in *yóga*, can regularly visualise *Kuṭastha* at a particular moment of practising *Kriyāyoga*. Therefore the *Upanisháds* have stipulated — ***Bālāgrasāhasraṃ ardhatasya bhāgasyabhāgasaḥ. Tasyabhāgasya bhāgārdhaṃ tadjñéyanca nirañjanam.***[1] The measurement of the dotlike *aṇu* within *Kuṭastha* is equivalent to one-half of one thousandth part of the tip of a hair strand or one-fourthousandth part of the tip of a hair strand. That *Brahma-Aṇu* is so subtle that it cannot be ascertained by intelligence, therefore it is the inexplicable state or if a living being does not attain the *Śivá* state, the self cannot be conscious about it. ***Sūkshmatvāttad vijñyeyaṃ***. (*Gītā* 3/16) — implying that due to subtlety or amorphousness He is incognizable. *Brahma* is existent in living beings below *Kuṭastha* in the form of the dynamic *Prâṇá* and above *Kuṭastha* in the Divine Region as a still *Prâṇá*. He is both animate and inanimate. Since He exists in an extremely subtle

1. Brahmopanishad Chapter 6.

manner in the form of *Brahma-Aṇu*, He is unknowable, He can be comprehended in a special manner then, therefore He is ***Jñānātītaṃ nirañjanam*** i.e. beyond knowledge and immaculate. Since the ignorant ones are unaware of the Omnipresent God-essence, *Brahma-Aṇu* remains distant from them, but since the knowledgeable ones are skilled in the soul-essence, He remains constantly in close proximity to them. He is knowledge, He is worth knowing. Again through *sādhana*, He is cognizable. Thus Yogiraj has written — ***Ujiyāle mey sūkshmabastu kā dárśana hotā haye, andhiyāle mey nahi — jayse sūryake jyot mey koi gharke bhitar ched hoke āye to yo dhul sab urtā haye ek ek karke sab dekhātā haye, lekin chāye mey kuch nahi — Brahma sūkshmānusū-kshma haye, isliye pratham jyot mey dekhlātā haye — phir jab andhakār ke ānkh hotā haye tab andhakār sab cij dekhne mey ātā haye — yāne vijñāna pad.*** — Subtle objects are perceptible when there is light and not perceptible in darkness; just as when sunlight enters a room through a slot then each speck of dust in the air can be noticed, but cannot be observed when the slot is shaded. *Brahma* is subtlest of the subtle. Therefore He can be perceived in the effulgence. Again when the path of vision is concealed by self-manifested darkness (where there is no day or night) then everything can be visualised in this darkness and that is the state of science. Whatever path one follows to know about the true essence of religion,[1] he has to come to this eternal path demonstrated by sages.

1. It has been earlier discussed that *yógaśāstrá* has been established upon science. According to Indian mathematical science, the lowest measure is *aṇu* (atom). 2 *aṇus* = 1 *daṇuk*, 3 *daṇuks* = 1 *trasareṇu* (minute body containing 6 atoms), 8 *Trasareṇus* = 1 tip of the hair strand or a dust particle. The dimension of mind is synonymous with that of *aṇu* and it's measurement is forty eight times more subtler than the tip of a hair strand. The dot within *Kūṭastha* is four thousand times more subtler than the tip of a hair strand. Thus the mind's motion is absent there. Only the Omnipresent Soul is present there.

One who is absorbed in comprehending his subtle mind is a *Muni*.[1] What is actuated by the mind is opinion. By practising regular *Prânákarma* such a deep engrossment arises that the desire for speech disappears, that is the actual state of science. But if the desire to talk persists, yet speech is not made and this is expressed indirectly, it is not the true reticence. When desires are eliminated the silent state automatically arrives, but if desires are existent silence cannot be maintained. As long as endeavours are made to visualise the truth (the soul) with the help of the kinetic mind, till then the indivisible truth's visualisation remains far removed. To realise that soul-truth, cessation of mind is required. In that state of cessation, the resplendence of the soul's manifestation is reflected. With the help of imagination-power the mind divides that resplendence and converts it into different mental moods. This is the disposition of the mind. To attain the non-alternative supreme truth (soul-truth) one has to go above the mind. In this state there are no questions regarding opinion, because when the mind is absent, can opinion be present? If the motion and settlement of the two entities of mind and *Prâṇá* can be caused in the same manner in *Ātmadhyāna*, then true devotion and attainment of God is possible. But this cannot be achieved without prolonged *sādhanā*. To proceed in the path of God-attainment, the primary requisite is to perform actions in accordance with soul-orientation i.e. soul's engrossment for then achievement of knowledge will occur. After knowledge is derived, devotion automatically dawns through that knowledge. Therefore Yogiraj would state — ***Guḍer maylā ṭānte ṭānte sādā haye, temni Prâṇâyāma korte korte nirmal haye*** — This indicates that jaggery is refined by a clarification process, similarly by practising regular *Prâṇâyāma,* purification is gained. Educating His devotees, Yogiraj further expressed — ***Ulto likhe āynā diye dekhle***

1. Opinion, rapt comprehension of the subtle mind are all metamorphoses of *mánas* (mind) conjugation.

sojā dekhāye, tadrūp dehastha vāyuke ulṭāileo svárūpa dekhāye — suggesting if any alphabet is written reversely and viewed through the mirror, it appears to be straight, similarly if the body air is reversed, one's own form can be viewed. Pure devotion is true devotion. This pure devotion cannot be acquired until ignorance is exterminated. Therefore Yogiraj would state — ***Oshṭha kanṭha danta prakṛitite vāyur jor Prâṇâyāme poḍile jñāner svānuvab howyār nām bhakti*** — signifying that with the force of *Prâná* and *Apâná* airs while practising regular internal *Prâṇâyāma*, the vital powers of the lips, throat and teeth cease giving rise to knowledge which results in soul-realisation and this is referred to as true devotion. But how can ignorance be removed? Yogiraj would remark likewise — ***Uttam Prâṇákarma karite thākile āpnā hoitei ajñāna dūrībhūta hoibe*** — implying that if excellent *Prânákarma* is practised ignorance will automatically be removed. It is the soul-religion. Therefore God has stipulated —

Śreyān svádhármo biguṇaḥ paradhármād svanusṭhitād
Svádhárme nidhanaṃ śreyaḥ paradhármo bhayābahaḥ. (*Gītā* 3/35)

This denotes that the soul-religion even if fraught with faults is greater than the skillfully executed sensory disposition. For initial practitioners there will be shortcomings. It is exclusively dependent on practice. By practising this *Ātmadhárma* or soul-religion if one expires, it is still better; but the sensory disposition is perpetually terrifying, because *Prâṇá's* vibratory motion creates a distance from God's proximity. It is for this reason, birth and death are inevitable.

Yogiraj would expound — Barring direct visualisation; love, devotion, affection are not born, just as it is not possible for a childless person to have parental love. Again, does love and affection evolve from the very moment a child is born? Certainly not. The more one sees the child and rears him the more love and affection towards the child will develop gradually without the parent realizing it. How is true love and devotion by conjecture possible for the God you have not seen? Perhaps this type of love can dawn in one in a million as a result of acquiring the propensities of previous births. If the *Prâṇákarma*-like dexterous *yógakarma* is practised regularly, some or the other *Ātmajyoti* can definitely be visualised. The more you will regularly visualise the *Ātmajyoti*, the more you will develop love and affection towards it, without you being aware of it. The desire to visualise that wonderful ever-pure *Ātmajyoti* will persistently arise, for it cannot be noticed in the perceptible world. In this manner the more the direct visualisation is augmented, the more the love and devotion towards it will be enhanced. Subsequently by becoming engrossed in *Ātmajyoti* visualisation steadfastly, a thorough raptness in love and devotion will occur. It is then that ignorance will be severed and true pure devotion will be born. Thus barring visualisation of the God-entity, actual love and devotion are not possible. It is exclusively dependent upon *Prâṇákarma*.

In *Mūlâdhāra cakrá* of every human being, the *Kuṇḍalini* power is dormant. Until this power is awakened through *Prâṇákarma*, *sādhana* is directed towards material objects. The objective of *sādhana* is not to enjoy the Divine bliss and Divine wealth after death. This type of enjoyment can be derived without *sādhana*. Through *sādhana* a living being by abandoning the endless snare of delusion can achieve the state of *Śivá* or stillness or attain the complete essence. For this reason, a *yogi* has to arouse the power of *Kuṇḍalini*. The soul of a living being is like *Śivá* pervaded with benignancy but is shrouded with illusion and ignorance. This *Śivá*like soul exists latently in the essence of space or *Viśuddha cakrá* in the form of Death. This latent state has to be awakened. By *Prâṇákarma* the moment when the internal air becomes still in

Viśuddha cakrá, the dormant state disappears. In this manner when a *yogi's* air is stilled in the *Viśuddha cakrá*, he will become *Nīlkaṇṭha*, the *Śivá* state. The five *cakrás* are the centre for the five essences — earth, water, fire, air and space. Power is of the same content in all five *cakrás*. But when power is awakened in *Mūlâdhāra cakrá*, that aerial power is driven upwards in the path of *Sushumná* and gradually all power within the *cakrás* being aroused completely in the ultimate state, liberates five *cakrás*. Then even a hint of ignorance does not exist. Then the soul's ignorant illusory impediment is removed and an union between *Śivá* and *Śakti* (the Female Principle partaking in creation) occurs. In the *Ājñā cakrá*, this is the sublime union between *Śivá* and *Śakti* or between the Primordial Male Energy and Primordial Female Energy or it is the eternal union between stillness and dynamism, this is *samādhi*.

Chapter 7

THE SUBLIME GURU

Everyday in the morning, Yogiraj would go for a holy dip in the Ganges at Ranamahal Ghat accompanied by His faithful devotee Krishnaram. That day also, after the dip Yogiraj was returning home alongwith Krishnaram through an alley. Suddenly He mentioned — "Krishnaram tear off a cloth."

Krishnaram could not follow what his Guru Maharaj (the Gracious One) was telling him.

After walking a few steps, a brick from the terrace of a house fell on the foot of Yogiraj. One of His toes was grazed and blood started oozing out. Quickly, He tore a piece of cloth from His attire and bandaged the toe. Krishnaram assisted Him in doing this.

After this, Krishnaram with folded hands enquired — "Maharaj, if you knew before that the brick would fall, why didn't You avoid it? For then, You wouldn't have suffered this injury."

Yogiraj replied — "That is not possible Krishnaram. If I had avoided it, I would have had to suffer the pain with interest at any other time. I have to receive what is destined, therefore the earlier it is completed, the better it is."

Krishnaram had two sons and one daughter. On lying down after dinner his wife reproachingly told him — "The time for the holy thread ceremony of the youngest son is almost lapsing, have you made any arrangements for this? Make due arrangements as early as possible."

Krishnaram was a poor Brahmin, his family expenditure was managed somehow. Where was the money for celebrating his son's holy thread ceremony? He was an ardent devotee of Guru Maharaj.

He never gave a thought to all those facts. Comforting his wife he said — "When the Guru Maharaj will shower His grace, then surely arrangements for the ceremony will be made. I have no money. What is the use of baseless anxieties? Let Him worry Whose anxiety it is."

The next day like every other day, Krishnaram went to the house of Yogiraj in the morning to accompany Him to the Ganges where the Latter would go for a holy dip.

Yogiraj was seated on His Own *āsaná*. The moment Krishnaram paid his obeisance, Yogiraj brought out thirty rupees from under His seat and giving it to Krishnaram said — "With this money, perform your son's holy thread ceremony according to the scriptural codes. There is no need for ostentation."

Krishnaram hesitatingly replied — "O Guru Maharaj, You are always gracious to me. I am unable to properly serve You even. Why should You give me money?"

Yogiraj remarked — "Look Krishnaram, there is only One Who can give and He gives through the medium of someone. Now He is giving through My medium, why won't you accept it ?"

Krishnaram accepted this providence wholeheartedly.

Panchkari Bandopadhyaya was a favourite devotee of Yogiraj and was quite advanced in *sādhana*. Because it is extremely difficult to practise *sādhana* by dwelling in the vicious environment of domestic life, he had developed an apathy towards everything. He had mentally decided to forsake his domestic existence. But for this the consent of his Gurudeva was imperative. Bandopadhyaya *Mahāśaya*, one day came to Yogiraj and prayed for His consent for becoming a *saṃnyāsin*.

Hearing everything, Yogiraj stated in a grave tone — "Which weighs more, your holy thread or matted hair? Do you want to publicize yourself as an ascetic so that people respect you and you can earn some money? Look, if people could become ascetics by donning the saffron robe, then donkeys and horses could become ascetics. Why should not the asses and horses whose colour is more or less saffron be termed as ascetics? Abandon all that madness and remain in the family, spend your livelihood by earning for yourself and practise *sādhanā*. Never maintain your existence on other's contributions."

With bowed head, Panchkori Bandopadhyaya left.[1]

Yogiraj would comment — "There is no dearth of skeleton-like *maṭhas*, missions and *āśramas* in the spiritual world of India. Establishment of *maṭhas*, missions, etc. does not entail *sādhanā* practice for these act as a deterrent in *sādhanā*, as then the objective is centred on the further expansion of *maṭhas* and missions." Therefore Yogiraj laid much importance on *sādhanā* to be practised in seclusion. He would state that by donning saffron robes, people can distinguish a person as an ascetic, and this impedes *sādhanā*. By donning ordinary attire, recognition is absent and *sādhanā* can be well practised. The life of *saṃnyāsins* is an extremely difficult one, therefore He never consented to any of His devotees becoming *saṃnyāsins*. But He had devotees who were *saṃnyāsins* from before. He asked householders to remain within the precincts of the home and advised *saṃnyāsins* to stay in their *āśramas*. His advice was that *Ātmasādhanā* should be practised by men in their respective habitats, there was no need for change, for then only they would be benefitted. He forbade the change of attire and would advise that by wearing saffron robes and becoming an ascetic, it is not possible to attain God. It is good to maintain the garb and environment one is accustomed to, remaining within the same habit *Ātmasādhanā* should be practised for then only life will become successful.

1. He later became famous as Keshabananda Brahmachari.

Once the wife of Kedarnath De, one of His devotees was stricken with cholera. She was dying, the family consisted of few small children and it would be a terrible mishap if she left her husband alone in this state. Kedarnath rushed and prayed with folded hands at the Lotus Feet of his Gurudeva — "O Master, please save my wife, otherwise I shall be in deep trouble with my children." Kedarnath became dejected with cries.

Yogiraj keeping in accordance with the social customs said— "Call, a good doctor."

Kedarnath in a lugubrious tone submitted his prayer — "There is no use of calling a doctor. Unless You shower your grace, it will not be possible to save my wife. I have surrendered to You, do whatever You have to do."

The Sublime Yogi was infused with mercy. He stated — "Can you do whatever I tell you?"

Hope flashed in Kedarnath's mind. He said — "I shall do whatever You command."

Yogiraj said — "Go and bring a bottle of rose water."

Kedarnath immediately purchased a bottle of rose water.

Yogiraj stated — "Go to the toilet and mix a little of your stool in the rose water and immediately feed this to the patient."

Kedarnath obeyed in verbatim and the patient revived.

Yogiraj always in accordance with social norms never impeded the functioning of the medical profession for He advised all to consult doctors when necessary. The medicines which He imparted apparently had no medicinal value, but His tendering them carried implicit significance.

This Sublime Yogi Who is rarely attainable even to the gods and goddesses constantly bared Himself for the welfare of His devotees.

He would advise them at all moments and impart education so that they could achieve advancement in *sādhanā*.

Yogiraj would state that the six *cakrás* are prevalent in all human bodies. The dynamic *Prâná* flowing through these six *cakrás* confines everyone. If you can become supportless with the help of *Prânákarma* or take recourse in the void, the six *cakrás* will become non-functional. Then you can realise that the obstructions of the six *cakrás* have been released. Void means nothingness and settling in this nothingness clears all impediments. The company of internal breath is true company, because as long as this is existent a living being's entity exists, therefore breath is real. If an association is made with this breathing, settlement in the void occurs, then authority, thoughts, sins, virtues, desires are all exterminated and soul-orientation hence soul-engrossment is derived. *Kuṇḍalini* is the source of power, she is dormant. She exists by taking support in grossness. She has to be deviated from the gross support for then she can take recourse in *Śivá* or the void and become independent or supportless. ***Nirāśrayaṃ māṃ jagadīśa raksha***. This means, my supportless state is the state of Controller of the Universe and only this state can save me. Initially, a living being considers the gross essence to be the shelter. But the actual shelter for a living being is the void essence, where there is no support. A living being attains eternal safety if he can achieve settlement in the *Ājña cakrá*. Above the *Ājñā cakrá*, it is inexpressible and beneath it is expressible.

The technique of Yogiraj in imparting education was a distinct one. He would perpetually render subtle scientific interpretations to the spiritual facts. For this reason, it would impress *sādhakas*. He would express — That which stills the breathing motion is *dhárma* and it's reverse is *adhárma(*kineticism*)*. Action can never be the cause for bondage. Hoping for the consequences of action, is the cause for bondage. There is no difference between the good and bad of action. If one attaches oneself with material cravings and performs external actions then result of the performing actions will be evil. The means by which settlement is attained in *Kūṭastha* is auspicious and by which this is not achieved is inauspicious. Ordinary man does not practise *Ātmakarma* (soul-action), therefore their sensory powers remain unrefined. The human body has not been borne only to suffer or enjoy the consequences of evil or good actions respectively. This human body has been borne for the practice of pure, passive, *Ātmakarma* which is beyond sins and virtues. Until *Ātmakarma* is complete, till then the human shape has to be acquired, it's necessity will not end. Everyone has to practise *Ātmakarma*, whether it is practised in this birth or the next birth. *Ātmakarma* cannot be practised without the human body. The body is termed to be the field. ***Idaṃ śarīraṃ Kaunteya kshetramityabhidhīyate.*** (*Gītā* 13/2) — O *Kaunteya*, this body is known as the field, because it is the germination ground for knowledge, as religion and action are accomplished by this body. Whatever exists in the material world is prevalent in this body. Therefore this is the microcosm. If the body can be cultivated with the help of mind and *Prâná,* good result is derived. Therefore the great soul Ramprosad has proclaimed — ***Eman mānab jamīn raila patit ābād karle phalta sonā***. — meaning such a body field remains uncultivated; if cultivated, golden result would accrue. If fulfilment is derived in this body, a living being becomes *Śivá*. The action which is performed to fulfil is the true action or *Karmayoga*. If a *yogi* becomes attached in *Ātmakarma,* his sensory enemies are gradually eliminated with the influence of that action. The motion towards arriving at *Brahma* never ceases for the one who practises *Ātmakarma* and by the medium of *Ātmakarma* if once the state of going beyond the body-consciousness is achieved then supratemporality and the state beyond the cycle of birth-death occur. This body is the bow and breath the arrow. One who directs this bow and arrow is *Ātmârāma*. That *Rāma* is indestructible. Since He dwells within the body-chariot characterised by the ten senses, He is known as *Dāśarathi*. Thus Yogiraj has written — ***Jihvā tāluke bhitar gaḍāy diyā — ómkāra dhvani yo sunātā haye soi mūlmántra Rāmanām haye*** — implying I have placed the tongue in the palatal cavity. In this state, by constantly practising *Ātmakarma* the *Ómkāra* sound which I can perceive now, is the fundamental *mántra* (internal chanting of *Rāma's* name). He has again written — ***Ab bālam khirā milā jihvā tālumūlme lagnese ṭhāṇḍā mālum hotā haye*** — denoting that if *Khecari* is accomplished, then the access for visualising *Brahma* opens. *Bālam khirā* means tender cucumber. Just as the inside of a tender cucumber is empty, so also is the palate cavity. Thus Yogiraj notes that the correct path for *Khecari* is established and if *Khecari* is accomplished in this manner coolness in the palate cavity can be felt.

Action is principal to *yogis*. God in the *Gītā* has similarly declared — ***Jñānayogena sāṃkhyānāṃ karmayogena yoginām*** (*Gītā* 3/3) — meaning the followers of *Sāṃkhya* philosophy attain fulfilment through *Jñānayoga* and *yogis* attain fulfilment through *Karmayoga*. Hence action to a *yogi* is *Karmayoga* i.e. *Prâṇákarma*.

The true "I" can be ascertained through *Sāṃkhya*. The word "I" neither implies the self nor the body. The one 'Who' is present in this body, in the form of soul can be truly termed to be the self. The existence of this body depends upon the vital breathlike action's presence. Through this action when the state beyond action i.e. the state of knowledge is achieved, the true 'I' can be realised, that is *Sāṃkhya*. In the state beyond the aforesaid action settlement of the vital breathlike *Sāṃkhya* or numbers takes place. Numbers or *Sāṃkhya* have commenced from times immemorial. Time is infinite, it is countless. But that time becoming existent in the body is being converted into the vital breathlike number and this number occurs 21,600 times within the body day and night. The state of the number of vital breathings is the present state of a living being. A living being does not pay attention to this number but remains ensnared by his state, hence is involved in illusion. If the number of vital breathings can be observed, the state beyond it can be achieved and the true self can be known. Therefore it is termed to be the *Sāṃkhya* philosophy. By paying attention to the aforementioned numbers or to the breathing motion, the *Prâṇá* motion can be observed and when the state beyond this motion arrives, the state of knowledge dawns and those who pay attention to *Sāṃkhya* attain settlement of the mind. This settlement is derived through *Jñānayoga* for the followers of *Sāṃkhya* philosophy. *Yogis* attain settlement through *Karmayoga —karma* means *Prânákarma* (*Prâná*-action). It is action of *Prâṇá's* continuous vertical ascent and descent motion i.e. *Ātmakarma*. For *yogis*, by practising continual *Ātmakarma*, action's union is achieved i.e. *Iḍā's* and *Piṅgalá's* motion becoming one merges in the path of *Sushumná* and in this state beyond action, mind's settlement occurs. By this *Karmayoga*, *yogis* attain settlement. "Through *Jñānayoga*, the followers of *Sāṃkhya* and through *Karmayoga, yogis* attain settlement" — if this is superficially noted, it seems as though God has mentioned about two types of action by which settlement is achieved. But in actuality, it is not so. They are the same and both the states are the same state, because God has clearly expressed — ***Na karmaṇāmanārambhā-nnaishkarmyaṃ púrushoaśnute*** (*Gītā* 3/4) — signifying that without executing action man cannot achieve a passive state, or else barring *Ātmakarma* or *Prâṇákarma* the passive state beyond action cannot be attained.

* * * * * *

Bhutnath Sen, an engineer and a disbeliever in idol-worship was employed in Assam. Here he had heard the name of this Household

Yogi. Bhutnath was immensely eager to learn about Indian *yóga-śāstrás* and had studied a number of scriptural texts. Eventually he understood that by reading the *śāstrás,* the true essence of religion and *yóga* knowledge cannot be known. He visited many *sāṃnyāsins* in that region, but failed to satisfy himself. It seemed as though Bhutnath was interested in knowing and deriving something more. Therefore one day he arrived at Kashi and presented himself before Yogiraj.

The moment Bhutnath completed paying His obeisance, Yogiraj enquired — "You have come to Kashi, have you taken a holy dip in the Ganges and paid a *dárśana* to Lord *Vísvanāth*?"

Bhutnath being a non-iconodulist replied — "I have not come to pay a *dárśana* to the *Śivá* idol but to pay a *dárśana* to the living Vísvanāth."

Yogiraj stated — "You do not have the correct knowledge in this regard. You first go for a holy dip in the Ganges and pay a *dárśana* to *Vísvanāth*, then come here."

After the holy dip in the Ganges, Bhutnath went to the *Vísvanāth* temple and while he was rendering homage to the idol of *Vísvanāth*, he saw the idol of Yogiraj in that place. He realised his mistake.

Yogiraj would in this manner ask everyone to abide by the prevalent practices. He would say —"Until settlement through *Ātmakarma* is achieved, it is better to abide by the prevalent practices."

The next day Bhutnath again appeared before Yogiraj.

Yogiraj was smiling. Bhutnath paid his obeisance and sat down.

Yogiraj uttered a few essential truths to Bhutnath and imparted advice under the guise of a story.

Bhutnath was quietly listening to these till now. When Yogiraj halted, Bhutnath expressed with folded hands — "Whatever I had required to know, I had jotted them down on a piece of paper lest I forget and kept it in my pocket. It was my wish that I would learn about them one by one. But all this time you were answering to these questions of mine. I do not any longer need to know anything, I have received all the answers."

Bhutnath was fascinated and obtained *yóga* initiation from Yogiraj.

Yogiraj at the time of imparting initiation would accept Rs. 5/- only and Rs. 10/- from widows as a mark of penance. He maintained this rule throughout His life and commanded His future *sādhakas* to also follow that rule. Such has been noticed that when any poor devotee desirous of obtaining initiation but failing to acquire Rs. 5/-, Yogiraj Himself would pay this as advance. Seeing this, one of the wealthy devotees of Yogiraj who stayed a long distance away from Kashi, kept Rs. 100/- with one of the disciples of Yogiraj residing in Kashi, so that when the time necessitated, the poor devotees could be given assistance. Yogiraj would keep the money derived from imparting initiation separately. The *Gurúdeva* of Yogiraj, Babaji *Mahārājá* would sometimes send one of his *sāṃnyāsin* devotees to Him to collect that money. This money would be expended towards the necessities of the group of *sāṃnyāsins* of *Bābāji Mahārājá*. There is a scriptural injunction that before taking initiation an expiation of sins is a must by superficial *yajñá* but there are many complicated paraphernalia pertaining to this. For this reason, Yogiraj had decided that the initiation amount obtained from those initiated as a mark of penance would be sent to His *Gurúdeva* for serving him or his accompanying *sāṃnyāsins*. This would be beneficial for those initiated as per the scriptural injunction.

Yogiraj had written to one of His devotees — **"I am not materially attached, for this reason not disappointed also. Show**

this letter of mine to my friend Sri Ramdas Maitra and pay regards to him. Take initiation from him and pay him Rs. 5/- as a mark of penance and later come and meet me when it is convenient for you. Each stage of My *Kriyā* is *dhárma* which can be derived directly from *Gurú*. If the mind is elsewhere other than in *Brahma* it is a sin — otherwise there is no sin. Through devotion towards *Gurúdeva* a wholeness can be derived, but it is rare. If the mind cannot be stilled and controlled by existing in this difficult world, self-realisation is not possible; to visualise and become conscious that the soul is the Infinite Soul and *Nārāyaṇa*, a constant true knowledge of *Brahma* occurs and the sins and virtues of the person concerned are absent because he sees *Brahma* in everything. Settlement in the equal state — to be effected in practice; if it is effected only through talking it will be merely talking — everything is *Brahma* — I am Infinitesimal."

Bābāji Mahárājá would often eulogize about His favourite disciple, Shama Churn to his group of sages. By this once envy was roused in the mind of one of his *sāṃnyāsin* devotees. He told *Bābāji Mahárājá* — "Shama Churn is a householder, why do you extol Him so much?"

Bābāji did not reply but after a few days sent that *sāṃnyāsin* devotee to Yogiraj to collect the money which had accrued from initiation. The *sāṃnyāsin* came to Shama Churn. He mentally decided to avail the opportunity of testing Shama Churn. Shama Churn also understood this. Sitting in the parlour of Yogiraj, both discussed many essential facts. There was a potted Valerian tree beside. A leaf was plucked from this plant and taking the leaf as an objective, discussions about the Male and Female Primordial Energy, illusion and *Brahma* continued. They entered into such deep discussions that they became oblivious of the fact that the night was over. Suddenly Yogiraj stated — "It is already dawn now, let us go and have a holy dip in the Ganges."

The unfathomable depths of Yogiraj dispelled the *sāṃnyāsin's* mistake. He understood why *Bābāji Mahārājá* would eulogise so much about this Household-Yogi.

A little distance away from the residence of Yogiraj was the house of Jaipal, the milkman. One of his sons had a sudden attack of cholera. There was little chance of his son surviving. The poor and ardent devotee Jaipal arrived in the presence of his Guru Maharaja. He came and saw that his Guru Maharaja like other days was seated on His Own seat with half open eyes. Jaipal rendered his obeisance from a little distance and sat down. After a few minutes, the Sublime Yogi opened His eyes. Jaipal, in a quivering tone prayed for saving his son's life.

In Kashi then, *jilebis* (a wheel shaped sweetmeat) made from *tikhur* was available. *Tikhur* is an acquatic fruit of the water chestnut variety. Yogiraj stated — "Feed him to the full with *tikhur jilebis* immediately."

Jaipal immediately administered this and his son was cured.

Yogiraj had given His younger daughter, Harimohini and youngest son, Dukari marriage in Bishnupur of Bankura district. In this context, He had merely gone twice to Bishnupur and then many obtained initiation from Him. In May 1886 on account of His daughter's marriage, He came to Bishnupur for the first time. In the last week of May 1886, at nine in the night He boarded the train at Kashi, alighted at Panagarh station the next day at five in the evening and taking a cow-drawn cart from there arrived at Bishnupur. Panchanan Bhattacharya *Mahāśaya* met Him at Panagarh. After this, on May 1891, He came to Bishnupur again on account of His youngest son's marriage. This time also Panchanan Bhattacharya *Mahāśaya* met Him at Panagarh station.

Kailashchandra Bandopadhyay who was a poor Brahmin, used to live in Bishnupur. He was employed as a private tutor in the house of Sibdas Bhattacharya. Kailashbabu became extremely eager to obtain initiation from Yogiraj. But he did not have the stipulated amount of Rs. 5/- for initiation. Therefore he approached Sibdas-babu and asked for an advance of Rs. 5/-. Listening to everything, Sibdasbabu jestingly replied — "I will give you the money if you tell me in detail about the initiation you will obtain."

Kailasbabu agreed to this and accepted Rs. 5/- as advance.

Kailasbabu came to obtain initiation from Yogiraj. Suddenly Yogiraj expressed — "You have promised to state in detail about initiation, I will not give it to you."

Kailasbabu vowed he would not tell anyone. But Yogiraj did not agree to this. Subsequently, Kailasbabu went to Sibadsbabu and told him — "Yogiraj has been able to know everything, He will not give initiation."

Sibdasbabu jocularly said — "You do not have to say anything about initiation. I had jokingly told you. You can take initiation now."

After this Kailashbabu obtained initiation. This Kailashbabu later became a famous *yogi*.

In 1892, Dukari Lahiri the second son of Yogiraj, suffered a mental derangement. In spite of being treated by many specialists of Kashi, there was no alleviation. Many advised medicines to be brought from Goddess Kali's temple of Tirol in Burdwan district. Though being *Brahma*-conversant, He would abide by the popular customs and practices. Thus through a letter to one of His devotees, a station-master of Tarakeswar, He was informed that Tirol was almost 18 miles away from Tarakeswar station and the road was not good, whereas from Burdwan station Tirol was about 17 or 18 miles away and the road was good. So in December 1892, He arrived at

Burdwan station from Kashi. Panchanan Bhattacharya *Mahāśaya*, being present there from before had arranged for a palanquin. Yogiraj went to Tirol in that palanquin and acquiring the medicine from Kali temple there, returned to Kashi. But Dukari Lahiri was not cured by that medicine also. Observing this, Kashimani Devi stated — "You being present what is the necessity for other medicines?" After this Yogiraj administered a root of *apāmārg*. Taking this, His son was cured.

* * * * * *

In Kashikhanda within Skandapurana, there is a rule for Kashi peregrination. It is known as *pañcakrośi yātrā* or *pañcakrośi parikramā*. About 50/60 miles have to be traversed on bare foot and it normally takes five to six days for this. Carrying foodstuff alongwith them many peregrinators together chant "*Jai Śivá Śambho*" and proceed. This peregrination takes place each year.

Once Ramprosad Jaiswal, a lawyer and ardent devotee of Yogiraj decided to undertake that *pañcakrośi parikramā*. He would come regularly to pay *dárśana* and obeisance to his Guru Maharaj. Therefore he set thinking that these five or six days he could not pay a *dárśana* to his Guru. Becoming anxious, he came to his Guru Maharaj and prayed for His consent and blessings that he complete the peregrination within twenty four hours and again come and pay homage to Yogiraj.

Yogiraj explained to Jaiswal what the actual *pañcakrośi parikramā* meant. The quintuple cells[1] (divisions) of the soul is the mainstay of this body only, which is Kashi. Thus this quintuple-

1. The quintuple divisions are :—

   (a) *Ānnamaye* (gross essence); (b) *Prâṇámaye* (dynamic essence); (c) *mạnasmaye* (mental essence); (d) *vijñānamaye* (scientific subtle cogitative essence) (e) *ānandamaye* (Divine Communion beatific essence).

celled body should be peregrinated through the medium of *Ómkāra Kriyā* and this is the real '*pañcakrośi parikramā*'. If this peregrination can be performed *Prâná* air attains settlement in the *Sahasrâra*. That is the essence of void or essence of *Śivá*. It is then that the presiding gods and goddesses of Kashi can be visualised. The external *pañcakrośi parikramā* abounds in superficiality. Soul-visualisation does not occur through this. But Yogiraj never forbade anyone to execute the superficial religious rites. He would remark it is better to perform them by which the mind is purified. Therefore He consented to Jaiswal's peregrination and blessed him.

Taking the blessings of his Guru Maharaj, Jaiswal proceeded for his peregrination the next day at dawn and returning within twenty-four hours again paid a *dárśana* to his Guru.

The blessings of a true Guru were achieved in this manner in Jaiswal's life.

Yogiraj would expound that the only *Ātmakarma* is true *karma*, others are non-*karmas*. But to maintain one's livelihood some actions (*karmas*) require to be performed. Therefore actions cannot be forsaken completely. He never advised to forsake one's own wife or wealth; He Himself also maintained this. Instead He used to say a domestic person requires both wealth as well as spiritual attainment, none can be disregarded. Those who renounce the world are feeble-minded. Remaining amidst everything perform such actions that will dispel material attachment. This attachment only is the deterrent, absence of attachment cannot create deterrents. Attachment originates from desire, desire originates from kinetic mind and the kinetic mind originates from dynamic *Prâṇá*. But there are not any billows in a still *Prâṇá*. Thus mind, desire, attachment are all absent. Nevertheless carnality, wealth remain, the disposition or attachment towards them being absent they no longer pose as an impediment. In a word, one has to go beyond desires or be passive.

As long as volition persists, till then attachment and impediment will obviously remain. Therefore through *Ātmakarma* annihilate volition or aspiration first. When desires are annihilated a state of non-attachment will arrive, then carnality, wealth and the material world will not act as deterrents. Therefore Yogiraj laid stress on — ***Khecari karṇe se indriya daman hotā haye*** — meaning by practising *Khecari* all the senses are controlled.

He would remark — A woman can never pose as an impediment to man. If woman acts as a deterrent to man, then it is imperative that man would also pose as an impediment to woman. Both have been created by God and to maintain the creation both are required. Both have the equal authority to practise *Ātmasādhanā*. Thus none act as deterrents to the other. Reckon upon the Maxim of God, He has noted —

Māṃ hi pārtha byapāśritya jeapi syuḥ pāpyonayaḥ.
Striyo vaíśyāstathā śūdrā steapi yānti parāṃ gatim. — (*Gītā* 9/32)

O Partha(Arjuna), those who are born of sinful progenitors or the downtrodden like *Vaiśyas, Śūdrás*, even if they take shelter in Me, shall surely attain salvation.

Money is required for food, clothing, medicines, etc. One should execute one's existence on one's own earnings rather than depend on others, but at the same time it is not proper to become a slave of money in any manner. You consider that earning an immense amount of wealth is a mark of manly prowess. It is not so. True manly prowess is how spiritedly you can practise *Ātmasādhanā*. Reorient a portion of the mind you constantly keep engaged in the earning of wealth, towards *sādhanā* and endeavours should be made by all for this. You say that you do not derive any time for *sādhanā*, this is not correct. Everyone should make efforts to find a certain amount of time off from his daily routine for the practice of *Ātmasādhanā*. Therefore the compassionate *sādhaka* has expressed —

Yabtak jindegī rahegī, phursad nā milegī kāmse;
Kuch samay aysā nikālo, lagan lagā lo Rāmase.

This implies that as long as life exists you will not derive any spare time from work; you have to reserve a certain amount of time from work to unite yourself with God.

Establish a yogic bond with *Ātmârāma* and remain united with Him in *Kūṭastha*.

Attachment cannot completely be relinquished with the help of the present kinetic mind because as long as *Prâṇá* remains dynamic, the mind remains kinetic. As long as the mind is kinetic, attachments will prevail till then. Passion, anger, greed, illusion, arrogance, envy, mind, intelligence, intellect, pride, hunger, thirst, sleep, sloth, visualisation, audition, olfaction, thoughts, anxieties, attachment, love, affection, vanity, body consciousness etc. all types of physical and mental propensities and dispositions which are existent have all been derived from the dynamic *Prâṇá*. In a word, all that can be observed in a living state, have all originated from the vibratory *Prâṇá*. Immediately after birth, *Prâṇá* becomes active and breathing commences. As long as *Prâṇá* will remain dynamic, till then breathing will continue and a living being will remain alive. Therefore as long as *Prâṇá* remains vibratory or breathing continues, till then all the aforementioned types of physical and mental propensities and dispositions will be prevalent. Again the more *Prâṇákarma* is practised, the more *Prâṇá* will progress towards stillness. The more progress is made towards stillness the more those propensities and dispositions will decrease. In this manner when *Prâṇá* becomes completely still or there is a cessation of vibration, then none of them will exist as in a still *Prâṇá* any type of propensity or body-consciousness does not prevail. This is the true purification of the elements. After vibration has been exterminated, this five-elemental body becomes purified. Therefore the dead loses all kinds of differentiation. Again this is the real *Upavāsa* (fasting). *Upa* means near. When *Prâṇá* becomes still, settlement occurs near the soul. Abstinence from food is not the actual fasting or *Upavāsa*, again *Prâṇá* is the *Puróhita,* (*Puró* means body-abode and *hita* means benefaction) because He is the only One to dwell in this body-abode and when He becomes still the actual benefit or welfare to a living being occurs, therefore He is regarded as the living being's Benefactor. *Prâṇá* maintains an equilibrium on either side, one is dynamic, the other still. If one side increases, the other side decreases.

Thus one devotee asked Him — "By what means can this restless mind remain quite well?" Yogiraj rejoined — "If there is an absence of the mind's existence."

Love, devotion, affection all these depend upon the existence of *Prâṇá's* dynamic state in the body. The love between mother and child; between husband and wife; the devotee's love towards God; the root of all these is that *Prâṇá*. Body cannot love body. *Prâṇá* loves *Prâṇá* because the source of love is *Prâṇá*. In a body sans *Prâṇá*, there is no love or affection. The source by which one embraces one's wife, the same source is adopted to embrace the daughter. Therefore you must first love your own *Prâṇá,* nurse Him (by practising *Prâṇákarma* only, one can serve Him), observe Him (by practising *Prâṇákarma* one can observe Him). If this is performed the universal *Prâṇá* can be comprehended, then you will have an equality of vision in all creatures and all elements. Just as knowledge about the sea can be acquired by observing it from the seashore, it is not necessary to see the entire sea; similarly if own inherent *Prâṇá* is realised knowledge of sublime *Prâṇá* can be attained.

* * * * * *

Like other days even on that day Yogiraj went for an evening promenade along the banks of the Ganges at Ranamahal Ghat with Krishnaram. Sometimes a little distance away, the helmsmen could be heard steering their boats with a splashing sound. At a moderate distance away in a temple, above the cemented ghat, *Śivá* - invocation by assembled devotees could be heard. A newcomer arrived and paying obeisance with folded hands to Yogiraj, started developing an acquaintance with Him. The newcomer said — "I have heard Your name before, but I did not have the fortune to meet You all these days."

Yogiraj smiled and engaging in a pleasant conversation with him, enquired about his name, his habitat etc.

While walking, the newcomer suddenly asked — "If You give me courage, can I ask You one question."

Yogiraj said — "Surely, you can."

The newcomer humbly enquired — "I have heard You practise *dhyāna* in Your room. But of which God do You practise *dhyāna*?"

Yogiraj smilingly replied — "I do not know about that."

The newcomer further enquired — "You must be practising *dhyāna* of *Śivá*, *Kṛishṇa* or *Kālī*?"

Yogiraj answered — "I practise *dhyāna* of that One Who is prevalent in *Śivá*, *Kṛishṇa* or *Kālī*, you, Me and everyone else."

The newcomer was amazed and stated — "I could not follow what You said."

Yogiraj replied—"Neither can I explain, nor can you understand."

Chapter 8

DIVINE ABSTRUSE CAUSATIONS AND SENTENTIOUS SAYINGS

Those who practise the *Kriyāyogasādhanā* as bestowed by Yogiraj are known as *Kriyābāns* or *Kriyânvitas*. With *Kriyābāns* He would discuss and explain the various aspects of their lives — food, sleep, copulation etc. He would stipulate pure food to be the best. Pure food implies that which enhances the virtuous qualities. Pure food keeps the body and mind tranquil. To practise *yóga*-action, one must eat less and consume easily digestible food. Consuming excess food impedes *yógasādhanā*. Hot, cold, pungent, spicy, bitter, stale food in their extremities should never be consumed. *Kriyāsādhana* should be practised three hours after having full meal. Five to six hours of sleep regularly is a must. Married people should have coitus twice a month. By this the mind is at rest and *sādhana* is also practised well. But waywardness in life should never be indulged in at any cost. If carnal desire strikes, three or four forceful *Prâṇâyāmas* should be practised. Regularly *Prânákarma* should be executed by keeping the two sets of teeth firm. If *Prâṇákarma* is executed with force, *Prâṇá* attains stillness soon. Therefore He would remind everyone repeatedly — ***Kaske Prâṇâyāma karnā cāhiye***. *Prâṇâyāma* should be practised with fortitude. *Prâṇá* air is the principal air amongst the forty nine airs. If the vital *Prâṇá* air is stilled through *Prâṇákarma*, the other airs become still. Then nothing remains, be it relinquishment or acceptance.

He would say that for the practice of *Kriyā* there is no rule pertaining to direction, place or time. *Vedānta* has noted in this regard — ***Yatraikāgratā tatrābiśeshād.*** (*Vedānta* 4/1/11) — meaning there is no rule pertaining to direction, place and time for the practice of *Kriyā*. It is the duty of all to practise *Kriyā* when the body and mind are fit. The fact that *Kriyā* should be practised at a particular time is not necessary but for beginners if a particular time and direction are observed, *censtá*(see footnote page 50) is propitiated. But once settlement in *Kriyā* is achieved, there is no rule. Texts concerning *Kriyā* should be studied. By keeping the waist, chest and neck in an upright position *Kriyā* should be practised with the flow of *samāná* air. By this, knowledge about *Brahma* can be gained. *Yóga* practitioners should not bathe at dawn, should not carry heavy weight, should not walk very fast, should not undertake a rigorous fast, should not be awake till very late at night, in a word should not perform such an action which will accelerate or lengthen the breathing motion. When there is thunder, *Kriyā* should not be practised. *Kriyā* in the morning annihilates the sins of the night and *Kriyā* in the evening annihilates the sins of the day. Practice of *Kriyā* should be enhanced during winter and spring. If a great deal of *Kriyā* is practised a deep engrossment arises and a sound can be heard within the occiput which is known as *Nādá-Brahma*. ***Prâṇâyāmamanumatvā unmattabad caranti***. (*Jablok Upanishád*). Being rapt in the engrossment of augmented *Prâṇâyama*, settlement in *Brahma* can be achieved and one can detachedly wander in this world. Practising *Prâṇákarma* renders establishment in Godhood.

Kriyāyóga has five items — *Tālavya, Prâṇâyāma, Nābhikriyā, Yónimudrā* and *Mahámudrā*. These five items total the first chapter of *Kriyāyoga*. When a devotee can complete the first chapter he is eligible to obtain the second chapter. In total, *Kriyāyoga* has six chapters. *Ómkāra-kriyā* features from the second till the sixth chapter. The mystery of *Kriyāyogasādhana* can be derived exclusively from the *Gurú*. Through *Tālavya*, the obstruction of the tongue is released; through *Prâṇâyāma*, *Prâṇá* and *Apâṇá* airs are stilled; through *Nābhikriyā, Samāná* air achieves a state of evenness; through *Yónimudrā*, soul-realisation occurs and through *Mahámudrā*,

Vyāna and *Udāna* airs achieve a state of settlement. By conquering the five *Prâṇás* in this manner, settling in the void essence at *Kūṭastha* and by arriving at the state beyond action the *Kriyābān* is capable of wandering in the realm of his self.

Yogiraj was imparting advice. The devotees were enquiring what they required to learn. One devotee asked — "What is *Karmayoga*?"

Yogiraj expounded — "The action which causes an union with God is *karma* and to remain united with that *karma* incessantly is *Karmayoga*. Others are all inactions. God is not an Object Who has descended from the sky, this is a state. This is the still state of *Prâṇá*. Still *Prâṇá* in a living being deriving vibration has assumed the forms of intelligence, mind, senses etc. and remains enchanted by this. This is a living being's deviated state from his original form or else this is the state of declension from still *Prâṇá* to dynamic *Prâṇá*. Stillness is a living being's original form. Dynamism represents a living being and stillness represents *Śivá*. Therefore the action which terminates that dynamism and reverts a living being again to stillness or the action that causes a living being's state to be extinct and elevates him to the state of *Śivá*, is known as *Karmayoga*. Nothing occurs without action. Whatever we desire to obtain or give are termed to be actions. Without action nothing can be acquired, thus without action God also cannot be obtained; implying stillness cannot be achieved. Some actions have to be performed to achieve God. Can God be found through the medium of different types of actions performed materialistically? Certainly not, because a little of these types of actions are performed by all. Then why do they not find God? *Jápa*, vows, fastings, chanting together, virtuous acts, undertaking pilgrimages, helping others, serving guests, compassion for living beings etc. are all actions which are performed by everyone in small degrees, but then why do they not obtain God? Thus God cannot be achieved by performing these actions because these actions are incapable of causing soul-visualisation. But performing these actions purifies the mind of man, these act as aids in the path of *sādhana*. Thus these actions are necessary. Action will produce consequences, this is the disposition of action. Evil actions produce bad consequences and for good actions good consequences are inevitable. The results produced are in equation to actions performed. Just as, if hunger is to be appeased the action of taking food is necessary, any other action will not be feasible. Similarly to attain soul-realisation, *Ātmakarma* is necessary." God in the *Gītā* has stated — ***Gahanā karmaṇo gati*** (*Gītā* 4/17), implying that the result of action is incomprehensible. It is extremely difficult for an ordinary man to understand the real action by which union with soul can occur. Therefore God has expressed —

Kiṃ karma kimkarmeti kabayoapyatra mohitāḥ
Tad te karma prabakshyāmi yajjñātvā mokshyaseyaśubhād.

(*Gītā* 4/16)

This signifies, be it proper action or inaction, conscientious people are fascinated by this. I shall tell you that action which will free you from evil, the sensory attachment. Because ***saṃnyāsastu mahābāho duḥkshamāptumyogataḥ.*** (*Gītā* 5/6) — Dear *Mahābāho* (Arjuna), barring *Karmayoga* (*yóga* of action), achieving *saṃnyāsa* (renunciation) is impossible. The state beyond action can be termed to be true renunciation. Then actions are absent. This *saṃnyāsa* or state of renunciation can be attained through action only. Nothing can be achieved without action.

Therefore Yogiraj has written on 19th June, 1873 — ***Ab baḍā majāse bekām haye soi kām huā — yāne kuch nahi karnā ehi kām huā — baḍā āścarya ki bātne isime hamesā garaf rahanā cāhiye*** — implying that now with ecstasy inaction occurred, this inaction became the real action or not performing anything has now become

My action. It is a peculiar fact that it is imperative to always remain in this inaction. Thus the worldly actions which ordinary men consider to be action are regarded as inaction by *yogis*. Common man is unaware of the transcendental state of *Kriyā* or the state beyond action, therefore that still state is inaction to them; but to a *yogi* it is the real action. Yogiraj has further recounted on 25th June 1873 — ***Tin konā āur car lakir — tin konā yāne tino nādi iḍā, piṅgalā, sushumná — cār lakir yāne kshití, áp, téjas, maruta — iha sabko choḍke śūnyáme dhyāna lagānā — ehi asal kām haye — āj to bilkul śvāsā gayā — baḍā bhāri neśā huā*** — Tin *konā* means the three nerves *iḍā, piṅgalā* and *sushumná* and *cār lakir* signifies earth, water, fire and air; thus by overcoming these three nerves and four great elements and engrossing on the fifth great element of the infinite void or the void within the void is the true action. By continually practising *Prâṇákarma*, the breathing motion today has completely ceased and achieving this type of *kumbhaka* state, a deep engrossment arose.

By practising this type of *sādhana*, what state did He cause Himself to achieve? He has remarked on this on 23rd August 1873 — ***Āj abhay sab karmame — akarma yo soi merā karma haye*** — signifying that He is devoid of fear in all actions, therefore He is fearless in all actions because what is inaction for the common man, that transcendental state of *Kriyā* or the state beyond action has now become His only action, inferring His perpetually remaining in *Kriyā's* transcendental state. God has similarly stated —

> ***Karmaṇyakarma yaḥ paśyedakarmaṇi ca karmaḥ yaḥ.***
> ***Sa budhimān manushyeshu sa yuktaḥ kṛidsnakarmakṛid.***
>
> (*Gītā* 4/18)

One who sees inaction in action and action in inaction, is the most intelligent amongst society and although he is the performer of all actions, he is united in *Brahma*. Thus the one who considers the consequence-oriented worldly action to be inaction and the inactionlike passive *Prâṇákarma* as action which is devoid of consequences and which is regarded apparently as inaction by ordinary men, is the most intelligent amongst human society. Although he performs all actions, he perpetually remains united in that passive *Prâṇákarma* state beyond action that is Still *Brahma*. Then he achieves intelligence due to that *Prâṇákarma* and by constantly remaining united in *Brahma* performs all actions detachedly, then all his attachments are eliminated or when in the nasal passage, *Prâṇá's* inhalation-exhalation action by deriving a settled state causes settlement of *Prâṇá* in the state beyond action, only then it is the true state of relinquishment of action. Therefore Yogiraj has detailed on 19th June 1873 — ***Howā aysā upar carā ki barā jor sāṅge uthānekeliye. Āb baḍā majā se bekām haye soi kām huā — yāne kuch nahi karnā ehi kām huā — baḍā āścaryaki bānte isime hamesā garaf rahanā cāhiye*** — inferring the *Prâṇá* air rose upwards in such a manner that it seemed as though the body would be lifted upwards with force. Now inaction is achieved with ecstasy implying I have become devoid of action and remaining in this passive state is My action or not performing anything is My action. It is indeed strange that it is necessary to constantly exist in that inactive state implying this to be *Kriyā's* transcendental state, a constant existence in this transcendence is imperative.

Worldly actions cannot be completely forsaken. Therefore God has expatiated to Arjuna —

> ***Niyataṃ kuru karmatvaṃ karmajyāyoayakarmaṇḥ.***
> ***Śarīrayātrāpi ca te na prasidhyedakarmaṇḥ.*** (*Gītā* 3/8)

This verse signifies thus — perform all responsibility-oriented actions because it is better to perform some action than not perform any action at all. By relinquishing all actions, bodily existence cannot be maintained. That action which if not performed tantamounting to a fault is the imperative action. This vital-breathlike *Prâṇákarma* is the imperative action, because with the help of *Prâṇá* air the body is maintained, therefore vital-breath *Prâṇá* air is the life-span of a living being. Even if all actions are abandoned, the breathing action will continue. There is no alternative other than that action. The body does not exist if that breathing action is non-existent. It is derived from *Prâṇá* and without it a living being cannot survive. It is the external manifestation of *Prâṇá*. All types of action executed by man are desirous; desires and aspirations are inevitably wrapped with it. Only the breathing action is passive action, because it is not enveloped by any desires or non-desires. Whether it is desired or not, the breathing action will continue. The aspiration-oriented action will subsist as long as the kinetic mind which has originated from the dynamic *Prâṇá* exists. The action which is performed with the mind's attachment is bound to be replete with desires. But the action which occurs without mental attachment is passive action. When man is steeped in deep slumber and desires or non-desires are both absent, even then the breathing action continues. "I shall sleep" is a desire, similarly "I shall not sleep" is also a desire. When both these desires are absent, the action occurring even then is passive action. Thus the breathing-action is passive action. Since all other actions are derived from the mind, they are replete with desires. The mind itself is sensory, therefore actions executed through the senses can never be passive. God in the *Gītā* has stated about this passive *Prâṇákarma*. Because the *Prâṇá* air which is travelling within a living being is a living being's present state, that is the vital breath *haṉsá* . External motion of *Prâṇávāyú* is action in opposition to *haṉsá* which results in aberration thus causing a living being to perpetually remain in a state of aberration. Because of it's externally oriented motion alongwith the decline of lifespan, the body also decays. But through the medium of vital breath *hansá's* internally oriented motion, if the *Hansá Kriyā* (*Prânákriyā*) can be practised in accordance with it's rule, the externally oriented action which acts in opposition can be resisted and soul-engrossment or normal state being achieved all types of aberrations are eliminated. Thus Yogiraj has recounted in His diary on 21st July 1873 — ***Āj āur baḍā sthir gharkā hāl milā ākh āp bund huyā jātā haye āur Brahma sāf dárśana hone lagā — tríkūṭā yāne jihvāmūl — upar tālukā ched bund kartā haye āur jihvākā agrabhāg tālu madhyame lagtā haye āur jihvākā mūl tāluke nice lagtā haye isi tarhase bilkul bāharkā śvāsā bund hotā haye dhanyabhāg uskā jisko iha hoye*** — the significance of this is that today I have received the trace of a more tranquil state, the pair of eyes is automatically closing and *Brahma* could be envisioned more clearly. *Tríkūṭa* implies the three peaked mountain or the famous pilgrimage. But Yogiraj is expatiating — *tríkūṭa* implies the root of the tongue, this tongue by being raised upwards closes the hole of the palate cavity, the tip of the tongue enters the middle of the palate and the root of the tongue remains fixed beneath the palate, in this manner in the *khecari* state by continually practising *recaka purākalike Prâṇákarma*, the external inhalation and exhalation of breath by completely ceasing, Yogiraj has effected Himself to achieve *kévala kumbhaka*. Therefore He states that he is blessed who attains this type of *kévala-kumbhaka*. When is this *kévala-kumbhaka* achieved ? Giving it's immaculate calculation, He has said — ***Daślākh ekshaṭ hājār Prâṇâyāma me kévala-kumbhaka sidh hotā haye.*** — signifying that in 10,61,000 *Prâṇâyāmas, kévala-kumbhaka* can be achieved. When a *yogi* by regularly practising *Prâṇâyāma* is capable of completing the stipulated number of *Prâṇâyāmas* only then *kévala-kumbhaka* is automatically achieved. Thus that *kévala-kumbhaka* state will be his natural state, whether this is practised in the present birth or in the subsequent two to three births.

Who will perform this action ? God has stipulated —

Nirāsīryatacittātmā tyaktasárvaparigrahaḥ,
Ṡārīraṃ kévalaṃ karma kurvannāpnoti kilvisham. (*Gītā* 4/21)

This verse denotes that the one who practises *kévala* named action through this body becomes passive, is engrossed in the soul and relinquishes all the sensory propensities, is devoid of sin.

Thus it can be clearly understood that God has termed that *kévala-karma* to be the true *Karmayoga*. Elsewhere God has stated this action to be *sahajá-karma*. Therefore what is *kévala-karma* is *sahajá-karma* and this is *karmayoga*. God through the medium of Arjuna has advised mankind to follow this *karmayoga*. But how can this *karmayoga* be performed? What is it's inherent feature? In this regard, God has more or less clarified about this. More or less because it is knowledge which is derived from the *Gurú* and cannot be achieved by reading books.

Apâne juhavati Prâṇáṃ Prâṇeapânáṃ tathāpare.
Prâṇâpânágatī ruddhā Prâṇâyāmaparāyaṇāḥ.
Apare niyatāhārāḥ Prâṇān Prâṇeshujuhavati. (*Gītā* 4/29)

This verse implies that some offer oblation of *Prâṇá* air in the *apâná* air and *apâná* air in the *Prâṇá* air. By practising likewise through the medium of *kévala* named *kumbhaka*, *Prâṇá's* motion is arrested denoting that the person concerned becomes an adept in *Prâṇâyama*. Some others by becoming skilful in *Prâṇâyāma*, control all the senses and offer oblation of *Prâṇá* within *Prâṇá* or practise *Óṃkāra Kriyā*. This is the actual oblation. By practising in this manner, he attains the state :—

Sparṡān kṛittvā bahirvājhyāṃṡcakshuṡcaivāntare bhruvoḥ
Prâṇâpânáu samau kṛittvā nāsāvyantyarcāriṇau. (*Gītā* 5/27)

The significance of this verse is that by keeping the whole gamut of material facts like form, taste etc. externally and placing the Third Eye between the eyebrows (*śāmbhavī* state) he becomes a traveller of inner motion. The action of *Prâṇá* or *Prâṇákarma* is incessantly continuing through the nasal passage in the form of vital breath, by this *Prâṇákarma* all the airs within the body are stilled and the upward and downward motions are spontaneously arrested and movement occurs within the nasal passage. In June /July 1871, Yogiraj recounted His *sādhana* experience — ***Ānkh upar sthir hogiyā Brahma dekhne lagā — śvāsā bhitar bhitar calene lāgā mánas sthir bhayā — praṇām kariyā bindi ānkhke upar do hāt tafādke thaḍi picheke praṇāmke bakhat khāli ānkhse dekhā sabere dekhā, sabereke bakhat āb praṇām karenekā erādā nāhi kartā āpke āp praṇām hotā haye — bhitar bhitar jihvā galeke bhitar baiṭh gayā*** — denoting that His eyes have now been stilled above, vibrations have ceased (the *śāmbhavī* state), in this state He is visualising *Brahma*. The breathing motion is now in the *sushumná*, therefore the mind being arrested has become still. While paying obeisance in the morning, He visualised the dot with naked eyes three feet away; but since His kinetic mind has settled in the still mind, the desire to pay obeisance is absent and now obeisance is being automatically paid towards His Own Self. In the pit of the throat, that is in the palatal cavity, the tongue has attained a position of settlement. There being no desires or thoughts in this state, duality is non-existent and duality being non-existent, who will pay obeisance to whom? Since the universe becomes pervaded by *Brahma*, an automatic obeisance is being paid by the self to the self. If obeisance is paid, duality occurs. Therefore *Prâṇákarma* or soul-action is the true *karmayoga* or else if the external motion of the function of *iḍā* and *piṅgalā* which is continually occurring in a living being is made internally oriented and it's union caused, that is *Karmayoga* or *yóga* of action. In this manner, ***Sarvacintāparityāgo***

niścinto yóga ucyate. (Jñānasaṅkalinī taʹntra) meaning *yóga* is the abandonment of all thoughts. Elsewhere, sages have noted ***yógaścittabṛitti nirodḥ. (Pātañjala yógasūtra samādhipād slóka 2)*** — inferring that the state of cessation of all types of propensities of the mind is known as *yóga*. By practising regular *Prâṇákarma* the airs are stilled and the vibratory *Prâṇá* becomes still. The moment *Prâṇá* attains stillness, the present kinetic mind becoming tranquil settles in the still mind. In this state since the present kinetic mind is absent, that thought-free state is known as *yóga*. Therefore God advising Arjuna to be a *yogi* has stated —

> ***Tapasvibhyoadhiko yogi jñānibhyoapi matoadhikaḥ.***
> ***Karmibhyaścādhiko yogi tasmādyogi bhavārjuna.*** (*Gītā* 6/46)

This verse signifies that in God's opinion *yogis* are greater than hermits, knowledgeable and active persons; thus O Arjuna, become a *yogi*, because only a *yogi* by causing an union between *iḍā* and *piṅgalā* thus inducing an attainment of the still state of equilibrium or the state beyond action is capable of achieving settlement i.e. a constant union of the Infinite Soul essence in the state of science. The causing of the union of the soul with the Infinite Soul through soul-action (*Prâṇákarma*) or the *Kriyā* practice of attainment of settlement is the *yóga* practice.

One of the devotees of Yogiraj enquired — "It has been stipulated in the *śāstrás* that by showing compassion towards living beings, service towards God can be rendered. Kindly explain how it is possible to show compassion towards living beings."

Yogiraj stated — It is absolutely true that showing compassion towards living beings, service to God can be rendered. But what you consider to be compassion towards living beings is not the true compassion and showing compassion in that manner, soul-attainment is not possible. Normally, you shower compassion or render service to poor, distressed, helpless, afflicted persons by providing wealth, food, clothes, medicines etc. Actual kindness or service is not rendered towards living beings in this manner because it is impermanent and the person who showers this compassion does not gain soul-attainment. It is merely a temporary compassion towards the body of a living being. The body of a living being is not the real living being. Apart from this, the particular necessity for which kindness was showered towards someone can recur again in the future. For instance, if a hungry person is provided food, he can feel hungry again. Moreover, hunger is an affliction of the body. Thus this type of service is service towards the body and not towards God. It is true that He dwells in this body but serving the body cannot render service towards the God within. For instance, if the renovation of a decrepit temple is accomplished, worship of the deities within the temple cannot be accomplished. By this type of compassion a person's earthly afflictions cannot be eliminated. But keeping in accordance with social norms, this type of compassion should certainly be exhibited. But the *śāstrás* have not stipulated the showering of compassion towards living beings in this manner. To comprehend the significance of the scriptural statements or to comprehend the meaning of the actual compassion towards living beings, one must first understand what a 'living being' denotes. *Prâṇá* is basically still. When that still *Prâṇá* derives vibration, only then He is termed to be a living being or else the dynamic state of *Prâṇá* in the body is known as life. As long as this life is existent or *Prâṇá's* dynamism is existent, till then a living being remains alive. Therefore compassion towards living beings implies providing compassion towards that dynamic state of *Prâṇá* and this is service to God. In other words, through *Prâṇákarma* by providing compassion towards the dynamic state if this is again transformed into the still *Prâṇá*, service towards God is rendered because still *Prâṇá* is God. To serve still *Prâṇá*, dynamic *Prâṇá* is necessary.

Just as dynamic *Prâṇá* can extirpate dynamic *Prâṇá*, similarly a thorn can be uprooted by another thorn. Service to *Prâṇá* is possible by *Prâṇá* exclusively and is not possible through the medium of material objects. ***Tan mánas vacaná karma lāgāoe — isiko ahiṃsā kahate haye.*** — The state which evolves by unifying or stilling the body, mind, speech and action is known as *ahiṃsā* or the malice-free state. ***Nāsikā dvārāy ye śvāsa āsiteche tāhā kanṭher dvārāy lakshya kariyā balā.*** — A living being's existence depends upon the breathing motion occurring through the nose. Therefore everyone speaks by fixing attention on the function of the throat air. *Karma* (action) means *Prâṇákarma* (*Prâṇá-action*). This type of *ahiṃsā* can be achieved only through *Prâṇákarma* and absence of malice in body, mind, speech and all actions causes *ahiṃsā*.

The fact that Yogiraj would visualise God in all elements has been noted in His diary — ***Eysā Chāyā Púrusha ghaṭme ghaṭ dekhā*** — *Chāyā Púrusha* infers the Supreme Being, He is *Nārāyaṇa*, He is *Purāṇá Púrusha* (Primordial Being) — He is prevalent in all bodies. *Yógis* can see Him with a steadfast gaze. On 12th August, 1873 Yogiraj wrote — ***Ek Ādi Púrusha khaḍā dekhā. Ādi Púrusha śūnyáme*** — inferring I could envision the Primordial Being standing in the infinite void. After this He has written — ***Cnādme ohi Purushôttamakā rūpá rātbhar dekhā kabhi hāt payer bhi haye*** — I saw the Form of the Supreme Being throughout the night within the Soul-Moon which can be visualised in *Kūṭastha* and sometimes I saw Him to be having hands and feet also. ***Nákshatra ek ādmike chātike bhitar dekhā*** — signifying I saw that eternal star within the chest of a person.

Oke bhajan kare sādhana kare ke kār kibā kare,
Oki sādā mānushṭi, oki kālo mānushṭi,
Oje sādār upar kālo sāje emon mānushṭi.

Describing the Primordial Being, Yogiraj stated — "Barring that

Primordial Being, nothing can be performed, therefore who can adore Him, who can practise His *sādhana*, without Him can anyone perform anything? Is he a White Being or is He a Black Being? He is such a Being Who is white but has assumed blackness.

Bhelkī lāge dekhle tāre,
Tāre tāre dāko tāre.
Ómkārer par jyoti ākāre,
Se je āche sākār nirākāre.

This denotes that one is spellbound by observing Him, invoke Him through the strings of *iḍā, piṅgalā* and *sushumná*. After the *Ómkāra* sound ceases to exist, the Effulgent Form appears. He is amorphously and inamorphously pervasive.

In what manner can one know the Being Who is above brightness and darkness and Who induces a spellbound state while being seen? Yogiraj has stated — ***Sthir buddhise mālum hotā haye — jyoti svárūpa baḍā nesā baḍā ānand. Ómkāra dvārā jāhā jānite icchā kare tāhā tār haye*** — I can understand through the still intellect — that like the effulgence there is deep engrossment and deep ecstasy. Through the medium of *Ómkāra Kriyā* one achieves what he wishes to know.

Yogiraj possessed a boundless devotion towards His *Gurú*. There is no evidence that He had gone to have a *dárśana* of His *Gurú*. Thus barring the time of initiation, there is no authenticity in the fact that He had achieved a *dárśana* of His *Gurú* in the latter's gross form. In His diary of fourteen years, nowhere can mention be found of the fact that He met His dear *Gurú Bābāji Mahárājá* in his gross form. Since He had recounted each and every incident daily in His diary, it is certainly expected of Him to recount His experience of meeting *Bābāji* in the gross form either in His own house or elsewhere. Instead, many such incidents of His union with His dear *Gurúdeva (Bābāji)* through the medium of *sādhanā* have been noted in His diary. Therefore if *Bābāji* had given *dárśana* to Yogiraj in the gross form at least once, Yogiraj would have mentioned this. But this evidence is absent everywhere. On 17th May, 1873, in Diary No. 3 He drew a human face and inscribed beneath it — ***Bābājike rūpá, ehi yáma o dhárma.***— It is the form of *Bābāji*, he is *yáma* (regent of death) and *dhárma* (religion incarnate). A few months prior to this, in the same Diary No. 3, He has noted on 13th December, 1872 while staying at Danapur — ***Jab Prâṇávāyú śirke upar carā tab Bābājise milā, jab Bābājise milā tab kyā nahi kar saktā haye*** — signifying that while practising *sādhanā* when the *Prâṇá* air arose above the head, then I was united with *Bābāji*. When I was united with *Bābāji*, then I experienced the confidence of doing anything and everything or else tasks which could not be accomplished were now accomplished.

Giving introduction about His *Gurú Bābāji Mahárājá* in His Diary No. 3 on 16th February 1873 He has noted — ***Jo Kisun so Buḍuā Bābā*** — implying that Who is Krishna is the Revered Old Father or *Bābāji Mahárājá*. From this it can be deduced that His *Gurúdeva* was not an ordinary *sādhaka* merely. He was Krishna Incarnate.

While residing at Kashi, He had written in Diary No. 9 during the second half of December 1871 (date not specified) — ***Khod Bābāji kāldaṇḍ liye upar súrya candrámāke bhitar dekhlāi diyā*** — in other words *Bābāji* himself alongwith the staff of death could be visualised within the Soul-Sun and Soul-Moon above, that is in *Kúṭastha*.

In April 1872, while staying at Kashi, through the medium of *sādhanā* He had met His dear *Gurúdeva* and this experience has been remarkably expressed in His Diary No. 9 — ***Gurúkā ādarbhāo sushumná jāgā bicbicme āot haye kabhi kabhi jyot mālum hot haye khāli ākhse sushumná dekhā jāgarit sapan***

sushupti gurú se bātcit bhayā — implying *sushumná* was awakened by the affection of the *Gurú*, sometimes it is appearing, sometimes the effulgence can be experienced, I saw the *sushumná* with naked eyes, in the states of awakening, dreaming and deep slumber, I held a conversation with *Gurúdeva*.

Professor Taraknath Sanyal, son of the brother-in-law of Yogiraj obtained *Kriyāyoga* initiation from Him and achieved an elevated state in *sādhanā*. One day he had prayed to Yogiraj — "Kindly bring Your *Gurúdeva*, the noble *yogi Bābāji Mahárājá* once, we wish to see him."

Yogiraj replied — "I shall inform you after asking *Bābāji*." A few days later, He informed Taraknath — "*Bābāji* does not wish to come."

From this evidence it can clearly be inferred that *Bābāji Mahárājá* never appeared before Yogiraj in the gross form. *Bābāji* would sometimes send a *saṃnyāsin* of his following to Yogiraj to collect money accumulated from initiation. It is for this reason, that many harbour a wrong notion that *Bābāji* would appear before Yogiraj in the gross form. From the diary written by Yogiraj it instead is proved that *Bābāji Mahárājá* was a Krishnalike incarnation. A *yogi* of this stature does not require to come in the gross form. Specially he had promised to Shama Churn while imparting initiation to Him that he would himself appear when necessary and give *dárśana* to Yogiraj in the spiritual manner. Thus it is correct that he had given innumerable *dárśanas* to Shama Churn through *sādhanā's* medium and blessed Him. Shama Churn also has acknowledged this fact in His diaries written during a period of fourteen years.

Forty six songs, poems and Hindi couplets all composed by Him have been registered in His diaries. He has expressed His name either above or below them as "Shama Churn" or "Shama" or sometimes only "Sha". An exact representation of some of them have been incorporated here.

He has composed a beautiful hymn to denote what true devotion towards the *Gurú* is and what the glory of the *Gurú* denotes and if the significance of this can be understood, the complete *sādhana* essence can be realised —

Gurúnām sadā niyejā majā
Dekhe yā sadā dhvani śunejā
Cor kuṭhrīr bhitar majā
Lutejā buker jore
Ātmārāmake Rāmanām
Sunaiejā — ye jābār se
Yāk baye tui āpan karma karejā —
Tor habe bhālo śeshe tui sthir
Ghare cale yā.

Obtain the glory of *Gurú* with happiness constantly, visualise it and hear the *Ómkāra* sound within, capture the ecstasy of the secret realm with all your strength and make *Atmārāma* listen to the glory of *Rāma*. Do not bother about the one who is going astray, practise your own action, this will be good for you and eventually you will merge in the still state.

By habiting this worldly wilderness noble *yogis* even have to sometimes discipline their minds. Yogiraj also had disciplined his mind and composed an excellent hymn —

Yethāy āche baḍa majā
Ānanderi uḍāiyā dhvajā
Loṭa tume sarvānge majā
Tāhār nāi anta
Mánas cole yā tui āge beḍe cole yā
Sukh niścay habe abhay pada pābe
Dekhe śune pābe baḍa majā.

Sri Shama Churn bhane sadā
Rekho savāyú mane
Ihātei ante habe majā.

When a great amount of joy prevails raise it's symbol; seize the endless joy throughout the body. Dear mind depart, go ahead, surely you will gain happiness and the fearless state and experience the joy. Sri Shama Churn constantly narrates to bring *Prâṇávāyú* into reckoning for this will eventually impart bliss.

Common man considers a *yogi* to be extremely hard-hearted and harsh, without a hint of love and affection. But Shama Churn is not such a Yogi. He is a Yogi Who had a magnanimous love for all. Describing what that Godly love is and in what manner it can be achieved, He has composed a pleasant hymn in this regard —

Premer ghar kothāy
bal dikin,
Prem ki amni mele
mehanat kar kichudin.
Hāte hāte cnād pābe
milan habe yedin.
Dīnvābe theko sadā
ānande rātdin.
Ānander nāiko sīmā,
tākāo yeman mīn.
Kālācnāder preme paḍe
habe nāko kshīṇ;
Keno beḍāo edik odik
ore buddhihīn.

Thus — Can you tell me where the state of love abounds; love cannot be acquired so easily you have to strive hard for it. One day you will be united with that state of love, you will obtain anything you desire. Constantly exist in a humble manner hence in perpetual ecstasy. There is no limit to this ecstasy which when acquired will lead to a steadfast gaze. Even if you are in love with Bhagavan Krishna, this ecstasy will not wane. O ignorant one, why do you wander here and there?

Regarding what Kashi is, where it's settlement is and what *Víśvanāth* is, Yogiraj has composed two hymns and while reciting it, it's immense beauty and replete spirituality can be observed —

Sādher premeśvarī dīpyamān Hari,
Āsen yān khusī jakhan dekhān camadkārī.
Hari vinā nāiko gati vrajeśvari,
Jagadmoy dekhi āmi vyāpak Hari,
Hari jānen kata rañj bhaver kāṇḍārī,
Harir upar Har āchen Trīpurāri,
Dhanya Trípurāri Kāśīr sthiti triśūlopari
Yekhāne sab kichu nāi divāśarvarī.

The desirable God of love is the resplendent *Hari*; He arrives and departs in accordance with His wish and renders marvellous visualisations. There is no alternative other than *Hari* Who is Master of *Vrajá*; I see the all-pervasive *Hari* in the creation Who is aware of the histrionics of the universe, He is the Pilot in the voyage of life; *Śivá* is *Trípurāri* (the Destroyer of the vibrations in the lower, middle and upper portions of the body as well as of creation) Who prevails on *Hari*; O Glorious *Trípurāri*, You are the settlement of Kashi above the Trident (*Kúṭastha*, the conjoining place of *iḍā*, *pingalā* and *sushumná*) where nothing exists, not even day and night.

Mero mánas ānand kānan kāśī,
Yāhnā virāje sadā ānand śaśī,
Adhaḥ ūrdhvá bic sthir ghar haye,
Yāhnā khare Víśvanāth avināśī.

This still mind of Mine is the blissful garden and the abode of Kashi where the moon of joy constantly prevails. The still state exists throughout the body; in the upper, lower and middle where the Imperishable *Vísvanāth* reigns.

Yogiraj often referring to the couplets of Kabir would explain many essences to His devotees. The *sādhana* essence of Kabir and that of Yogiraj are more or less the same. It is for this reason, there was a popular belief at that time that Kabirdas himself had desended in a high Brahmin family in the form of Shama Churn Lahiree. Though enough evidence regarding this fact cannot be found, He Himself has penned at one place in His diary — ***Yo Kabirā soi sūrya soi Brahma soi Hum*** —implying the One Who is Kabir is the Soul-Sun, He is *Brahma* and He is Myself. Again He has noted — ***Yo Kabirā sūryakā rūpá soi avināśi Brahma soi Hum*** —signifying that the one Who is the Soul-Sun Kabir is the Imperishable *Brahma*, again He only is Myself. In another context He has recorded — ***Kāyāke virá Kabir yāne śvāsā.*** *Kāyā* means body. The principal strength of the body is breath and that breathlike strength is Kabir.Elsewhere He has recounted — ***Satyáyugame Kabir sāhebka nām—Satyá Sukṛit; Trétāme—Munīndra; Dvāpárame — Karuṇāmoy; Káliyugame Kabir*** — meaning Kabir in the *Satyáyuga* had descended in the form of *Satyá Sukṛit*, in the *Trétāyuga* as *Munindra*, in the *Dvāpárayuga* as *Karuṇāmoy* and in the *Káliyuga* as Kabir, therefore from His Own statement at that time, it has been proved that those popular beliefs were correct. The one who was Kabir is Shama Churn. Of course at a later date, many have used the term Kabir to mean the soul of the living being. Further proofs about the fact that Yogiraj knew about all the incidents of His previous births, can be gleaned from His diaries. For example, He has written inoneinstance— ***Āmār strīr pūrvajanme bhagini cile tāhāte āpanke bhālabāsa***—implying that My wife was My sister in the previous birth, I love My Self within her self.

*　*　*　*　*　*

Like every other day, that day also Yogiraj was sitting engrossed in *dhyāna* in His room. Normally He would not meet anyone in the mornings. But that day one devotee came to meet Him out of acute necessity and seeing Him in the engrossed state from the door, paid obeisance to Yogiraj from there and went to the Dasasamedh market nearby. While shopping, the devotee suddenly saw that at a little distance his Guru Yogiraj was also shopping. The devotee thought that perhaps he was making a mistake. He saw properly again — no it was not a mistake, it was his adorable Guru Mahatma Shama Churn. But the mind does not seem to agree so easily. Therefore to dispel any doubt, he again went to the house of his Gurudeva. Reaching there he saw that his Gurudeva was sitting engrossed in *dhyāna* as before. The devotee realising his mistake, bowed down in obeisance and said — "O God it is difficult to understand Your Divine Activity, it is You Who know about it. For a meagre person like me, to realize it is mere impudence." Thus the fact that Yogiraj would wander at different places at one and the same time, has often been proved. This is not an impossible task[1] for noble *yogis* who have gained spiritual attainment are emancipated and remain constantly united in *Brahma*.

One devotee would reside a few miles away from Kashi. One day he set out with his family towards Kashi in a bullock-cart to have a *dárśana* of his *Gurú*. In the middle of the journey, the wheel of the cart broke down and the cart stopped moving. The cart -puller made many attempts to repair the wheel but did not succeed. The devotee became anxious as he had his wife and children with him and another three or four miles more was required to reach Kashi. Again if Kashi could not be reached before dusk, there was the fear of dacoits. Therefore to save themselves from this danger, he started ardently praying to his compassionate Guru. At this moment,

1. In the interpretation of *Vyāsa* in *yóga* philosophy, evidence and rationality of this yogic ubiquity have been explained.

suddenly the bullock started pulling the cart. All noticed that the cart started moving normally. Though all were astonished by this unexpected incident, none paid attention to it and arrived at the house of Yogiraj at dusk. After this they entered the house of their Guru, paid obeisance to Him and sitting at one side, started repeatedly narrating the problem they faced on the road, to their Guru. Everytime Yogiraj answered — "Hmm." The devotee thought that perhaps his Gurudeva was not paying attention, therefore He did not listen properly. Thus he loudly started repeating the problems he faced on the road. Then Yogiraj replied — "Can't you see, how much I am sweating? Fan Me a little. Who was pulling your cart all along?"

Thinking about the boundless mercy of Gurudeva towards His devotee who was involved in difficulty, the devotee's eyes welled up with tears and the other present devotees were stupefied with amazement. He would dispel the problems of His devotees who were in difficulty in various ways. The *Brahma*-knowledgeable noble *yogis* can accomplish any difficult feat it is true, but they do not always desire to show much miraculous graces. But due to necessity or to eliminate the miseries and afflictions of the poor, distressed and sheltered disciples, such Godhood-repleteness being aggrieved by their distress lent His endeavours. Yogiraj has also been noted for doing this many a time.

This is an episode of another day. This Mahapurusha Whom nature even could not affect remained within the family precincts yet stayed perpetually detached from the world, domestic affairs and body-consciousness. Like other days, that day also in the morning He was returning home after taking a holy dip in the Ganges. In the middle of the road, a person told him — "Your foot is injured and bleeding."

Yogiraj taking a piece of cloth bandaged the wound and

coming home, as usual entered His room and gradually became engrossed in *samādhi*. A few hours had elapsed. The housefolk while moving along the room noticed that a narrow stream of blood was trickling down the outlet of the room. They saw that the blood was trickling from the room where the Sublime Yogi was in *samādhi*. Being worried, they entered the room and after innumerable calls broke His *samādhi* and enquired Him whether He had a wound in any part of His body.

Yogiraj did not remember anything, therefore He said — "There is no wound in any part of the body." But the housefolk were still anxious. They asked — "Then from where is this blood coming?"

Suddenly, the Great Yogi recalled. He answered — "While returning home after a holy dip in the Ganges I had injured My foot, but bandaged it." Later it was observed that instead of bandaging the wounded toe He had bandaged the toe of the wrong foot and as usual blood was oozing from the wound. He had attained such a stature of going beyond body-consciousness.

In this regard, He would remark to His devotees — "By practising regular *Prâṇá* action when the *Prâṇá* air is permanently centred on the head, then *yogis* lose their body-consciousness. It is then that a *yogi* achieves complete static settlement in *Kū́ṭastha* and attaining a state of being rapt in *yóga* is constantly united in *Brahma* and achieves a detached state from the material world. You can achieve this, if you make endeavours." Therefore He would advise all — "Perform all actions by remaining in *Kriyā's* transcendental state or in the state beyond action. Just as Rajasthani belles carrying pitchers on their heads crack jokes on the way yet their mind is fixed on the pitcher, similarly place the mind on *Kū́ṭastha* and perform all actions. But remember that without practice those women could never carry pitchers on their heads in that manner, similarly without *sādhanā*, the mind cannot be placed on *Kū́ṭastha* and all actions performed. It is exclusively dependant on *Prâṇákarma*."

One of His favourite disciples resided a little distance away from the house of Yogiraj. The disciple's ardent wish was that he invite his Gurudeva to his house and treat Him to a delectable meal. One day expressing this wish to his Guru, the Latter agreed. The disciple prepared many dishes including fish curry and arranged them in great quantities for Yogiraj to eat. Yogiraj happily ate what He desired and cast away the existing remnants from His plate. The devotee's wish was that as there would be remnants on the plate of Yogiraj it would act as *prasāda* for the other family members of the house who could have a share of this *Gurúprasāda*. For this reason, he had served immense quantities of food on Yogiraj's plate. But seeing Gurudeva cast away the existing remnants, quietened everyone. After ablution, Yogiraj suddenly remarked — "There is no use of eating the *prasāda* on the plate. Look God has clearly stated in this regard — ***Prasāde sarvaduḥkhānāṃ hānirasyopajāyate.*** (*Gītā* 2/65) — All miseries are eliminated by this *prasāda*, for do you know what that *prasāda* is? That *prasāda* is *Ātmaprasāda*. Since *Prâṇá* is dynamic a living being undergoes a great deal of harm, miseries and afflictions. Through *Prâṇákarma* when the vertical motional vibration of *Prâṇá* is ceased, stillness accruing from the state of cessation of action is achieved, that is *Ātmaprasāda*. By achieving this *Ātmaprasāda*, all types of sorrows and afflictions are annihilated and a complacent state arrives. Try to obtain that *prasāda*." He would never allow anyone to take ort, the remnants of His plate. He has written in His diary — ***Galeme miṭhā ras uparse nīce girtā nākse lahugi galeke bhitarse khokike sāth — isikā nām amṛíta — isiko pinese amar hotā haye*** — inferring that by raising the tongue upwards, placing it in the palate cavity and practising regular *Prâṇákarma*, I could experience a sweet juice in the throat which flows down exuding from above or the *Sahasrâra* and enters the middle region of the throat and nose while coughing, this is known as nectar. Drinking this ambrosia causes immortality. The gods had drunk this ambrosia, while churning the sea. Gods or the *Kriyābāns*, by practising excellent *Kriyā* can drink this ambrosia and attain immortality.

Another of His devotees being present there also wished to treat his Gurudeva to lunch at his house. Gurudeva agreed to this and the disciple prepared many varieties of fish dishes alongwith other items, devotedly offered these to his Guru and sitting beside Him, started fanning Him. Yogiraj contentedly commenced eating all these. The disciple in order to please his Guru, repeatedly kept on imploring—"Father kindly take the hot hilsa fish curry, the rich rohu fish curry etc." After imploring three or four times, Yogiraj suddenly stopped eating and arose. The disciple thought that perhaps he had committed an offence and enquired —" Father, most of the food remains untouched?" Yogiraj replied — "Do I eat fish? Why did you serve fish to Me?"

The disciple with folded hands fearfully said — "Father, I had seen You consume fish in another disciple's house the other day, therefore I derived the courage to offer fish."

Yogiraj amazingly stated — "When did I eat fish? I am a vegetarian."

Yogiraj would in this manner remain aloof from the realm of the mind.[1]

---

1. God has declared observing this state —

Naiva kiñcīd karomīti yukto manyet tattvavid.
Paśyan śṛinvan spṛiśan jighrannaśnan gacchan svapanď svasanď.
Pralapan bisrijan gṛihannannunmishannimishannapi.
Indriyāṇīndriyārtheshu bartanta iti dhārayan.
Brahmaṇyādhāya karmāṇi saṅgaṃ tyaktvā karoti yaḥ.
Lipyate na sa pāpena padmapatramivāmvasā.. *(Gītā 5/8-10)*

This verse signifies that the person who goes beyond the state of action is united in *Brahma* and being conversant with the soul-essence, he is especially knowledgeable about essence; he sees, hears, touches, eats, copulates, sleeps, breathes, speaks,

The late Gangadhar Sen renowned Ayurvedic practitioner of Calcutta had a student named Pareshnath Rai. Paresh Babu later coming to Kashi, commenced his Ayurvedic practice and was capable of gaining immense fame and wealth. He was famous not only in Ayurvedic practice but attained a great deal of glory in poetry, grammar, philosophy etc. and became renowned, therefore he was quite vain about this.

Pareshbabu had quite a lot of intimacy with Rajchandra Sanyal *Mahāśaya*, brother-in-law of Yogiraj. By this merit, Pareshbabu got introduced to Yogiraj. Pareshbabu had composed an annotation of *Caraká*. Once this annotation was discussed in the presence of Yogiraj. There, quite a few *paṇḍitás* conversant with the *śāstrás* were also present. After reading and explaining the annotated part, he desired to know the opinions of everyone present to which the *paṇḍitás* highly eulogised. But noticing Yogiraj to be silent, Pareshbabu asked — "How is the annotation, You did not remark anything?"

Yogiraj in a solemn tone stated — "Everything is faulty."

None had the audacity to raise an objection to the renowned and arrogant Pareshbabu in this manner, therefore being nonplussed they started exchanging glances. The infuriated Pareshbabu controlling himself a little said — "What do You know about *Cáraka*?"

Yogiraj rejoined — "I know what is correct."

Pareshbabu who had been hit on the nail spent a few days

---

forsakes, accepts, awakens or bats an eyelid; he affirms himself that the sensory faculties are engaged in sensory actions, yet settles himself with the thought "I do nothing" thus being detached from conceit spontaneously remains passive. In this manner, by surrendering to *Brahma* and due to constantly remaining in the state beyond action, the person who can abandon the craving for consequences and perform actions, is perpetually united with the still *Prâṇá-Brahma* and is not involved in virtues or sinful actions, just as a lotus leaf though remaining in water is not drenched by it.

agonisingly, after which one day he came to Yogiraj and said — "My teacher late Professor Kaviraj Gangadhar Sen, while teaching *Cáraka* to us stated that though he taught what he knew in this regard, the true significance of *Cáraka* essentially was known to *yogis* only. If you ever meet such a *yogi*, only then can you comprehended it's intrinsic meaning."[1]

After this, Pareshbabu was converted into a devoted disciple of Yogiraj. Pareshbabu would tell many that he had bowed his head to only three persons — they were respectively the Supreme Being, Whom he did not know, secondly his Ayurevedic *Gurú*, late Gangadhar Sen and thirdly Shama Churn Lahiree. He would never bow down before a fourth person after this.

This Pareshbabu eventually had achieved such a height of progress in *yogasādhanā*, he would often enter into *samādhi* and to break this *samādhi*, Yogiraj Himself had to go to his house. Pareshbabu thought that perhaps this brought pain to his Guru, therefore he purchased a house near the abode of Yogiraj and started residing there.

Before his death, Parashbabu bequeathed a greater portion of his immovable property to Tinkari Lahiri *Mahā́śaya*, the son of his Guru.

One day, one of the female disciples of Yogiraj asked for a photograph of Him. Yogiraj giving one of His photographs, remarked — "If you consider this to be only a photograph it will be so; but if you regard this to be a girdle of protection, then it will be that."

A few days later, this lady disciple alongwith another female disciple, were reading the *Gītā* placed on a table. That photograph of Yogiraj was fixed on the wall in front of them. At that time a

1. Yogiraj later had rendered an esoteric explanation of *Cáraka*.

thundershower commenced and these two ladies being awestruck started praying with folded hands in front of the photograph — "O Gurudeva, please save us from this danger."

All on a sudden thunder struck nearby and the ladies thought they were singed by it. Later both the ladies had stated that it seemed as though someone had encircled them with blocks of ice.

Yogiraj would perpetually protect devotees under His Aegis in this manner.

Another favourite disciple of Yogiraj, Panchanan Bhattacharya *Mahāśaya* came to Kashi and started habiting in the house of Yogiraj.[1] Attaining an advanced state in *yógakarma*, he had gained the capacity to gauge menfolk.

One day after taking a holy dip in the Ganges he was returning to the house of his Guru. While walking on the road, he noticed a high-ranking *sādhaka* walking a little ahead of him. Thus developing an interest in striking up a conversation with him, Bhattacharya *Mahāśaya* started walking briskly. To catch hold of him, the moment Bhattacharya *Mahāśaya* started running, that *sādhaka* disappeared. Bhattacharya *Mahāśaya* regretted this intensely. He thought that despite his Guru being present, he was driven towards another *Mahātmā,* hence was guilty of transgression. Lamenting this, the moment he came to Yogiraj the Latter laughingly enquired — "Could you not catch him?"

The repentant Bhattacharya *Mahāśaya*, becoming even more ashamed fell at His Lotus Feet and started weeping.

Yogiraj remarked — "Do not cry, he is one of your fellow disciples. If you desire to see him then tell Me so for if I recall him, he will come."

---

1. When Tinkari Lahiri *Mahāśaya*,the eldest son of Yogiraj came to Calcutta he would often stay for long periods at Bhattacharya *Mahāśaya's* house.

Bhattacharya *Mahāśaya* collecting himself said — "I do not wish to see him anymore."

Yogiraj gently smiling remarked — "He is one of your Muslim fellow disciples[1], he is also not eager to meet anyone lest Hindus become dissatisfied."

An old Brahmin, having retired from service was staying at Kashi and would spend most of his time in worship and studying the scriptures. Like other days, one day after taking a holy dip in the Ganges, he came to Yogiraj and prayed to Him with folded hands, for obtaining yogic initiation.

Yogiraj replied — "Do what you are doing now. You will receive initiation when the time comes."

The old Brahmin went away dejectedly.

A few days after this, an old lady came and ardently prayed to Yogiraj that she desired to obtain *Kriyāyoga* initiation.

Yogiraj said — "Come tomorrow morning after a bath."

One such devotee who was present on both the days enquired Yogiraj after the old lady left — "I know that old Brahmin to be extremely religious yet he did not obtain initiation, but this lady will receive initiation, what is the reason for this?"

Yogiraj in a placid tone explained — "The religious feeling in that Brahmin has awakened only recently, therefore it is advisable for him to engage himself in external worships and the studying of scriptural texts, but the lady had obtained *yogic* initiation in her previous birth, but neglected it. In this birth she has completed the consequences of her past actions and come to Me, therefore it is necessary to impart yogic initiation to her."

---

1. He was Abdul Gafoor Khan

Harinarayan Mukherjee, a disciple of Yogiraj was employed in the Post and Telegraphs Department at Kashi. One of his intimate friend and colleague Kalibabu, was a debauch inspite of having a beautiful wife. Harinarayanbabu felt sorry for this and tried explaining to his friend in order to steer him away from this wrong path. But this evoked no results. He then thought that if he brought his friend to his Gurudeva, then he would no longer go in the wrong path. Therefore he one day told his friend — "Come let us go and meet Yogiraj."

The friend refused to go and started making different types of adverse comments about Yogiraj.

Harinarayanbabu was his friend's well-wisher. His belief was that if his friend was brought to his Gurudeva by any means, he could not go in the wrong path. Therefore although Harinarayanbabu did hear various adverse comments about his Gurudeva he did not lose hope and started making endeavours to reform his friend. After making such endeavours his friend eventually agreed and one day in the evening, both went to Yogiraj.

Yogiraj was then surrounded by many devotees and was imparting advice. Both the friends after arriving, paid obeisance, sat in a corner and started listening to the advice. Hearing the advice replete with knowledge, the friend was satisfied and went away for that day.

The next day Kalibabu himself told his friend — "Come, let us go today also and have a *dárśana* of Yogiraj."

Harinarayanbabu becoming thrilled took his friend to Yogiraj again. In this manner, for a few days he accompanied his friend to Yogiraj. After this, Kalibabu reformed himself, started maintaining a noble existence and a few days later obtaining yogic initiation from Yogiraj, entered the path of *sādhana*.

It can be thus noticed that many erring persons would instantly change the motion of their minds the moment they came into contact with Yogiraj and were compelled to maintain an honest existence.

The aforementioned Harinarayanbabu was a famous Indian classical singer. Many years after the Departure of Yogiraj, in 1937 a marble statue[1] was installed in His house, in the room He would habit. Arrangements had been made to celebrate this occasion. Satyacharan Lahiri *Mahāśaya*, grandson of Yogiraj had invited Harinarayanbabu on that occasion and requested him to deliver songs. But Harinaryanbabu shamefully replied — "Do not ask me to sing here, one should not make fun here." The reason for this being asked, Harinaryanbabu said — "One day, I alongwith my music teacher and disciple of Yogiraj, Ramdas Goswami *Mahāśaya* of Serampore had come to pay obeisance to Yogiraj. The Latter had then started discussing with keen interest the tune, rhythm and harmony of music. While discussing, suddenly He withheld His speech and evoked a bass sound, which still rings in my ears. My tune is nothing compared to that. That day He had demonstrated the respective vocal origins of respective tunes and respective notes. This is why I do not have the courage to sing in His presence."

---

1. Now that marble statue of Yogiraj and the statue of His eldest son, Tinkari Lahiri *Mahāśaya* have been installed in 'Satyalok', D22/3, Chausattighat, Varanasi.

Chapter 9

ESOTERY OF YOGASADHANA

The Sublime Guru, was sitting surrounded by devotees imparting advice. One devotee enquired — "Barring mother, father and other close senior persons who else are worthy of respect? Who should reverence be administered to and which persons are fit to receive this?"

Yogiraj expatiated — "Parents are great *gurus*, they are worthy of reverence." Apart from this *Mánu*[1] has observed —

Cakriṇo daśamaīsthasya rogiṇo bhāriṇaḥ striyāḥ
Snātakasya ca rājñáśca panthā deyovarasya ca.

(*Mánurahasya* Chapter 2)

This denotes the one who is travelling in a car implying one who is proceeding by remaining in *Kúṭastha*; one who has fixed his *Prâṇá* air between *Viśuddha* and *Ājñá Cakrás*; one whose inner vision has become powerful; one who experiences the feeling of weight on the head by practising continual *Prâṇákarma*; one whose *Prâṇá* air has attained a settlement from the *Mūlâdhāra Cakrá* to the *Sahasrâra* and as a result experience the feeling of a veil being pulled on the head; one who is constantly and perpetually immersed in *Kúṭastha*; one whose tongue has reached the palate behind and one who proceeds practising the *Ómkāra Kriyā Prâṇákarma*; are all worthy of obeisance. They should not be impeded while walking, way should be made for them to proceed first and none should sit before they are seated. *Mánu* has further expounded on this matter —

Teshāntu samabetānāṃ mānyou snātakapārthivou.
Rājasnātakayośaiva snātako nṛipamānabhāk.

(*Mánurahasya* Chapter 2)

1. One of the fourteen sons of *Brahmā*, regarded as the father and first lawgiver of mankind.

This signifies that amongst all the aforesaid respectable persons, the one whose tongue has reached the palate behind and the one who remains perpetually engrossed in *Kűṭastha*, are the greatest. Between the two, the latter is supreme. Therefore one should not harbour enmity towards such personage. Even if they are junior in age, due respect should be administered to such persons.

One devotee asked — "We have no dearth of *Mahǻtmās* in our country. Many assume the guise of a *Mahǻtmā*. Under these circumstances how can one easily recognize a *Mahǻtmā*? From which person can one obtain religious advice?"

Yogiraj explained — "Note that the persons mentioned above, are all worthy of imparting religious advice. You should easily recognize him as *Mahǻtmā*, the one whose tongue has reached the palate behind."

Brāhmasya janmanaḥ kartā svádharmasya ca śāsitā.
Bāloapi biprobṛiddhasya pitābhabati dhármataḥ.

(*Mánurahasya* Chapter 2)

This verse implies that soul-disposition is *Svádharma*[1]. One who advises and teaches about *Svádharma* and *Kriyā* should be regarded as a father even though he is junior in age.

Another devotee enquired — "Unknowingly, many a time we

1. *Svádharma* signifies one's own intrinsic religion. Here religion does not infer the prevalent systems of faith and worship. Each and everyone is dependant upon their own-soul or *Prâṇá* and has a right to know it. Here religion infers the endeavour to know the own-soul or *Prâṇá*.

The Indian word *dhárma* means religion in English. The lexical explanation of religion stipulates the prevalent systems of faith and worship. But the actual implication of the word *dhárma* does not conform to this explanation. *Dhárma* implies the endeavour to know the omnipresent soul or *Prâṇá*. Thus this soul or *Prâṇá* permeates the total creation in the animate and inanimate. *Dhárma* is one, *Prâṇá-dhárma* or soul-*dhárma*. *Dhárma* is an afferent word while the English word religion is efferent. Therefore religion can never be a synonym for *dhárma* which in English cannot be explained in one composite word.

commit sinful acts. For instance while walking on the road many creatures are trampled upon without our being aware of it. How can we be saved from such sinful acts committed despite a non-inclination to do it?"

Yogiraj rejoined saying that in the *śāstrás, Mánu* has clearly stipulated regarding this —

Ahṇā rātrayā ca shāñjantun hinastyajñānato yatiḥ.
Teshāṃ snātvā viśuddhyathaṃ Prâṇâyāmān shaḍācaḍed..

(*Mánurahasya*)

— implying that the devotee who by not knowing commits the aforesaid sin if he practises *Prâṇâyāma* six times according to the scriptural injunction will be particularly purified of that sin because internal *Prâṇâyāma* is the absolute austerity in the path of six *cakrás*.

Prâṇâyāmā brāhmaṇasya trayoapi vidhivadkṛitāḥ.
Vyāhṛitipránarvaiktā vijñeyaṃ paramantapaḥ.

(*Mánurahasya*)

This verse denotes the practice of *Prâṇâyāma* thrice[1] as per codes of *Kriyā* with intra-*Ómkāra* sound by the *Kriyābān* which is the absolute austerity.

Dahyante dhnyāyamānānāṃ dhātunāṃ hi yathā malāḥ.
Tathendriyāṇāṃ dahyante doshāḥ Prâṇásya nigrahād..

(*Mánurahasya*)

Just as metal is purified by fire, similarly all the senses are purified by *Prâṇâyāma*. The present kinetic mind is engaged in sinful actions. When *Prâṇá* becomes still through *Prâṇâyāma*, the present kinetic mind also becomes still. After the present kinetic mind attains stillness, all the senses become still, then achieving a

---

1. The objective of mentioning three *Prâṇâyāmas* signifies the minimum quantity to be practised.

cessation of actions, they all become purified. This is the sanctified state of the senses, because if they lack function, who will perform the evil actions? Thus Yogiraj would say — ***Jihvā uthnese indriya daman hotā haye*** — meaning when the tongue reaches the palatal cavity, the senses are controlled. This is known as the *Khecari* state or releasing the obstruction of the tongue or is spiritually known as the consumption of beef. It is the principal facet of *yógasādhana*. The *śāstrás* have not stipulated to give a calf in oblation and consume the veal, though apparently that seems to be it's significance. *Yajñá* means oblation of *Prâṇá*, i.e. to merge the dynamic *Prâṇá* in the still *Prâṇá* through *Prâṇâyāma*. This *Prâṇá-yajñá* is the true *yajñá*. To perform this, *gó* meat has to be consumed. *Gó* implies tongue here, not the veal.

Gómāṃsaṃ bhojayennityaṃ pibedamaravāruṇīm.
Tamayaṃ kulīnaṃ manye itare kulaghātakāḥ.
Góśabdenoditā jihvā tadprobeśo hi tāluni.
Gómāṃsabhakshaṇaṃ tattu mahāpātakanāśanam.

(*Haṭhapradīpikā*)

This infers that one who constantly consumes beef by releasing obstruction of the tongue and one who drinks ambrosia exuding from the Soul-Moon is pious, others are not. By consuming such beef, even the sins of greatest sinners are destroyed. Again aiming at this, the *Vaishṇavá śāstrás* have noted —

Góbhojane mahāpunya,
Jāyā thākite gṛihaśūnyá.
Gurú mere svargávās,
Hari bhojle sarvanāś.

This implies that by consuming veal in this manner a great virtuousness is achieved, all types of material attachments alongwith carnal attachment are withdrawn; the vibratory *Prâṇá* is *Gurú*, by causing a cessation of the existence of *Gurú,* inferring merging in still *Prâṇá* is the Heavenly Abode and one who worships *Bhagavān Hari* in this manner loses everything that is, there is a cessation of the function of the senses by which a living being enjoys material pleasures. *Bhagavān Hari* (Still *Prâṇá*) then destroys the sensory oriented mind of a *sādhaka* by seizing these material pleasures.

In ancient times all sages would consume veal in this manner. The authors of the *śāstrás* would visualise God in all living beings and have advised murder to be extremely sinful. When sages envisioned God in all living beings they could never advise murder because they were established in *ahiṃsā* (the malice-free state). The authors of the *śāstrás* have expressed all these in the form of innuendos, but at present all advice has been reduced to superficial facts.

While teaching the precepts of *yógasādhana*, Yogiraj would counsel all His devotees — "*Kriyāyoga* is an extremely subtle action, therefore it is imperative for everyone to repeatedly come into close proximity with the *Gurú* and show him the *Kriyāyoga* and obtain repeated advice about this. Otherwise, it is difficult for all to initially comprehend the subtle *Kriyāyoga* and there is every possibility for committing a mistake. If anyone thinks that he has understood everything at the first instance, it is incorrect. It is absolutely necessary for all devotees to totally surrender to their *Gurú*. The more one can surrender oneself to the *Gurú*, the more he can ascertain the subtlest of the subtle techniques of *yóga* from his *Gurú*. Without surrender, nothing can be derived from the *Gurú*. Going to the *Gurú* or any deity empty handed is not proper and should never be executed. Modesty is imperative in the vicinity of *Gurú*. Sitting before he is seated, expressing anger if he is enraged, expressing the feeling of being a great *paṇḍitá* or apparently being conversant with many *śāstrás* and arguing with him regarding the *śāstrás* are all forbidden. Whatever he says regarding soul-knowledge, should be imperatively accepted with a spirit of self-surrender."

He would also note — "Those who practise *Kriyā* regularly, they are more or less free from disease. The basis for religion, wealth, desire, salvation is sound health; but disease destroys health, salvation and life. Thus if *Kriyābāns* keeping in accordance with the advice of their *Gurú* practise enough *Kriyā* then they will be free from disease, spiritual consciousness will be augmented and consequently will attain the state of salvation. Therefore always abide by the command of *Gurú* to foster protection of the body. The internal air is God and practising *Kriyā* retains that God. It is the duty to retain the body and soul in this manner. If *Kriyābāns* are faced with adversities then they will be freed from them if they practise *Kriyā*. It is advisable to always keep tongue in an uplifted position and the total *Kriyā* has to be practised by raising the tongue. Coition should be executed by uplifting the tongue. Women should not practise *Kriyā* during menstruation. After meals, one should lie down on the left side. If this *Prâṇâyāma* is practised perfectly there will never be any afflictions of the heart."

What is termed to be *'Sadgurú'*? (true *Gurú*). Yogiraj has replied in answer to this — "*Gu*" means darkness and '*rú*' means light. One who annihilates darkness and causes an enlightinment, he is the *Gurú*. The internal motion of breathing-air only can eliminate this darkness, therefore this breathing-air the producer of light from darkness is the actual *Sadgurú*. *Kūṭastha* is *Śrīgurú*, the unbounded greatness.

People belonging to all the different sects like *Śākta* (worshipper of the female principle of creation, *Śākti*), *Śaiva* (worshipper of *Śivá*), *Gāṇapatya* (worshipper of *Gaṇeśa*), *Vaishṇavá* (worshipper of *Viśhṇu*) and *Saúrya* (worshipper of the Soul-Sun) should be devoted to *Ātmakarma* which produces religious wealth, desire, salvation and spiritual attainment. The *śāstrás* similarly denote that —

Jápecchāktaścaśaivaśca gāṇapatyaścavaishṇávaḥ.
Saúryaśca sidhidaṃ devī dhármārthakāmamokshadam.

— (*Gurú Gītā*)

Yogiraj would impart *Kriyā* to married couples together, because He would say that if *yógasādhana* was obtained alongwith wife, there would be less impediments in *sādhana*. He would further remark this *Kriyāyoga* to be above all types of irrational beliefs.

* * * * * *

Haranchandra Roy would reside afore the Abode of Yogiraj. He would daily urinate after dusk towards the Abode of Yogiraj from his terrace. This would cause a lot of inconvenience for the family members of Yogiraj. One day Yogiraj forbade Haranbabu not to commit this nuisance. For the one whose time had drawn near, refusing to listen to the statement of the Mahapurusha is but natural.

Haranbabu stated — "You do not have to bother whatever I do in my house." Apart from this he hurled many obscenities at Yogiraj.

Yogiraj hearing all these was hurt and without uttering a single word raised a wall on that side the next day.

After a few days, suddenly Haranbabu expired. Later it was noticed that none survived in Haranbabu's family.

In support of this *Mánu* has observed —

Sukhaṃ jhabamataḥ śete sukhañca pratibudhyate.
Sukhaṃ carati lokeasminnabamantā vinaśyati.

(*Mánurahasya*)

This signifies that the person who is above honour, taking recourse in the Supreme Being peacefully and without anxiety, in other words if the one who realises stillness and wanders blissfully on earth is insulted, the insulter is destroyed. The insulted person himself does nothing because he is beyond respect and insult and becomes exclusively dependent upon God, thus for him it is God who looks after everything. Therefore if such a person is insulted and attempts are made to harm him, God punishes the wrong-doer. God punishes the wicked and cares for the righteous. Thus Yogiraj would tell all His devotees — ***Jo Bhagavānko hāmesā dhyāna kare, usko kām woh kartā haye*** — this infers that the one who is perpetually engrossed with God, his work is performed by Him.

At the moment of *samādhi* — place, time, name and form are all absent. Then all merge harmoniously together. All these that are within the limits of name and form cannot be permanent. Therefore Yogiraj would say — Drown yourself in the quest for soul-essence and through the medium of *samādhi* settle in that tranquil state. Then you will note that the name and shape of the world no longer remains. By calming the petty feeling of pride, you can realise the indivisible still entity as your own form. The knowledge which dwells in duality is insignificant because it is sensory knowledge. I am the devotee and You are God is also trivial knowledge. But true knowledge is that which sees the same soul-entity within everyone. The soul-entity which is stationed within everyone cannot be known with the help of the present kinetic mind and intellect. If the *Vedānta* ascertainable realization or knowledge is achieved Godhood cannot be ascribed merely to person, place or idols. Then God can be realised in all living beings and in all elements. Then the discrimination amongst Hindus, Muslims, Christians or amongst Brahmins, Sudras or high and low castes is absent. Then by visualising the infinite *Prâṇá* everywhere, it becomes the *Brahma*-pervaded universe. Thus it can be noticed that though being born in a high ranking Brahmin family; Hindus, Muslims, Christians or Brahmins, Sudras or the rich and the poor were all equal to Yogiraj. He had given shelter to everyone. Men belonging to different sections of society had become His disciples. Casting away all types of superstitions and degraded customs, Yogiraj effected a concord in religious dissension as He had observed the fundamental truth of all religions of the world in oneness. In His observation, everyone is the ambrosial son, none small or great. A few other great men like Chaitanya, Kabir, Nanak, Dayanand etc. did not maintain any discrimination and were able in harmonising all religions. The pragmatic experience of Yogiraj in this regard was marvellous. By arriving at this state through the medium of *sādhanā* He has recounted in Diary No. 5 — ***Jyotke bhitar nilā, nilāke bhitar ek safed bindi dekhā uske bhitar ādmi wahi bahut kisam ke Hindu, Ingrej hotā haye*** — this denotes within the resplendence of *Kūṭastha* there is a blue colour, within this blue I saw a white dot, within that dot, I saw a man. He is the Supreme Being. He only has become different types of Hindus, Christians etc. In another place Yogiraj has recounted —***Dama par dama Allāh — damake pare jo dama haye so Allāh yāne sthir ghar*** — implying that within the inhalation and exhalation, stillness comes once. If explained clearly, it is when inhalation is complete and exhalation commences, and when exhalation is complete and inhalation commences, at both these moments stillness arrives once and that still state is *Āllāh*. But none notice that still state. *Āllāh* means *Khodā*,[1] what is primary or the root that is *Khudā*. The word *khud* means the self or the root. By practising excellent *Prâṇákarma*, the still state of *Prâṇá* which occurs is the root or the cardinal or the self which exists in all living beings and that root or the *Khodā*like still *Prâṇá* becoming vibratory results in the living being state. Everything originates from the still *Prâṇá*, He only is Primordial Energy *Brahma*, He only is *Khudā*. At the end of *pūraka* and the beginning of *recaka* and at the end of *recaka* and beginning of *pūraka*, the still state which is experienced and which only the *yogis* are conversant about should

1. *Khod* — The word has been derived from the Persian etymology "Khud".

be increased by *Prâṇákarma* and settlement achieved, that is the root or the prime, that is *Kriyā's* transcendental state. — ***Khodā yāne khod — ā jab āpnese ātā haye. Allāh — ālā baḍā yo sabse baḍā*** — implying that by practising continual *Prâṇákarma* when the still state automatically evolves, He is the Prime or *Khodā* and that is the still infinite void. He being all pervasive is all extensive, therefore He is *Āllāh*. Thus Yogiraj has again noted — ***Bedamame yo dama haye soi asal dama haye***. — *Bedama* means a state of cessation of breath. If breathing is not arrested wilfully and continual internally oriented *Prâṇâkarma* practised, the *kévala-kumbhaka* state automatically arrives and this state is *bedama*; then the externally oriented breathing motion ceases completely. This is wholly dependent on *Prâṇákarma*. That breathing state is the actual breath (which can be learnt exclusively from the *Gurú*). In this internal *Prâṇâyāma* the action of external inhalation and exhalation is not present. At the beginning of this *Prâṇâyāma*, by abandoning the *Iḍā* and *Piṅgalā* the action involves the *Prâṇá* and *Apâná* airs within, the external airs remain external and the internal airs remain within. The Supreme Being in the Form of a root within *Kúṭastha* exists in the same manner in all human beings. He is not different as a Hindu, Christian or Muslim etc. Fundamentally everyone is the same, the difference occurs only in dualism. By settling in non-dualism or in stillness no difference remains. Therefore it can be noticed that along with Hindus belonging to different castes, many Muslims like Amir Khan, Rahimullah Khan, Abdul Ghaffar Khan etc., many Christians like the Commissioner of the state of Coorg in India, an Englishman; the Police Superintendent of Hazaribagh, Mr. Spencer and other Englishmen obtained initiation from Yogiraj and this has been noted in His diaries. Thus we deduce that He is the Salvator for all.

* * * * * *

Abinashbabu, a disciple of Yogiraj was employed in the Bengal Nagur Railway (now the South Eastern Railway). Once he desired to have *darśana* of his Gurudeva and therefore applied for a week's leave to his higher authority. His higher authority then was Bhagabati Charan Ghosh, father of Paramahamsa Yogananda. Bhagabatibabu called Abinashbabu and said — "You cannot progress in your service if you constantly trouble yourself thinking about religion. Concentrate properly in your office work."

Abinashbabu was returning home walking, in a disheartened state. On the way he noticed Bhagabatibabu was going in a palanquin. Coming closer, Bhagabatibabu alighted from the palanquin and started walking together. As a ruse for offering consolation and letting know the procedure to gain material benefits, Bhagabatibabu started explaining to Abinashbabu. The latter was listening to him in a stoical manner and was praying mentally to his compassionate Gurudeva so that he could meet Him.

Both of them were walking across the field. The rays of the setting sun then illumining the entire region created a blazing spell of illusion. Suddenly a few yards away, they saw Yogiraj descend assuming an Incorporeal Form and remark — "Bhagabatibabu, you are extremely merciless towards your subordinates." Saying this He disappeared. Abinashbau started praying with folded hands.

Bhagabatibabu was astounded by this unexpected incident. After keeping silent for a few minutes, he said — "Your leave begins from tomorrow, go and have a *darśana* of your Gurudeva. If you take me also alongwith you it will be better. I would like to see that Sublime Yogi."

The next day Bhagabatibabu alongwith his wife and Abinashbabu boarded the train for Kashi. Arriving at the house of Yogiraj, they saw Yogiraj seated in *padmâsana* and paid their obeisance to Him.

By opening His transcendental eyes, Yogiraj smiled and said — "It is improper to prevent anyone from proceeding in the religious path."

After this Bhagabatibabu alongwith his wife obtained *Kriyāyoga* initiation from Yogiraj and they were blessed.

A few days after the birth of his second son Mukundlal, Bhagabatibabu alongwith wife and infant arrived in Kashi at the house of Yogiraj. The *dhyāna*-rapt Yogiraj was then sitting surrounded by devotees. Holding the child in her arms, Bhagabatibabu's wife paid obeisance to Yogiraj and at this moment the Noble Yogi taking the infant in His arms placed him on His lap and commented — "Your son will become a *yogi* and show several men the path for the quest of God."

With the blessings of the Omnipercipient Sublime Guru, this Mukundlal later became famous as Paramhamsa Yogananda.

Swami Pranabananda (previously Nilmadhab Mukhopadhya), another favourite disciple was employed in the Railways. After achieving an exalted state in *sādhanā*, he was perpetually rapt in the ecstasy of *Brahma*-bliss thereby being unable to perform his official functions properly. He contemplated that if he could obtain retirement from service by any means, he could then concentrate a greater deal on *sādhanā*. Therefore he prayed to his Gurudeva that he be granted exemption from service.

Yogiraj replied — "Take grant for your pension."

Pranabananda stated — "My period of service does not entitle me to obtain pension, what reason can I show for this?"

Yogiraj remarked — "Show any reason you like."

The next day Pranabananda submitted an application for pension stating the cause for this as physical illness and immediately and unexpectedly the departmental doctor and the authority consented. Pranabananda obtaining retirement from service, concentrated on his *sādhanā* with a new spirit. This Pranabananda acquired immense renown as the subsequent *sādhaka* of Yogiraj.

Yogiraj would always sit on a charpoy in *padmâsana* in His parlour with all the disciples seated in front. He would maintain reticence. Sometimes opening His eyes, He would fix His gaze on any devotee seeking an answer mentally and give him a brief answer. It was not necessary to always ask Him a question, He would answer His devotees by gauging their innate dispositions. Some devotee perhaps would come to Him with questions pertaining to his difficulty, knowing his predisposition He would give a facile and simple answer and remove all his doubts. Any mental wave of any of His devotees would not remain unknown to Him. He would never explain any *śāstrás* through the medium of theoretical knowledge. He would express to His devotees all what He had derived from His *sādhanā* realizations. The philosophical and scientific essence of the complicated *śāstrás* like *Vedas, Vedānta, Upanishads, Gītā* etc. would be explained by Him to all in a dexterous manner through the medium of His Own realizations. He would comment that all these ancient *śāstrás* were a storehouse of practical knowledge of the ancient sages. Only those to whom such realisations occur, can offer exact explanations of those *śāstrás*.

When devotees and visitors would frequent His place in the evening, He would courteously welcome everyone and extend hospitality towards them. He would not give special treatment to wealthy or talented persons or neglect poor or illiterate persons. He looked upon everyone in an egalitarian manner. Arrogance or vanity are absent in *Brahma*-knowledgeable persons and they find wonderful unity amidst everyone. The basis of an equality in vision of the sages is soul-knowledge. All His statements elucidate a penetrating keenness in knowledge. The heads of all would automatically bow down due to the glory of His Divinity. When Yogiraj would remain silent or discuss facts pertaining to the complexities of religion then it would be noticed that He would infuse inexpressible knowledge amidst His devotees. If any devotee would visit Yogiraj in an anxious frame of mind, his mental condition would change without him knowing it so much so that the moment the devotees had a *darśana* of Him, they would experience the taste of mental peace and bliss. He was never seen to be perturbed by misery or ecstatic due to happiness. If anyone recounted his past misdeeds to Him, He would advise them to forget all the past sorrows, afflictions and pain and concentrate on *Ātma-sādhanā*, make endeavours for spiritual advancement, for if all these are accomplished a general well-being in all spheres could be achieved. Therefore He would constantly remind everyone the necessity of practising *Kriyāyoga*. He would never ask anyone to perform His personal tasks and would never accept anyone's gift or assistance if there was a dearth of sincerity, the reason for this being He was more or less financially independent. He served as a Government employee, obtained pension and also engaged Himself as a tutor. Generally it can be observed that other *Gurús* who do not earn their own living and possess no financial independence are either directly or indirectly dependent on the wealth of their disciples. But since Yogiraj maintained His livelihood with His own earnings, He did not have to be dependent on others. He did not expect the favour of others. Amongst His established ideals, this ideal is regarded to be the greatest and He would advise all His devotees to act likewise.

Yogiraj would profess that the *yógasādhanā* through which inclination towards God does not evolve is not *yóga* at all. If the correct and excellent *yógasādhanā* is practised then surely devotion towards God will arise. Alongwtih covetousness, aspiration, jealousy, malice, greed, envy all other types of sensory and mental dispositions will spontaneously be controlled. Therefore *Kriyāyóga sādhanā* has been termed to be the greatest. If devotion towards God is derived through the medium of *Kriyāyóga sādhanā*, then the existence of God in everything external can be felt. The one who has not developed an interest in the quest for God within the self, will not attain anything despite him undertaking several pilgrimages.

To achieve reverence, faith, devotion, knowledge etc. independent endeavours are not required. If these are acquired through the medium of independent endeavours, then it will be impermanent. But if *Prâṇákarma* is practised in an excellent manner, these will be achieved automatically and will be permanent. That permanent devotion is pure devotion and permanent knowledge is rationalism. On the contrary if the attempt by the mind to abandon all types of devilish propensities like covetousness, anger, jealousy, greed, attachment etc. which act as impediments in the path of *sādhana* is made, it cannot be abandoned. Whatever relinquishment is accomplished, it will be impermanent. But if superior *Prâṇákarma* is continually practised the devilish propensities are relinquished on one side, on the other the virtuous propensities evolve and to abandon or accept anything an independent or mental endeavour is not required, for devilish propensities will be eliminated and the virtuous propensities will automatically appear. If relinquishment is made through the superior type of *Prâṇákarma* desire or the existing kinetic mind have to be destroyed. Nothing will remain in that state beyond desires and this should be regarded to be the true relinquishment. Therefore He would ask everyone to heed — ***Khudhārter nikaṭ anna yatakhāni prayojon, mumukshur nikaṭ Kriyā tatakhāni prayojon*** — *Kriyā* is important to the person desirous of salvation, just as food is important to the famished.

Many a time as has been observed, Yogiraj with the purpose of destroying the accumulated afflictions or sins of others would bring these upon Himself. Therefore sometimes He would be taken ill. Exalted *yogis* through spiritual means would be able to absolve the sins or diseases of others by undergoing the sufferings themselves. In this manner, when necessity demands *yogis* absolve their disciples from the consequences of their actions. When the great *yogis* realise that it is necessary for any advanced disciple to make further progress, it is then that they act likewise. It is true that by this the *yogis* suffer temporary afflictions but do not suffer any spiritual loss, instead it proves to be beneficial for them.

In the letters addressed to some of His advanced disciples, Yogiraj many a time has detailed these facts. Sometimes He has written — ***Āmi ār kata kariba. Āmār loker janya asukh kariyāche, tāhār upar sab kāj āche. Kriyā karun, bhay nāi*** — How much more can I do ! I have fallen ill for the sake of man, apart from this I have other tasks. Practise *Kriyā*, don't be afraid. Again He has written to someone — ***Nijer ei śarīre tāhār katak rog bhog kariyā chilām. Pradīpey taila nā thākile tāhār nirvāṇalāv haye. Prakṛitir biruddhe dehe katakshaṇ jīvana thākite pāre. Ātmār mṛityú nāi kāraṇ Ātmāi mahākālsvárūpá. Sthitipad kālero upare. Mahākāl samudrasvárūpá gatihin, jīva nadīr nyāye sei samudre paḍe. Kāle satarka thākile mṛityú ghaṭe nā*** — this implies I had suffered other's illness in this Form of Mine. If there is no oil in the lamp, it will be extinguished. How long can life exist against nature? The soul is immortal because it is like the static void. The static state is supratemporal. The static void is motionless like the placid sea, a living being enters into this sea like a river does. If one is conscious about the passage of time, death does not occur. To another disciple Yogiraj wrote — ***Akālmṛityú baliya śok kariyo nā, jīver pakshe kālākāl mane haye, kāler akāl nāi, ejanya jīver kartavya samasta kālei kālrūpī haṃser śaraṇāpanna hoiyā thākā***. This signifies thus — do not grieve because of untimely death, a living being considers about the propriety and impropriety of time, there is no impropriety of time, for this reason it is the duty of a living being to take refuge in the timelike *Haṃsa*[1] always.

The noble *yogis* many a time in order to impart welfare to their devoted disciples by taking their afflictions upon themselves, release them from the sufferings. This can be termed to be causeless mercy. It was noticed many a time that Yogiraj had similarly displayed such benevolence for the benefit of His devotees. Therefore He would note that the infinite dynamic void which is incessantly continuing is indivisible. This indivisible void seems to be divisible only during the inhalation and exhalation of breath; but in actuality it is not divisible. That static void by settling in the body is prevalent in the form of *Haṃsa* (breathing form) in a living being. It is for this reason He would advise everybody to take refuge in the breathinglike *Haṃsa*, for then there is no propriety or impropriety of time, or else death is absent.

So among the disciples who were residing away from Kashi, the willing ones who could express their intention to have a *dárśana* of Yogiraj and seek His consent regarding this, Yogiraj would reply to them thus — ***tomāder Kūṭasther madhyei yakhan Āmi sarvadā āchi, takhan ei hāḍmāṃser dehaṭāke dekhte āsār kon prayojon?*** — When I am constantly present in your *Kūṭastha*, then what is the necessity for coming to see this Form of flesh and bones? He has similarly written letters to others — ***Dekhā karār janya eto vyasta keno? Āmār ei hāḍ-mās dekhiyā lāv ki? Kūṭasthe lakshya rākhun, tāhāi Āmār rūpá, Āmi hāḍmās bā 'Āmi' ei śabdao Āmi nahi, Āmi sakaler dās.*** — Why are you so anxious to see Me? What is the use of seeing My flesh and bones? Observe *Kūṭastha*, that is My Form, I am not flesh and bones or the word "I" is not Myself, I am

1. Breathing is the timelike *Haṃsa*. By taking refuge in it, one can become supratemporal.

everyone's slave. To some He has written — ***Guru sab cālāitechen. Āmi Kūṭastharūpe sarvadā saṅge āchi.***[1] — The *Gurú* is controlling everything. I am constantly present amidst everyone in the form of *Kūṭastha*. He has written to another disciple of His — ***Māyā kartṛik hāḍmās dekhā jāiteche, tāhā yata śīghra yāye arthād māyār bishay yata śīghra jāye tatai bhāla. Bhāla manda tathāy nāi. Āmār bolite yāhā kichu āche tāhā guruke arpaṇ karā cāi. Arpaṇ hoile tāhāte ār sattva thāke nā. Yakhan deha arpan korechen takhan nijer deha dekhlei ta Āmākei sthūlete dekhā haye. Eirūpá bhābe Āmār deha sab. Śraddhā o bhaktir sahiṭ Kriyā karun***. — This implies flesh and bones can be seen due to illusion and the sooner illusion goes, the better it is. There is no good or evil in it. The totality of the self should be offered to *Gurú*. The moment offering is made, the prerogative towards it is lost. When you have offered the totality of your body to Me, then by observing your own body, you can perceive Me in the gross form. In this manner, My Form is an embodiment of everything. Practise *Kriyā* with respect and devotion.

He would address His devotees thus — ***When you strive to become a yogi, why are you so weak-willed? No one has taken the tree's shelter and none will take river water away from you. Why are you so worried about transitory things? It is your duty to abandon all future and past thoughts; keeping attention towards Prâṇá, perform all present functions. No one has achieved happiness through wealth and never will. It is the provocation of the mind which impels man to earn money. Why are you so anxious about the future? All behave like puppets and rave and rant for money. The world is a place for ordeals. One must be skilful in all aspects and a constant feeling of want should never be harboured. Now it is imperative to increase the mental strength,***

1. All these statements are exact representations of what He has addressed to His devotees in His letters. The names of the devotees have not been published here to avoid intrusion into their privacy.

all actions have to be performed dexterously, to be afraid of anything is not desirable. The devil is perpetually present within the mind, you should be aware that the mind should not concentrate on anything else other than the soul. Practice of Kriyā is the actual study of Vedas. By regularly practising Kriyā, the transcendental state of Kriyā occurs, this is the actual Vedānta philosophy.[1] *One should realise it by practising Kriyā. What is the use of reading books? Kriyā only is yajña (an oblation). Kriyā is the only truth, everything else is untrue. Everyone should perform this yajña. The cessation of mind is known as mántra. No one is ignoble, only the mind is ignoble. Nārāyaṇa exists in all living beings. No one performs anything, God performs everything, a living being is merely a pretext. Make endeavours to concentrate on that Guru-Bhagavān in accordance with the Kriyā-code, for this will impart welfare. Soul is the Guru. Kriyā should be practised with this type of fortitude — I do not belong to anybody, nobody belongs to me. It is definite that one day, everyone will have to relinquish everything. It is completely uncertain when and to whom that particular moment will come. Man remains unaware about this but when that moment suddenly arrives, everyone laments. Thus the objective of life has to be set right and everyone then has to aim to proceed towards that destination. In fact, if a person does not yearn for God, the strength to internally invoke Him does not arise. The immortal, imperishable Guru (the soul) only is the example of causeless love. He is inherently present in everyone always, but even then none make proper endeavours to find him. A living being is oblivious of what good is, for only after knowing this he will become Śiva. Not knowing what good is, the*

---

1. The *Vedas* denote knowledge. The person who has realised *Kūṭastha* is conversant about *Vedas*. The terminal state of knowledge is *Vedānta*. Then there being an absence of any type of *Kriyā* or action, the state of cessation of action is *Vedānta*. Then there is neither knowledge nor ignorance. Breath is *Gāyatrī*, the origin and personified female energy worshipped in *Vedas*.

good at times seems to be evil. In pre-transcendental state of Kriyā (the state beyond action) when the conation of the inhalation and exhalation of breath does not perpetually remain, the mind should be emplaced there. This aforesaid state is termed to be Bhagavan Krishna. The word Krishna infers this aforesaid state only[1]. The state of cessation of the inhalation and exhalation of breath which occurs incessantly is Prâṇákrishna. Those who practise sādhana secretly are known as gopīs.[2] The secret sādhaka, gopī constantly awaits the manifestation-like arrival of this Prâṇákrishna in his body-Vṛindāvana. It is not necessary to seek grace from Gurú, it automatically comes without seeking if his instructions are conscientiously followed. Thus scrupulously adhering to Gurú's maxim, God-consciousness semblant of Gurú's advice evolves in one's own still Prâṇá. By having faith in the maxim of Gurú and performing actions, one day it will be directly perceptible, this is certain. If mental strength is lacking then it has to be acquired by staying in a place which will impart it. Kriyā should be practised there. If Kriyā is practised with fear, it is not Kriyā at all and one cannot save oneself with the help of that Kriyā. Everyone can

---

1. *Śrī* Krishna — *Śrī* = beautiful. *Ś* = breath, *Prâṇá* air; *r* = the seed of fire — the essence of heat (which exists in the Third Eye); ī = power. In other words by executing a powerful *Prâṇákarma*, the air attains stillness in the Third Eye and the state of non-vibration (***Dṛishtiḥ sthirā yasya bināhalokanam*** — *Jñānasankalinī Tántra* — Settlement of vision akin to the supportless state) occurs in the Third Eye, that beautiful state is *Śrī* Krishna — *Kṛi* conjugation means to cultivate, *ṇa* — signifies cessation. Or else by continually cultivating this body-field through *Prâṇákarma* the state of non-vibratory permanent stillness with an aura of detachment which is achieved is *Śrī* Krishna. That *Śrī* Krishna is indestructible and prevalent in all living beings.

2. Therefore Yogiraj advised everyone to avoid tumult and practise *Ātmasādhana* in a *gopī*like manner in silence. *Mahátmā* Ramprasad has similarly noted — ***Jnāk jamake korle pūjā ahaṇkār haye mane mane, lukiye tāre karbi pūjā jānbe nāko jagadjane*** — denoting if worship is performed ostentatiously, pride does arise in the mind, but you should worship Him secretly for then none will know about it. But it is rather unfortunate that at present this ostentatiousness is the principal facet of worship.

protect themselves by practising sincere Kriyā. Feed the Kriyābāns, for by feeding them you will be feeding all gods and goddesses. Kriyābāns only are devátās, all devátās are practising this Kriyā. To attain salvation in this life itself, Kriyā has to be practised according to it's rules and discipline, for only then what is prayed for is granted by the grace of the Gurú. Those who profess to only obtain bliss and longevity, not salvation, are steeped in deceit. They desire for blessings but it is not to be.

Many a time through various means He would draw destined devotees towards Him. He would often undertake both earthly and spiritual responsibilities and make *sādhana* the focal point of their lives. He would teach His devotees how to bring about a spiritual transformation in their lives through the medium of self-surrender. His torrents of mercy would often flow through the medium of love and affection or through the medium of any Divine bestowals. Seeing all these incomprehensible acts of Divine mercy, the devotees were filled with endless amazement. He was the true Benefactor and Beacon for everyone. Therefore He would perpetually explain in an easy and simple manner the underlying concept of God and the intrinsic *yógasādhana* essence to His devotees. By His advice and blessings man would find the true path of bliss. Many would hasten to Him with their material problems or with the hope of finding the spiritual path and Yogiraj also would always direct them into the true path of salvation. By being cohesive with their actions, behaviour and thoughts, He would keep a keen watch on His disciples.

If anyone questioned Him about His Divine bestowals, He would stipulate — ***Satyikār viśwāsa niye tomrā yadi Āmār śaraṇāpanna hao, tāhale yata dūrei Āmi thāki nā keno upasthit nā hoye upāi ki? Kriyā ye kare Āmi tār kāche upasthit thāki.*** — If you take refuge in Me with true faith, then no matter how far I may be, does any alternative remain other than not being present? I am present to the one who practises *Kriyā*.

He would state — When everyone goes to the temple then do they pay obeisance to the temple only or do they pay obeisance to the presiding deities of the temple? A temple has no value without idols. Again God is Omnipresent, thus just as it is true that He exists within that idol, similarly that He exists within you is also true. Moreover the Absolute Truth is He is within you because you are ambulatory. Therefore instead of making a quest for distant objects, it is better to make a quest for the nearest. When He is present within you and when His presence is the nearest, then making a quest for the nearest is an act of intelligence. Therefore God has expressed — ***Īśvará sárvabhūtānāṃ hṛiddeśearjuna tishṭhati.*** (*Gītā* 18/61).

The above *slóka* signifies that though God is prevalent in all the elements, He indwells in *Kūṭastha*. In this regard *Mahátmā* Ramprasad has said — ***Dub de mánas Kālī bole, hṛidi ratnākarer agādh jale*** — infers you can attain God by immersing yourself in *Kūṭastha*, not externally.

Yogiraj would expatiate that everyone has the desire, propensity and right to perceive feminine charm alongwith the other splendours of creation, but simultaneously with this perception the Creator has to be observed, the One Who has created with His inimitable skill and artistic dexterity. It is not proper to forget the Creator and marvel at His aesthetic Creation. If His creation is so beautiful, then how much more beautiful is He? Therefore in this manner, attempts to perceive the Creator amidst creation should be made, for then life will become blessed. It should be remembered that without *sādhana* the crystalline vision will not occur to anyone. It is not an incidental remark. No matter how much you make efforts with the help of the mind, permanence will not arrive. But the more *Prâṇákarma* is practised the more kinetic mind will be stilled and as much as the mind is stilled, the more that type of crystalline vision will occur. Then amidst all forms and beauty, you will perceive Him.

*   *   *   *   *   *

Brahma-conversant persons do not require to perform idol worship. Yogiraj Himself also never undertook it. The *śāstrás* have stated regarding this fact thus —

Uttamo Brahmasadbhābo dhyānabhābasta madhyamaḥ;
Stutirjápoadhamovābo bahiḥpūjā adhamādhamaḥ.

(*Mahánirvāṇa Tántra*)

This signifies that settlement in *Brahma* is the supreme, *dhyāna* or engrossment is medium, chanting praises and doing *jápa* is inferior and the most base is gross or superficial worship.

But despite this, He never forbade anyone to worship idols. Instead He would say that for an ordinary person idol-worship is absolutely necessary. By worshipping idols, devotion and respect for God are augmented and later when he will obtain *Ātmasādhanā* then he need not practise idol-worship. All idols are symbols of *Prâṇá*-God. All the forms which the sages have visualised through the medium of *dhyāna* have been established in the shape of idols and drawing the common man towards this, the sages have instructed them to engage themselves in idol-worship. These common men are oblivious of *Ātmakarma* and for this reason they fail to visualise those forms within the Inner Eye. Everything consists of two aspects; one external, the other internal. In the sphere of *sādhana* also these two aspects are present. Idol-worship, pilgrimages, vows, fasting, taking a holy dip in the Ganges, *jápa*, group chanting, singing in praise of God, serving guests, tending the poor and the hermits etc. are all the external facets of *sādhanā*. Only *Ātmakarma* is the internal *sādhanā*. Just as there is progress in sphere of service, similarly a living being also undergoes gradual upliftment in successive births. The compassionate sages have introduced external *sādhanā* because all men do not have the insight. All men do not yearn for God. They are contented if they acquire material benefits through God's grace and consider these benefits to be God. These type of men are several in number. It is for them that the sages have introduced the practice of external *sādhanā*. By regularly practising external *sādhanā* in this manner, a living being will be purified after several births and will be able to gain introspective vision of internal *sādhanā*, it is then that he will be deemed fit to obtain internal *sādhanā (Kriyāyóga)* and by executing this internal *sādhanā* can establish himself in the realm of the soul-self.

Yathāgādhanidherlabdhow nopāyaḥ khananaṃ binā.
Mallāveapi tathā svatmacintāṃ muktvā na cāparaḥ.

(*Pañcadasi* 9/153)

This verse denotes that though it is known that many gems lie underground, to acquire those gems excavation is the only method, similarly barring soul-cogitation or *Ātmakarma* there is no other alternative by which one can be in communion with the soul.

External *sādhanā* is bound by ritual discipline, breaking it tantamounts to offence. But internal *sādhanā* has no ritual discipline. For instance, in order to worship any idols in external *sādhanā*, first a clean set of clothes have to be worn. Wearing unclean clothes no idols should be worshipped, for if this is executed it becomes sinful. For this type of *sādhanā*, flowers, holy Ganges water, several leaves of the basil and bel plants etc. are required. But all these are not at all required for internal *sādhanā*. Even if clean set of clothes are not worn, there will be no offence. None of the external articles used in religious offerings are required. Only the mind and *Prâṇá* are necessary for practising internal *sādhanā*. Both of these are inherent in everyone. Thus *Prâṇákarma* is the principal feature of internal *sādhanā*. God has stated — ***Nehā-bhikramanāśoasti pratyavāyo na vidyate***[1].— This passive *Karmayóga* (*Prâṇákarma*) has no ritual offence, it being passive action lacks covetousness. It is spontaneously and automatically continuing, it has no new beginning. It can be attained from the moment of birth.

Taking a holy dip in the Ganges is a part of external *sādhanā*. Everyone can take a holy Ganges dip, there is no impediment here. Taking this holy dip in the ever-flowing Ganges is beneficial for the health of one and all. But if one while reciting a verse in praise of the holy Ganges takes the holy dip with devotion, then alongwith health improvement a little more devotion will dawn. This will be his extra gain. Nothing else will occur other than this. If anyone intends to visualise the presiding goddess of the River Ganges he will obtain it through *dhyāna*. But if anyone wishes to fulfil this human life, he has definitely to bathe in the three sacred streams within his own body. These three sacred streams are the three nerves — *Iḍā, Piṅgalā* and *Sushumná* prevalent in every human being. They are respectively known as the rivers Ganges, Yamuna and Sarasvati.

Iḍā Bhagavatī Gáṅgā Piṅgalá Yamúnā nadī,
Iḍāpiṅgalayormadhye Sushumná ca Sárasvatī..
Trívenīsaṅgamo yatra tīrtharājaḥ sa uccate.
Tatra snānaṃ prakurvīta sarvapāpaiḥ pramucyate.

(*Jñānasaṅkalinī Tántra*)

This verse implies that *Iḍā* is the Ganges, *Piṅgalā* River Yamuna and the *Sushumná* nerve within (*Iḍā-Piṅgalā*) is River *Sárasvatī*. Since *Ājñācakrá* is the confluence of the three nerves, it is known as

1. *Gītā* 2/40, *Iha* — this passive *Karmayoga (Prâṇákarma)*, *Abhikramanāśaḥ* — no fault at the inception, *na asti*—absent, *pratyabāyaḥ* —sin or an impediment, *na vidyate* — which does not occur.

Tríveṇī-Prayāga, and is the prime pilgrimage. If anyone can bathe there where the ambrosial cascade exuding from *Sahasrâra* becomes confluent, he will be liberated from all sins. But how can one bathe there ?

Manaḥ sthiraṃ yasya vināvalamvanam
Vāyu'ḥsthiro yasya binā nirodham.
Dṛishtiḥ sthirā yasya vināvalokanam.
Sā eba mudrā bicarantī khecari.

(*Jñánasankalinī Tántra*)

This verse denotes that stilling the kinetic mind without any support, stilling the breath without any obstruction or support that is concentrating on *Kū́ṭastha* without visualising anything with the help of the mind or imagination, one should bathe in the realm of the supreme pilgrimage and this is known as settlement in *Khecari.* God has described this to be *manmanā*[1] or reposing the mind in the soul and remaining engrossed in it. Thus the kinetic mind is a living being's present mind. The present mind makes a living being execute all actions. If that present mind is made tranquil through *Prâṇákarma*, the present kinetic mind's existence being lost will be converted into the still mind. It is then only that the kinetic mind will settle in the still mind. When this occurs, only then can one become the true devotee of the soul and by being worshipper of *ātma-yajñá* (i.e. worshipper of *Ātmakarma*) will pay obeisance to the soul or else pay obeisance to his own-self and realise his ownself. Therefore when *Prahlād* visualised God then he paid obeisance to his adorable God as ***Namastubhyaṃ namo majhyaṃ tubhyaṃ majhyaṃ namo namaḥ***. (*Víshṇupurāṇá*) — "I worship You within myself and also worship within You."

Bathing in the external Ganges can be accomplished by immersing the body, but the body cannot be immersed in the internal

1. ***Manmanā bhava madbhakto madyājī māṃ namaskuru.*** (*Gītā 18/65*)

Ganges. The mind and *Prâṇá* have to be immersed there. If the mind and *Prâṇá* are immersed in this manner and bathed in the *Kūṭastha*like juncture of the three rivers, life will be blessed, all earthly afflictions will be elliminated and cycle of births and deaths cease. Yogiraj in His *Kriyāyóga sādhanā* has stipulated the manner by which the mind and *Prâṇá* should be immersed and bathed in the confluence within the *Ājñācakrá*, which is the supreme place of pilgrimage. That is internal *sādhanā* and is the foremost duty of every human being.

Yamo vaivasvato devo yastavaisha hṛidi sthitaḥ.
Tena cedavivādaste mā gángām mā kurūn gamaḥ.

(*Mánurahasya* 8/92)

This denotes that for the one who has achieved a constant permanence in his *Kūṭastha* through internal *sādhanā*, it is not necessary for him to bathe in the superficial Ganges or in *Kuru-kshetra*, the field of action.

This path of *sādhana* introduced by Yogiraj is scripturally regarded as soul-knowledge, spiritual knowledge or *Brahma*-knowledge. But He had Himself named it as *Kriyāyoga* or *Kriyā* in brief. This *Kriyāyoga* is logical and scientific. The fact that it is entirely scientific is because Yogiraj has described it to be as accurate as mathematics. He would state that it is correct that without devotion one cannot practise *sādhanā*, but how many possess such a devotion? Such devotion does not evolve initially. Thus how will those having a dearth or an absence of devotion practise *sādhanā*? Interest in *sādhanā* cannot grow in them. They have to acquire devotion. Just as when there is a lack of appetite, there is a disinclination towards food, but the moment food is consumed the latent hunger is exterminated, similarly despite a disinclination to practise *Kriyā* if continual practice of *Kriyā* is executed, soul-communion is inevitable. Then true devotion will automatically ensue. Initially due to lack of practice it is true that *Kriyā* will be improper or there will be less interest, but regular practice of *Kriyā* will positively make the person develop a liking for it. *Kriyā* means action. Yogiraj has termed the *Karmayoga* of *Gītā* as *Kriyāyoga. Karma* also infers action. Nothing can be achieved without action, therefore much stress has been laid on *Karmayoga* in the *Gītā*. The name of *Kriyāyoga* has been mentioned in the *Pātañjala yóga* philosophy and in many other places in the *śāstrás*.

Tapaḥ svādhyāyeśvara praṇidhānāni Kriyāyoga.
Sahi Kriyāyogaḥ samādhi bhāvanārtha kleśatanukaranārthaśca.
(*Pātañjala Yógasūtrá Sādhanapād* 1,2)

Kriyāyoga is the profound engrossment, attentive study and austere endeavour. This *Kriyāyoga* is the solemn action leading towards *samādhi* and annihilates all afflictions. By continual solemnization leading towards the state of *samādhi* through this type of *Kriyā*, all the physical and mental afflictions are alleviated, later the *Nādá* sound emanating from *Brahma* can be heard excellently and no type of imagination appears in the mind. Later by attaining the state of the virtuous being, a keen profound wisdom occurs. Therefore Yogiraj would express — ***Śarīrer kashṭa holei bujbhe sādhanā ṭhik hocche nā.*** — If there is bodily discomfort, it should be understood that *sādhanā* is not being properly practised. This is that immortal *yóga* which all sages would practise in ancient times. This *Kriyāyoga* existed before the Advent of Bhagavan Krishna, it exists today, will always exist, therefore it is immortal *yóga*. Sometimes due to the onslaught of time it declines, it is then that a Sublime Soul makes His Advent and revives it. This immortal *yóga* having become extinct once, Bhagavan Krishna preached to the masses through the medium of Arjuna. Later the practice of this sublime immortal *yóga* suffered a decline due to a long period of neglect. It was then that Krishnalike *Bābāji Mahārājá* again made it easily obtainable to the masses through the medium of Shama Churn. ***Jo Kisun so Buruā Bābā*** — The one who is Krishna is *Bābāji*. This is definitely an authoritative statement of Yogiraj[1]. Not only this, He has further written — ***Bābājike rūpá, ehi yáma o dhárma***. From this it can be deduced that His *Gurú* was not only a noble *yogi*, but he himself was root of death and *dhárma*. Therefore God Almighty instilling hope has remarked that whenever a decadence of religion will appear or when this sublime immortal *yóga* will become obsolescent due to onslaught of time, only then will He descend in the Form of a noble human being and establish it. The Advent of Shama Churn was due to this objective.

God has adduced —

Sahajaṃ karma Kaunteya sadoshamapi na tyajed.
Sarvārambhā hi doshena dhūmenāgniribābritāḥ. (*Gītā* 18/48)

This *Kriyāyoga* is that *sahajákarma* or *Prâṇákarma* which is instinctive. When fire is lighted the ensuing smoke conceals the flame, but when the smoke subsides then the fire assumes a blazing form. Similarly, initially due to lack of practice this *yógakarma* may be fraught with faults but nevertheless it should not be abandoned,

1. When Brahma-Shama Churn descended as Jiva-Shama Churn He notified His initial manifestation *Kūṭastha-Bābāji* or Krishna-*Bābāji* (*Kūṭastha* is Krishna) to remind this immortal *yóga* to Jiva-Shama Churn in due course; because it was obvious to Brahma-Shama Churn that the moment He would mark His Advent as Jiva-Shama Churn He would remain oblivious about this immortal *yóga*. For this reason *Bābāji* is Krishna and later Shama Churn Himself declared — ***Humhi Krishna; Humhi Kisunji; Humhi nirākāra Brahma; Humhi Sūrya, Humārei prakāśita sab jagad; Humārai rūpáse jagad prakāśita; Humhi Brahma haye Humhi Ādi Purusha Bhagavān; Sūrya Nārāyaná Bhagavān Jagadvisvar sárvavyāpi Hum haye. Sūrya hi Krishna, Hum sūrya haye— Mahādevá.***— I am Krishna; I am Kisunji; I am Amorphous Brahma; I am the Soul-Sun, the entire universe is My creation; the total creation has manifested from My Form; I only am Brahma; I only am God, the Primordial Male Energy; I am the Soul-Sun, Nārāyaṇá, God, Controller of the universe and am Immanent; the Soul-Sun is Krishna, I am the Soul-Sun-Mahādevá.

because all actions in the initial stage are fraught with faults. Therefore a specific utterance by Yogiraj could be heard most of the time. He would tell almost everyone — ***Banat banat ban jāye***. — If *Ātmakarma* is regularly practised, one day you will reach the state beyond all actions, or the source or origin which is the objective and then you will have a communion with the Infinite Soul and realise yourself.

This *Prâṇákarma* revived by Yogiraj has been described by *śāstrás* thus —

> ***Prâṇâyāmo mahắdhármo vedānāmapyagocaraḥ.***
> ***Sárvapuṇyasya sārohi pāparāśitulānalaḥ.***
> ***Mahắpātaka koṭināṃ tad koṭināñca dushkṛitām.***
> ***Pūrvajanmārjitaṃ pāpaṃ nānādushkarmapātakam.***
> ***Naśyatyeba Mahắdevá dhanyaḥ soavyāsayógataḥ.***
>
> (*Rudráyāmal* Chapter 15)

This implies that *Prâṇâyāma* is the *Mahắdhárma* (ultimate religion)* which is incomprehensible even to the *Vedas*, it is the essence of all virtues and the destroyer of all sins. By this millions of misdeeds and all the sins of previous births are destroyed. The one who practises this *Prâṇâyāma* is blessed.

Extolling the virtues of this *Prâṇáyāma*, the *yóga śāstrás* have given a clarion call to mankind — ***Ānando jāyate citte Prâṇâyāmī sukhī bhabed***. — meaning the one who practises *Prâṇâyāma* lives blissfully in this earthly world.

But this *Prâṇâyāma* is not practised by pressing the nose (it is derived exclusively from the *Gurú*), because by this the air is arrested perforce and *Kumbhaka* occurs against the natural tendency and this incurs a risk of disease. ***Bālabuddhibhiraṅgulā-ṅgushṭhāvyāṃ nāsikāchiddramabarudhya yaḥ Prâṇâyāmaḥ***

* See Foot Note chapter IX Page - 156

kriyate sa khalu śishtaistyājyaḥ. (Explanation of *Rig Veda*) — this denotes that the *Prâṇâyāma* practised by less intelligent persons of blocking the nostrils with fingers is abandoned by *yogis*.

Yogiraj has stipulated that just as one and one equals two, this is inevitably true, similarly twelve excellent *Prâṇâyāmas* cause withdrawal from the senses, 144 excellent *Prâṇâyāmas* result in realisation or soul-oriented visualisation. If the mind is completely drawn from the senses, soul-realisation occurs, 1728 excellent *Prâṇâyāmas* result in *dhyāna* or being fixed in soul-visualisation and 20,736 excellent *Prâṇâyāmas* result in *samādhi*, all these are also inevitably true.

Prâṇâyāmadvishaṭakena pratyāhāra prakīrtitaḥ.
Pratyāhāradvishaṭakena jāyate dhāraṇā śuvā.
Dhāranādvādaśa proktā dhyānaṃ dhyānabiśāradvaiḥ.
Dhyānadvādaśakenaiba samādhirabhīdhīyate.

(*Gorakshasaṃhitā*)

Just as food causes appeasement of hunger, similarly *Kriyāyoga* causes attainment of God. It is not known whether anyone else has been capable of imparting such a mathematically accurate scientific path of *sādhana* before. This also is another speciality of the path of *sādhana* bestowed by Yogiraj.

How much scientific this *Kriyāyoga sādhana* conferred by Yogiraj is, has been elaborated in an account by Him that an ordinary person inhales and exhales 21,600 times in twenty four hours. This is the life span of a living being. Everyone inhales and exhales fifteen times per minute. The longevity of a living being is reduced by this manner. When there is a depletion of the resources of breath, a living being expires. But the time taken for one *Prâṇâyāma* is 44 seconds. By this calculation a *yogi* practises 1964 or 2000 *Prâṇâyāmas* in 24 hours, meaning a *yogi* inhales and exhales 2000 times in a day whereas an ordinary person inhales and exhales 21,600 times. By practising continual *Prâṇâyāma*, when a *yogi* achieves the static state then his breathing becomes motionless. Therefore Yogiraj would note — ***Yakhan chay cakrete mánas nā diyā āpnā āpni Kriyā haibe takhani sabkichu baliṭe pāribe*** — implying when *Kriyā* will automatically occur without placing the mind on the six *cakrás*, then that person will be able to state everything or else whatever that person will state will be true, because he will then attain the state of union. Yogiraj has further mentioned regarding this — ***21,600 śvāsako roke. 100 din roke to yo icchā kare sidha hoye — tab yattā roj cāhe jiye*** — Stop the natural flow of 21,600 breaths. If stopped for 100 days then whatever is wished will be fulfilled — then the life span can be extended as desired — or else if this type of *Kumbhaka* occurs, a *yogi* acquires the state of leaving his mortal frame at his will. ***Pūraka recaka chuṭe tab Kévalakumbhaka bāhalāoe*** — While regularly practising *Prâṇákarma* the inhalation and exhalation of breath will be absent; the static state will occur; it is only then the *kévala-kumbhaka*like ecstatic state will evolve. God has stated —

Nāsti buddhirayuktasya na cāyuktasya bhābanā.—(*Gītā* 2/66)

This signifies that the person who does not remain united in the soul does not possess soul-knowledge and being disunited with the soul does not have proper *dhyāna* also, because a living being's present disintegrated intelligence or kinetic intellect is untrue. Thus the intellect ensuing from this dynamic state is also untrue. When breath is the longevity of a living being then it can be easily deduced that a *yogi* through *Prâṇákarma* exhausts less of it and can augment longevity at will and in this manner become capable of controlling dȩath also. The person who practises a greater number of *Prâṇâyāmas* will acquire more longevity and sound health. Therefore the state of *samādhi* or the tranșcendental state of *Kriyā* also is termed to be death, because there is an absence of breathing then. An absence of breathing tantamounts to death.

This *Kriyāyogaic* breathing action is an ancient science. In almost every line of *Vedas, Upanishåds, Gītā* and the *śāstrá* of *Tántrayóga*, their esotericism and expedience have been expounded. The symbol of *yóga* is reflected in *yajñá*, regular worship and in all types of religious actions. At present, just as the deities are concealed under the symbols, similarly under the influence of *yajñá* and superficial worship, *Prâṇá-yajñá* has become concealed. With regard to the *Purāṇic* historical viewpoint, Krishna imparted this *yóga* to Arjuna. Many great souls had practised *sādhana* in this path of *yóga* throughout the world and achieved immense spiritual fulfilment. Amongst them the renowned were Kapil *muni*, King Janaka, Vyasadeva, Sukhdeva, Patanjala, Socrates, Jesus Christ, Saint John, Saint Paul, Dadudayal, Kabir, Ruhidas, Nanak, Jnaneswar, Tukaram, Ramdas Swami, Ramprasad Sen, Gautama Budha, Mahavira Jain etc. God has stated that when He had once descended in the past, He had imparted this sublime imperishable *yóga* technique to the Soul-Sun (*Sūrya*). *Sūrya* had given it to *Mánu* amd *Mánu* to *Ikshāku*. The great sages in this manner handed down this *yóga* to successive generations; but the *yóga* has lost it's significance due to the onslaught of time. Thus the still *Prâṇáic Prâṇá*krishna, had imparted this immortal *yóga* to *Sūrya* — ***Āditya ha bai Prâṇaḥ*** — *Prâṇá* is *Sūrya* (Soul-Sun); the motion of *Prâṇá* occurs in the *Iḍā* and *Piṅgalā* and this *Piṅgalā* is known as the sun nerve and *Iḍā* is known as the moon nerve. Therefore the airflow of *Prâṇá* within the *Piṅgalā* nerve is *Sūrya*. God mentioned to *Sūrya* or else that inexpressible state of the still *Prâṇá*krishna by entering the nerve of the sun in the form of dynamism, manifested Himself dynamically or the still *Prâṇáic Prâṇá*krishna who reveals Himself as the dynamic *Prâṇá* in the nerve of the sun is the explicit state of *yóga*. After this *Sūrya* imparted this to *Mánu, Mánu* means the mind. When *Prâṇá* becomes vibratory, this vibratory state acquires a designation of the mind and that mind becomes the expr ssive state of imperishable *yóga* in that designation. The still state of air is the state of *yóga* union. From that still sate, vibration evolved and in the sun nerve and mind the state of expression or manifestation of *yóga* appeared. This is clarified thus, the still *Prâṇá*like soul deriving vibration was expressed as *Sūrya* in the *Piṅgalā* form, from the *Sūrya* to the mind, from the mind to *Ikshāku* signifying that this sublime eternal *yóga* became manifest within the external air of the nose. Amidst the fourfold lives from celibacy to relinquishment of four social orders, the *yóga*-culture was positively maintained by people belonging to the different strata of society. Almost all the kings of the Raghu dynasty eventually departed abiding by the path of *yóga*. That sequence in our country was unimpaired till the time of the great poet Kalidasa. In the first great epic of the Raghu dynasty the evidence of this fact can be underlined from the statement — ***Yóganāntye tanutyajām***. Later due to the onslaught of time it became extinct. Shama Churn preached this sublime *yóga- sādhana* to humanity by again disentangling it from the clutches of time, by amending it's austerities and making it suitable for the present spiritually debilitated mankind. This is His supreme bestowal to the whole of humanity and to the universal storehouse of knowledge.

* * * * * *

Because of the existence of the soul; earth, water, fire, air and space are perceptible. When the mind attaining stillness settles in *Kūṭastha-Brahma*, by practising *Ātmakriyā* salvation occurs. Thus salvation means nothing else other than constantly remaining in *Kriyā's* transcendental state. By remaining in *Kriyā's* transcendental state in this manner, the body consciousness remains detached. Likewise, if you keep your body aloof and place your intellect, mind etc. on *Kūṭastha-Brahma*, then you will obtain repose from the kineticism of the mind and later perpetually exist in the beauteous *Brahma*. Existing here, you do not exist and none of your belongings also exist. Thus the mind is freed from being otherwise confined. In actuality, you do not belong to the Brahmin caste, you are not a hermit, you are amorphous, you are not visible, you have no desires; thus you exist perpetually in the Absolute Void Brahma as a percipient of this world or exist in *Kriyā's* transcendental state, that is your only function. For one who has visualised this Infinite Void even for a split moment, his life has become fulfilled. Religion and irreligion, happiness and sorrow etc. are all functions of the mind, but the Infinite within you is devoid of everything. You are not the master, enjoyer or sufferer; authority, enjoyment and suffering occur through the mind, when that kinetic mind merges in *Brahma* or when it permanently settles in *Kriyā's* transcendental state, then definitely there is eternal salvation. You are perceiving substance in Unsubstantial-*Brahma* everywhere; but as long as you are the viewer, the mind has not become *Brahma*, till then you are envisioning. Since the viewer and the view are twoness, the mind continues vacillating. In this manner the viewer or mind is being confined, that is your state of bondage. Considering yourself to be the master you are seeing *Brahma* or else you are seeing everything in your fore, that is self-conceit; this self-conceit is impinging upon you, therefore you are undergoing all the pains and restlessness of this world. Since you are not deriving mental peace in any manner you are praying for advice. Therefore you are not the authority, the enjoyer or the sufferer and this faith automatically appears by remaining in *Kriyā's* transcendental state. Drink this faith-semblant ambrosia and remain constantly in the beauteous *Brahma* or in *Kriyā's* transcendental state. This is the state of salvation and it's reverse is the state of bondage.

This world is merely a fantasy of the mind, just as a rope is fallaciously regarded to be a snake. Again when the rope is regarded as a rope, happiness ensues, similarly when you remain in *Kriyā's* transcendental state, then you become the personification of your own consciousness. That 'you' is like the Percipient, Infinite and Complete. Being Complete, oneness occurs and being one there is salvation. Then you are passive, beyond desires and aspirations, therefore still and tranquil. The earthly bondage is being caused only due to fallacy. The feeling 'I' occurs because you are perpetually in bondage with bodyhood. Annihilate that present-self with the *Kriyā*-falchion and when the self becomes extinct in *Kriyā's* transcendental state, it is then that egotism will be removed, merging in *Brahma* will occur and you will be blessed. Then you will not perform anything because there will be no actions then. Then all types of desires will be absent and you will become detached. This is the true state of detachment, because then there being no desires, no type of sensory attachment exists. Then you only become the selfmanifested immaculate form. You are the pure, the knowledgeable in *Kriyā's* transcendental state, being infinite, your mind should not be finite. Remain in that *Kriyā's* transcendental state where there are no earthly possessions, no aberrations, no fear and that is the place of tranquillity and rest. The consciousness of the present-self before this results in the world being perceptible, but in the transcendental state of *Kriyā* when the present-self is absent, this type of self-knowledge or soul-knowledge occurs and the world becomes imperceptible. In this type of *Kriyā's* transcendental state only the Brahma-self exists, then how and to whom will the self pay obeisance? Then the self pays obeisance to the self through the medium of *Ómkāra-Kriyā*, because the Soul-self is not perishable. Paying obeisance to another causes dualism, again the one to whom obeisance will be paid is perishable, therefore the self pays obeisance to ownself.

If another exists othcr than the self, duality ensues. This duality is the cause for all great miseries. There is no remedy for this misery other than *Kriyā's* transcendental state..Duality evokes imagination. This body, heaven, hell, bondage, salvation, dread, covetousness, aspiration are all fantasies. Ridding the mind of such fantasies, when there is oneness in the transcendental state of *Kriyā*, then there is neither desire nor non-desire; bondage, salvation are all absent, then the tranquil supportless form does not remain, then where is bondage? Being united in *Kriyā's* transcendental state is known as knowledge and for the one who has achieved that knowledge or remains affixed, that knowledge acts as his bon ami. The one who remains affixed in the transcendental state of *Kriyā* is devoid of mundane or extra-mundane desires, all yearnings have ceased for him. But the one who is conscious about the permanent and the transitory yearns salvation, this also is duality. But the equanimous one existing in *Kriyā*'s transcendental state executes nothing, yet executes everything. Therefore Yogiraj has portrayed — ***Pnāc daṇḍa rodh hole karma habe*** — or else by continually practising *Kriyā* even if for five *daṇḍas*[1] only, the *Prâṇá*-air ceases or the five *daṇḍas-Kévala-Kumbhaka* state is achieved, the state which will originate will be action or not existing in that state of cessation is inaction. Such a composed one always remains tranquil in the soul. He does not possess content or discontent, bondage or salvation. He is not enraged even if he becomes a victim of vituperation and is not elated by praises. When desires cease, expectations also disappear. Expectations ceasing and by remaining in *Kriyā*'s transcendental state, he is constantly gratified. Such a person is termed as a *Mahātmā* and this type of *Mahātmā* is nonpareil. King Janaka has described this type of *Mahātmā* thus —

1. One *daṇḍa* equals 24 minutes.

Yadpadaṃ prepsabo dīnāḥ śakrādyāḥ sárva devatāḥ.
Aho! tatra sthito yogi na harshamupagacchati.

(*Ashtābakrasaṃhitā* 4/2)

This signifies that the state which all gods and goddesses humbly wait to achieve are attained by the serene *yogis*. Despite this attainment, elation cannot hold sway over them.

For the person who exists in *Kriyā's* transcendental state, sins and virtues cannot affect him, he is wise and he only is capable of truly forsaking volitions and non-volitions. Considering this world to be ephemeral like effervescence, regarding both happiness and misery, hope and despair, and the alive and dying state to be equal, practise *Kriyā* and merge in the transcendental state of *Kriyā*. Then you have no acceptance or relinquishment, births or rebirths, inhalation and exhalation. What is the continuum is age, because continuum and age both denote time. Keep an observation on the passage of time and regularly observe the timelike breath continuing. When this breath becomes still, the universe will be pervaded by *Brahma* and there will be an equality in *Kriyā's* transcendental state. Worldly existence is nothing but desire. Abandoning all cravings or desires results in settlement, then material attachment is absent and this is dependent upon *Prâṇákarma*. Thus desire is worldly existence and bondage. In *Kriyā's* transcendental state desires being absent material attachment is also absent, that is salvation.

The transcendental state of *Kriyā* beyond the three attributes is soul-communion. When there is no soul-communion hence *Kriyā's* transcendental state, it is degradation and this degradation is dearth. The absence of soul-communion occurs due to mental aberration, thus if the mind is kinetic, mental aberrations arise and then not existing in *Kriyā's* transcendental state, there is an absence of soul-communion. But by practising regular *Kriyā*, the dearth is removed and spontaneous *Kriyā* ensues, then a type of inexplicable condition occurs within the head, that is deep engrossment. After this acquiring settlement, aberrations cease and by this a state of stoicism arrives. Stoicism results in tranquillity and being tranquil, attachment no longer remains and no type of afflictions plague, therefore it is restful. Worrying brings misery but *Kriyā's* transcendental state being free from anxieties makes the person happy and calm.

Calm yourself by abandoning thoughts about good or evil, happiness or misery, rest and toil, what has to be performed and forsaken or else remain in *Kriyā's* transcendental state, for then you will derive true rest. But remember if you meditate on that inconceivable form also, then you would be worshipping thought, therefore the thought 'let me attain the transcendence of *Kriyā*' has also to be relinquished and you have to become calm and quiet, become thought-free and abandon both relinquishment and acceptance. Then by remaining beyond desires, there will be no good or evil, you will not exist in form or formlessness yet you will exist in statice. Then you will perform all the actions of eating, sleeping, going etc. yet not perform anything. For instance, just as an inebriate expresses an euphoria of detachment after inebriation, similarly in *Kriyā's* transcendental state a marvellous state of non-attachment is achieved. Then the desire for spiritual attainment and the gratitude on achieving spiritual attainment would be absent. This type of relinquishment automatically occurs while practising *Kriyā*. Then both desires and non-desires being non-existent; material possessions, the earthly world, scripture, science are all non-existent, confinement or release are also absent, because the desire for salvation is non-existent. For instance, if the longing to acquire a particular object arises, the idea of the means by which it can be derived appears. If that longing or idea remains unfulfilled, malice is evoked. All these are dispositions of the mind. But when the mind merges in the soul in *Kriyā's* transcendental state, then malice, covetousness, imagination, mind are all absent and therefore there is a complete absorption into the Infinite. Then wandering in the beauteous *Brahma*, relinquishment occurs.

Advising His devotees He would further espouse — the soul within you is the soul which pervades all elements. Therefore the soul of all the elements exists within you. There is no difference, thus it is you who becomes the all pervasive soul, *Jagannātha* (Master of the universe). The moment you specially realise this in *Kriyā's* transcendental state, you can realise the mental inclinations of everybody and it is then by achieving omniscience you will automatically learn about the attributes and actions of all elements. Then by being Omnipotent all actions can be performed with a non-desirable wish. By this type of profound *Kriyā*, realisation of the subtlest of the subtle *aṇu*like self occurs, leading to the removal of pride and a prideless state will be achieved. You are *Kūṭastha*, pay reverence to Him, it is repeated again — pay reverence to Him. Do not desist from paying this reverence because you only are *Kūṭastha*like Almighty Soul and you are beyond the five essences, the mind, intellect and self-conceit. When you become one in *Kriyā's* transcendental state then you only are the Supreme pervading the universe, without you the world does not exist, thus good, evil and imagination do not exist. If you attain oneness, you are the imperishable and indestructible one, the tranquil pure consciousness and immortal. Then where are your birth, action, propensity and pride? Therefore by abandoning the divisions of this and the fact that everything is the self, become doubtless positively about this in the transcendental state of *Kriyā*. You are perceiving the world because you are not within yourself, but in *Kriyā's* transcendental state when you will remain within yourself then you only will become the reality i.e. *Jagannātha*. Just for once contemplate on the fact that barring you, everything is absent, you are materialistic and non-materialistic because when you concentrate on extraneous matters you are materialistic, again by remaining within yourself or in the transcendental state of *Kriyā*, you are non-materialistic. Everything evolves in this universe in accordance with your volition; in *Kriyā's* transcendental state after the cessation of desires you will positively know that the universe is a fallacy merely and by obtaining the knowledge that the entire universe is pervaded by *Brahma* you will attain equilibrium. Then you are neither in bondage nor are liberated and being crowned with success in this manner you will wander in beatitude, this is the maxim of *Kriyāyoga*.

No matter how many *śāstrás* you peruse or hear, how many churches or temples you visit it will not bear any result. You will have to forget all this, but becoming oblivious is not possible without remaining in *Kriyā's* transcendental state and the expectations of the mind do not cease. Aspiration brings misery, but the person who by receiving the initiation of *Kriyā* practises it resulting in a cessation of desires is blessed for he attains material detachment and none is as happy as he is. Such a person loses the interest to put his eyelids into motion, he then becoming nonchalant and devoid of the propensity for action, just inhabits in the realm of placidity. Thus salvation is achieved when there is a freedom from thoughts, then religion, wealth, passion, salvation and everything become neutral. Then he is neither disappointed nor enraged, because of the cessation of acceptance and relinquishment. Actually this state is not known to all, the one who has attained it can comprehend, no matter how much is explained or written it cannot be understood, thus the cessation of judging good and evil and desires destroys the root of earthly attainment. But in order to mitigate misery by abandoning domestic existence if anyone wishes to go to the forest, mountains, caves, *maṭhas,* missions or *āśramas* and considers the acquisition of happiness by going there, he also is bound because his desires are existent; but the one who even by habiting this domestic existence practises *Kriyā* and is successful in causing a cessation of desires by achieving *Kṛiyā's* transcendental state has neither any happiness nor sorrow, any bondage or salvation. But as long as attachment and desires persist within the body, till then he is not knowledgeable or liberated but is the recipient of sorrow only. Positively know that until you achieve a cessation of desires in *Kriyā's* transcendental state by practising *Kriyā* or attain total oblivion, even if the Holy Triad of *Brahmā*, *Víshnu*, and *Mahêśvara* themselves descend and impart advice, nothing will accrue from it. The one who is beyond desires constantly communes solely, duality is eliminated from him because he becomes pervaded with *Brahma*, since his desires for enjoyment and salvation are absent, he is high-souled and such a person is scarce. Then he does not visualise anything yet perceives everything, because his vision then exists in the void *Brahma*. He then is neither awake nor asleep, his eyes are neither open nor closed. This is a wonderful state for he regards happiness and misery; prosperity and adversity; men and women, gain and loss, bondage and salvation as equal. To him these divisions do not exist. He has everything then, but since desires and attachments have ceased nothing exists, he eats only when he obtains food, otherwise remains unfed. The intellect then remaining in void *Brahma*, he stays within himself, he himself pays obeisance to himself. Then by existing in soul-disposition or in *Kriyā's* transcendental state, joy and absence of joy are both non-existent because they are merely the imagination of a thought-oriented living being.

Thus by abandoning them you should remain passive or beyond desires. You do not need to know, express or do anything. Therefore the ones who are *yogis* are beyond resolutions and apprehensions and being perpetually united in the positive state that everything is soul-pervaded, dwell statically. In *Kriyā's* transcendental state, this type of calm *yogi* has no distraction and distraction being absent, actions are also absent. The will to perform something is not present, then the assumption evolves that since nothing has been performed, *dhyāna* is non-existent also. Before the transcendental state of *Kriyā*, you were visualising this universe but merging in *Brahma* in *Kriyā's* transcendental state, the self becomes extinct, thus who will be covetous? By merging in *Brahma* in this manner, what other anxiety remains ? Thus, then the thought-free state prevails only, the self then becomes non-dual, nothing else other than the self is visualised then, I am *Brahma* then.

The one whose mind is distracted observes diversity, therefore he strives to arrest the distraction by practising *Kriyā*. But that very one by practising *Kriyā* becomes high-souled in *Kriyā's* transcendental state and his mind is no longer distracted, thereby causing the non-existence of *sādhana*. Because on practising prolonged *sādhana*, when a permanent settlement occurs in *Kūṭastha*, then what else can he do? Then he has nothing to perform. Because endeavours are made for this achievement and when achievement results, then the necessity for endeavours are not present, thus there is a termination of all actions. Then by being staid and still, attachment is extinct, thus the strife for *samādhi* is absent, then the mind being free from distractions, one remains engrossed or thoroughly rapt within himself in *Kriyā's* transcendental state. Being devoid of joy and joylessness he is perpetually contented in *Kriyā's* transcendental state, being free from both desire and non-desire he performs the action which comes his way, then he has no future and past. When he is not bound by domesticity despite maintaining a domestic existence, when he is incorporeal despite being corporeal, he does not desire to achieve or destroy anything, he remains in the mindless state of *Brahma* and can perform whatever he wishes, he is free from respect and disrespect. Since he is above ratiocination, he is free from deliberation, knowing, hearing, seeing, he does not aspire for the state of salvation, then his thinking attains a vacuous state. But one who possesses thoughts, though he does not perform anything physically performs everything through these thoughts. In *Kriyā's* transcendental state, the settled person is neither worried nor unworried, neither proud nor humble, is neither the authority nor the non-authority and relinquishes expectations and doubts. He does not practise *dhyāna*, he is neither ignorant nor knowledgeable, he does not have any feasance or non-feasance, he then becomes the immaculate form of *Brahma*. When desire is present salvation does not occur, the practice of *Kriyā* is also a wish. But that person is blessed who by practising regular *Kriyā* causes a cessation of *Kriyā*, achieves *Kriyā's* transcendental state, becomes passive and does not perform any inclination oriented action. Desire is the root of all evils. Therefore the erudites[1] eradicate the root of desires, which is possible only on practising *Kriyā*. The ignorant ones aspire to achieve peace. Therefore their aspirations being present fail to achieve peace. But one who is in *Kriyā's* transcendental state, he being still and beyond desires constantly remains in the serene frame of mind and becomes akin to Absolute *Brahma*. He does not perceive the soul then because visualising the soul is based upon support. *Kriyā's* transcendental state is supportless, therefore who will visualise whom? Those who are ignorant[2] and possess evil-will[3], they are the ones who wish to perceive the pure, non-dual soul and contemplate on the soul, but they are unaware of the fact that nothing exists in *Kriyā's* transcendental state. The one who is perpetually affixed in *Kriyā's* transcendental state is characterised by intrepidity and apathy, thus remains within himself; this is a marvellous state. He first by battling with desire through the medium of *Prâṇâyāma* conquers it and constantly remains fixed in *Kūṭastha*. Whatever he observes in this world is destructible, but the Void *Brahma* in *Kriyā's* transcendental state is imperishable, all

1. Here 'erudite' signifies those having intra-vision equanimity.

2.& 3. Here 'ignorant' and 'evil-will' infer those who lack the knowledge about the state of oneness of soul; the supportless soul and that the self is the soul.

afflictions dissolve remaining within it because he then being free from all desires, this universe though existing is absent thus body-consciousness also is absent. Then both the existence and non-existence of the body are equal. When he himself is non-existent then he is devoid of attachment but speciously performing all actions does not perform anything. This type of *yogi* neither has worldly delusion nor manifestation of any consciousness, he does not crave for Heaven or Hell, he is neither bonded nor liberated, ignorant or knowledgeable; he does not have any gain or loss; lamentation or repentance, commendation or condemnation, happiness or misery; feasance or non-feasance, bliss or sorrow, he is neither alive nor dead, he is devoid of love and affection, satisfaction and dissatisfaction, conflict or doubt, attachment or detachment, to him a clod of earth and gold are equal, he perpetually communing in *Kévalakarma* and merging in the infinite void *Brahma* does not perceive the soul, then he is beyond capability or *sādhana*, then he is the nonpareil. He then knowing does not know, seeing does not see, saying does not say, eating does not eat, lying down not lie, he is neither a family man nor a renunciate because everything for him has become extinct. Nothingness pervades him then. Remaining in this *Kriyā's* transcendental state is known as knowledge. Then though by attaining *samādhi* is not into it because despite remaining in this state he performs all actions inertly, but being inert is not passive because by being an inhabitant of the Absolute Void *Brahma* he can see everything and is Omniscient therefore though being erudite is not so, he is neither dual nor non-dual. How much more can be expounded? One who has learnt all the essences by settling in *Kriyā's* transcendental state in this manner is a *Mahāśaya*. He is not present in anything yet is Omnipresent.

*　　*　　*　　*　　*　　*

Yogiraj would mention that while proceeding on a distant and inaccessible place of pilgrimage, variegated scenes of beauty and other pilgrimages can be observed. If anyone being entranced by the splendour there pauses, he then fails to visualise the object of his aim. Therefore Yogiraj would note that by practising regular *Ātmasādhana*, automatically many gods and goddesses can be perceived. If anyone conceives that visualisation of these deities has made his life successful, then it is a misconception. He has to proceed further, he should not stop. If he proceeds without stopping then all those deities will patronize him. It is those deities who will enable him to reach his destination. Therefore *Mahātmā* Kabir has remarked — ***Is rāsteme bic musāfir aksar māre yāte haye*** — meaning, in this manner all travellers seeking salvation in the path of interminable travel fail to reach their destination.

Visualisation will become absent after reaching the place of destination, because the mind and intellect will cease to function, therefore then visualisation; knowledge; the self and God; the devotee and God; happiness and unhappiness; sorrow and misery; affliction and disease; birth and death; weal and woe; knowledge and ignorance; bondage and salvation and all deities are non-existent. This is an inexplicably soul-conscious state. This is the state of non-duality. Keeping this state in mind, *Mahātmā* Ramprosad has noted — "It is an abode apogean where *Gurú* and disciple unite into one." Yogiraj has termed this to be the "transcendental state of *Kriyā*." One who experiences this state, he only can comprehend. Because if one exists, the other is compelled to exist. Only nothingness prevails in that state. None exists there to state about nothingness also. Yogiraj would say — "You will then become the 'Absolute Void'. I assert that everyone has to go there at one time, whether you strive for it or not. But to achieve this you have to travel millions of births. But O dear *sādhaka*, judging by the mind and intellect which God has bestowed upon you, do you want to travel millions of births? Intelligent *sādhakas* will not aspire for it. If you are a wise *sādhaka* then consider the fact that since you have to reach your destination then instead of delaying, commence ardent endeavours to achieve it in this birth itself. O *sādhaka* amidst all of you the essence of valour is dormantly present. Awaken it by impinging or whipping. Convert that valour into a horse, mount it and gallop with heroic spirit. But do not take the reins in your own hands by mistake, give it to the Master just as Arjuna had done. Inhabit this material world but do not involve yourself in the turbid vortex of it. In the pit of covetousness, anger, greed, illusion, vanity, envy do not let six *cakrás* of the body-chariot be embedded in it. Abandon mental debility in all respects. Mental debility is a sin, it causes death. Do not invite your own death. O brave *sādhaka* you have become feeble-minded by constantly considering yourself to be so. But you are the ambrosial son. You are beyond birth, death, disease and afflictions. You have been forgetting about your own form. You have spent several nights supinely. Just for once consider, you will have to depart like this. Now sit with your backbone in an upright position. Heed the summons of this absorbed exalted inebriate. Practise *Kriyāyogasādhana*; for I speak with certitude, practising it will liberate you and not practising it will confine you. *Kriyā* only is the truth. As long as one enlightens oneself through *sādhana* till then the gods and goddesses will not patronize."

Sabāi eseche viśvamājhe
korte āpan khelā,
Sāṅga hole phire yābe
phuriye gele belā.
Kothāi duḥkha kothāi sukh
se ye kevala antar bimukh,
Dhara dhara tene sur[1]
pābe tumi ananta sukh.

1. *Tene sur* implies perfect *Prâṇâyāma.*

The inference of the aforesaid verse has been rendered below :—

In this world descends everyone
    To play their respective games,
On completion will return
    When time wanes.
Where's sorrow, where's happiness
    They're efferent from everyone always,
Hold the dulcet *Prâṇâyāma* sound perfect
    You'll derive infinite bliss.

The three attributes of *Sattva, Rájas* and *Támas* are perpetually in action in a living being. He is a slave to these three attributes. These three attributes are the three principal deities. The Rájas attribute is *Brahmā*, the Creator; the *Támas* attribute is *Mahêśa*, the Destroyer and the *Sattva* attribute is *Víshṇu*, the Protector.

Rájobhābasthito Brahmā
Sattvabhābasthito Hariḥ.
Krodhabhābasthito Rudrá
Strayodevā strayoguṇā. (*Jñánasaṅkalinī Tántra*)

Just as these three attributes are acting within the living being, similarly they are in action within this universe. In a living being the *Támas* attribute is beneath the navel, from the navel to the throat is the *Rájas* attribute, from the throat to the *Ājñācākrá* is the *Sattva* attribute and above it is the state beyond attributes or the attribute-less state. God has remarked —

Ūrdhvám gacchanti sattvasthā madhye tishṭhanti rājasāḥ,
Jaghanyaguṇabṛitasthā adho gacchanti tāmasāḥ. (*Gītā* 14/18)

The person invested with the *Sattva* attribute remains in the above portion of his body, the person with the *Rájas* attribute remains in the middle and the one with *Támas* attribute in the bottom.

This denotes that when a living being is controlled by a particular attribute then his mind settles in the respective place of that attribute and he remains eluded by it. In this manner the upward and downward motion from *Sattva* to *Támas* and vice versa is constantly occurring. The mind of a living being never wanders to the place free from attributes. Achieving settlement by reaching that place above attributes through *sādhana* can bring an attainment of the attributeless state. This state is *Brahma*. Here the deities of *Brahmā, Víshṇu, Mahêśa, Durgā, Kālī, Jagaddhātṛi* are all absent. Indians in origin regard these three attributes as the three gods of *Brahmā, Víshṇu, Mahêśa*. Followers of other faiths disregard those three deities, but everyone acknowledges the three attributes, because those three attributes are constantly engaged in action within everyone.

In this *Kriyāyoga sādhana*, the *yogi's* mind becoming still attains such a permanence in the attributeless state that he becomes capable of perpetually remaining there. Thus Yogiraj has recounted in His diary — ***Jattā piyoge ottā majuri milegā. Sabere cār ghari rāt rahate Prâṇâyāma karnā ācchi haye*** — In other words, the rewards will be commensurate with the amount of *Prâṇákarma* practised or else soul-visualisation will occur to the extent of stillness achieved. It is better to practise *Prâṇâyāma* a couple of hours before dawn, for during this period nature being calm it is an apt time for the practice of *Ātmasādhana*.

Yogiraj used to comment that the faculty of a river is to flow towards it's source, the sea. Whether it desires or not, at one point of time nature will force it.to merge in it's source. Similarly a living being's disposition is to proceed towards his source or origin, *Brahma*. Therefore Arjuna has noted —

Yathā nadīnāṃ bahavoambubegāḥ
samudramevābhimukhā dravanti.
Tathā tavāmī naralokavīrā
viśanti vaktrāṇyabhivijvalanti. (*Gītā* - 11/28)

This implies that just as all the rivers proceed towards the sea and enter it, similarly the valiant heroes (*yogis*) enter the repletely Effulgent-You.

Aeons ago, for some unknown reason man had deviated from *Brahma* or else had forgotten his own form, thus kept on wandering being born innumerable number of times. In accordance with the evolution of time, he commenced his birth from the small leaf, shrub, insect and bird till he attained the birth of a human being. In this manner, attaining a gradual progress in births, he keeps on proceeding towards *Brahma*hood or else his source, origin, *Brahma*. Whether he desires it or not due to the influence of time and through the medium of gradual evolution, he at one point of time has to reach his place of origin. This is the disposition of a living being. For this he has to traverse 84,00,000 births. To evolve into a human shape measuring the length of his own 84 fingers (average height of a human being) he has to traverse 84,00,000 births. Not only this, though he is born as a human being he has to strive to make his brain worthy of attaining *Brahma*-knowledge for which the evolution of another 10,00,000 years is required.

Therefore Yogiraj would state — *Kriyāyoga* is capable of greatly reducing the span of this natural evolution. Giving an accurate calculation of this, He has noted that by practising *Kriyā-yoga sādhana* for merely eight hours in one sitting, a *yogi's* brain becomes advanced by a thousand years of the evolutionary cycle.

The one who makes endeavours or practises *sādhana* is a *sādhaka* and the one who achieving that attainment has become one with it, has merged in it resulting in an united state, is a *yogi*. For this reason if there is no achievement then he cannot be termed a *sādhaka* or else in the *sādhaka* state knowing and visualising are existent because then also his mind or intentions act. Therefore Yogiraj has delineated — ***Yemata kona gharer madhye sūryer ālo***

yāye ebaṃ darajā bandha thāke bāire yadi pākhi uriyā yāye tāhār chāyā deoyālete dekhā yāye tadrūpá mone prakāś haile devátādi yāhārā āchen tnāhār diger dárśana haye — Just as sunlight filters into a room through a slightly ajar door and if a bird flies across, it's shadow is reflected on the wall, similarly when manifestation occurs in the mind, all the deities present can be visualised. In this state the two entities of *Brahma* and the self are prevalent or the one practising *sādhanā* and the one whose *sādhanā* is being practised are both existent. Thus Yogiraj has recounted — ***Kālī soc soc Kālī huyā ab Kālīkā Bābā honā haye Bābā yāne Brahma arthād yo śūnyáke bhitar śūnyá haye — ei sab súryako dekhneme miltā haye.*** — Constantly engrossing with Goddess *Kālī* I have become converted into *Kālī*, now I have to become the father of *Kālī*, father here means *Brahma* who is the Void within the present void or the Infinite Void from which the last element of the five elements – the present void, has originated. While visualising that *Ātmasúrya* the Infinite Void can be attained, but this is not meant for a *yogi* because *yóga* is the name for stillness and the one who has become still is a *yogi*. When a *yogi* attains *samādhi* or the transcendental state of *Kriyā*, then he is beyond visualisation, acquisition and non-acquisition. Therefore Yogiraj has mentioned — ***Uhate bemánas keman keman mánas na pāoye. Mánas choḍeto mánas nahi hāoye***. "*Bemánas*" means the cessation of mind and the mind is unaware of this state; but when attempts were made to be known the mind itself lost it's entity and there was no knowing. In this type of *Kriyā's* transcendental state the self being absent all actions are absent because the one who has to perform the action is non-existent. But for a *sādhaka*, the doer (the self); the act of doing (action) and the field of doing (the body) are all prevalent yet achievement of that One will suffice; that is *Brahma* Who is absent. But for a *yogi* actions being absent in *Kriyā's* transcendental state he is passive because in this state all attributes are passive being united in the void. The self being absent in *Kriyā's* transcendental state, the nature of the state cannot be known because the one who will know is non-existent. Then why is *Kriyā* being practised ? Since *Gurú* has commanded, it is being practised but it's ultimate result is beyond the scope of knowledge.

It is for this reason one devotee enquired — "Everyone performs actions to obtain something. But by practising *Kriyā* nothing can be gained, then why does everyone practise *Kriyā* ?"

Yogiraj commented — "Because they are fools." This signifies there is neither acquisition nor deprivation, gain or loss. Then the three attributes become one, hence the attributeless state. Since it is inexpressible it is lacking in virtue or else virtue and vice are extinct. Virtue and action being non-existent cannot be cited as an example. Just as when the virtue and propensity of water exists there is water, but when it's virtues and propensities are absent then there is no water. *Kriyā 's* transcendental state is similar. Since self is absent in this state the mind's disorientation and disposition are both absent.

Religion[1] denotes that which is perpetually present; for instance the breath for all living beings is religion. When this religion is exterminated it remains still in the soul. Thus Yogiraj has portrayed — ***Mánasko dusre taraf nahi jāne denā cāhiye mánasse mánasko dekhnā cāhiye. Mánas o cakshu sthir honese kyā hogā jabtak śarīr sthir na hoye. Āj śvāsā bilkul bāhar nahi nikaltā haye. Ab barā majā matoyālke māphik*** — The mind should not be allowed to proceed in a contrary direction, the kinetic mind should be understood with the help of the still mind. When the mind and eyes become still nothing will result until the body is still. Today breathing is not external at all. There is a lot of ecstasy now like that

---

1. See Footnote page 156.

of an intoxicated person. Those who accept or visualise anything have not acquired the knowledge of essence. Duality being absent, nothing can be accepted or observed. In *Kriyā's* transcendental state, duality being absent, it is a speechless state therefore a silent one. Digression of the mind is bondage and salvation is constantly remaining away from this bondage and abiding in *Kriyā's* transcendental state. By dwelling regularly in this liberated state, a detachment in all outward objects occurs and *Brahma* is perceived in all objects. This state does not contain religion or absence of religion, senses and the body, because the mind alongwith the senses becomes engrossed in the soul and the soul becomes engrossed in the Infinite Soul. In this state even the sound of thunder is inaudible. There is nothingness in *Kriyā's* transcendental state and this nothingness is *Brahma*. Thus not remaining in *Kriyā's* transcendental state is untruth. There is no segregation in this state. Visualisation and audition arise from segregation. The contrary of all that which can be observed is *Kriyā's* transcendental state where the state of shelter and sheltered is non-existent because this state is free from shelter. When *Brahmāṇu* attains grossness millions of times, it becomes *aṇu* of the earth. In connection with this gross *aṇu* all objects occur and this type of union manifests in all parts of the body, just as gravel is derived from *aṇu* of the earth. The *aṇus* of all gross images assemble together and function with harmony everywhere. All gross images are formed by this type of union; but cannot remain united due to restlessness and for this reason is impermanent, but settling in *Brahma* in *Kriyā's* transcendental state there is no impediment and becoming one there is not any origination of anything and due to this, the mind cannot attain infinite merging in the excellent manner if it concentrates on any other object, other than Brahma. But in the pre-transcendental state of *Kriyā* or in *savikalpa samādhi* everything being regarded as divisible is not *Kriyā's* transcendental state. The conglomeration of body, soul, mind and omneity is life; this life being sheltered within the fold of action everything occurs. The virtue of soul is the mind and this body being the abode of enjoyment and suffering; happiness, misery are all occurring with the help of the mind within the body. Thus Yogiraj has stated — ***Jalá jabtak ghaṭme to uskā kuch tākat nahi, jab Gáṅgāme milā to sab kare.*** — As long as water is confined in a container it possesses no strength, but when it merges with the river it attains full capacity to do everything. Similarly as long as the breathing-motion is externally oriented till then it has no capacity because externally oriented breathing is confined within the body container. But when it attains stillness by becoming internally oriented, then by merging with the Absolute Infinite Void becomes Omnipotent. Reaching this state, Yogiraj has reiterated thus — ***Barā majā sab áṅga ṭuṭne lagā*** — I felt intense joy and realised total corporeality losing existence. But when initially the mind is connected with the soul and then merged, visualisation and knowledge, that which is attainable or unattainable are all absent. Therefore He had noted on 28th July, 1871 — ***Ek nirmal śūnyá dekhā ohi Brahma haye usime mánasko laya karnā cāhiye. Jab do ek ho jāye to ek haye ehi Humjād haye.*** — I have observed a pure void, that is *Brahma*, the mind has to be merged therein. When two dissolve, there is oneness, duality no longer exists; that state of oneness is *Humjād* or the Supreme Being. On 30th July He has recounted — ***Nirmal rūpáme mánasko laya karnā cāhiye.*** — The mind should be merged in the Immaculate Form. Later on 26th August, He has written — ***Śūnyá nirmal dekhā usime mil jānā samādhi kahalāoye — ohi bāki haye — Purushôttamake āge Brahma haye — usime laya honā bāki haye. Laya bilkul nishkām na honese nahi hogā.*** In other words, what I am perceiving is the pure void, merging in this is known as *nirvikalpa samādhi* (profound engrossment in which man is totally absorbed with the Infinite) which yet remains to be attained; merging in *Brahma* beyond the Supreme Being state is yet to be achieved. Merging will not occur unless there is a total passivity. He has further recounted — ***śūnyá bhavaname laya ho jānā.*** — Merging should occur in that void state. That void state is real, merging there remain united and attain oneness. On September 2, He has mentioned —***Nirmal jyot mánas dekhtā haye lekan woh na laya huyā —wohā yāke abhi nirvāṇa nahi huyā*** or else the mind is still visualising that Pure Effulgence but has not as yet achieved merging; merging there, attaining complete emancipation (*nirvāṇa*) has not yet been achieved. Therefore Yogiraj has advanced further and noted the gradual progress—***ab Hum nirmal jyotme samāy gaye.*** —I have now merged in that Pure Effulgence. ***Bahut taraikā ghar darwājā dekhneme āyā — óm dhvanime laya honā cāhiye —*** I could observe many types of rooms and doors in *Kúṭastha* meaning the manifestation of the six *cakrás*. I have to merge in the *Ómkāra* sound of this state. He has further expounded —***Barā darwājā khulā — jaysā nalkā jalá Gáṅgāme milnese Gáṅgā ho jātā hay oysā śvāsā yāyke śūnyá bhakāme milnese ekākār ho jātā hay — ehi Brahma haye — ādi Brahma saccā — āphi āp Bhagavān rūpá haye — ab barā majā haye —*** This signifies that the main gate opened, just as when tap water merges in the River Ganges it becomes the Ganges, similarly when the breath mingles with that pure void then it merges, this state is *Brahma*, this Primordial *Brahma* is true, then the self becomes God. From where does that breath come? ***Śūnyáke bhitarse haoyā ātā haye iha mālum hone lagā.*** — I could understand that the breath is originating from within that infinite void. A few days later He portrayed — ***Āj abhay padá dárśana huyā — yāne mahásthir huyā, moksha huyā — phir woh śūnyá gharme raha karke sab kuch dekhe sab kuch kare. Yetnā indriya laya hotā hay ohi śvāsāme*** — Today I visualised the fearless state or else I attained sublime stillness and salvation. Remaining in the void state I visualise and perform everything. All the senses merge with that infinite voidlike breath. The fearless state denotes the place where there is a cessation of fear. Since that infinite void is supportless, it is the state of fearlessness. He has further noted — ***Ab Maye ānandkā ghar pāyā yāne śvāsā na āoye na jāye.*** — I have achieved that blissful state where by abiding, there is a complete cessation of extrinsic and intrinsic motion of breath. After this He has voiced an ultimate aphorism — ***Ab na ānā na jānā*** — Neither coming nor going will occur now. Arriving at that still state what happened to Him? He has recounted — ***Sthir gharme ṭhahare — ab aṭaknekā jagahi milā.*** — Settling in that still state, a place to perpetually remain united has now been attained. By remaining united here how did the world appear before Him ? He has delineated — ***Iha jīvana haye sab jhuṭ dekhlāi detā haye bāstabik kuch nahi — jaisā murdā camḍā lagā rahā dhokese mālum hotā haye ki merā śarīrme lagā haye āur merā haye — oesehi jagad saṃsārko mālum hotā haye. Iha mālum huyā ki iha saṃsār svapnavad haye. Sab tuch mālum huyā. Ab dusre padārthpar tākneka erādā na kare.*** — By intra-vision it has been visualised that this life is totally untrue and practically there is nothing. Just as scurf on the body is mistakenly regarded as one's own skin, so also this material world is similar. It has been further comprehended that this material world is dreamlike and futile. The desire to waste any glance on any object no longer exists. ***Ab iha erādā kartā haye cupcāp paḍā rahe***. — Now the desire is to remain inactive. Therefore He chanted —

Ragaḍme kabhi kasar mat karo,
Ragaḍme mano kāmnā pūrṇa tero.
Mánas dusre taraf kaṭhin dharo,
Śūnyáke dhyānase sab kāj nikāro;
Dekhoge āścarya sāmarth tero,
Picheme sabkuch banegā tihāro.
Udās mánas tum kaṭhin phiro,
Āgar tum jāno ho husiyāro;
Lage raho snāiyāse bhalitaro,
Tujhe snāi peyār jarur karo.

Nirantar snāijikā dhyāna dharo,
Hoyegā jarur kām terā puro.

Do not neglect the practice of austere endeavours for if you do strive to practise, your aspirations will be fulfilled. Be firm to prevent the mind from involving itself in material attachment. Perform all activities remaining in the void state; for then you will realise your own marvellous capacity. Later, you will achieve everything automatically, you will wander apathetically and apparently you will seem to be devoid of any emotion. You will be aware of everything from before but you should be careful not to divulge it. Be united with God in a superlative manner for then He will positively bestow graces upon you. Perpetually remain attached to Him through *dhyāna*, because this will definitely make all your actions fruitful.

That Shama Churn is only a Yogi is not correct. Instead, He had Himself in seclusion and solitude divulged His actual identity in His confidential diaries. None was aware of His identity during His lifetime, because He was averse to propaganda. Like other days, recounting His *sādhanā*-derived experiences, on 13th August, 1873, he wrote — ***Āj Hum Mahāpurusha huye*** — today I have become Mahapurusha. On 17th August, after delineating a human face, He has written — ***Mahāpurusha Hum haye — sūryame aisā dekhā Humhi Brahma haye*** — I am the Mahapurusha and I have visualised within the Soul-Sun that I only am *Brahma*. On 18th August, He has noted — ***Humārāi rūpáse jagat prakāśit — ab bahu gāḍhā Prâṇâyāma huyā. Humhi ek Púrusha haye āur koi nahi*** — The world has manifested from My Form, now a deep *Prâṇâyāma* has been executed. I only am the Primordial Male Energy, there is none else. On 22nd August, He has mentioned — ***Humhi Ādi Púrusha Bhagavān — kuch peṭme nā tākatse darad haye — ab śvāsa āur bhitar gayā — ab Caturbhūj honekā lakshmaṇ huyā — iha mālum hotā haye ki iha dono hāt choḍāi***

aurbhi śaktimoy nirākār dui hāt bhitarse niklā. — I am the Primordial Being, God Almighty; there being a decline in strength in the stomach, I am experiencing pain; now the breathing has deeply entered internally; now I received the indication of My becoming the quadrumanous Narayana; I could realise that apart from My present pair of hands, another pair of immensely infinitely powerful amorphous pair of hands emerged. On 25th August, He sketched a sun and wrote beside it — ***Sūrya Nārāyaṇá Bhagavān Jagadīśvara sárvavyāpi Hum haye. Ek jyot bhitar mālum hotā haye yo sūryase ātā haye sūryahi Hum haye. Yo Hum soi woh rūpá nirākārkā. Yo buddhike pare anantrūpá ohi Bhagavān — āur nirmal. Hum hi akshar Púrusha.*** — I am the Soul-Sun, Narayana, Bhagavan, Controller of the Universe, Omnivalent. I am also that Effulgence emanating from the Soul-Sun which I visualised. What is Myself is that Amorphous Form. The vast *Kūṭastha*like Infinite Form beyond the intellect is God Almighty and this is sacrosanct. I am that Imperishable Being. *Akshar* means imperishable; the soul of a living being becoming attributeless or beyond attributes is inseparable from the infinite soul and merges there, only then can he be termed imperishable. Yogiraj has further recounted — ***Kūṭastha akshar amar ohi Sūrya Nārāyaṇá haye — ehi Hum haye āur ehi Sūrya haye. Kūṭastha akshar ādi āur Hum haye. Sūryahi mālik āur majā āur sāf. Akshar Sūrya haye ohi Hum haye.*** — *Kūṭastha* is imperishable and indestructible, that is the Soul-Sun *Nārāyaṇá*; that *Kūṭastha* is Myself and the Soul-Sun. That imperishable *Kūṭastha* is eternal and Myself. That Soul-Sun is the Supremity, this has become more clearer and more blissful. That vast imperishable *Kūṭastha* is the Soul-Sun and I Myself am that. On 23rd August, Yogiraj comments — ***Hum jab Sūrya hay tab yo Hum kahe so Veda haye — yāne niścay jāne.*** — When I am that boundless *Kūṭastha*like Soul-Sun, then whatever I assert is the *Vedas,* definitely know this. Thus *Vedas* is not of human origin. On 24th August He penned thus — *Humhi Krishna* — I am Bhagavan Krishna. On 27th August, He recounted — *Yo Púrusha ādityame so Mayehnu. Brahmarūpá Súryaká Humārā haye.* —The Primordial Energy within the Soul-Sun is Myself. The Soul-Sun Form of *Brahma* is emanating from Me. On 3rd October He wrote — *Hum Súrya haye Mahádevá.* — I am the Soul-Sun, Mahadeva. On 12th November, He recounted—*Humhi Mahápurusha Purushôttama.* — I only am the Supreme Being, the Absolute. On 8th January, 1874 He penned —*Súrya Brahma ehi sthir ghar pahucātā haye* — *Ab sthir gharme gaye, usikā nām amar ghar haye.* — The Soul-Sun is *Brahma* and it's visualisation enables a *yogi* to reach the still state, now I have arrived at the still state and it is termed the immortal state. On 29th January, He further portrayed —*Ab sutokā dil cāhatā haye* — *āur khāli Brahmako dekhe yāne śūnyáke bhitar śūnya* — *ab sthir gharme Maye gayā ab mālum hotā haye jaisā śarīr upke haoāse nicese uṭhtā haye jaisā hukkā pike pāni phek denese niceke ched ynahāse piyā jātā haye onhāse dhuā nikas jātā haye oyesāhi hoyegā. Ab agam. ghar gaye* — *ab ajar gharse amar ghar gaye* — *ab kuch nahi khāli Mālik.*— I desire now to simply lie down, I keep on visualising that Absolute Void *Brahma* in the void within the void, now I have reached the still state, now the body is overflowing with airs and through the medium of airs this overflowing condition proceeds from bottom to above. For instance after the hookah is smoked while casting away the water through the hole from where the hookah is smoked, smoke pipes out overflowingly; the state is similar to this. Now I have reached the inaccessible abode, from there I procceded to the ageless state and finally to the immortal state, where everything is absent, excepting Void *Brahma,* the Supreme. Yogiraj has further noted on 2nd May thus—*Brahmarūpá Humārā yāne yo śūnyá bhitar, mánas, soi śūnyá bāhar* — *phir mánas dekhne lagā bāharkā Kûṭastha akshar phir wohbhi gayā* — *ab raha gayā khāli*

śāntipadá iha śūnyá jab Brahma huyā yāne iha mama āur Kūṭastha akshar Brahma haye tab śūnyá mánas Brahma huyā.— *Brahma* Form is Mine or else the mindlike void which is internal is also external, again the mind perceives the external imperishable *Kūṭastha*, that also has disappeared, now only the Absolute voidlike *Brahma* or the peaceful state is existent, in this state alongwith My Entity the imperishable *Kūṭastha* and everything became *Brahma* and mind also then merged in this Voidlike *Brahma*. Regarding this He blissfully addressed His Own Self and chanted —

Ab calo payare Amarpur calo
Choḍ jagajañjāla vishayrasa tyāgo
Āur bhaṭkat phiro kneo tum bhulo
Vishay rasase kuch majā nahi haye
Āphi āp tum samāy lo
Phirte dolte rahe ekelā
Hardam snāi[1] pāś hājiri delo.

O dear-self, now proceed towards the Immortal Abode and relinquish the worldly refuse and all material attachment. Why do you forget your own self and wander aimlessly? Worldly pleasures do not entail any mirth; you should immerse yourself only in your own self; you only shall exist in that state of vacillation; constantly be present before thyself.

How can one attain that fearless state ? Yogiraj described this in His diary on 15th August, 1874, thus — ***Abhaypadá Gurú binā miltā nahi — śūnyá bhavaname sthir rahanā, binā sthirme ghusnese nahi hogā.*** — The fearless state cannot be acquired without the divine influence of *Gúru*; one has to remain static in the void state; without stillness entry is not possible there. The Sublime Yogi espoused to mankind —

1. *Snāi* = Master

Nām sumir leo amṛita vāṇī
Tum bhuleho āp Brahma na jāni
Kahoto hāt knyākar hi hilāni
Mánashi mánas tumāhi hilāni
Hilo kisme oke kaṛo bakhāni
Śūnyáme bicār dekhehu hilāni
Kohilāowe woh to kaho śuni
Śvāsa hilāowe ehi sat vāṇī.
Kneo hile ihate kaho hum śuni
Icchā hetu hile iha jñāni ki vāṇī
Śvāsa kneo hile se varṇo ham śuni
Haowā svabhābataḥ sthir nahi jāni
Iha śvāsa niklā kanhuse bhulāni
Śūnyáse niklā māyā āye milāni
Niklekā kyā kāraṇ kahahu jñāni
Karmaphal bhog janya bhule phirāni
Isliye karma phalāphal choḍāni
Dhyāna karo sadā Brahma mánas milāni
Tab tadrūpa hoge sadne bakhāni
Hardam dekhe svárūpake nisāni
Iha ānand mūl jāne Brahmajñāni.

Take refuge at the feet of God, this is the eternal message, you yourself are *Brahma* and not being conversant about this state you have forgotten yourself; by moving your hands to and fro what do you prattle about? The kinetic mind and thought make you vacillate; abandon the objects of your vacillation; envisioning vacillation judge the void; who is the vacillator; breath is the vacillator, this is the maxim. The reason as to why the breath causes vacillation should be known; the dictum of conversant persons is that volition causes vacillation. Describing as to why breath vacillates, enlightenment should be caused; it is known that normally air is not motionless; it is unknown from where the breath emanates for it causes misguidance; it originates from void and causes fusion in illusion; O wise man, enlighten the cause for it's emanation; the cause is for undergoing the consequences of actions which results in the own self being forgotten and casts one in the vortex of the cycle of births and deaths; for this the consequences of actions should be abandoned; perpetually practise *dhyāna* on *Brahma* by merging the kinetic mind with the still mind, you will achieve the same form as *Brahma* as righteous persons denote; you will perpetually envision the symbol of your own form; a *Brahma*-conversant person is completely aware of this bliss.

* * * * * *

Yogiraj Himself would never do *jápa* of any names or *mántras* and would not impart these to His devotees. He would never don His forehead with a sectarian mark and would attire Himself in the normal garb. He did not favour these gross actions or any form of ostentation. He would practise *Ātmasādhana* Himself and would impart this to His devotees. He would say that ostentation does not reap any benefits because through this soul-visualisation is impossible. When what is incapable of bringing about soul-visualisation then what is the use of performing those and wasting time ? The *Śrīmadbhāgavata* has similarly expressed —

Ahaṃ sarveshu bhūteshu bhūtātmābasthitaḥ sadā.
Tamabajñāya māṃ martyaḥ kurutearcābiḍamvanam.
Yo māṃ sarveshu bhūteshu sant mātmānamīśvaram.
Hitvārccāṃ bhajate moudhyādbhasmanyeva juoti sḥ
Ahamuccābacaidra baiḥ kriyāyādpannayānaghe.
Naiba tushyearccitoarccāyāṃ bhūtagrāmābamāninaḥ.
(*Śrīmadbhāgavata* 3/29/21, 22,24)

This verse signifies that I am the Soul of all the elements and am constantly immanent in them. Ignorant persons disregard that Soul and worship idols. The person who due to ignorance abandons

Me (the Soul) and worships idols, his action is rendered futile. I am prevalent in all the elements, disregarding this the person who worships idols with extraneous objects deluding himself with the concept of worshipping God truly, I am not pleased by his worship.

Yogiraj would state that human birth is scarce to obtain and is transient. Therefore such a *sādhanā* should be practised which will enable man to obtain release from the clutches of birth and death in this birth itself. It is for this reason He was never noticed to have observed fasting or performed gross worship. Only for the purpose of teaching mankind, He would fast once in a year on *Śivárātri* day. He would state that if He abstains from doing this, the people also would follow suit. But this does not imply that He is an unfeeling prosaic Yogi. He is a Rajayogi and an Incarnate of love and mercy.

Yogiraj would remark that if one had to travel to a distant place for a few days, some requisites would be necessary. In this instance, the traveller is conversant about the place and period of stay. Yet without the prescribed requisites, travel is impossible. But when this body is abandoned and you have to proceed to an unknown path for an indefinite period of time, then how many requisites would be necessary? No material objects will be required then. The destination and duration of stay is unknown. That requisite has to be acquired in this present life through *yógasādhana* and carried over and that *sādhana*-derived experience will be the only requisite in the form of reformation. This requisite is imperishable. Regarding the person who takes this alongwith him and in rebirth derives it again, God has assured in the *Gītā* that a person who has deviated from *yóga* due to untimely death is reborn in a noble family or in the *yogi* lineage. He has become attached to *yóga* with full devotion and never digresses or else the noble person neither faces deviation resulting in adversity nor suffers the degradation of birth and he does not distance himself from *Brahma*. To the one who executing this *Ātmakarmaic* holy action, God has addressed such a person imparting confidence thus — ***Nahi kalyaṇkṛit kaściddurgatiṃ tāta gacchati*** (*Gītā* 6/40) —The one who brings about his own welfare with the help of this *Ātmasādhana* is the true person who imparts welfare. This author of *Pañcadaśī* scripture has similarly expressed thus —

Iha bā maraṇe bāsya brahmalokeatha bā bhaved.
Brahmasākshādkṛitiḥ samyagupāsīnasya nirgunam.
(*Pañcadaśī* 9/150)

This denotes that for the worshipper beyond attributes visualisation of Absolute *Brahma* definitely occurs, be it in this life or in the life after death or in the *Brahma*-Abode, the result of his worship will surely be achieved.

Yogiraj has been a Sadhaka of sublime fortitude. He never indulged in idleness or postponement of actions. He would work during the day, teach students in the evening, manage the different aspects of family life and yet was able to engage Himself in social welfare activities. In the evening till 9 p.m. He would discuss the spiritual essence with His devotees. Amidst all this apart from His *sādhana*-derived experiences, He would note down almost all daily incidents in His diaries. He would Himself reply daily to the letters of His several devotees. Apart from this, He had to solve various problems of many. Performing all these, He practised such a *sādhana* secretly that enabled Him to mount it's highest pinnacle. From this it can be deduced that He and mental fortitude were synonymous. He had thus mentioned in His diary — ***Ab rātbhar jāgnekā erādā hotā haye*** — now the desire is to practise nightlong *sādhana*. Again He has written — ***rāt me nid kam ātā haye — baḍā sthir baḍā nesā.*** — During the night there is less sleepiness — the feeling is of immense stillness and deep engrossment. This implies from this time onwards He would practise *yógasādhana* throughout the night and being completely absorbed in *Kriyā* would remain in the state of cessation of all attributes.The descriptions conferred on His state of *sādhana* during that period makes one amazed. He recounted — ***Agam panthme pag dharā. Ohā na mālum śvāsā ātā haye na mālum jātā haye saṃg sabkā choḍe. Āur dhvanimune Rādhājikā dárśana bhayā. Ab anmol dhan milā.*** — Permanence has been attained in the inaccessible abode or the still state. In this state it cannot be understood whether there is an existence of breath or else achieving *Kévala-Kumbhaka* all attributes alongwith the senses have been forsaken. *Rādhā* inherently descending from the *Sahasrâra* through the sound current was visualised. Invaluable wealth was derived now. In this manner He would delineate the images of various gods and goddesses and describe them in accordance with His visualisations.

A few days later describing another state elsewhere He wrote — ***Bilkul bāhar kā śvāsā bandh hotā haye. Dhanya bhāg uskā jiske iha hoye.*** — The external inhalation and exhalation which incessantly continues in the nasal passage has completely stopped. The one who attains this type of permanent cessation or *Kévala-Kumbhaka* is blessed. From this it can be ascertained that after commencing His life of *sādhana*, He did not waste any time and practising austere *sādhanā* progressed fast towards the zenith of *sādhanā*. Exactly a few days after this He has written — ***Sa śarīrme sidhe jaláke upar jānā kuch kaṭhin kām nahi haye, jab Prâṇâyāma karte karte Prâṇávāyú ruk gayā doghaḍi se upar tab yatte jalá par cāhe otte jalápar cale jāye āur yette dūr tak cāhe otte dūrtak — kneo ki jab jalá śūnyá o sūrya sab ek rūpá āur Humbhi ohirūpá tab vāyúke rokneke ghor sahaje me iha śarīr halak karke ujay le jāye — iha bāt tab hotā haye jab Kévala Kumbhaka hoye*** — This implies that walking across water is not a difficult task. While practising *Prâṇákarma* when the *Prâṇá-air* ceases or the breathing motion ceases for at least an hour, then no matter how deep the water is or how distant it is it becomes possible to walk across it because then the essences of water, void and that of the Soul-Sun are the same and then the self also attains the same form. When *Prânâ* air is stopped easily from the external motion, then it is possible to make this body light and walk across the reverse water-current also. This state arrives when *Kévala-Kumbhaka* occurs.

History denotes that only a few renowned great *yogis* achieving this state were able to walk across the river or sea under the guise of holy sport like Jesus Christ, Tailangaswami etc. But this Sublime Household Yogi though achieving that state in the path of *yóga* never demonstrated this. The sages have similarly noted this path of *yóga*-state in our *sāstrás* — ***Udānajayājjalápaṅkakaṇtak-ādimbasaṅga udkrāntiśca*** (*Pātañjala Yógasūtrá Bibhūtipād* 40) — this signifies that if the *Udāna* air in the throat is conquered the upward air being arrested causes a cessation of the downward airs as well and the body becoming light does not come into contact with water, mud or thorns etc., then the to and fro motion over these become facile. ***Kāyākāśayoḥ sambandha saṃyamyallaghuta-lasamāpatteścākāśagamanam.*** (*Pātañjala Yógasūtrá Bibhūtipād* 43). The relationship between the gross body and the void or else control in the virtue of essence i.e. when the air ceases from the *Mūlâdhāra* to the *Viśuddha*, the body becomes featherweight and the power to frequent the void is achieved. This type of person is regarded as an essence-conversant person.

Apart from His *sādhanā* realisations He would recount almost all daily incidents candidly in His diaries. These daily recountings were exclusively secretive. None had the authority to read those diaries during His lifetime. But this Noble Yogi being compassionate has described His daily *sādhana*-derived realisations in His diaries which is not exactly known in the case of any other

Mahāpúrusha. All these diaries provide an invaluable wealth in the universal storehouse of knowledge.

The fact that He has been extremely simple, naive and frank can be ascertained from His writings. In the initial stages of *sādhanā* He had written in some place in His diary — ***Āj kām mujhe ākramaṇ kiyā*** — today I was attacked by carnal passion. In some place He has written — ***kām praval huyā ab sāmālnā cāhiye*** — carnal passion has intensified, it should be controlled now. Again He has remarked — ***Āj kāmse cittá cañcal huyā*** — carnal passion made My mind restless. Further He has stated — ***kām baḍā jor kiyā*** — vehement carnal desire is insistent. Again He has denoted — ***Kām-devá phir jagā — āur nid bahut gherā. Āur bhūk baḍā lagā.*** — The deity of carnal passion has appeared again — sleep has trapped me intensely and I am feeling very hungry. How much candid is He who can make such comments in His diary! Because it is quite natural for these diaries to fall in the hands of His future generation. Thus everyone keeps such matters secret. But going through His diaries one can understand that He did not conceal any facts of His life, made recountings of that only which necessitated and whatever *sādhanā* realizations were effected by Him, He noted them with blunt forthrightness. He never disacknowledged any aspect of human life.

What occurs to each and every human being, that is the various impediments one has to overcome while progressing in the path of *sādhana*, have all been noted by Yogiraj in a disciplined manner for the welfare of humanity. Despite being the Absolute, in order to set an example for mankind, He fostered these occurrences in His Own life. He never advocated to forsake hunger, thirst, slumber, carnal desire etc., alongwith other sensory dispositions through the medium of austerities superficially, instead He established for the masses the medium of *sādhanā*, which is basically scientific and does not incur physical or mental detriment. Denial and abandonment is one facet and conquest another. Advice has been dispensed by Him to win over these inherent hurdles in the path of *sădhana* which torments everyone. In this manner eventually He caused the carnality and attribute cessation state in Him thus facilitating the state of sublimity of a Yogi to blossom upon Himself.

The aforesaid realisations are intended exclusively to spiritually enlighten the masses. In a human being's journey towards stillness he is bound to be plagued by such impediments. Yogiraj assuming a Human Form rigorously maintained this discipline and enumerated these realisations. We must always remember that essentially, He performed all actions without actually being involved in them or that apparently sensory aflictions plagued Him without Him being actually plagued.

Sanătána Dhárma eternally preaches the afferent withdrawal of the sensory faculties. But due to decadence of the age, it has degenerated into the superficial withdrawal of senses. The present teaching is either to suppress or to relinquish the sensory stimulus or else remain aloof from it. This is not afferent relinquishment, and the senses cannot be controlled because the sensory stimulus forcibly being absent, there is no means for gratification, such an efferent state arises. On the contrary, when afferent relinquishment through the medium of *sădhana* evolves, there is total withdrawal of mind from the sensory stimulus despite it being present, this is the true afferent detachment or abandonment. Yogiraj has set forth this teaching for humanity.

Carnal passion is a physical disposition. As long as *Prâṇá* is dynamic in the body, till then that physical disposition will exist, no matter how great a soul, one is. When *Prâṇá* becomes still or the breathing motion ceases then alongwith passion all types of physical dispositions are eliminated. Then though he possesses the body, he conquering passion is capable of going beyond all types of physical and mental dispositions and the three attributes. Yogiraj administered this similar state upon Himself.

In His *sādhana*-life, He shortly reached it's summit. Therefore He has sometimes quoted — ***Āj sonekā Kālīse bheṭ huyā.*** — Today I have visualised Goddess *Kālī* in the golden form. Sometimes He has written — ***Chinnamastā rūpá dekhā.*** — I have visualised the beheaded form of the Goddess. This beheaded form is the symbol of the aggressive Female Energy, Controller of the universe. One living being derives nutrition by consuming another living being; this implies the drinking of one's own blood by self-beheading i.e. annihilating evil in all it's entirety within the self, because everything is derived from that still *Prâṇá*. Due to the differences in the body-containers, it seems separable. Basically, one living being consuming another living being implies the self devouring the self, *Prâṇá* devouring *Prâṇá* because the one consuming and the one being consumed are both the same. The threefold essence of inherent nature i.e. the enjoyer, the enjoyable and the enjoyment are merged. While practising continual *sādhanā* at the juncture of the extermination of all types of enjoyment, a terrifying awful feeling becomes manifest in a *yogi*. Practising regular *Prâṇákarma* when *Prâṇá*-air becomes still and *Sushumná*-oriented, achieving a permanent settlement in *Kuṭastha* all types of enjoyment of a *yogi* are exterminated and the state which emerges is the state of the beheaded form. In this manner the recourse to which essence should be taken and as to how *sādhanā* should be practised which will enable achievement of the intrinsic condition of each *cakrá* have been meticulously and dexterously delineated by sages through the medium of images of deities. All these are immanent realisations of *yogis*. For instance the garland of 108 heads of Goddess *Kālī* represent the destruction of the 108 bestial propensities of a *sādhaka*. The lolling tongue of Goddess *Kālī* is the symbol of internal *Khecari Mudrā*. The falchion in her hand represents the annihilation of ignorance or else it is the knowledge-falchion. In this manner, it should be understood that all the essences of the deities are latent within the body.

Sometimes He has recounted — ***Śūnyá Brahma najar parā*** — I have visualised the Absolute Void *Brahma*. Sometimes He has remarked — ***Brahma sāf dárśana hone lagā*** — *Brahma*-visualisation was becoming clearer. He further wrote — ***Yo Brahma soi śūnyá soi Sūrya jyoti*** — One Who is *Brahma* is the Void and He again is the Soul-Sun's Effulgence. Again He has remarked — ***Óm nirmal bhitar śūnyá — ekṭho ādmi Āpne māphik baiṭhā dekhā*** — Within the *Ómkāra* is the pure crystalline void — I visualised someone like Me seated there. Again — ***Ehi ilāhī illillā*** — He is the Supreme *Āllāh*. Further He has expressed — ***Ehi Āpnā rūpá haye, phir ehi nirākār Brahma Ómkāra haye*** — This is My Own Form, what is My Own Form is the *Ómkāra*like Amorphous *Brahma*. Here He Himself and *Brahma* merged together and became One, His living being state achieved mergence and became established in Oneness. This is the ultimate state of a *yogi*. In this state none remain to express about duality. Therefore He would say as long as duality is perceived it is vile. He has made another significant aphorism — ***Rātdin jab rodh śvāsākā hogā tab Rāmanām ko pāoyegā, āur sab sidh hogā*** — Yogiraj here denotes — What will be the result of loudly chanting the name of *Rāma*? While executing *Ātmakarma* when the external motion of breathing has permanently ceased, only then the actual essence of *Rāma's* name can be achieved and then everything will become spiritually attainable and liberated. Thus a living being hears external sounds through the medium of the senses, he cannot hear the intrinsic sound because the senses have no capacity of entering here. These are the *Ānahāta* and *Ómkāra* sounds which are continually intra-occurring within the total creation. But none pay attention to this. By practising regular *Prâṇákarma* when *Prâṇá* air attains stillness then one can hear or maintain that incessant sound-current of *Ātmârāma*. Then the actual chanting in praise of God occurs within. There is no necessity to verbally chant. In this state, the tongue, lips, eyes, mind and *Prâṇá* will become static and non-vibratory. Under these circumstances, who will verbally chant? This chant in God's praise is the cardinal chant. Loud chant is secondary. With the latter if there had been no tune, rhythm or instrument, none would have executed it. To loudly chant in praise of God or to externally search will not facilitate the quest for *Ātmarāma*, this has been asserted by *Mahātmā Kabir* —

Kabir ākhḍiyā jnhāi paḍi, panth nihāri nihāri
Jihvḍi ānchālā paḍe, Rāma pukāri pukāri.

Kabirdas infers that a constant keen attention on the different spiritual paths in the quest for God has confounded him so much that observation failed him and constant chanting of *Rāma's* name made him weary of speech.

In this regard, Yogiraj has noted a remarkable fact — ***Bājāse jab jānyar mast hoye tab ādmi óm me na mast hoye tó gadhā haye*** — All the animals are enraptured listening to music but if man does not become enraptured listening to the *Ómkāra* sound within him, then he is a blockhead. Thus if one does not aspire to hear the *Ómkāra* sound then his human existence is rendered fruitless. For instance a donkey being a beast himself carries grass for other beasts, but such is his luck that he is deprived of the fodder himself, similarly the person who does not intend to listen to the *Ómkāra* sound, he also fruitlessly labours for material benefits. The *śāstrás* have similarly expounded —

Anātmabuddhiśaithilyaṃ phalaṃ dhyānāddine dine.
Paśyannapi na ced dhyāyed koaparoasmād paśurvad.

(*Pañcadaśī* 9/156)

In other words, the soulless knowledge which persists despite remaining in the soul is gradually removed by *dhyāna*. Inspite of becoming conversant with this direct consequence, if still the person does not practise *dhyāna* who else can be a beast other than him?

Can God be achieved by invoking Him? Explaining this question of one of His devotees Yogiraj expounded — Name and form belong to the body or any object, by what name will you invoke God? He is beyond name and form. The body is destructible, hence name and form are also destructible. But the One Who is God is devoid of origin and is imperishable. Is God a distant object ? Is He without you that you have to loudly invoke Him? Distant objects are beckoned by their names. Who else is nearer to you than Him? He dwells within you, therefore how can you loudly invoke Him? For instance, if you have to invoke the name God, *Prâṇá* must be dynamic in the body. If *Prâṇá* is non-existent in the body-temple in a dynamic form, the lips and tongue are rendered incapable to invoke God. Therefore to invoke Him it is necessary for *Prâṇá* to exist in the vibratory form in the body. But there is no action in the still *Prâṇá*. The word 'God' does not connote God, similarly the words '*Hari*' and 'water' do not connote *Hari* and water. If the word water comprises the attributes of water then thirst would be quenched by crying aloud for water. But this does not occur. Thus by loudly invoking *Hari*, response from Him cannot be derived. *Hari* means One Who seizes everything, where there is a complete absence of the sensory attachment. When *Prâṇá* attains stillness or after the extinction of the dynamic state everything is seized, the living state of a living being is eliminated, a state of cessation of all types of senses is achieved, therefore still state is termed to be *Hari*. Thus Yogiraj has remarked — ***Darpaṇke bhitar jo nadí usse piyās nahi jātā,*** meaning thirst is never quenched by merely observing the reflection of the river through a mirror.

Does any person call himself by his own name ? It is not

necessary. When *Prâṇá* Himself is God, then how will *Prâṇá* invoke *Prâṇá*? What is the necessity for invocation ? Because He is the Master of invocation, again One Whom He will invoke is He Himself only. Thus where is duality? This *Prâṇá*-God is prevalent in all living beings in a still state. But a living being deriving vibration has deviated from his consciousness and forgotten his own self. Therefore it is imperative for everyone to eliminate dynamism through *Prâṇákarma* and again achieve the still *Prâṇá*like self-consciousness or else bring a transformation from the present vibratory state to the still state.

When everyone pays obeisance to God they fold their hands and place them on the forehead between the eyebrows. Due to ignorance being unaware of it, everyone actually pays obeisance to the *Kűṭastha*. As a matter of fact none pay obeisance to the external deities because the place of settlement of all gods and goddesses is that *Kűṭastha*. There is no alternative other than paying obeisance to the *Kűṭastha*, paying obeisance to Him results in obeisance being paid to all deities. Therefore it is observed that *Brahmā*, *Víshṇu* and *Mahêśvara* are all rapt in *dhyāna*, they also pay obeisance to *Kűṭastha*.

'My house' is a commonly used epithet. I, myself am not the house, I merely reside there. Similarly everyone says 'my body'. From this parlance it can be deduced that this body is not the self, I just dwell within it. Within this body a separate self-entity is present, which is termed to be the real self. That self is the true self. If that true self is absent, the person's self is also absent. That self is the soul, that self is God, that self is beyond births and deaths and is indestructible. How will that 'self' invoke the 'present self'? What is the necessity for invoking? Merely try to know yourself, that is *sādhanā*. When you will know yourself then you will become liberated from the fetters of earthly bondage, thus you will become

Śivá yourself. Knowing oneself in this manner is the ultimate and supreme fulfilment of human life.

How will you eulogize God? It is equivalent to praise or flattery. Is He fond of sycophancy like you? He never wants flattery, He makes His devotees akin to Him, establishes them like Himself. Therefore to obtain Him, you have to station yourself at engrossment in statice, because the static state is the state of the cessation of vibration, this purports that stillness is *Brahma*. Thus try to become static through *Prâṇákarma*, that is the settlement in *Brahma*. Then you yourself will become *Brahma*. The action that reaches you to that static state is *sādhanā*, that is *Karmayoga* (action of *yóga*). Resort to that *Karmayoga*, celebrate it, in other words practise *Ātmakarma*, the passive *sādhanā*, for then you will achieve everything. Thus *Kriyā* is true and everything else is untrue. ***Purā ṡvāsame piyā āpnā knhoj kare bhāi. Janma janmakā saṃsār tumhārā sabe chuṭ jāi*** for instance, after drinking a glass of water it goes within, without being externally noticed, similarly practising regular *Prâṇákarma*, the externally oriented breathing completely becomes internally oriented and still and the state of *'Kévala-Kumbhaka'* is attained. Drink the breath completely in this manner (in the *Kévala-Kumbhaka* state), then search for yourself or in other words one's Dear One exists in that still state of breathing, achieving Him or the still state will annihilate the material aspirations of all births and the cycle of births and rebirths will be removed.

The tongue itself is sensory and the hymns in praise of God performed with the help of this sensory faculty is the indirect chanting. Therefore Yogiraj would observe that for those who have not achieved the technique of direct chanting it is better to perform the indirect chanting. By performing this type of indirect chanting, a living being will gradually be purified and devotion, reverence, faith will emerge in his mind. Later automatically the moment will arrive when by the grace of *Gurú* he will become aware about the actual chanting or he will derive the *Prânákarma*like *sādhanā* from *Sadgurú*, then it will not be necessary for him to perform the indirect chantings. Thus Yogiraj would remark that those who have fortunately acquired the *Ātmakarma sādhanā* or the path of direct chanting, for them the indirect chanting or idol-worship is no longer necessary. They can then realise, know and visualise everything within themselves. The *śāstrás* have similarly expressed—

Dehasthāḥ sarvavidyāśca dehasthāḥ sarvadevátāḥ.
Dehasthāḥ sarvatīrthāni Gurubākyena labhyate.

(*Jñānasaṅkalīnī Tántra*)

All types of knowledge, deities and pilgrimages which are prevalent within this body can be derived from *Gurú* through the path of six *cakrás*. *Iḍā*, *Piṅgalā* and *Sushumná* are the three steps. The three worlds of heaven, earth and hell are located in this body itself. Hell is from and beneath the navel; earth is from navel till the throat; above this is heaven.

Brahmāṇḍalakshaṇaṃ sárvaṃ dehamadhye byavasthitam.
Sākārāśca vinaśyanti nirākāro na naśyati.
Nirākāraṃ mano yasya nirākārasamo bhaved.
Tasmād sarvaprayatnena sākārantu parityajed.

(*Jñānasaṅkalīnī Tántra*)

This verse implies that everything in the universe is existent in this body. Form is destructible but formlessness is indestructible. In the amorphous mind a holy knowledge of *Brahma* is born. Therefore the knowledge of any form is impermanent, all endeavours to abandon all forms should be made.

Mántra pūjātapodhyānaṃ
Homaṃ japyaṃ balikriyām.
Saṃnyāsaṃ sarvakarmāṇi
Loukikāni tyajedbudhaḥ.

(*Jñānasaṅkalīnī Tántra*)·

This signifies that knowledgeable persons easily relinquish all types of popular religious customs like *mántras, jápas,* external worships, religious austerities, oblation, sacrifice and becoming an ascetic.

In this regard, there is a remarkable story. The king of Sagar in Madhya Pradesh in order to establish a vast lake completed the task of excavation. But all attempts to fill the lake with enough water failed after which the king sought the directive of the *paṇḍitás*. They advised that if human sacrifice was accomplished the lake would be filled with water. The king announced accordingly that if in lieu of immense wealth anyone was willing to offer their infant son for sacrifice, they could do so.

A poor Brahmin had many sons. Hearing this announcement he thought if one son would be offered for sacrifice, then the immense wealth accruing from the sacrifice would sustain the lives of the other members of his family which would be better than gradual death due to starvation. Therefore he offered one of his infant sons to the king.

The king took this infant son near the lake and after making arrangements for the sacrifice asked — "Dear boy, what is your last wish?"

The son replied — "I have no wish and even if I have, it is no use telling you."

The king stated — "I am the king, if you have a last wish tell me I shall fulfil it."

The child answered —

Mātā-pitā dhanki lobhi
Rājā lobhi sāgarā
Devī́-devátā balike lobhi
Mama śaraṇāgati Mádhavā.

The parents are greedy for wealth, the king greedy for the lake and the gods and goddesses greedy for the sacrifice, I have surrendered to *Mắdhava* (one of the appellations of *Víshṇu*).

The raised falchion descended. The lake becoming inundant inundated the whole town. Observing this condition the king again enquired the *paṇḍitás* — "What is the means by which the town can be saved from this?"

The *paṇḍitás* replied — "Ask that lad for it's he only who can save."

The devoted lad prayed to *Mắdhava* and said — "O God they do not know what they require; save them."

After this, the flood abated.

Imparting spiritual enlightenment about the esoteric mystery of idol-worship Yogiraj would explicate to His devotees — "Look at the Image of Bhagavan Krishna. The sages to explain the essences of this *yógasādhana* to common men have made remarkable arrangements. Krishna holds a flute in His hands and this flute has six holes. This is allegorical of the six *cakrás*. Above there is another hole, it represents the *Sahasrâra cakrá*. Krishna is piping His flute, this implies the internally oriented airs' actions that is *Prâṇákarma* in the path of the six *cakrás*. Practising this *Prâṇá-karma* regularly, *Kűṭastha* is visualised. Therefore Krishna dons peacock feathers on His head. The eye design in the feather is symbolical of *Kűṭastha*. He stands in the *Tríbhaṅgamurāri* position (standing posture of Bhagavan Krishna having three bends at head, waist and legs) representing the release of obstructions of tongue, *Anāhata* and *Mūlâdhāra cakrás* which in turn symbolises releasing the obstructions of *Brahmā*, *Víshṇu* and *Mahêśa* respectively. He stands on His left leg and His right one is aslant across it, this is symbolical of *Ómkāra Kriyā*. Know that the complete *yóga* essence pervades the images of Bhagavan, in this manner. One who worships Krishna likewise is the true worshipper of Krishna. Again

Goddess *Durgā* possesses ten hands. These represent the manner by which the *sādhaka* controls his ten senses or divisions of *Prâṇá*. These ten divisions denote *Prâṇá, apâná, vyāna, udāna, samāná, nāga, kūrma, kṛikara, devadatta* and *dhanaṃjaya*. With the help of these ten *Prâṇás* or ten senses, all actions are accomplished. At the feet of Goddess *Durgā* lies the lion, king of the jungle. She controls or restrains him, for the lion represents passion. He has not been completely annihilated for then creation will not be maintained, but She has controlled him. She has exterminated *Ásura* (the Devil). *Ásura* symbolises anger. It is imperative for the *sādhaka* to eliminate anger. On the right is Goddess *Lakshmī*, whose mount is the owl. Here a *sādhaka* is being cautioned that while practising *sādhana*, when he achieves the *Lakshmī* state, he should be careful that he does not become like the owl because the owl is day-blind and is nocturnal. In other words, dear *sādhaka*, be careful for when you achieve spiritual and material wealth you may attain the state of the owl. Aiming at this state Kabirdas has expressed—

Kanaka kanaka te śaoguṇi mādakatā adhikāya.
Iye khāye bourāt hyāye uha pāye bourāye.

Kanaka implies *datūrā* or gold. Consuming the *datūrā* (thorn-apple) makes a person insane. It infers deriving gold or immense wealth makes man insane, he does not have to consume it, it's intoxicating effect is so intense.

On the left of Goddess *Durgā* is Goddess *Sárasvatī*, her mount is the swan and it's function is to segregate milk from water if mixed. When a *sādhaka* arrives at an exalted state of *sādhanā* then deriving the correct knowledge he achieves that state. He then becomes capable of extracting the essence from the murky material world. This state is known as the state of *Paramahaṇsá*. But the *sādhaka* has to proceed further because he has not as yet established himself in non-duality. Beside *Sárasvatī*, is the commander-in-chief of the gods, *Kārtikeya*. He symbolises heroism. A *sādhaka* has been advised to practise *sādhanā* heroically. *Kārtikeya's* mount is the peacock. The eye design noticed in the plume of a peacock represents *Kūṭastha*. If a *sādhaka* heroically practises *sādhana*, he will surely visualize *Kūṭastha*. *Kārtikeya* has a bow and arrow in his hands. The arrow represents breath and bow represents the body. One who guides the arrowlike breath within the body valiantly and executes the airlike *Prâṇákarma* is *Kārtikeya*. Since a *sādhaka* practises *sādhanā* with austerities, he deserves fulfilment or salvation. For this the one who grants success is *Ganeśa*. But his mount is the mouse. The disposition of the mouse is to cause harm without any reason. Therefore in that state since a *sādhaka* has not yet attained settlement completely in non-duality, he has to remain away from the harmful ones, for if this is not done fulfilment or salvation will not come to him. *Śivá* is above all. He is the essence of void. Though He is *Vísvánāth*; or else Controller of the universe, He has no place to dwell. This infers that when a *sādhaka* completely establishes himself in the essence of void or in non-duality then by attaining this state, nothing belongs to him. *Śivá* does not wear any garb, He sits with ashes smeared all over His body, this implies that type of relinquishment regarding all aspects which comes to a *sādhaka*. *Śivá* holds a small drum in His hand and from it's two ends an uniform musical sound emanates. This symbolizes the *Ómkāra* sound, a *sādhaka* becomes rapt and merges in it. *Śivá* holds a trident in His other hand, this represents the three attributes of *Sattva, Rájas* and *Támas* or the achievement of the attributeless state of a *sādhaka*. Snakes entwine His waist and throat. Snake symbolizes malice. This denotes that a *sādhaka* has controlled malice alongwith other senses and has completely attained the state of non-malice. The mount of *Śivá* is the bull. The bull signifies *dhárma*. It has four legs—disposition, wealth, passion, salvation; these are the symbols[1] of the steps of *dhárma*. *Śivá* means the void essence. In this manner by settling in the void essence, a *sādhaka* achieves liberation. The void infers emptiness and this state of emptiness is *Brahma*. Practising *sādhana* and becoming conversant about the deity-essence will bring forth fulfilment or salvation. Yogiraj has elucidated — ***Hṛidayame jab apânávāyú āoye daś prakārke anahad sunāoye — ci, ci ci, kshudra ghaṇṭā, saṃkha, vin, tāl, murlī, pakhāoj, naghabat, dīrgha-ghaṇṭā*** — When *Apâná* air enters the *Anāhata cákra*, then ten types of *Anāhata* sound can be heard — chirr, continuous chirr, small bell, conch, lute, rhythm. snake-charmer's flute, wooden tom-tom, concerted drum music, prolonged bell. All types of instruments played in the gross worship are an allegory of these internal sounds. Exclusively the *yogis*, can internally realize these sounds. Yogiraj has further clarified — ***Knāśarkā āwāj huyā — galeme cinike māphik miṭhā mālum huyā — ānkhke sāmne bijli camkene lagā — Ómkārkā dhvani bahut dertak sunā*** — The sound of the dish of bell metal could be heard within; I could experience a sugary taste in My throat; lightning started flashing before My eyes; I heard the *Ómkāra* sound for a long period. Again He has illustrated — ***Ragke***

---

1. ***Catushpād sakalo dhármaḥ satāñcaiba kṛite yuge,***
Nādhármeṇāgamaḥ kaścinmánushyān pratibartate.

(*Mánurahasya* 1/81)

In other words, *dhárma* is divided into four steps — first step is releasing obstruction of the tongue; second step is releasing obstruction of the *Anāhata cakrá*, the third step is releasing the obstruction of the *Maṇipūra cakrá* and last step is releasing obstruciton of the *Mūlâdhāra cakrá*; these are the four steps of *dhárma*; *sakala*, *s*—voice, *ka*—head, *la*—practising *Kriyā* with the forceful sound emanating from head; truth is *Kúṭastha*, absorption occurs next, then science and eventually *samādhi*. Then the kinetic mind merges in the still mind by these four types of true unions, resulting in *Brahma* realisation. *Na dharme* — irreligion; *agam* — settlement; *kascid* — non-occurrence, *púrusha* — the realisation of those who have excellent *Kúṭastha* visualisation. Or else in irreligion that is barring *Kriyā*, settlement in *Kúṭastha* will never occur which all sincere, devoted *Kriyābāns* realise..

dono nestarke ek āwāj nikastā uchikā nām anahad bājā usse choṭā bāyā joki uparke koṭise gābāpar caḍke mālum hotā haye hāmesā yesā sānāikā sur dete haye usse kuch kam āur āwaj haye iha mālum hotā haye ki bahutse ādmi istroekā knāshar ghanṭā bājāy rahe. Baḍā ghanṭākā āwaj śirke bhitar piche mālum huyā. — This denotes that from either side of the temples a sound is emanating known as the *Anāhata* sound. A slighter sound was emerging from within a little above the temple on the left. I could understand that the sound was milder than the shenai note and it seemed as though many people were playing the dish of bell metal together. The sound of a big bell could be heard within the occiput, Yogiraj has stated — ***Bṛishākārke upar Mahādevá caḍhne gaye āur kyā bāhan prathivi nahithā—bṛishākār yāne iha śarīrrūpi bṛisha iskā dui siṃ Prâṇâyāmake haoyā se nikastā haye — āur kām barjit hotā haye isliye iha śarīrko bayel kahate haye isike upar Mahādevá haye arṭhād Brahma*** — *Mahādevá* mounted the bull, but why? Could not the world serve as a mount for Him? The bull signifies this body having two horns, i.e. the *Iḍā-Piṅgalā* like two horns which come out during *Prâṇâyāma*. Practising the *Iḍā-Piṅgalā* action the state of relinquishment of passions can be achieved. This exists within the body, that is the reason why this body is termed bull. *Mahādevá*, the still *Prâṇá-Brahma* exists in this body. *Mahādevá* implies the vast space or the Still sublime void which is all pervasive.

Yogiraj has detailed another acme of His *sādhanā* realization in His diary which had occurred to the sages of ancient times also. Yogiraj has expressed — ***Ādi Purāṇá Kishunji se bheṭ huyā*** — I met the original Primordial Krishna. Again — ***Ādi púrushase bheṭ, jihvá āur āge jaye ke ṭhaharā, śūnyá bhavana me mánas gayā*** — implying I merged with the Primordial Being. The tongue was raised further upwards and stopped. When I attained this *Khecari* state then My mind entered the void. Void means nothingness. In that state of nothingness or in the supportless, amorphous, attributeless state, I achieved the state of settlement of the mind. This state occurs when there is *Kévala-Kumbhaka* and is also known as '*Khecari* attainment.' Yogiraj has again referred to this void state as — ***Śūnyá asal cij haye, śvāsā bhitar bhitar caltā haye*** — that Void is the truth or *Brahma*, because everything originates from there and merges there. Yogiraj has further mentioned — ***Súrya śūnyá haye śūnyáme miljānā haye.*** — That Soul-Sun is the void, one should dissolve and merge in that Void. ***Humhi āsmānkā súryarūpá — Hum choḍāy dusrā na koi nahi woh kahatā haye sab choḍāyke baiṭho — ek majā maithunkā payerse sirtak hotá haye. Yo śūnyá bhitar soi bāhar. Ab śrif śūnyá hojānā haye.*** — I only am the Origin and Form of sun in the sky. There is none excepting Me. An instruction from within to forsake everything alongwith the senses and sit quietly engrossed occurs. In that state the joy of consummation is experienced from toe to head. The infinite void which I can visualise within can be noticed externally also, thus the internal and external have become the same, I can perceive the Absolute Void *Brahma* everywhere. Now I shall have to abolish My Esse and completely become the Void.

' Who is *Purāṇá Púrusha, Purāṇá* Krishna or *Ādi Púrusha*? *Upanisháds* have explained thus — ***Ajo nityaḥ śāśvatoayaṃ purāṇo.*** (*Kambalākshyā Upanishád's Uttar Balli* and *Gītā* 2/20). One Who is eternal, Who has none before Him, is, was and will be perenially present, One Who does not undergo any metamorphoses, One who is indestructible and beyond the cycle of births and deaths He only is *Purāṇá Púrusha, Purāṇá* Krishna and *Ādi Púrusha* (the Primordial Being). When a *yogi* enters the cave of *Kúṭastha* everything becomes pervaded by *Brahma*, then everything becoming one, there remains no duality. If duality is absent, is birth existent ? If there is no birth, where is death? He is the Supreme Being, He is eternally Primordial. One should remain merged in

Him. He is the *Ādidevá* (the Origin) or *Devādidevá* (the Prime). Therefore Yogiraj would stipulate that without practising *Prâṇákarma*, one cannot reside there, for that only is *dhárma*. Practising *Prâṇákarma* and settling in the state beyond actions or *Kriyā's* transcendental state is the eternal state, the Immortal Abode. By perpetually abiding in the eternal state or in the state beyond action, the person concerned himself becomes eternal. *Mahātmā* Kabirdas has corroborated —

Kabir yo woh ek na jāniyā,
Tao sab jāne kyā hoye.
Ek hnite sab hnot hyāye,
Sabte ek na hoye.

This implies that without knowing that One, it is futile to know everything else. Everything has been created from that One, that One pervades everything. He has further expressed —

Ekhi sādhe sab sādhe,
Sab sādhe sab jāye.
Yo tu snice mūlko,
Phule phale aghāye.

This signifies that by executing the *sādhanā* of that One, *sādhanā* of all is accomplished, but practising *sādhanā* of all, everything is rendered fruitless. For instance, if the root only of a tree is watered, flowers and fruits blossom in abundance.

Ekaṃ bhūtaṃ paraṃ Brahma
Jagad sarvaṃ carācaram.
Nānābhābaṃ máno yasya
Tasya muktirna jāyate.

(*Jñānasaṅkalinī Tántra* 84)

This denotes that only *Brahma* is prevalent in all elements and the whole creation. If the mind is plagued by various thoughts it deters salvation, instead knowing that One makes salvation imperative. Thus *sādhanā* of One should be practised. If various deities are worshipped the feeling that this god is great, the other is small arises. ***Guhāṃ prabishṭau parame parārdhe***. (*Kaṭhopanishád* 3/1) — implying if the *Prâṇá*-air can be entered into the *Kūṭastha* cave, merging in Absolute *Brahma* occurs, then material attachment is exterminated, thus an all-conversance arises. In accordance with the codes of discipline, Yogiraj caused this to occur in His Own yogic Esse.

Áṅguṣṭha mātra Púrusha madhye ātmani tishṭhati. (*Kambalākshyā Upanishád's Uttar Balli*) — Within *Kūṭastha* dwells the Primordial Being Soul akin to the diminutiveness of a thumb-tip. Thus Yogiraj would counsel His devotees that the thumb-tip Primordial Being which they perceive in *Kūṭastha* can be noticed by practising excellent *Prâṇákarma* for He is the Soul, the Fearless and Supreme State, He is *Brahma*. Practising regular *Kriyāyoga* gives rise to such knowledge that the Supreme Being is the self. He Himself only is *Purushôttama* (the Supreme Being), He again is the Effulgence of all effulgences. All effulgence is manifested from Him, He is the Soul-Sun, therefore if He does not exist there is not any effulgence. Thus whatever is being observed, the entirety is His Form because all forms emanate from Him. Therefore a living being is *Śivá*like, if the soul had been absent everything else would have been absent. Since soul exists in the form of *Brahma*, the entire creation persists, therefore soul is *Brahma* and *Brahma* is soul and if knowledge of this type is acquired, then the whole creation becomes pervaded by *Brahma*. Thus the sages of *Upanisháds* have noted — ***Aṇoraṇiyān mahatomahīyān ātmāguhāyāṃ nihitasya jantostamaḥ kṛitaṃ paśyati bītaśokā.*** (*Bṛihannārāyaṇa Upanishád* Rule – 1) — He is infinitesimal again the infinitude. If the mind enters the soul which is latent within the *Kūṭastha*-cave, all miseries are dispelled. He nurtures all living beings subtly. Then Yogiraj states that practising excellent *Prâṇákarma* enables visualisation like the unquivering flame of the lamp within the eyebrows of this *Ómkāra* body; a threadlike lustre can be observed, He only represents the potential female energy, He only is the Soul-Sun form of *Kūṭastha,* He only is the innate-void. This breath is the root of speech, she is *Gāyatrī* (the personified female energy worshipped in the *Vedas*). The dulcet note which can be heard while practising *Prâṇákarma* is the *praṇáva* sound (mystic syllable) or the sound of Krishna's flute. Being thoroughly rapt in that *praṇáva* sound, the *Prâṇá*-air rises upwards and settlement in *Kūṭastha* is achieved. That is the immortal state.

Hṛídisthitaṃ paṅkajamashṭapatraṃ,
Sakarṇikaṃ keśara madhya nīlam.
Añgushṭamātraṃ munayo vadanti,
Dhyāanti Vishṇuṃ Púrushaṃ Purāṇám. (*Ómkāra Gītā*)

If permanence is achieved in the *Anāhata* lotus, within it's stamen of eight seed-vessels the blue thumbesque Primordial Being exists, such is quoted by the sages and they practise *dhyāna* on that Primordial Being *Víshṇu.* He is known as *Purāṇá Púrusha.*

Dhyānābasthitatadgatena mánasā paśyanti yaṃ yogino.
Yasyāntaṃ na biduḥ surāsurgaṇā devāya tasmai namaḥ.
(*Gītā Dhyāna*)

This infers that settling in *dhyāna* and being thoroughly rapt in this state enables *yogis* to visualise the Primordial Being. The God, Whose beginning and end even gods and demons are unaware of, such a God should be paid obeisance to.

On 15th July, 1873, Yogiraj has penned — ***Pnāc indriyoko pare mánas yāne śvāsā — mánaske pare buddhi yāne bindi — buddhi se pare Brahma nirākār śūnyá nirmal.*** — The state of the mind occurs beyond the five senses. As long as breathing exists, the kinetic mind is also existent. When the breath becomes still the kinetic mind loses it's existence. The mind's existence depends on the existence of breath. Thus the breath becomes still and intellect persisting, settles in the *Kūṭastha* dot. Beyond that intellect or dot is the Amorphous *Brahma* Who is Pure and the Void. The *śāstrás* have rendered a similar stipulation —

> ***Sparśanaṃ rasanaṃ caiba ghrāṇaṃ cakshuśca śrotaram.***
> ***Pañcendriyamidaṃ tattvaṃ mánas sādhanyamindriyam.***
> (*Jñānasaṅkalinī Tántra* 28)

Touch, taste, smell, sight and hearing are the five essences of the five senses and beyond this is mind, the principal sense.

Therefore Yogiraj has written on 17th May 1873 — ***Bindúme āṭak rahanā kām haye.*** — One should constantly remain united with the dot beyond the mind, for then settlement in the void is executed. What will occur after this? He has already stated on 3rd March, in the same year — ***Āj Hum ujiyālā ghar cale — jayse koi dipak bār diyā. Śvāsā bhitar bhitar calā.*** — I have entered into the state of manifestation, it seemed as though someone had lit a lamp there. Breathing is continuing internally, or in the path of the *sushumná*. In this state which resembles the sky at dawn or the twilight sky which lacks the radiance yet is self-manifested, everything can be perceived. The near and distant can be envisioned. After this *samādhi* state arrives. Therefore Yogiraj recounting His *sādhana* experiences described on 13th January — ***Śūnyá bhavana āur safā jihvā āur upar uṭhā ab baḍā majā ek ujiālā usise sab dekhlātā haye āur kuchvi nahi dekhlātā haye usise mánas ṭhahar jāneko nām samādhi.*** — The void state in the *Sahasrâra cakrá* could be seen clearly, the tongue was raised further upwards and remained united in the palatal cavity, then a feeling of ecstasy emerged, I could visualise everything in the tranquil brilliance of the sky at dawn, again nothing could be visualised because in this state visualisation is absent, the mind who would see is absent. Therefore Yogiraj states that the settlement of the mind in that state is *samādhi*. The Soul-Sun which is revealed then has been addressed by Him thus —

Sūrya hi Krishna. That *Ātmasūrya* is Krishna. The experience in that peculiar state has been described by Him thus — ***Yon deśme rāt nahi haye wonhā ek ādmi ke māphik dekhā woh ādmi na kuch bole na kuch cāle — khāli khaḍā haye — tumi sutra ācho se dnāḍiye āche — kevala se premer bhusho — prem korile tnāhāke pāoyā yāye.*** — Yogiraj infers the state which has no nights. Which state does not undergo nights ? Such a state is not existent. If there is no night, then is day only present? This also is not possible, because if there is day, there has to be night. Again the reverse is imperative, if night prevails, day also has to prevail. If one exists, the other also has to exist. Just as if only happiness is desired and not misery, it is not possible. Happiness and misery co-exist. The existence of one gives rise to the existence of the other behind it. Thus Yogiraj is quoted to have said — ***Yon deśme rāt nahi***— meaning where there is neither day nor night, in the conflictless state of self-manifestation like the sky at dawn, I saw a Being who did not speak a word or move but merely kept on standing. Then I realized that since He is the fundamental source of everything He was standing, or else He is *Purushôttama*. That *Purushôttama* is the Incarnate of love; if He is loved properly, He can be achieved. When does this love occur? The more *Prâṇákarma* is practised, the more the amorphous form will become condensed and the more condensation takes place, the more visualisation with the Static Eye (in *Kūṭastha*) occurs resulting in being attracted towards Him, eventually that attraction will be intensified into love. This love is pure and holy. Holy love before this is impossible. The great soul Ramprasad has chanted — ***Ūrdhvá jihvā kari ānanda sāgare bhāsite*** — If tongue is raised upwards on the palatal cavity, one can float in the ocean of ecstasy. Commenting on it's later state or the aforementioned state, *Mahātmā* Ramprosad has proclaimed — ***Ye deśete rajanī nei mā sei deśer ek lok peyechi, ebār bhālo bhābīr kāche bhāb śikhechi.*** — I have found the Being belonging to the state which has no night, I have become conversant about love from the Mother of love. Due to Ramprosad's propensities at birth, he would prefer to refer to Soul-*Brahma* as 'Mother', therefore in all his statements he has used the address 'Mother'. In actuality, He is the Mother and Father. On 1st March 1874, the sublime glorified state of *sādhanā* was achieved by Yogiraj and has been portrayed by Him thus — ***Na śvāsā lenā na pheknā — baḍā sukh — ehi Brahma. Sūrya ko jyoti nahi rahā.*** — Practising *Prâṇákarma* continually, He arrived at such a state when inhalation and exhalation of breath was eliminated and attaining the *Kévala-Kumbhaka* state completely, He became still. Then He was exremely blissful and that ultimate happy state is *Brahma*. When the river enters into the sea, it's current no longer exists, similarly Yogiraj also caused His permanent settlement in *Brahma*. He has described that state as bliss not joy. There is a difference between bliss and joy. In joy there is a meagre trace of bliss, but in bliss, a total joy is prevalent. To remain merged in the Void *Brahma* majestically is bliss and remaining far from that Absolute Void-*Brahma* is misery, in other words, abiding in *Kriyā's* transcendental state imparts bliss, not abiding in *Kriyā's* transcendental state imparts misery. Thus bliss is a much more exalted state than joy. Therefore He has specified this state as bliss. When He settled in that *Brahma*-bliss or Void-*Brahma* and after descending He explained that state thus — ***Sūrya ko jyoti nahi rahā.*** — Then there was no effulgence of the *Ātmasūrya*, only self-manifestation prevailed, because the perceptible sun and moon could not express the effulgent form, everything evanesced.

God has delineated this state thus —

Na tadbhāsayate sūryo na śaśāṅko na pāvakaḥ.
Yad gatvā na nivartante taddhāma paramaṃ mama. (*Gītā* 15/6)

This signifies that the resplendence of the sun, moon or fire are absent there because their resplendences are not able to manifest that state. It is a supremely effulgent place, self-manifested and inexplicable. That state which after being achieved by *yogis* does not entail rebirth, this is My Supreme Abode.

The *Kaṭhopanishád* has stated — ***Natatra súryo bhāti na candrátārake neme vidyuto bhānti kutoayomagniḥ. Tameba bhāntamánubhāti sarvaṃ tasya bhāsā sarvamidaṃ bibhāti.***— In that state where the rays of the sun, moon or stars cannot reach, when the flash of lightning cannot be more brilliant, then it is but obvious that fire is negligible. Therefore since this *Ātmasúrya* is eternally aflame, the perceptible sun, moon and stars are resplendent in His Omnilucence.

* * * * * *

Yogiraj would never advocate practice of so-called *dhyāna*, but would advocate the practice of *Kriyāyoga sādhana. Gītā's Karmayoga* is *Kriyāyoga. Dhyāna* commonly means being engrossed in the thought of an imaginary or desired deity in the *Ājñācakra* and progressing gradually towards *samādhi* in this manner. But the path of Yogiraj is not so. He has taught the technique of the movement of *Prâṇá* air by means of *recaka* and *pūraka* through the six *cakrás* afferently, if the movement of *Prâṇá* air is internal, an automatic '*Kévala Kumbhaka*' state will arise and all types of dynamism being exterminated, the true base for *dhyāna* will be established. After this by *yónimudrā*, engrossment will ensue in soul-visualisation and if further progress is made the state of *samādhi* will appear. Since no type of discomfort occurs in this practice, *Gītā* has clarified —

Rājavidya rājagujhyaṃ pavitramidamuttamam
Pratyakshyāvagamaṃ dhármyaṃ susukhaṃ kartumvyayam.

(*Gītā* 9/2)

This verse signifies that since this knowledge is scientific, it is the supreme knowledge, it is extremely esoteric and holier than the holiest. This *Prâṇákarmaic dhárma* is direct and explicit, it can be practised at ease and in comfort and is imperishable, it does not suffer destruction. Thus Yogiraj would remark — ***Kashṭa holei bujhbe Kriyā ṭhik hocche nā*** — implying if there is discomfort it should be understood that *Kriyā* is not being practised properly. Executing this *karma* terminates the necessity for all *karmas*. *Prâṇávāyú* attaining vibration gives rise to all sorts of actions. Again when it attains stillness all actions become absent, thus this is known as the state beyond actions which Yogiraj would refer to as *Kriyā's* transcendental state. This transcendental state is the aspiration and be-all and end-all for everyone, that is the supreme abode. Therefore He would counsel everyone to remain in *Kriyā's Parābasthā* (*Kriyā's* transcendental state) for a prolonged period because there is nothing greater than this as that Still State is *Brahma*. ***Niścalaṃ Brahma uccate***—the static or the void state is *Brahma*.

On 16th August 1873, Yogiraj has penned — ***Āj jeyādā dertak dáma bund rahā — Humhi Súrya Bhagavān. Humārā rūpá Kālācnād.*** — Today My breath ceased for a long time. I only am the Soul-Sun God, My Form is the black Soul-Moon. On 19th August sketching a black moon He wrote beside it — ***Kālācnādkā rūpá, Krishna yāne Kālācnād.*** The black Soul-Moon which is perceived in *Kúṭastha* and which is perceptible only to *yogis* is the form of the black Moon; this dark Moon is Bhagavan Krishna. A few days later He delineated a face of Krishna and wrote beside it thus — ***Ie cehārā bhitarkā miṭ yātā haye piche hājār Krishna najar paḍātā haye bhayānak baḍe bhayānak surat sab najar paḍātā haye baḍā bhāri Krishna isme dahayat mālum hoti haye.*** — The Image of Krishna which I am visualising in *Kúṭastha* has evanesced, later I visualised a thousand[1] Krishnas. After this the gigantic Krishna which I envisioned was extremely terrifying and it seemed as

1. Here thousand infers countless.

though there was a blazing sensation within. ***Ek jyot bhitarse dekhā uskā varṇan nahi ho saktā uho jyot seoyāye āur kuch nāhi — ab kaṭhin kābārā haye — baḍā ānand yehi āur Brahma birāṭ mūrtikā rūpá haye*** — I envisioned an effulgence within, which is indescribable; there is nothing else excepting that effulgence. Now a difficult state arose and in this state there was immense bliss, this is *Brahma* and the Form of infinitude. Advancing further He wrote on 31st August, 1873 thus — ***Uha Krishna śūnyáme mil yātā*** — implying that Krishna also merged in the infinite void or in the void within the void. Eventually, no form exists, all merge into the infinite void. Thus He mentioned — ***Yata rūpá dekhā yāye sab aparūpá. Sab rūpá śūnyáme milyātā haye.*** — All the forms which are perceptible are basically amorphous and all of them merge in the void. Aiming at this, Arjuna has quoted — ***Ai devátā samūha tomā-tei prabeś karitechen.*** (*Gītā* 11/22). All the gods and goddesses are entering You and merging in You. How is that void? Yogiraj has expatiated thus — ***Bindú ghomṭār bhetar haite dekhā yāye arthād sādhāraṇ śūnyer āvaraṇ āche kintu mahá śūnyer āvaraṇ nāi tannimitte praṭhame dekhā yāye nā — mahá śūnyer bindúte samudāye dekhā yāye*** — Practising regular and prolonged *Kriyā*, a veil-like state appears on the head and then the dot can be visualized. The virtue of common space acts as a deterrent but the Infinite Void lacks virtue, hence the absence of deterrent, for this reason that dot cannot be visualized initially — the totality can be perceived within the dot of the infinite void. But how long does visualization persist ? Yogiraj expounded — ***Hum binā kuch nahi phir Humbhi nahi khāli śūnyá nirmal ohi āpne padá. Ab śvāsā bhitar bhitar cale lagā — ohi śvāsā Nārāyaṇá haye āur ohi kāraṇ bāri. Ehi kā nām pār utarnā kahate haye — isineseme yogilog paḍe rahate haye.*** — There is nothing excepting Me, again I also am absent, only the pure infinite void prevails, that is the own state or the own self-form. Now My breath flows internally or in the

Sushumná, this internal breath is *Nārāyaṇá* and is the source of everything. This is referred to as the transcendence of the material world, all noble *yogis* settle in this state. ***Humhi súrya Humārei prakāśit sab jagat*** — I am that *Ātmasúrya*, the entire creation manifests from Me. By abiding in this state He noted — ***Iha mālum huyā ki súrya Humāhi haye. Yaisā Hum súryarūpī āur Humāre sab téjas sárvavyāpi Brahma. Humārā na hāth haye na payer haye kévala maṇḍalākār Humārā téjas sárvavyāpi.*** — Now it has been realized that I only am that *Ātmasúrya*. When I am that *Ātmasúrya*, then My entire Effulgence is all pervasive. I have no hands and feet[1]. I only am the Orbed Indivisible Infinity, My Effulgence pervades the whole creation. The *śāstrás* state —

> ***Akhaṇḍa maṇḍalākāraṃ vyāptaṃ yena carācaram***
> ***Tadpadaṃ darśitaṃ yena tasmai Śrīgurave namaḥ.***
>
> (*Gurúgītā* 27)

Obeisance should be paid to such a *Gurú* who has shown the path to realize the indivisible infinite *Brahma* pervading creation.

This state is truly termed to be the *Gurú* state. Therefore Yogiraj has delineated a sun and inscribed beside it — ***Ehi Gurúcaran haye.*** This is the Lotus Feet of the *Gurú*. Again He has written — ***Ehi Gurúka rūpá haye yāne súrya — iha pratakshya Gurú yāne Mahádevá.*** This *Ātmasúrya* is the form of *Gurú*, this is the real *Gurú* or *Mahádevá*. *Mahádevá* is the Primordial *Gurú* ; Yogiraj Himself being that state of the Primordial *Gurú* wrote thus — ***Hāmesā kumbhaka Mahádevákā yóga svárūpa bhayā śira hāmesā bhāri ānkh upar tānā huyā khicnese jaldi nahi ṭuṭṭā, nahi bolnese baḍā phaydā.*** — Just as the Reigning-God *Mahádevá* is constantly

1. Here hand symbolises action and feet motion. Mankind cannot function or move barring hands or feet, but since Yogiraj is Almighty, Omnipresent and has descended as a Human Being, He can execute all actions despite hands and feet. In this regard He expressed — "I only an Omnipotent, I can execute anything I will." This purports that Yogiraj is Omnifunctional.

engrossed in *dhyāna*, similarly Yogiraj also being engrossed in the *Kevala Kumbhaka* state was rapt in *dhyāna* like *Mahādevá*. His head was perpetually heavy, His eyes like those of *Śivá* were raised upwards so much so that pulling them downwards even would not result in them being pulled down.[1] There being a cessation of speech in this state desire to talk is absent, thus this refrainment of speech is beneficial. Therefore He reiterated — ***Moun honā acchā mālum hotā haye.*** — I have realised that it is better to abstain from speech. There is no desire of speech in this state, who will converse then when desire is non-existent ? Therefore He has become silent. To achieve that state He would advise His devotees — ***Ek okta harroj yattā sake ek āsaná baiṭhe.*** — Practise *Kriyā* daily at least once as long as practicable for then everything can be achieved. He further remarked that if anyone aspired to achieve salvation in this birth itself it would be possible if he practised this *Kriyāyoga sādhana* with sincerity, respect and fortitude.

* * * * * *

The *Prâṇâyāma* revived by Yogiraj has been divided into three stages by Him — inferior, medium, superior. Initially due to lack of practice, a *sādhaka's Prâṇâyāma* is inferior; a great deal of perspiration occurs at this time. Later further practice results in medium *Prâṇâyāma*. Yogiraj has explained this fact thus — ***Camak uṭhe bicme ṭhelā diyā usise śarīr knāpā — isiko madhyam Prâṇâyāma kahate haye.*** — The body jerks occasionally, an internal push makes the body quiver and waver, when this occurs while practising *Prâṇâyāma* it is referred to as the medium type of *Prâṇâyāma*. After this when excellent *Prâṇâyāma* occurs then the

1. It should be mentioned here that *Śrī* Ramakrishna described the eyes of a *yogi* to *Śrī* Mahendranath Gupta as he had opined — "A *yogi's* mind is constantly engrossed in God and rapt in Soul. His eyes have a vacuous gaze like those of a bird's who sits apathetically hatching her eggs — her attention is concentrated on the eggs. Can you show me that picture?" *Śrī* Gupta replied — "I shall try my best to find it." — (*Śrīśrī Ramakṛishṇa Kathāmṛita* 3/2)

body attaining levity levitates. In this excellent *Prâṇâyāma*, a whistling sound emanates, that is known as the *praṇáva* sound. Thus He has written — ***Ṡi ṡabd jorse niklā.*** The whistling sound emerged with force. He has depicted the form of this excellent *Prâṇâyāma* thus — ***Yettā recakakā āsal bāsubli yāne bāsulikā āoyāz hotā haye ottā pūrakakā āoyāz nahi hotā haye — joki ṡūnyá rūpá ohi asal Brahmakā rūpá — āb āur majā — jiv āur caḍhā jātā haye — ṡabdke suratme laya lagānese karma vrom sab jātā haye.*** — In the commonly prevalent *Prâṇâyāma*, the three functions of *recaka, pūraka* and *kumbhaka* exist, but in the *Prâṇâyāma* of *Rājayoga* or in the one revived by Yogiraj only the two functions of *recaka* and *pūraka* prevail, it is not necessary to cause *kumbhaka* by striving for it — if the two actions of *recaka* and *pūraka* are internally practised, an automatic *kumbhaka* will result. All inhale and exhale through the nose. If the nasal passage is blocked for some reason, then breathing takes place through the mouth. It is for this reason that inhalation and exhalation through the nose or through *pūraka recaka* and ceasing for a while causing *kumbhaka*, is the common prescript. But in *Rājayoga* or in the *Prâṇâyāma* revived by Yogiraj, inhalation or exhalation of breath through the nose or mouth is taboo. This infers that through the *Iḍā* and *Piṅgalā* or through the medium of the two nostrils the function of the inhalation and exhalation of breath is absent, it is wholly internal; the action involves the internal *Prâṇá* and *Apâná* airs. *Iḍā* and *Piṅgalā* attract a living being towards the material world; therefore the *Iḍā* and *Piṅgalā* should in the very beginning be abandoned and this *Prâṇâyāma* occurs through the *Sushumná*. It is extremely comforting and can exclusively be derived from the *Gurú*. There is no possibility of any risk or harm in this. Therefore in the above quotation Yogiraj explains that while practising excellent internal *Prâṇâyāma* at the time of *recaka*, a wonderful flutelike sound emanates but does not occur at the moment of *pūraka*. What is form of void is form of *Brahma*. Now there is an enhanced happiness, the tongue is being raised further upwards. If the mind can be merged in the whistling *praṇáva* sound which emerges during *recaka* of this internal *Prâṇâyāma*, all types of fallacies pertaining to actions evolving from dynamic *Prâṇá* are eliminated. Regarding this excellent *Prâṇâyāma* He has recounted His realizations from 1871 to 1873 on different days in various modes — ***Kriyā korte korte āp uṭh khaḍā huye — phir hos karke baiṭhe choḍā śvāsāko.*** — While practising *Kriyā*, I spontaneously stood up. When I regained consciousness or became aware, then I sat down on My *āsaná* again and exhaled breath internally. ***Siddhā sanáme baiṭhke karte karte uṭh āsanáse khaḍā huyā*** — sitting in the *Sidhāsaná* posture while practising *Kriyā*, I suddenly stood up from My *āsaná*. He again wrote — ***For instance a big and heavy stone can be lifted with the strength of a few, similarly the body can be raised with the force of internal air, but does not leave the earth or the Mūlâdhāra cakrá, for this reason a small portion of the buttocks, or legs remain attached to the Mūlâdhāra cakrá, when all the airs merge in the void, then the yogi can with the help of the void go everywhere. When a yogi sits in āsaná, mind can be present everywhere with the help of his static mind and he becomes omnipresent, then he can know everything, eventually becomes omniscient due to the universe being pervaded by Brahma. Later continually concentrating on the soul and the mind merging a little, dhyāna results, practising dhyāna in this manner, knowledge of samādhi dawns, thus by deriving many types of knowledge a purity and true love apear.*** Again Yogiraj has mentioned — ***Baḍā majā — badan jarā halkā.*** Practising this type of excellent *Prâṇâyāma* I sensed a great deal of happiness, the body became a little light. ***Āj haoyāse śarirko dhakel diyā.*** Continual *Prâṇâyāma* made the airs still resulting in an internal push to the body. He penned on 2nd September 1873 — ***Śarīr bahut dhilā ho gayā.*** Practising excellent *Prâṇâyāma*, the body became internally slack and light. The airs being still in this state all the joints and flesh of the body become non-functional, after which the body-consciousness gradually disappears. Therefore Yogiraj has repeated — ***Pisāb nā hoke uṭhke ṭapāṭap āpse āp girne lagā.*** —Being rapt in *Kriyā* for a prolonged period, I did not micturate. But the body has become so slack that the moment I stood up the urine flowed spontaneously. ***Majhuke māphik sūryake taraf ómkāra rūpá dekhnese nicekā payer tin cār dafe uṭh khaḍā hotā haye ṭhik majhuke māphik śarīr samet tin cār dafe āge kudtā haye āp se āp — vāyūke gatise iha sab premki lakshman.*** — I attained the state of a frog, for while visualising the *Ómkāra* form within the Soul-Sun I had to stand up three or four times and in this state, the body leapt like a frog three or four times. Practising regular *Prâṇâyāma*, the moment airs become still this type of frog-leap occurs which is the indication of love. ***Āj jaminse calte okta payer uṭhe lagā***. Today while walking, My feet lifted from the earth. ***Āj sūrya dekhte okta payer jaminse uṭhne lagā.*** —Today while visualising the Soul-Sun, My feet were being raised from the ground. ***Koi hat pakaḍke uthatā haye.*** — It seemed as though someone was lifting Me by holding My hands. ***Ākhse aihi Brahmasvárūpa najar paḍātā haye — ucepar uṭhnekā tabiyat kartā haye ucekā hāoyāse dar mālum hotā haye — baḍā ānand.*** — I can perceive the void crystalline *Brahma* with the naked eye, such a state arrived, the body became light and weightless due to practice of *Prâṇâyāma* so much so that it was levitating, the upper air within the body being still I feel a slight amount of fear, again a great deal of happiness. ***Iha mālum hotā haye ki kumbhakase badan hālkā hotā haye.*** — When *Kumbhaka* occurred automatically while practising *Prâṇákarma*, I realized that the body attained buoyancy and lost weight. ***Āb upar khaicke lejātā haye.*** — Achieving this type of *Kévala Kumbhaka* state the body is being pulled upwards. ***Āj kévala bhitar bhitar se calā — āur baḍā majā mālum huyā — āur eysā mālum huyā ki āsaná leke uṭhe jo dhvani ādhi rātko sunātāthā sodhvani aksar sunātā haye ohi dhvani ohi śūnyá ohi Brahma.*** — Today I have severed all connections with superficial nature and am travelling exclusively within, immense bliss is ensuing from this. I could further comprehend that now I was levitating with My *āsaná* posture intact. The *Ómkāra* sound which I could hear at midnight can now be heard at all times, that sound is the Infinite Void and this again is *Brahma*. ***Padmâsana sāmnekā uṭhā.*** — Sitting in *padmâsana* and practising *Kriyā*, the front portion arose. ***Āsaná āpse uṭhā.*** — While

I was practising *Kriyā* sitting in the *āsana* posture, I automatically levitated. ***Tiluyār gur tene tene hālkā haye jeman temni śarīre śvāsa tene tene śarīr hālkā haye — se yeman dudher upar bhāse temni śūnyer upar śarīr thāke. Kichudiner par aṇute miliye yāye.*** — After jaggery is refined it becomes light, similarly regular practice of *Prâṇákarma* makes the body light and just as the jaggery floats on milk, similarly the body floats in space. A few days later it merges in the *aṇu*. Advancing further in *sādhana*, on 13th September 1873, He remarked — ***Ek tarhakā bhāri neśā jisme bekhabar ho jāne paḍtā haye.*** — Such an intense engrossment occurred that the self-entity was lost or body-consciousness alongwith the senses were abandoned; the mind, intelligence, intellect, pride were all eliminated. Because the mind, intellect and intelligence are observers, when they are non-existent who will observe whom, who will collect information of whom? As long as this mind is kinetic, till then various visualisations result, but when it is still, there is a total absence of everything. This type of engrossment makes a *yogi* intoxicated. Pertaining to this intoxication, He has elaborated —

Khāoyā bhule jete dekhine,
Eman premto koi dekhine.
Neśār upar neśā dhare,
Dukhkha sukh yekhāne hare.
Eman neśār bolihāri,
Theko tumi ei neśā dhari.

Due to the intensity of love food intake being forgotten is a rare phenomenon. If intoxication due to engrossment is further enhanced, then misery and happiness cease. Drown yourself in such a marvellous intoxication.

The *yogis* ascribe this type of engrossment related intoxication to be the true love. Superficial love or proclamation of love is not true love. Thus He has noted — ***Yār yeman mánas se temni dekhe*** — Perception is in accordance with mental disposition. Describing this mind or desire He has written on 6th March 1873 — ***Bapu***

hṛidayke kahate haye — yāne chātike āge yo māṃsa haye — inhā se icchā udpatti hotā haye tab laḍkā paydā hotā haye — jab icchā rahit ho jāye tab āphi Brahma ho jāye; sūrya Brahma Ohi Mālik. — *'Bapu'* signifies the body; here desires emanate from the bosom and from desire a child is born, because coitus with wife can never be performed without desire. But on continually practising *Kriyā* when the state of cessation of desires is achieved or the transcendental state of *Kriyā* is consummated then the self becomes *Brahma*. The *Ātmasūrya* is *Brahma*, He is the Master. If the breath ceases, desires cease. A *yogi* can perform all actions in the desireless state. ***Haṃsá Ómkarā so mánas hoi — phir śvāsā rahit ho jāye tab mánas sthir hoye arthād kshar akshar o niaksharkā dubdhā jāye — mūl arthād śvásā śirpar caḍhākar dālpāti sab dekhe.*** — What is *Haṃsá* is *Ómkāra*, which is the mind and in this state the mind is *Brahma*. When this mind becomes still it is *Brahma*, again when it becomes kinetic it is the mind. Continual practice of *Prâṇákarma* and *Ómkāra Kriyā* arrest the breath; when the external motion of breath is ceased and the *Kévala Kumbhaka* state achieved, the mind also becomes still. It is now that all types of transitory, perennial and ignorant doubts disappear, then there is neither duality nor non-duality because when the mind is absent, there is none to state about duality and non-duality, then everything merges in the Absolute Void *Brahma*. Only the one who undergoes this state can realize it but cannot know it, for knowing about it results in duality. Breath is the basis or actual. Because barring breath, this body cannot exist. Through *Prâṇákarma* and *Ómkāra Kriyā* raise that fundamental breath on the sinciput in the *Sahasrâra* and observe the root and leaves beneath i.e. after arriving at the basic still *Prâṇá* from the vibratory *Prâṇá*, all the senses, vices, organs which were functional then due to their habitat in the vibratory *Prâṇá* and the medium by which one would perceive this material world have become passive now, that state of theirs should be noticed, they are the branches of the trees. This can be explained by the example of a sudden radical transformation a person has undergone from abject poverty to affluence, living in a highrise he now empathetically observes the poor (his past condition) from this height. Hence the static state is the state of affluence whereas the kinetic state, the state of poverty. Observing this state of a *yogi*, God has remarked —

Ūrdhamūlamadhaḥśākhamaśvattham prāhurabyayam.
Chandāṃsi yasya parṇāni yastaṃ Veda sa Vedabid.

(*Gītā* 15/1)

Trees are deemed to possess branches above and roots beneath. But God has here stated the reverse : that the root is above and the branches are beneath. A tree of this reversed syndrome cannot be noticed anywhere but since God has referred to this, it definitely exists which is comprehensible to *yogis* only. Above the *Ājñācakrá*, the fundamental truth is the Infinite Soul essence and beneath is the body-like peepul (*Aśvatthá*) tree characterised by hands, feet, the senses etc. and it is about this which God has expatiated. *Aśvatthá* means transient, existent today, may not be existent in the future; this type of body is the *Aśvatthá* (peepul tree). From the root of this tree i.e. the area from *Ājñācakrá* to *Sahasrâra* which is the place of settlement for the still *Prâṇá-Brahma* and from here the dynamic *Prâṇá*-air by the manifestation of one's actions has extended; actions of the branchlike hands, feet and senses beneath again have proceeded from below to the different nerves till the head. All the *Vedas* are the leaves of this tree or the three attributes are like the leaves of this body-tree. One who is conversant in this manner about this body-like *Aśvatthá* tree's knowledgeable body essence, is the only *Veda*-conversant person. Thus Yogiraj has advised to halt the breath at the origin, the head and remaining in this state to observe the lower organs and the senselike branches beneath, for then the fallacy about the world will disappear and *Brahma*-knowledge will dawn. ***Śvāsā rahit yāne Kévala-Kumbhaka rātdin mánas leāoye āur āpnehiko āp dekhe — isikā nām Brahmajñāna.*** — *Kévala-Kumbhaka* is the state of cessation of breath which automatically occurs while practising regular *Prâṇâyāma*. Therefore perpetually keep the mind above for then the self can perceive the true-self, this is termed us *Brahma*-knowledge. Yogiraj has reiterated —

Halonā halonā halonā,
Pechan phire habe keman kore
Tā balanā balanā balanā.
Tríkoṇer madhye mánas pora
Upare caḍe dāine hoite bnādik pheranā,
Jaḍiye dhore mánas linger bhitar yoni
Tene dhore ṭhelā madhye madhye denā.
Ek hole ye majā se mukhe balā yāye nā;
Yoni linga ek hole eki majā mánas bai
Anya keha jāne nā. Kothāye linga
Kothāye yoni kemane milan haye balanā.

While executing *Ómkāra Kriyā* many a time apprehensions occur regarding the exactness of the performance of *Ómkāra Kriyā*. Generally kinetic mind remains substantially in front side of the body; it's existence at the back of the body is marginal. But *Ómkāra Kriyā* has to be executed at the back of the body. Therefore question arises in the mind as to how the mind will place itself at the back of the body and perform *Ómkāra Kriyā*, this the mind itself has to answer. Yogiraj then caused *Kūṭastha* to provide the answer that the kinetic mind has to be reposed in the triangle within *Kūṭastha*. The mind has to be mounted on the *Ājña Cakrá*, then rotated from right to left. After this the phallic kinetic mind has to be entered by intermittently thrusting into yonilike *Kūṭastha*. In this manner when the mind will enter *Kūṭastha*, the supreme bliss which will emanate is inexplicable. When the kinetic mind is united in *Kūṭastha*, the beatitude which originates can be explained by none other that the still mind. Then track of the entities of kinetic mind and triangular *Kūṭastha* is lost.

Through the medium of *Ómkāra Kriyā*, *yogis* can visualise a triangle within *Kūṭastha*. That triangle is the primordial source or origin, everything originates from there. The mind has to be entered there — the mind is the phallus. If the phallic mind is caused to enter, a dot or *Brahmāṇu* is visualised — that is the seedlike place of origin of the entire universe. He is *Bhagavān* (God). *Bhag* means the source, the origin or *Kūṭastha, vān* implies arrow and breath. Conducting breath inwardly, in other words continual practice of *Prâṇákarma* makes the mind still and the entrance into the *Kūṭastha* source or origin by the phallic mind gives rise to the tranquil state which is *Bhagavān*, God. *Kūṭastha* only is the source or origin and mind is the phallus and their conjoined symbol is the *Śivá Liṅgam* (phallus of *Śivá*). Therefore Yogiraj has quoted again — ***Bhagavad yāne bhagke māphik arthād jab jihvā nākke bhitar talumūlme jāye*** — When the tongue is raised upwards and enters the palatal cavity, the ecstasy derived then is *Bhagavad*, state of God. God has corroborated thus —

> ***Mama yonirmahadbrahma tasmin garvaṃ dadhāmyaham.***
> ***Sambhabaḥ sarvabhutānāṃ tato bhabati Bhārata.***
> ***Sarvayonishu Kaunteya mūrtayaḥ sambhabanti yāḥ.***
> ***Tāsāṃ Brahma mahadyoniraham bījapradaḥ pitā.*** (*Gītā* 14/3-4)

This verse denotes O *Bhārata*! My intense *Brahma* pervaded universelike state which exists is My source, because from that state everything originates. I place Myself in the manifestation of spiritual consciousness which is the cause for universal expansion i.e. the dynamic motion emanating from this state becomes the expression of different images. The Sublime *Brahma* pervasive consciousness of the *Prâṇá*-Soul which exists, can be expressed by *Prâṇákarma sādhana* when the mind is settled in the cave of *Kūṭastha* within the *Ājñācakrá*. The triangle within that glorious extensive *Kūṭastha* is the place of origin of that Sublime *Brahma* or the true place of origin. From this point of *Kūṭastha* the motion of vital breath is spread. The *Prâṇá*-Soul in that place of impregnation within that triangle by being settled in the form of *aṇu* or the dot later becomes distinguished as a body expansion of the dot. Thus from that magnificent *Brahma* place of origin, all elements are created in this manner. Likewise, whatever is being created from different wombs is the root of all Creation i.e. the Absolute *Brahma* or else motion being derived from that state many images arise from various wombs and He is prevalent as the Master in all these. Whatever occurs from small innumerable wombs, all such wombs are separable but the inseparable *Brahma* is the Supreme Place of Origin, for this reason He is the Mother; and I only am the Father because in the aforementioned triangle the form of the dot which exists subtly like an *aṇu* is Myself, thus I dwell within Myself in this manner. As an expansion of that dot, I express many images which are similar to the transformation of *Kūṭastha*, thus My fatherlike self is born as the son; the metamorphosis of the father becomes the son, therefore I only am the Master of impregnation, the Father. Thus Yogiraj has reiterated — ***Tríkon téjas rūpáki balihāri jāi*** — The Absolute *Brahma*like triangular place of origin is intensely effulgent. Yogiraj has further penned — ***Jyotirmoy yoni dekhā*** — I have visualised the resplendent place of origin. Again — ***Jyotirmoy yoni — raktavarṇa kāmbīj dekhā*** — I saw the effulgent place of origin and the blood-red seed of passion. Sometimes He has remarked — ***Bhagavatīkā yoni Mahādevakā liṅga dekhā*** — I have seen the place of origin of *Bhagavatī* and the phallus of *Mahādeva* from where creation emanates. Again He has written — ***Ek baḍā choṭā sarsoke māphik bindi ohi baḍā dipakke māphik huyā phir ek choṭā nákshatrake māphik huyā. Iha bindihi asal haye — ehi sab khel dekhlātā haye.*** — An extremely minute mustard seedlike dot could be envisioned within that triangle. This only became like a big lamp or became manifest, later I observed it became like a small star. That dot is real for that only shows the play of birth, death etc. On another day He has noted — ***Jyotirmoy liṅga dekhā — ehi Mahādevakā liṅga āur Kishnjikā ūrdhapuccha*** — I envisioned the resplendent phallus, the symbol of which can be seen in the material world in the form of *Śiváliṅga* and in the form of the peacock plume on *Bhagavān* Krishna's head. It's allegory is the sandalwood or clay paste painted on the forehead of *Śaivas* and *Vaishṇavas*. It originally symbolises the three folds occurring on the forehead (*Trāṭaka*) during *Kriyā* practice. He has repeated — ***Ūrdhapuṇdra Vísvánāthkā liṅga dekhā*** — While I was in *trāṭaka* position, I perceived *Vísvánāth's* phallus. Drawing a triangle and a resplendent phallus, He has written beside it — ***Óm tríkoṇ — jyotirūpá lāl dorā sushumnākā kināre mehin dekhā — pahale jyotirmoy liṅga dekhā phir śūnyame samāye gayā — barā majā roknese chaycakrá jyotke bhitar dekhlātā haye. Apūrva jyotirūpá praṇām korite dekhāye. Sarpākār jyotirūpá liṅger upar dekhāye*** — I visualised beside the *Sushumná* a fine resplendent red stripe within the *Ómkāra* triangle. I first saw the resplendent phallus, later it merged in the Infinite Void. When there is a cessation of breath then immense happiness ensues and within the resplendence, the six *cakrás* of the *Sushumná* can be perceived. While practising *Prâṇâyāma* a wonderful resplendence can be visualised, again resplendence resembling the form of a serpent can be noticed on the phallus. ***Ek sundarī kāmbīj dekhā*** — I perceived a beautiful seed of passion. ***Yonirūpā ādyāśakti dekhā*** — I envisioned the magnificient *Brahma* Primordial Female Energy which was like the place of origin also, from where everything originates. ***Cār Veda o Brahmā Víshṇu Mahêśa virājmān yonike bhitar dekhā.*** — I envisioned a triangle which is like the Primordial Female Energy and Sublime *Brahma* where four *Vedas* and *Brahmā*, *Víshṇu* and *Mahêśa* are prevalent. Because of the augmentation of the *Sattva* attribute all the deities can be perceived. This is not the end, further advancement has to be effected, the attributelesss state has to be achieved for the *Sattva* attribute also is an attribute. The *yoni* and the *liṅga* have to be united and made one but how? ***Arjuna madsyaveda vāna mārnā cāhiye — Prâṇâyāmase Brahmajñāna hotā haye — tiske bād Ómkāra — Ómkāra so Rāma haye sādho karo bicār — pahale śi aysā āoj bhitarse hoye, piche óm isise sohaṃ kahātā haye — Paramáhaṇsa kahe — uskebād Ómkāra iha agādh mat — yāne samādhi haye — pávanako suratme mánas lagāke burā bhalā sab mālum ho jāye — isike anubhav kahate***

haye. — On executing excellent *Prâṇâyāma* with a definite aim similar to the shooting of Arjuna's arrow aimed at the reflection of the fish's eye, knowledge about *Brahma* can be derived, after this *Ómkāra Kriyā* is practised, that *Ómkāra* is *Rāma*, *Kriyābāns*, should consider this. Execution of excellent *Prâṇâyāma* results in a *śi-śi* sound (a similar sound occurs if a key-hole is blown) which is the *Praṇáva* sound. Continual practice of this and merging with the *Praṇáva* sound results in the achievement of 'I am He' state. After this in the *Ómkāra* or in *Nirvikalpa samādhi* when imagination or alternatives do not exist, if one arrives at such a *samādhi* everyone harbours only one singular opinion, because non-duality becomes absent then. In this manner by practising excellent *Prâṇákarma*, there is a cognition of the substantial and insubstantial objects or of good and evil, this is perception. Thus Yogiraj chanted —

Mánas āynā monete dekho.
Cnād badani cokhete.
Lāgā mánas Ómkārete.
Pābe majā kata se dhvanite.

See the kinetic mind within the mirrorlike serene mind through the beautiful *Kūtastha* in all His glory. If the mind adheres to the *Ómkāra* sound, a great deal of joy can be achieved.

Mánas jāsne mánas jāsne jāsnere kothā.
Mánas diye mánaske dekhle habe sakal bṛithā.

The mind should not deviate. If the kinetic mind is perceived with it's kineticism, then everything will become fruitless.

Indir karma indir kare,
Mánas keno knede mare;
Āchāḍ kheye paḍe mare,
Madhye madhye nakal kare.

The senses perform their sensory functions; influenced by the senses the mind becomes dependent on this. Emulating the senses, the mind loses it's ability to distinguish between the right and the wrong; thus it becomes the recipient of happiness and misery.

It is the disposition of the kinetic mind to emulate whatever it sees or whatever appears in it's presence, in this manner it vacillates, thus suffers anguish. But the moment the kinetic mind is stilled, nothing else remains. Where is the place of origin of this mind ? ***Dhvanike antargat jyot yo jyotiki sūryase ātā haye — uske bhitar mánas haye — ohi mánasme laye honā Víshṇukā yo padá haye — isime śvāsā samāye jātā haye.*** — The effulgence within the sound is emerging from the Soul-Sun, the mind is settled within it. This is the still mind. To merge with this mind is the state, *Víshṇu*; the breath merges in this state of *Víshṇu* or what is the still mind is the *Víshṇu* state. The breath commences and ends here. Yogiraj has again mentioned — ***Jyotke bād mánas nirākar rūpá Nirmal rūpáme mánasko laye karnā cāhiye.*** — The place of settlement of the still mind is beyond the pure Soul-Effulgence which is amorphous. The kinetic mind has to be merged in that pure form. ***Manete yeṭā haye śarīreo seiṭe haye, maner āvaraṇ gele śarīrer āvaraṇ yāibe kramaśaḥ.*** — What occurs mentally occurs physically also, when the mental illusion is removed, the physical illusion will gradually be removed. Thus He intoned —

Ómkāra dhvanir śonre sur
Yekhāne jyoti pracur.
Dekha dekha surer bhitar kaṭa sur
Mánas sadā taite pur.
Abhyāsete habe sabur
Dárśana habe Mahāprabhur.
Dhara dhara ṭene sur
Kāṭa sab diye ai kshur.

Kriyābāns, keep on listening to the *Ómkāra* sound, where a great deal of effulgence abounds. Observe the various deities within the *Ómkāra* sound. Perpetually keep the mind on the *Ómkāra* sound with patience, this can be developed through continual practice and subsequently *Bhagavān* can be visualised. Hold that *Ómkāra* sound, worldly delusion has to be severed with that razor.

Mánas bāre bāre jápa sadā tāre
Yejan antareri antar
Sadā thāke antare.
Bhāb bine bhāb kemane habe
Cintay sei dhvanire.
Yakhan dākbi tāre
Biralete dhyāna dhare.
Mánas niye mánas deto sure
Advutá rūpá dekho antare.

The mind should constantly think about *Bhagavān* Who is Inherent and perpetually dwells in the innermost realm. How can love emanate without love; it will occasion itself by ruminating upon that *Ómkāra* sound. When you remember Him in a secluded atmosphere through *dhyāna*, place the kinetic mind with the help of the still mind on that *Ómkāra* sound, for then there will be an intrinsic marvellous visualisation.

Kase dhare ṭān ṭāno
Kena śono ven venāno
Amūlya dhan Kālī jeno
Hṛidpadme base āchen
Cesṭā kare dharanā keno
Kare ekānta manano
Dudh ghi khāonā keno
Nirjanete ṭān ṭāno.

Why do you pay attention to the constant prattle, instead it would be better to practise *Prâṇákarma* doggedly. Know that

Goddess *Kālī* is the invaluable wealth. She dwells in the *Anāhata* lotus, why do not you strive to retain Her in deep concentration; consume milk and it's products like butter, ghee etc. which impart strength and practise *Prâṇákarma* in solitude.

The *śi-śi* sound of *Prâṇákarma* is the razor, everything has to be severed with that razor, for then stillness will be attained and attaining stillness will result in the attributeless state (absence of *Sattva, Rájas, Támas*) which will cause the conquest of the cycle of births and deaths. Therefore He asserted — ***Mánasme kuch nahi, dhyāna dharo sabkuch haye.*** — There is nothing in the mind, concentrate in *dhyāna,* everything can be achieved. He further declared — ***Dhokā denā — yāne mánas yo khāli haye uskā deke mánasme yo Paraméśvarakā rūpá ho jānā — isiko Bāṅglāme phāki diye neyā kahātā haye.*** — Deceiving infers the offering of the vacuous mind after it reaches the vacuous state, that is reposing the kinetic mind in the still mind, then the still mind becomes the embodiment of the Form of the Supreme Being. This in the Bengali language denotes attainment through deception. Here the kinetic mind is deceived into entering the still mind which is the attainment. ***Jisko bātkā ṭhikānā nahi uskā bāp yāne Bhagavānkābhi ṭhikānā nahi*** — This implies when the mind is kinetic words have no significance, it constantly vacillates. Thus as long as the mind will remain restless, it will be remotely distant from the still *Brahma.* Regarding the offering of the mind, the tenth chapter of *Śrīmadbhāgavata* has a remarkable narrative. While visiting *Bhagavān* Krishna, the *gopinīs*[1] desired to take some offerings alongwith them. But what offering should they take? He possesses everything. The *gopinīs* contemplated that they have to offer Him such an object which He did not possess. Eventually, they discovered that *Bhagavān* has everything excepting the mind, which they possessed

1. *Gopis* and *Gopinīs* infer the male and female devotees respectively of *Bhagavān* Krishna who practise *Ātmakarma.*

in abundance. Therefore they offered their minds completely to *Bhagavān*. This denotes that *Bhagavān* does not possess the kinetic mind, therefore He has no mind, but this mind is borne by the *gopinīs*. They ceased their restless mind through *Prâṇákarma* and reposing the restless mind on the still mind, stilled their restless mind or became mindless. This is known as the offering of mind to God. ***Bhīshma yāne dar — yabtak śirme tin bān arthād iḍā piṅgalā o sushumná nahi milā tabtāi uha sthir nahi hot haye joki agni yāne téjas karke na māre piche Ómkāra dhvani varṇame sunātā haye.*** — *Bhīshma* infers existence of fear (fear to practise austere *sādhana*), until the three arrows of *iḍā*, *piṅgalā* and *sushumná* do not merge ín the head, till then there is no tranquillity and as long as the air is not stilled, fear will persist. Thus if excellent *Prâṇákarma* is executed with force the air becoming still eventually, the *Ómkāra* sound becomes audible and remaining absorbed in it will give birth to the still state. Thus as long as the dynamism of *Prâṇá* persists a human remains petty, but the moment he achieves the still state he metamorphoses into supremity. In this regard, Yogiraj chanted —

Śarīrer dharma śarīr kare
Tumi kena mara āmi āmi kare,
Yadi keha haite tumi esaṃsāre
Akhaṇḍa brahmāṇḍa jagadmaya tumi,
Tomā binā āche ke jagater svāmi.
Amūlya dhan mánas tāhāke bujha tumi,
Sei karāye tomāye jagader svāmi.
Āmi bale berāo jagate tumi,
Tomā chāḍā āche ke jagate Prabhu,
Tannimitte āpnāke āpni dekha sei Prabhu.
Tabe pāibe ānandámayī ānandá,
Takhani tomār habe paramānandá.
Cintā kara kena dibānisi mánas,
Tomā binā bandhu nāhi anyajan.

The functions of the body are performed by the body itself but how can you contemplate that it is the self which performs; in actuality you do not pertain to this world for you are the pervasion of the indivisible universe, who else other than you is the Controller of the universe? The mind is invaluable, try to comprehend it, for it will make you the Absolute. You are obsessed with egotism, but barring you in the real self who else is the Master, for that reason regard yourself as the Supreme. You will acquire the blissful ecstasy when you will attain the state of supreme bliss. O mind, why do you perpetually concern yourself with material thoughts, excepting you there is no real friend.

On 4th January 1873, Yogiraj recounted — ***Sūryanārāyaṇá Ómkārakā rūpá dekhā — śarīr bahut halkā huyā saphed pardā ānkhke sāmne mālum huyā phir sūryake bhitar Kisunkā rūpá — ohi jagadmay — sattva, rájas, támas rūpá pnāc tattvame milā padārth āur sab tattva usse nikasā —yane nirmal Brahma.*** — I visualized the *Ātmasūrya Nārāyaṇá*like *Ómkāra* Form, the body became light by regular practice of *Prâṇákarma* and then I realized a whitish opacity before my eyes. After this illusion disappeared, I saw the Form of Bhagavan Krishna within the *Ātmasūrya*, Who was Omnipresent, that was the form of the three attributes of *sattva, rájas* and *támas*. All elements mingled in the five essences and I also viewed that those five essences were emanating from that *Ātmasūrya* which is the pure crystalline *Brahma*. On 19th April 1873, He wrote — ***Āpnāhi Svárūpa Nārāyaṇákā dekhā. Ehi Āpnā Rūpá haye phir ehi nirākār Ómkāra haye. Ohi Ómkāra ādi Veda haye.*** — I saw *Nārāyaṇá* , My Own Form. This is the own form and again this is the amorphous *Ómkāra*. That formless *Ómkāra* is the *Vedas* in it's origin. Yogiraj delineated on 3rd June 1873 — ***Ab Svárūpa dárśana huyā — woh Rūpá tríkūṭike bhitar haye — haṉsá usko kahe jab saṉsai jāye āur safed dekhe āur sudh bhitar bhitar āoye āur jāye yo āj huyā — baḍā majā*** — Now the visualisation of the reality of self occurred, this visualisation occurs within the triangle of *Kūṭastha*, that is known as *Haṇsá*, then all types of scepticism are eliminated and everything appears to be white because white does not pertain to the category of colour. It infers neutrality. That only is the holy state which arrives and departs from within, this occurred today. I derived immense pleasure from this. Yogiraj penned His realizations further on 19th June 1873 — ***Kūṭastha akshar Nārāyaṇáke rūpá hojātā haye*** — The imperishable *Kūṭastha* became the form of *Nārāyaṇá*. The next day 20th June, He wrote — ***Āpnā Rūpáse bhinna rūpá dekh paḍā. Nārāyaṇákā rūpá antar dṛishtime mālum hotā haye*** — I envisioned a different form within My Real Self. The form of *Nārāyaṇá* can be visualized in the intra -vision. He remarked on 8th July 1873 — ***Ek Svet Púrusha Āpne māphik dekhā*** — I perceived a white Being akin to Myself . On 28th July 1873, He wrote — ***Āpnā rūpá dekhā — Nārāyaṇákā Rūpá haye — baḍā majā — ab kām karṇeme āskat huyā.*** — I perceived the self in reality which is the form of *Nārāyaṇá*, now I feel very blissful and am lazy to perform actions, it seems that I should remain passive. During this period, He would execute *sādhana* throughout the night, thus He effected endeavours on His part to conquer sleep. Therefore He portrayed on 11th August 1873 — ***Āj bnāsulikā āoāz ācchā huyā śūnyá bhavan mil rahanā cāhiye — rātkā sonā kaise na ho — iskā kosis kareṅge. Nesā āur gāḍhā o śūnyá āur sāf*** — The flutelike sound emanating in excellent *Prâṇâyāma* which is known as the *Ómkāra* sound has occurred splendidly today and through the medium of this *Ómkāra* sound I arrived at the Infinite Void (*Brahma*) which is beyond that sound, I have to mingle and merge there; but to attain this mergence the time for prolonged *sādhana* which is required, cannot be derived while maintaining a family existence, thus *sādhana* has to be continued throughout the night and to execute this sleep has nevertheless to be conquered, now I am striving for this. Now the engrossment in *Prâṇákarma* has intensified and the void *Brahma* has attained more clarity. 14th August 1873 — ***Ab rātme nid kam ātā haye — baḍā sthir baḍā nesā.*** — Now I am experiencing less sleepiness in the night, practising continual action I have become extremely tranquil and am undergoing a deep engrossment. On 7th October 1873, He wrote — ***rātko nid na āoe.*** — Sleep is no longer plaguing Me in the night, it has been conquered wholly, thus there is no inconvenience now to practise *Prâṇákarma* throughout the night. Body-consciousness is prevalent as long as *Prâṇá* is vibratory, thus sleep is also required then. But when regular practice of *Prâṇákarma* stills *Prâṇá*, sleep is not required thereby making a *yogi* accustomed of being in *samādhi* for a long period of time in this manner. He does not require oxygen also. All beings inhale oxygen and exhale carbon dioxide. Inhaling oxygen likewise makes each cell active and since they are active, carbon-dioxide has to be exhaled. But when a *yogi* through *yóga* action is capable to cease the function of each and every cell of his body, then he can exist without oxygen, exhalation is absent then. In this state though the cells remain non-functional for a prolonged period they are not destroyed. When a *yogi* returns to his normal state or the awakened state then again all the cells alongwith the heart, lungs and brain resume the intake of oxygen thus rendering all these organs active, the motion of external breath commences functioning which is referred to as the dynamic state of *Prâṇá*. Ramprosad keeping this in mind is quoted to have said — ***Yār ghum tāre diye ghumere ghum pāḍāyechi.*** —Sleep is necessary in the vibratory state of *Prâṇá* and not in the still state. Therefore the sleep in this vibratory state was returned to this state itself and he achieved stillness or arrived at *Kriyā's* transcendental state.

Yogiraj would expand — ***Sakala dhármer gupta marma ye mahādyuti Kūṭastha tāhāke jānā cāi. Dhárma arthād Kriyā. Satyá, Tretā, Dvāpára balite kramaśaḥ Kriyār hrās haye arthād samādhi***

haite vijñānapad, vijñānapad haite jñāna, ār jñāna haite Kriyā kam. Satyáyuge Kūṭasthe thākā, Tretāte Kūṭastha dekhā, Dvāpáre Kriyār dvārāye ānanda lāv karā, Káliyuge Kriyā deoyā. — The sublimely radiant *Kūṭastha* which is the abstruse significance of *dhárma* should be realized. *Dhárma* implies *Kriyā* (*Prâṇákarma*). In the *Satyá, Trétā* and *Dvāpára* ages this *Prâṇákarma* gradually declines, in other words the state of *samādhi* declines to the state of highest knowledge, the state of highest knowledge to knowledge and from knowledge to the decrement of *Kriyā*. The *Satyá* age represents permanent settlement in *Kūṭastha*; the *Trétā* age represents visualisation of *Kūṭastha*; the *Dvāpára* age symbolises happiness derived from the practice of *Kriyā* and *Káliyuga* symbolises the imparting of *Kriyā*. He further explained — ***Satyá arthād Kriyār parābasthā, Tréta arthād Kriyār parābasthār par, Dvāpára arthād Kriyā karār samay ebaṃ Káli arthād Kriyā nā karā abasthā.*** — *Satyá* signifies the transcendental state of *Kriyā*; *Trétā*, the pre-transcendental state of *Kriyā*; *Dvāpára*, the period of practice of *Kriyā* and *Káli* signifies the state of not practising *Kriyā*. Thus these four ages have to be comprehended within this body itself. Commenting about the esotericism of the *śāstrás* He has quoted — ***Veda samudāye dhármer mūl arthād kriyār dvārāye sab jānā jāye. Śruti arthād binā kathāye yāhā sonā yāye, smṛíti arthād śune ye smaraṇa karā ihāi marma kathita, mánushyete sthir kariyāche Kriyā kariyā kirtike pāye ihaloke mare Brahmete līn haiyā param sukh prāpti haye.*** — The four *Vedas* are the basis of *dhárma*, or everything can be comprehended through *Kriyā*. *Śruti* implies that which can be heard without being spoken, *smṛíti* denotes remembering by hearing or the significant truth; man has determined that practice of *Kriyā* leads to glory and Supreme bliss can be attained by dying in this mortal world and merging in *Brahma*. He has further expatiated — ***Kathā binā yāhā śonā yāye tāhār nām śruti tāhā jānār nām Veda, tāhā smaraṇa kariyā yāhā ek padārth arthād Kriyā tāhār nām śāstrá; ai Veder arthād śruti smṛíti mimāṃsā haibār yo nāi kāraṇ hathād āsiyā pare tāhāri***

dvārāye Kriyā karite karite prakāś haye. Veda smṛíti sadācār arthād Kriyā ār ātmār priya arthād sthir howyā ei cār sākshād dhárma — arthād Kriyār lakshman jānā yāye. — *Śruti* is that which can be heard without words, knowing this is the *Vedas*; remembering it is oneness, this is *Kriyā*, again this is the *śāstrá*; there is no means by which the settlement of *Vedas* or hearing and remembrance can occur because it appears abruptly, again it manifests by regular practice of *Kriyā*. The *Vedas*, remembrance, righteousness and *Kriyā* are dear to the soul or else these entail stillness. These four only are *dhárma* or by this way the characteristic of *Kriyā* can be learnt.

Having faith in the dictum of the *Gurú* if this *Kriyā* is practised like the act of ferrying , the material worldlike river can be traversed and Yogiraj has described it on 11th December 1873, thus — ***Ómkāra svetrūpá — ohi jaláká rūpá ohi ādi rūpá—sahajá svabhāb śūnyákā sahajá Gurú bākyame bíśvās karnese sahajá sahajá Kriyā kare to pār utre haye — jaisā koi dubtā haye āur koi taernewālekā kamar isārese pakaḍke dono taer karke pārlage āur lagāoe āur āgar woh jor karke pakaḍeto āp dube āur bacāne wālekobhi dubāoe waisehi Gurú celā — kneoki yo Gurú soi celā*** — The *Ómkāra* form which is colourless is the form of water, that is the Primordial Form, settling in that Infinite Void it becomes the natural disposition or the self form or the normal state and the present dynamic state of *Prâṇá* then goes beyond nature. Completely abiding by the *Gurú's* dictum if this *Kriyā* is regularly practised then the cycle of births and deaths of this material world can be overcome. For instance when someone is drowning and another person comes to save him, at that moment if the drowning person holds his rescuer's waist gently then both can get to the shore, but if he holds the waist with a firm grasp[1] then both drown; the

1. When the words 'gently' and 'firm grasp' pertaining to the *Gurú*-disciple relationship are used their implications are reversed. 'Gently' here conveys the spiritual interaction between *Gurú* and disciple and 'firm grasp' the material relationship between *Gurú* and disciple which is taboo.

relationship between these two persons is similar to the relationship between *Gurú* and disciple, because the one who is *Gurú* is the disciple. ***Ekke ānkh uṭhā bimāri dekhnese bahut der tak jaysā uskā chuyā chutse uskobhi ānkh ātā haye oyesā Kūṭastha aksharko dekhnesebhi ohi rūpá ho jātā haye — isme sandeha nahi.*** — When a person suffers from an eye inflammation if another observes this inflammation for a long moment or if there is direct contact his eyes become inflamed, similarly continual practice of *Kriyā* results in the regular imperishable *Kūṭastha* visualisation, thus the self becomes converted into the *Kūṭastha* state, there is no doubt about this. Therefore Yogiraj chanted —

Hari bhajan binā nāiko gati,
Jini agatir paramgati;
Sekhāne gele nāi punarāgaman,
Indriya sab habe āpni daman.
Sukh sekhānkār ke balbe keman.
Jār haynā kakhano nidhan,
Ye peyeche amūlya dhan;
Atul sukher ke koribe varṇan,
Bhakti hole pābe caraṇ.

There is no respite other than invoking *Bhagavān*, Who is the only Resort of the helpless; by achieving that state there is a cessation of rebirths. All the senses will become self-restrained; none can express the bliss of this state which is indestructible; who else can describe the supreme bliss other than the one who has achieved the invaluable wealth; everyone will gain access to the Holy Feet on acquiring devotion.

On 24th August 1873, He recorded — ***Vāsanā choḍ de to khud Vāsudeva hoye. Vāsu = vāsanā, deva = Mālik.***[1] ***Yab vāsanāko choḍe to khud Mālik hoye — Humhi sūryakā rūpá*** — If all types of aspirations are abandoned, the self can become *Vāsudeva* or the

1. *Deva* = Sanskrit conjugation *divá* meaning the void.

Master. While practising regular *Prâṇákarma* when the self-entity merges and everything attains the void essence, then the self attains Masterdom because that Crystalline Void *Brahma* is Omnipresent. He is the Master. Yogiraj thereby intoned —

Tum kabhi mad choḍo
uha snaiko
Jabtak na milāoye
āpko.

Never forsake God until you become confluent in Him.

On 3rd May 1873, He remarked — ***Humhi sũryakā rūpá nirmal jyoti — jab nirmal jyoti dekhte haye tab Hum choḍāy dusrā koi na dekhte haye — lekan ab nirmal jyotme samānā cāhiye*** — I am the *Ātmasũrya* Holy Effulgence, when I visualise that Holy Effulgence none but Me visualises it, but now merging should occur in that Holy Effulgence, the Effulgence and Myself have to become One and attain merging. The next day He wrote — ***Yo bindi soi sũrya — ab ghar ujiyālā hotā haye.*** — The cynosurelike dot which is perceived in *Kũṭastha* is *Ātmasũrya* and everything is becoming distinct in this *Ātmasũrya* visualisation. The next day on 5th May He commented — ***Nirmal jyoti Bhagavānkā haye — jyoti ākāśke māphik.*** — The Holy Resplendence of *Bhagavān* is like void. 12th August, 1873 — ***Āsmānke tríkuṭime akshar phir usise jyotrūpá — uskā baḍā nirmal rūpá*** — the voidlike triangle within *Kũṭastha* is supremely imperishable and later effulgence emanates from there, it is extremely pure. 28th August 1873 — ***Jihvá jab tālumūlme lagtā haye tab khaṭṭā miṭhā swād mālum hotā haye — āur gāḍhā — ab bahut sthir haye — āj Prâṇâyāma thoḍa huā — Ómkārkā dhvani piche taraf sunātā haye.*** — When the tongue is raised upwards and enters the palatal cavity then the sour and sweet tastes can be realized. Today, *Prâṇâyāma* being more intense, further stillness was achieved and the *Ómkāra* sound could be heard in the occiput. On 12th November 1873, He drew a dot within *Kũṭastha* and wrote beside it — ***Ehi agam sthān haye isime ṭhaharnā cāhiye.*** — The still dot within *Kūṭastha* is the inaccessible place, one has to pause at this still dot, if the mind is restless even for a brief while that dot cannot become still. Continually practising *Prâṇákarma* when everything ceases, then the state of going beyond the mind and desires is acquired and then dot also becomes still. The present kinetic mind and intellect of a living being are unable in reaching that static dot, thus Yogiraj expressed it to be the inaccessible place. One has to affix in that inaccessible still dot. He recounted on 7th December 1873 — ***Iha śarīrke bhitar dusrā ek śarīr haye aisehī lekin kālā*** — within this body there is another similar body but it is black. This is known as the visualisation of the own self. Just as the own body can be observed while standing before a mirror similarly practising continual *Prâṇákarma* when the mind becomes still before the mirrorlike *Kūṭastha*, then the own form is perceived which is the size of a thumb. That is the causal body. The body is of three types — gross, subtle and causal. The subtle body is within the gross body and the causal body is within the subtle body; at sleep the gross and subtle bodies release themselves from the senses and lie dormant, but the causal body does not lie dormant. It is the container and shelter for the other two bodies. Yogiraj chanted —

Māyā rakho maye choḍo
Satpar āge baḍho
Siḍhi siḍhi āge caḍho
Tab hogā sukh baḍo
Jhuṭe mansubā kyā gaḍo
Śrīmān sāmne khaḍo
Ohi ānkhpar paḍo
Phir ekhi ho paḍo.

Dispel illusion, abandon egotism and proceed towards the path of righteousness ahead; rhythmically ascend, for then you will derive immense happiness; what falsities does the mind entertain; a beatific vision of the Primordial Being has appeared; concentrate on Him for then you will merge and become one.

Galeme miṭhā mālum huyā āur bhitar bhitar calā āur baḍā neśā mālum huyā aisā hameśā cāhiye. — The tongue being lifted upwards entered the palatal cavity, then I derived a sweet taste and breathing continued internally. The deep engrossment which occurred in this state is constantly required. ***Nirmal Brahma Mālik, Brahma jalákā rūpá haye, Brahmai sárvamáya.*** — The crystalline non-illusory pure *Brahma* is the Master of everything because everything is created from that *Brahma*. *Brahma* is the form of water; because water is formless; it assumes the respective forms of the containers it is stored in. This type of Amorphous Void *Brahma* is Omnipresent. ***Sūrya Hamārā rūpá yo Ómkāra haye ohi sthir ghar yānekā rastā haye.*** — *Ātmasūrya* only is My Form, that is *Ómkāra*, that is the path for reaching the still state because repeated visualisations of that *Ātmasūrya* result in a *yogi* attaining the state of stillness, where visualisations and realisations are absent. ***Nākke upar tākke bhouke upar kapālke bicme tākke ṭhahar rahanā kaṭhin haye — isise sthitipad yāne samādhi hotā haye.*** — It is extremely difficult to be steadfast keeping the eyes in a raised position on the forehead above the nose between the eyebrows, but if one can remain in this manner the state of settlement or *samādhi* can be attained.[1] ***Jihvā dahine nākke chedme ghusā phir bāye chedke bhitar ek angul — ab khicnesebhi si aisā śabd ātā haye āur pheknesebhi.*** — The tongue being uplifted entered the right nostril, later entered a finger's width in the left nostril. In this condition inhalation and exhalation of internal *Prâṇāyāma* occurs, the *śi-śi* sound emanates during excellent *Prâṇâyāma*. ***Jihvā dono nākke chedme upar calā āur yo śūnyá bāhar soi bhitar dekhlāi detā haye.*** — The tongue was further uplifted, crossed both the

1. One should never practise this action by reading books or by not deriving education regarding this from the proper teacher. One should be seated in this position after prolonged *Prâṇâyāma*.

inner nostrils and went more upwards within. Executing *Prâṇákarma* in this state I could visualise the crystalline infinite void everywhere, externally as well as internally; the external and internal attained oneness. ***Ākāś Nārāyaṇá haye — Brahma dhyāna āsal haye hṛidayme sthita haye satya rūpá haye — māyā dhokā —*** This crystalline infinite voidlike sky is *Nārāyaṇá. Brahma-dhyāna* is veritable and everyone should perform it.[1] Through the dexterity of *Ṭhokar Kriyā* (which can be acquired exclusively from the *Gurú*) when the obstruction of *Anāhata cakrá* is released, then it attains a permanence and thus attaining causes the manifestation of truth, the illusory dynamism prior to this is a deception and untrue. ***Āur majā sthir gharkā ohā mālum hotā haye bahut dertak ṭhahare haye — nirmal ākāśbad Brahma mālum hotā haye.*** —Arriving at the static state, I derived immense ecstasy and I comprehended also that I settled in that state for a long period. I realized the crystalline, pure Absolute Void-*Brahma*. He has further noted — ***Sthir vāyute thākile hṛidaya emat nirmal haye ye kathā kohile hṛidaye dhākkā ihā anubhav haye. Khecari hoile ākāśetei caliyā jāye arthād calāye kona kleśbodh haye nā. Icchā haite ahaṃkār sei icchā sthir hoilei buddhi tini Īśvará. Alabdha dhan pāile yerūpá tṛipta mánas haye tad sahasragun samādhite mánas tṛipta haye — Brahma suddha arthād kono drabya hoite nirgata haye nāi arthād ucchishṭa naye.*** The *Anāhata* is purified to such an extent when remaining in the still air that while talking a thrust on the heart is sensed. After *Khecari* is attained access in the void takes place, this implies that in the sublime path the spiritually subtle movement is non-harrowing and effortless. Pride stems from desire and when this desire is stilled intelligence dawns which is *Bhagavān*. After attaining *samādhi* the still mind is steeped in contentment thousandfold more than the satisfaction derived from acquiring wealth which was not supposed to be achieved — *Brahma* is pure

1. The opinion which the *paṇḍitás* express is that *dhyāna* on the amorphous attributeless *Brahma* is not possible. This is a misconception, hence incorrect.

because He has not emanated from any source, thus is not ort. While worshipping *Nārāyaṇá* or *Śivá*, the holy ablution of the deities first has to be performed, then they have to be worshipped after which *dhyāna* on these deities should be accomplished as has been stipulated by the injunctions and rule of superficial worship. But Yogiraj declares — ***Mahādever prathame snāna tārpar dhyāna ihā asambhav, kāraṇ prathame dhyāna ucit chilo — matlab — Ātmāke jānā ucit Brahma tannimitta prathame snān āpnār ābaśyak pare dhyāna.*** — It is impossible to first perform Holy Ablution of *Mahādeva* and then *dhyāna*, because first *dhyāna* should occur — inferring that the soul should be comprehended i.e. the self should be steeped in the soul first, after which *dhyāna* should be practised. Likewise, He would lay greater stress upon internal *sādhanā*. Therefore it is noticed that though He has not undertaken all apparent pilgrimages, He has undertaken all pilgrimages internally. The internal pilgrimage symbolises the external pilgrimage. Yogiraj has proclaimed — ***Kūṭastha akshar āsal rūpá Ómkārakā yāne svāsā hamesā dhāraṇ karnese Baladevakā nām Haladhar huyā, uha candramārūpi Pravās tīrtháme (Candrakā uday honā pravās tīrthá haye) pahale snān kiyā piche phir sushumná uday honese Kūṭastha akshar dekhā tab Sárasvatī nadī snān kiyā — phir yab svāsā sthir huyā tab agnitīrthánāmāme snān kiyā — phir yab pañcaśrotā jab nikase tab Pañcabadarikā nāmā tīrthásnān kiyā.***— The imperishable *Kūṭastha* is the real form of *Ómkarā*, in other words if the breath is borne constantly or if *Kévala-Kumbhaka* is automatically achieved for a prolonged period, then the name of *Baladeva* becomes *Haladhar*, because *Prâṇá* air is strength, thus air is *Baladeva* and *Haladhar* (one who bears the plough). The dark moon visualised in *Kūṭastha* is the *Pravās* pilgrimage, I performed My ablution in that pilgrimage first; then when *Sushumná* emerged I envisioned the imperishable *Kūṭastha*, that is bathing in river Sarasvati. Later when breath became completely still, then I bathed in the fire-pilgrimage. Again when the five currents emerged or the current of ambrosia cascaded from the *Sahasrâra* then I bathed in the pilgrimage of the five *Badris*. Thus in this manner Yogiraj has effected all pilgrimages within His own body. Undertaking external pilgrimages does not cause soul-attainment. The *śāstrás* have similarly stated —

> ***Idaṃ tīrthámidaṃ tīrtháṃ bhramanti***
> ***tāmasā janaḥ.***
> ***Ātmatīrtháṃ na jānanti***
> ***Kathaṃ mokshaṃ barānane.*** (*Jñānasaṅkalinī Tántra*)

This implies that ignorant and vicious persons wander from one pilgrimage to the other. Dear *sādhaka*, until you are aware about the soul-pilgrimage, you cannot attain salvation.

Yogiraj has repeated — ***Gáṅgājiki lahar ānkh mudke thoḍā thoḍā dekhā*** — Closing My eyes I could view little of the waves of the *Sushumná*-Ganges. This is termed to be the play of *Sushumnā* waves. He has delineated the picture of *Hara-Pārvatī* Who exist on the peak of Mount Kailash and written beside it — ***Śirke ādhe upar Kailāś pāhāḍ yāne sahajádal padma jisme Har-Pārvatī birājmān dūrse dekhā yāye*** — Mount Kailash is located in the *Sahasrâra* where *Hara-Pārvatī* prevail and this can be distantly visualised. Kashi is situated above the Trident of *Mahâdeva*, the Trident is the three attributes of *Iḍā*, *Piṅgalā* and *Sushumná*. Kashi signifies the state of revelation and *Mahâdeva* signifies *Sushumná* which is the *Sattva* attribute. Drawing a sketch of the *Gomukhi* (a holy cave in the Himalayas shaped like a cow's mouth) He has mentioned beside it — ***Gomukhi dekhā*** — I envisioned the pilgrimage of Gomukhi in *Kūṭastha*. ***Nāḍi nákshatra ṭhik hoto saphal haye sab karma, nahito biphal hoto haye sab dhárma*** — If at the time of birth the planetary positions of the person concerned are right or favourable then all his actions will be successful and if unfavourable, then all material actions and spiritual progress will be unsuccessful. ***Jihvā uṭhke***

jaysā bilkul śvāsā bund ho gayā o miṭha mālum hone lagā — the tongue being raised and entering the palatal cavity external breathing ceased totally, thus the external inhalation and exhalation of breath became non-existent. In this condition I sensed a sweet taste on the tip of the tongue. ***Śushumnāye vāyú gele kuper matan galāye chidra anubhav haye*** — when *Prâṇá* air enters the *Sushumná* while practising *Prâṇákarma* then within the throat a pit similar to that in a well is experienced. This signifies that air within the pit of a well is non-vibratory, similarly the inner air within the throat becomes non-vibratory. ***Svaprakāś arthād āpnā āpni prakāś arthād icchārahit, icchā thākile kakhana kichu haye nā*** — spontaneous manifestation results with the cessation of desires. Until desires persist, there is no spiritual fulfilment. ***Ab baḍā majā huyā haye śvāsā ekdam sautak ghus gayā avināśi yāne tríkūṭike ṭikiyā yāne jñānacákshu har hameś ānkhke sāmne khaḍā*** — now I derived immense bliss, breath wholly entered till the end of *Sushumná*, then I realized that the immortal indestructible *Kūṭastha*-Eye of Wisdom is constantly prevalent to vision. ***Humhi nilkā koṭhi Humhi Kisunji*** — I only am the blue *Mahádeva* (another appellation of Srikrishna). I only am Bhagavan Krishna. ***Yo Kisun soi sūrya soi pāni*** — The One Who is Krishna is *Ātmasūrya* again He is the causal water. ***Bāre bāre Sūryake dekhte icchā kare*** — I aspire to see the Soul-Sun repeatedly. ***Yo Hum soi sūryakā jyoti*** — What is the Effulgence of the *Ātmasūrya* is Myself. ***Āpan Rūpá āsal*** — the Own Form is the truth. ***Jagadke sār Sūrya haye ohi rūpá tumārā haye*** —The essence of the universe is *Ātmasūrya* because everything is created from it, that is the form of yourself, Myself and everyone else. ***Tumhi tum ho tum choḍāye dusrā nahi tab laye sparśa*** — You are that You, when this state arrives while practising *Prâṇákarma*, only then the mergence came into realisation. Delineating a sun on the forehead of a human form He has written beneath it — ***Sūryakā dusrā rūpá yáma ohi Hum — Sūryai Hum. Yo svāsā soi Sūryakā jyot soi Hum — Sūryase iha***

svāsā ātā haye — iha samajnā jaldi nahi hotā haye. The second form of *Ātmasūrya* is death, again that only is Myself. What is breath is the Effulgence of *Ātmasūrya*, again that only is Myself because this breath emanates from that Soul-Sun, that is the place of origin of breath; though this cannot be comprehended soon or through a small amount of *sādhana*; for this austere *sādhana* is necessary. ***Sūrya o jyot phir ohi kāraṇbāri hotā haye usise sab udpatti āur usise laye. Ab svāsā bhitar bhitar jātā haye thoḍā bāhar bhi jātā haye. Āj mánas saṅga deśese ekdaphā khabār gayā isse Prabhukā dárśana o dhvani ājan dekhne sunā — strí púrushkā kāl haye iske taraf tāknā nahi, bhul karkebhi cāhiye nā*** — The *Ātmasūrya* and the Effulgence are the causal water, from this water the entire universe has been created and merges here. Now the breath is internally entering though a small quantity of breath is still external. Executing *Prâṇákarma* such a state arrived that the mind abandoned all the senses, in this state visualisation of the Master occurred and I envisioned and heard the manifestation of the *Ómkāra* sound. This only is like death for everyone irrespective of sex, never pays attention to it not even by mistake because *Prâṇá's* still state bears two aspects — one is *Víshṇu* the Protector or pervasion and the other is the Deathlike Destroyer. Yogiraj advised — A *yogi* should not observe this Deathlike Destroyer. Nevertheless, both the states will appear to a *yogi* and the knowledge of both the states has to be acquired but still it is a *yogi's* duty not to cast his glance on that Deathlike Destroyer, for by doing so he will fall into the jaws of death. Therefore He is cautioning every *yogi*. —***Āj kisike kuch kahese mánas dab gayā haye. Jihvá bilkul aṭak rahat haye āur svāsā bhitar bhitar caltā haye. Ab is kadar nesā hotā haye ki nesāke māre ānkhse subātā nahi — haraf likhnekā na najar paḍe — āur nid aisā nesā gher āoye*** — Today uttering something to someone has afflicted My mind. The tongue has completely been uplifted and entering the palatal cavity has become fixed there and since breathing motion has become internally oriented it is continuing within. In this state the *Prâṇá* air rising upwards caused such an intense engrossment that I could not see anything even the alphabets while writing and just as the drowsy stupor which arrives before sleep, a deep absorption similar to this enveloped Me. ***Kasāk bhitar bhitar praṇām karte bakhat ānkh bandhā ho jātā haye āur kuch bujhātā nehi baḍā nesā haye o baḍā majā haye.*** — At the time of internal *Prâṇákarma* executed with vigour the eyes spontaneously close, I cannot comprehend anything, now an intense absorption and immense bliss is emerging. Yogiraj has further expounded "Inhalation of each initial internal *Prâṇâyāma* causes uneasiness, there is discomfort ceasing it for a while, there is comfort at the time of internal exhalation, but the wind does not exist in the belly. In the second *Prâṇâyāma*, the air travels up the throat, nose and internally till the palate, the bliss of inhaling internal oriented *Prâṇâyāma* is similar to the bliss of cessation at both ends and to the exhalation but the dulcet *Ómkāra* sound which emanates at the exhalation moment causes the air to rise on the head and remain fixed, by this a heaviness in the head can be experienced. This state of heaviness is termed as engrossment. But why does not this engrossment occur to everybody? Just as passion to acquire a beautiful woman after being captivated by her ensues, (here the woman is the cause for passion) similarly heavy-headedness type of engrossment ensues on executing the internally oriented excellent *Prâṇákarma*. This type of Supreme Being or *Brahma* Who through the medium of illusion assuming a bewitching figure deludes the world and the passion which evolves observing the beautiful lady who is the shadowy form of the bewitching figure is far less than the enhanced engrossment evolving from visualising the Supreme Being, I perceived this while practising *Prâṇâyāma*." ***"Āte bakhat preṇāmse svāsa nāhi nikāletā āur yāte bahkat thoḍā nikālātā haye*** — At the time of inhalation of the internally oriented *Prâṇâyāma* no breath comes out but at the time of exhalation a small quantity goes out. Actually after practising *Prâṇâyāma* for a while breath does not depart at the moment of exhalation, it then travels internally. ***Praṇām karte bakhat parakh āste āste karte bakhat yarā hāoyākā kampher mālum hoye tab āpse āp rukyāye āur yettā dertak rākhenekā eredā hoye rākh seke — e mālum hotā haye monko nirthan karnese mārte mārte svāsāke tarha āisā āhubhāv bhāyā*** — While practising *Prâṇâyāma* in order to test it I was executing it gradually and I realised the disparity in the quantity of air. Practising *Prâṇâyāma* likewise, the breath automatically ceases and I can remain in this position as long as I desire. I further realised that if the mind being controlled proceeds towards the internally oriented breath, then a spontaneous replete still state appears. Thus Yogiraj has repeated regarding this state — ***Monseche tiran hoye uskā nām mántra. Tanseche bharaṇ hoye uchkā nām tántra haye*** — The present kinetic mind which is known to all as the mind, it's state of release or the still state is termed as *Mántra* and the medium by which the body is nurtured is *Tántra*. Thus by the constant flow in each and every nerve, this body is being nurtured, therefore that flow of air is *Tántra*. Yogiraj further stated — "Nothing is sweeter than the ambrosial cascade which flows from above; the head is quite heavy, remaining in *Kúṭastha* and executing *Prâṇâyāma* for a long period causes the causal water to flow down the *Sahasrâra*; the *Ómkāra* sound which could be previously heard while practising *dhyāna* or *Prâṇâyāma* can now be constantly heard. The opacity above the Soul-Moon within *Kúṭastha* is removed if regular *Prâṇâyāma* is practised and the crystalline amorphous Moon can be viewed, then the moment the eyes are closed that Moon can be clearly visualised within i.e. *Kúṭastha* but it can be visualised for a short while even now, it is not attaining permanence for a long period and now I have achieved the strength for practising longer *Prâṇâyāma* and the more the longer *Prâṇâyāma* is practised the more I can comprehend after a few days that breath is no longer external, I am feeling ecstatic at this state and I realised that everything comprises the state of cessation of the inhalation-exhalation of that breath or else the still state dawns or in other words this is the actual state of renunciation. Prior to obtaining this state, this renunciation is futile". ***Knāsar ghanṭākā dhvani kānme mālum hotā haye jab dhyāna kare*** — When I meditate or practise *Kriyā* then I can hear the jingling sound of the bell and the clinking sound of the dish of bell metal. — ***Khāli ānkhse candrá dekhā sabere praṇām karoth bakhat candrá sūryakā ekme milgāye haye phir khāli dekhā.*** — While executing *Prâṇâyāma* in the morning, I envisioned with naked eyes the Soul-Moon; I further noticed that the Sun and Moon merged into one, when merging into one took place then duality being absent everything was empty or vacant, thus I visualised the Infinite Void. This Infinite Void is *Brahma*. ***Sūrajme sab kāraṇbāri bharā haye*** — The Soul-Sun is replete with causal water. ***Jo bindi soi dhvanikā rūpá — ab dhvani samān haye. Āur Sūryai bindikā rūpá to Sūryai śabd haye.*** — The dot which is visualised within *Kūṭastha* is the form of the *Ómkāra* sound, now that sound has become equal and when that *Ātmasūrya* is the form of the dot, then that *Ātmasūrya* is the sound or the *Ómkāra* sound or what is *Ātmasūrya* is the dot and that is the *Ómkāra* sound.—***Ab agam sthānme gaye yāne sthir*** — Now I have reached that inaccessible place or still place where none can enter excepting *yogis*. ***Brahmāke kamuṇḍal me Harike caraṇse pāni girtā haye — ehi haye kāraṇbāri.*** — The water which is flowing from the Lotus Feet of Hari into the cornucopian water-pot of *Brahmā* is the causal water. The water-pot of *Brahmā* is the palatal cavity and *Hari's* Lotus Feet is the *Sahasrâra*. The ambrosia which flows on the palatal cavity at the tongue's tip (raised tongue) from the *Sahasrâra* is the causal water and by drinking this water one can attain immortality. Consumption of liquor is one of the five essentials of *Tántra* rites. According to Tantrism, drinking of this causal water is the actual consumption of liquor. It is not the superficial consumption of liquor.

The principal feature of Tantrism, is the *sādhana* of it's five essential rites. It is characterised by the three attributes of *sattva*, *rájas* and *támas*. Amongst them surely *sattva* is the most important. The five superficial essentials are liquor, meat, fish, wealth and coitus. Those who possess the *rájas* or *támas* attributes practise *sādhana* with the help of these five superficial vices, soul-realisation does not dawn through this; but the virtuous five essentials are different. The fact that the *rájas* or *támas* mode of practising *sādhana* of the five essentials is base has been explained by the *Tántra śāstrás* thus—

Madyapānena mánujo yadi siddhiṃ labheta bai,
Madyapānratāḥ sarve siddhiṃ gacchantu pāmarāḥ.
Māṃsabhakshaṇamātreṇa yadi puṇyā gatirbhabed,
Loke māṃsāśinaḥ sarve puṇyabhājo bhabantu ha.
Strīsambhogena debesi yadi mokshaṃ labheta bai,
Sarveapi jantabo loke muktāḥ suyāḥ strīnishebād.

(*Kulārṇabtántra* 2)

This verse denotes that if man attains salvation through consuming liquor, then the vilest drunkard should also attain salvation; if consumption of meat brings forth a virtuous orientation then all meat eaters should be blessed. Dear *sādhaka*, if salvation is achieved by copulating with wife, then let everyone become liberated by executing coitus with women.

Thus in accordance with the *sattva* attribute what is liquor, the first of the five essentials? *Śāstrá* denotes —

Somdhārā kshared yā tu brahmarandhrād barānane.
Pīttvānandamayastāṃ yaḥ sa eba madyasādhakaḥ.

(*Āgamsār*)

This signifies thus —Dear *sādhaka*, the one who drinks ambrosia which exudes from the *Sahasrâra* and is ecstatic is referred to as an inebriate *sādhaka*.

Yogiraj by drinking causal water would perpetually be rapt in *Bhagavān*-serenity.

In pursuance of the *sattva* attribute, what is known as the consumption of meat, the second essential ? *Śāstrá* stipulates —

> ***Mā śabdādrasanā jñeyā tadaṃśān rasanāpriyān.***
> ***Sadā yo bhakshayeddevī sa eba māṃsasādhakaḥ.***
>
> (*Āgamsār*)

Mā signifies function of the tongue, it's partial function is speech which is dear to the tongue. The person who devours the tongue or controls speech is known as the *sādhaka* who consumes meat. In accordance with the *Gurú's* instructions when the tongue is entered into the palate cavity, speech is arrested, in this state if enhanced *Prâṇákarma* is executed all desires are annihilated. Then desire being absent, who speaks ? Thus if the tongue is controlled, speech is arrested and the ardent *sādhaka* who strives to keep the tongue in a raised position is known as the *sādhaka* who consumes meat.

What is the third essential, fish ? *Śāstrá* states —

> ***Gáṅgāyamúnayormadhye madsou dvou carataḥ sadā.***
> ***Tau madsyau bhakshayed yastu sa bhabenmadsyasādhakaḥ.***
>
> (*Āgamsār*)

A pair of fish constantly swim within the two rivers of the Ganges and Yamuna, the *sādhaka* who devours that pair is a fish-eating *sādhaka*. The Ganges is *Iḍā* and Yamuna is *Piṅgalā*, the constant breathing which continues within these two nostrils is that pair of fish. The *yogi* who stills *Prâṇá* through *Prâṇákarma* and devours the breathlike pair of fish or stills them is the fish-eating *sādhaka*.

What is the fourth essential, wealth ? *Śāstrá* stipulates thus —

> ***Sahasrâre mahāpadme karṇikā mudritā cared.***
> ***Ātmā tatraiva deveśi kévalaṃ pāradopamam.***

Sūryakoṭi pratīkāśaṃ candrákotisuśītalam.
Atība kamanīyañca mahākuṇḍalinīyutam.
Yasya jñānodayastatra mudrāsādhaka ucyate. (*Āgamsār*)

The stem of the thousand petalled lotus is as unalloyed as mercury, it's manifestation is more intense than the rays of millions of moons and suns yet is soothing, extremely tender and the one who has realized the soul in union with the female energy or the *yogi* who as per his *Gurú's* advice has directly realized the Supreme Being through *Ātmakarma* is the *sādhaka* who worships spiritual wealth.

What is the fifth essential, coitus ? Commenting about the coital essence, *śāstrá* has purported —

Maithun paramaṃ tattvaṃ srishtisthityantakāraṇam.
Maithunājjāyate siddhirbrahmajñānaṃ sudurlabham.
Refastu kuṅkumābhāsaḥ kuṇḍamadhye byabasthitaḥ.
Makāraśca bindúrūpo mahāyonau sthitaḥ priye.
Ākārahaṃsamāruhya ekatāca yadā bhaved.
Tadā jātaṃ mahānandaṃ Brahmajñānaṃ sudurlabham.
Ātmani Ramate yasmādātmārāmastadocayate.
Ataeba Rāmanām Tārakaṃ Brahma niścitam.
Mṛityukāle Maheśāni smaredrāmāksharadvayam.
Sarvakarmāṇi saṃtyajya svayaṃ Brahmamayo bhabed.
Idantu maithunaṃ tattvaṃ taba snehād prakāsitam.
Maithunaṃ paramaṃ tattvaṃ tattvajñānasya kāraṇam.
Sarvapūjāmayaṃ tattvaṃ jápādīnāṃ phalapradam.
Shaḍaṅgaḥ pūjayeddevi sarvamántraḥ prasīdati.
Āliṅganaṃ bhabennyāsaṃ cumbanaṃ dhyānamirītam.
Ābāhanaṃ sitakāraṃ naivedyamupalepanam.
Jápanaṃ ramaṇaṃ proktaṃ retapātaśca dakshiṇā.
Sarvathaiba tvayā gopyaṃ mama prâṇâdhikapriye.

(*Āgamsār*)

This implies that the essence of coitus is the cause for creation, preservation and dissolution. Through soul-communion (coitus) spiritual fulfilment or the state of going beyond desires and the attainment of the unattainable *Brahma*-knowledge results. The *Maṇipūra-cakrá* alongwith the essence of heat by means of vital breath or *Prâṇákarma* when within the sublime place of origin in the *Ājñācakrá* the coital dot achieves union, or when settlement is attained in the *Ājñācakrá* then the supremely blissful *Brahma*-knowledge evolves. If such a settlement occurs in the *Ājñācakrá* communing in that still state which evolves is referred to as *Rāma*. This is the real *Rāma* chanting which can never be verbal. The soul-communing *sādhaka* constantly communes with the soul therefore it is definite that the name of *Rāma* is *Tārakabrahma* (this represents dot *Brahma*). Dear *sādhaka*, one should remain engaged in *Ātmakarma* so that at the time of death the name of *Rāma* can be remembered, for then after the relinquishment of all actions the name of *Rāma* is remembered at the moment of death and the person concerned himself becomes pervaded by *Brahma*. Aiming at this, Yogiraj has written — ***Ómkāra Ātmârāma ohi Rāma haye*** — The *Ómkāra Ātmârāma* is *Rāma*. This soul-essencelike coital essence is the supreme essence, acts as a cause for all knowledge and produces results for various disciplines of worship and *jápa*. All the *mántras* by the medium of this type of sixfold (six *cákras*) *yóga* action in accordance with the *Gurú's* advice become propitious or derive consciousness. The internal *Prâṇâyāma* when practised maintains the external air externally and the internal air internally, bearing this type of air in the *Ājñācakrá* is termed 'embracement' and to be absolutely rapt in the state of settlement is the act of 'kissing'. This type of *dhyāna* state occurs after practising 1728 internal *Prâṇâyāmas*. In the *Kévala-Kumbhaka* state 'invocation' occurs and by placing the tongue upwards, practising *Ātmakarma*, the ambrosia which exudes is the 'oblation'. The vital breathlike *jápa* action or *Ātmakarma* is 'spiritual communion' and communing continually likewise ambrosia exudes from *Sahasrâra* akin to semen ejaculation and the moment this takes place a satisfactory bliss evolves, that is *'dakshiṇā'* (tribute) or the state of achieving Absolute Bliss. This virtuous coital essence or the five essentials of *Tántra* rites had been stipulated by *Mahā́deva* (still *Prâṇā*) to *Parvati* (kinetic *Prâṇā*) and He advised Her to keep it an universal secret. But in the present age the *sattva* attribute is abandoned and the actions evolving from *rájas* and *támas* attributes are accomplished.

Yogiraj has remarked — ***Ei śarīri Ómkāra, ei śarīr hoite sakala udpatti*** — This body is *Ómkāra* and everything is produced from this body. He has remarked on another day thus — ***Āj mun cañcal hoke jaysā Prâṇâyāma kartethe so oysā nahi huyā — ab śvāsā bahut kum calne lagā —baḍā majā*** — Today the mind being restless to a certain extent, it prevented Me from practising the excellent *Prâṇâyāma* I used to but due to past prolonged practice, the breathing motion is reduced to a great extent and I am feeling ecstatic in this state. After this He has written — ***Āj ekdum dum bund — choṭā jihvā́ āur upar uṭhā — āur bicme pānikā sotā mālum huyā*** — Today My breathing completely ceased, the external breathing did not exist any longer. The uvula was further raised upwards and I experienced the flow of ambrosia in the palate. ***Jisne kāmko jitā usne sabkuch kiyā*** — One who has been able to conquer all types of cravings can perform every activity properly. The more the breathing motion is stilled by the practice of *Prâṇákarma* the more all types of covetousness will be conquered. ***Ohi ekrūpá Mahā́purushkā jo tamām brahmāṇḍ byāpik haye*** — That *Mahā́purusha* has the same form, He does not undergo any metamorphosis, I visualised that it is He who is pervading the entire universe. After establishing Himself in non-duality, merging and becoming confluent with *Brahma*, Yogiraj has stated — ***Sū́ryai Brahma Humhi Brahma sarvabrahma.***— That *Ātmasū́rya* characterised by the brilliance of a thousand suns is *Brahma*, I Myself am *Brahma*, everything is *Brahma*. Yogiraj declared that He Himself and *Brahma* becoming One, the creation was pervaded by *Brahma* Himself. ***Humārei Rūpá sab jagai — Hum choḍāy koi nahi, uha rūpá haye śūnyá me ohā na din na rāt.*** — My Form pervades the total creation or excepting Me nothing prevails in this Universe, barring Me there is a total absence of everything. This form of *Brahma* pervaded Universe is settled in the infinite void, i.e. the void within this void where day and night are absent but is spontaneous and self-manifested. This is the pinnacle state of a *yogi* and the ultimate of all *yógas* is *Layayoga* which is by merging with the vast entity there is an elimination of the small entity. This is the ultimate and principal aim of a *yogi*.

Normally Yogiraj never suffered from any serious afflictions but the existence of the body makes it liable to be plagued by some minor afflictions. Once Yogiraj was afflicted by an abscess, thus He revealed this fact in His diary — ***Āj Āpnā gāflise phoḍā huyā*** — I have developed an abscess due to My negligence. After a couple of days He recounted — ***Āj rojke māphik phoḍese Prâṇâyāma nahi huyā — avināśiko yāne Sūryáko rātme dekhā.*** — Today due to the abscess pain, I could not practise excellent *Prâṇâyāma* like other days, but I visualised the Imperishable *Ātmasūrya* at night. After another couple of days He expressed — ***Āj kuch durbal śarīr huyā lekin bhitar bhitar svāsā calā.*** — Due to the abscess which lasted for a few days, I became weak but the breathing motion automatically became internal. Delineating a sun, He wrote beside it — ***Humhi Hum haye. Sūryá dekhā ānkh mudke — Humhi Sūrya haye*** — I myself only am Myself or I dwell within Myself and even in this state by closing My eyes, I visualised the *Ātmasūrya*, I am that indestructible Soul-Sun. ***Alakh nirañjanakā jab kamal bikaśit hoye tab āphi āp dekhe — phir Āprūpi Bhagavān honā bnāki haye — tab Gurú samān dātā nahi mālum hoye.*** — While executing

Prâṇákarma, when the six cakralike lotuses flower from the *Mūlâdhāra cakrá* to the *Ājñācakrá* then the Glory of the Imperceptible Immaculate God is revealed and then one can himself perceive his own self. After arriving at this state, now solely the Own Form or the Self-Form-God-State remains to blossom. Then realization that none can equal the munificence of the *Gurú* dawns. After this advancing further, Yogiraj the Eternal effected a confluence between His Living-Being-State and God-State, firmly establishing Himself in non-duality in accordance with the *Vedānta* doctrine, mounting the highest pinnacle of *sādhanā* He penned in His secret daily recountings the Omnific words — ***Svayaṃ Bhagavān*** — In this manner by delineating a chronological sequence in His *sādhanā*, He has conveyed to mankind as to how He reverted from His present Shama Churn Living-Being-State to His Original Primordial State and thus made the ***Divine Apophthegm — SVAYAṂ BHAGAVĀN — It is My Own Self Who is God Almighty : the Supreme, the Absolute, Infinite, Infinitesimal, Creator, Universal-Sustainer, Destroyer, Salvator, Omnipresent, Omnipotent, Omniscient, Omniphile, Omniform, Omnigender. My Advent is to reorient mankind who albeit has deviated, essentially craves for salvation.***

* * * * * *

In 1871, in the month of August (date not mentioned) He noted — ***Kālā bindi ei sthir bahut der tak dekhā āur kahā Mātārīse ki bābā āvat prâṇáme marne lāge ekhi ehi kāhkarke royā tab sāmko Gurúne kahā upar likhā huyā Gurúne bātālāyā lekin ānkhse kuch nāhi dekhā ki kuch nāhi Brahma heya yāne mālum hotā heya ki mahā́vidyākā dárśana hogā*** — For a long moment I visualised the static black dot and cogitating on the fact that if I depart in the state of external breathing as is normal for humans at the time of death made me shed tears in anguish and I told *Mātāji* (Primordial Female

Energy) so. Later in the evening, I narrated to *Gurúji* (static state of *Prâṇá*) and he divinely explained everything. (Here evening marks the juncture state of dynamism and static *Prâṇá*). I visualised nothingness, exclusively *Brahma* prevailed or else I realised that now I would envision the state of Supreme Knowledge. In September, 1871 during the bright lunar fortnight, He has expatiated on the essence of space — "Now I am experiencing an intense bliss, everything originates from that *Ātmasūrya*, I was initially envisioning that very *Ātmasūrya* in the minuteness of a dot, now this very dot attained a magnitude comparable with the sun in the sky. This entire creation has originated from that *Ātmasūrya*, thus this gives wake to duality, again that very *Ātmasūrya* achieved dissolution within the Absolute Void *Brahma*, conversely this very *Ātmasūrya* again is originating from that Absolute Void *Brahma*. Therefore in this manner the eternal process of preservation and dissolution continues. The *Anāhata, Ómkāra* sounds alongwith other intrinsic sounds emanate from that *Ātmasūrya*, that Divine Sound is wholly the *Brahma*-Effulgence. This same *Ātmasūrya* metamorphosed into the Soul-Moon, therefore He only is the Master of the intense Moon-Effulgence, there alongwith all *Ganeśaji*, penman of the *Vedas* exists, He gives an apparent impression not to have written anything, conversely it is He only who explains the complete significance of the *Vedas* by the medium of His trunk (symbol of *Prâṇâyāma*). The type of sound which emanates while blowing into a keyhole is similar to the sound which is emanating while practising *Prâṇâyāma; Ātmasūrya* only is the verity, now there being an annihilation of desires, the will to execute any action is absent so much so that any type of yearning also has become non-existent. Now breathing is wholly continuing in

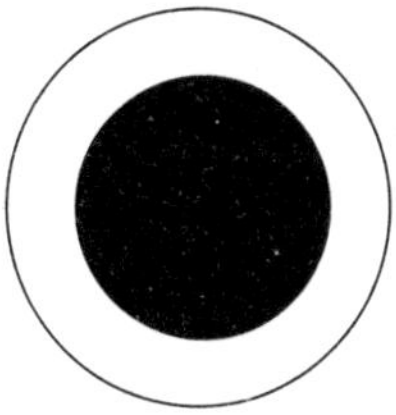

Sushumná and becoming rapt while envisioning the six *cakrás*, the external pair of eyes closed in this state, I realized I might fall ahead. In this type of engrossed rapt state, I visualised within the *Kúṭastha* mirror a terrifying image with monstrous hands and teeth which was seated, I informed this horrifying state that no matter how much of fright it tries to instil in Me, I will tenaciously remain united with the *Ātmasúrya* true-essence." He has commented after this — ***Ānkh bund karke dekhā cidme Prâṇávāyu haye āur Prâṇávāyume cid haye cid ṭhekāne rākheta kabhi nā mare ādmi dosrā sakasme kuc yod haye lekin sāf nāhi bhāyā.*** — Closing My eyes I visualised that in the dynamic state the *Prâṇá* air is prevalent and consciousness is present in *Prâṇá* air or what is *Prâṇá* air is consciousness and what is breathing is *Prâṇá*. If that consciousness or *Prâṇá* air is placed in the right position then none will expire, in other words the vibratory *Prâṇá* has to be stilled by *Prâṇákarma* for then none will expire. Because since that state signifies the cessation of births, who will expire then? When birth is absent, death also is absent. I envisioned that *Ātmajyoti* in all bodies though not very distinctly. He has later remarked — ***Nādche Víshṇuche milātā haye kneuki ākāshkā Víshṇukā ekrūpá hay āur sabad ākāshche nikālātā haye ichliye git shunneche sabkā dil khush rahātā haye keuki āp rūpáche sabke khuši payedā huti haye*** — The *Anāhata*, *Ómkāra* sound and the Omnipresent *Víshṇu* all merged in the infinite void, for that crystalline static infinite void being all pervasive, *Víshṇu* and the infinite void possess the same form or the same essence. *Nāda-Brahma* evolves from that crystalline infinite void, therefore every-one feels cheerful listening to songs since everyone's happiness emanates from one's own form. Thus, the source of origin for songs, bliss, *Víshṇu* and everything is that crystalline static infinite void. Yogiraj chanted —

Bhāla bhebe bhāla karanā o rasanā —
Miche kāje beḍiye baḍāo

Bhuleo tāke dākonā.
Se ye antare jāge
Sadā Ātmârāmare.
Tāhār bihane tumi
Raecho kemon kore ..

O dear mind, perform all actions with benevolence and love. You involve yourself in material actions which is basically a sham and wander about, but not once do you cogitate on *Bhagavān*. He constantly is present within us in the form of *Ātmârāma*. How can you exist without Him, in other words you cannot exist barring Him.

On the fourth day of the bright lunar fortnight (month not mentioned) in 1871 He detailed — ***Sūrya baḍā darvājā haye ucko caḍnevālākā nām darbeś haye āb hāoya upar khicātā haye gāḍhā pichekā śir baḍā bhārū yo rañj bindikā iyāne jickā nām nāhi haye aihi rañj praṇāmkā aihi rañj Prâṇákā aihi rañj Brahmakā yab esab rañj ek ho yāye tab āp rūpábhi Bhagavant dekhlāye.*** Soul-Sun is the principal access, one who mounts that access or the one who has achieved permanent settlement in that Soul-Sun is named *Darbeś*, (earthly detachment) because then not possessing anything of his own he is truly destitute. Now such deep excellent *Prâṇâyāma* is occurring that the bodily airs are being pulled upwards and an occipital heady feeling is being experienced. The minute dot or the cynosure can be observed in *Kūṭastha*, it's colour is being viewed but no name can be assigned to it, such is the colour of *Prâṇâyāma*, this nameless colour belongs to *Prâṇá* and this colour itself is the colour of *Brahma*. When all these colours mingle and merge into oneness then the own form also has become *Bhagavān* as is visualised. In 1871, during the eighth day of the dark lunar fortnight, in the month of October, He had sketched twelve Soul-Suns. The gigantic sun was in the middle and the remaining eleven suns were along the sphere. He has commented beside this — ***Sūryakā bhitar Nārāyaṇákā Sudarśaná Cakrá. Baḍkā bindime***

bicme jarad rañj okrebād beguni rañj ucke bād śapedī dusrā bindi kariyā rañjkā uckā bhitar ek khirike ticke bhitar mālum hotā haye Āprūpī Bhagavān isab Víshṇukā cakráme dekhā.— I envisioned *Nārāyaṇá's Sudarśaná Cakrá* within that Soul-Sun. The colour within the large dot or the extensive Sun was yellow, this yellow colour was encircled by purple and this purple colour was encircled by white. Beyond these three colours, the colour of the eleven suns in the sphere was black; I noticed an access within it and within that access I visualised the Own-Form-God. I visualised all these within the spherical *Víshṇu Cakrá*. He has reiterated — ***Dāhinā svāsā yabtak cale tabtak sabkuch dekhe phir binās hoye — lekan pahale dahinā calneke bād phir bāye calta haye yāne bnāowā yo ki sthir kālrūpá haye.*** — In the right nose or in the *Piṅgalá* as long as the breathing motion exists, it is termed to be the *rájas* attribute. This *rájas* attribute provides inspiration for all actions, therefore all actions are accomplished. A living being existing in this *rájas* attribute eventually meets death. But at first after breathing occurs in the right nostril, later breathing motion continues in the left nostril or in the *Iḍā*, this *Iḍā* also is deathlike, in other words existing in *Iḍā* also, death is inevitable. Thus through *Prâṇákarma* a living being has to go beyond *Iḍā* and *Piṅgalá* and enter the *Sushumná*, this *Sushumná* is the *Víshṇu* Abode. But this also is personified by the *sattva* attribute, therefore, a *yogi* goes beyond the *Iḍā*, *Piṅgalá* and *Sushumná* in the attributeless state where all the three attributes are non-existent and merges in that crystalline infinite void which is supratemporal and beyond conflicts, where *Brahmā, Víshṇu* and *Mahêśvara* are also absent, thus this state is beyond the clutches of birth and death. ***Ānkh yayese andhekā ṭhahar jaye oyesā vishayko jon dekhe kévala Brahmako dekhe uskābhi ānkhe thām yāye ābhyās bas ṭhahar jāye.*** — Just as eyes of a blind man stop functioning, so also a man thoroughly engrossed in material thoughts has a steadfast gaze, similarly the one who visualises *Víshṇu* attains a likewise state. Thus one who visualises *Brahma* in the same manner, his mind, eyes and everything become static, this depends on practice i.e. if *Kriyā* is regularly practised in a disciplined manner then stillness is attained. Stillness is *Brahma.* Thus *Kriyāsādhana* should be daily practised by all. Therefore He has repeated — ***Abhyās dvārāye kona karma nā karileo karā haye.*** — If any action is apparently not performed it is performed habitually. Extolling the virtues of *Kriyāyoga* He would reiterate — ***Tomār nijer bhāla kise habe tā tumi nijei jāno nā.*** — You consider that the actions which you perform will impart welfare to you but definitely it is not so, therefore you yourselves do not know the real action which will be truly beneficial for you. Practice of *Kriyā* results in total welfare. ***Eyesā mālum hotā haye ki kuch cij milā arthad tripta.***— Now I understood that I achieved something while practising *Kriyā*, this was the state of being appeased or attaining fulfilment. Then He chanted —

Meṭhāi kheye mon koi ṭripta holo nā
Eman dhan koi yāhā kakhana yāye nā
Gurú tumi bole deo bole deonā
Se ye sarvatrete āche birājmānā
Are tui dekhnā dekhnā dekhnā
Cákshur sanmukhe birāje śūnyashanā
Ai Brahmapad munete milāi nā
Ek hole bnāki kichu thākbe nā
Muner ānanda mune dharbe nā
Takhan Brahma binā ār habe nā
Epad pābenā mūl mántra binā
Yantri binā kévala yántra yántranā
Tāhā binā nāi anya ārādhanā
E ārādhanāye sukh atul nā
Ihā kadācit tumi bhuliyo nā
Bhulile pābe tumi yáma yántranā

Kalur cāke paḍe Prâṇá rabe nā
Ghorāmātra sār lābh kichui nā
Harinām[1] nite alas karanā
Noile parampad tumi pābe nā.

The consumption of sweet could not make the mind contended.
Does such wealth exist which never exhausts ?
O *Gurú*, kindly enlighten Me. He is ubiquitous.
You should constantly be observant
He is present in the vision as Void
That *Brahma* state is beyond the purview of the mind.
When oneness is attained everything becomes extirpated.
The bliss of still mind is beyond the ambit of dynamic mind
Then nothing exists other than *Brahma*
None will attain this state until *Kriyā* is practised
Barring *Kriyā* all other *sādhanas* are futile
No *sādhana* exists other than *Kriyā*
This *sādhana* imparts profound bliss
Never forget the practice of *Kriyā*
For non-practice of *Kriyā* will entail infernal agony.
The existence of *Prâṇá* will be annihilated by being ground by material constraints.
The cycle of births and deaths will recur but will not be beneficial
To practise *Kriyā* never be indolent
If not practised the Ultimate Supreme State will remain unfulfilled.

Kālī dekhe kāl bhay pāye
Se ye kichu naye athaca sarvamaye
Nirjane base bhebe dekha pābe sei dhan
Ye ki harebidhan o sakaleri nidhan
Prâṇá jāye jāk kshati nāi
Pāibe āmi sei dhan
Hari dhan amūlya ratan.

1. *Harinām* implies internal *Prâṇákarma*.

Dynamism is awed when stillness arrives
That stillness comprises nothingness yet is omneity
Practise *Kriyā* in solitude and then
The invaluable wealth will be achieved
Stillness seizes and destroys earthly attachment
There is no harm if *Prâṇá* departs from this mortal frame,
Static wealth will be achieved which is invaluable.

Hari mukhe hārā gela bāp
Ārto Prâṇe bācinā,
Prâṇá Prâṇá kare halām khun
Prâṇá yekhānkār sekhāneto gelonā
Sthirbhābe sthir hoi e munto
Ekhana sthir halo nā,
Lege thāka Haripade habe abaśya tnāhār karuṇā;
Jene śune tumi Hari balite kakhana ālasya karo nā.

At the juncture of stillness everything ceases
The feeling is that vibration of *Prâṇá* will not exist,
Desperation to achieve *Prâṇá* leads to exhaustion
Prâṇá does not proceed to His original still state
The desire is to become still in a still manner but the mind has not attained stillness as yet,
Regularly practise *Kriyā*, surely His clemency will be showered
Despite knowing this do not be indolent to practise *Kriyā*.

Se ye bisham ghaṭanā oprâṇá bnācenā
Yetechila āpan mandire sethai kare phelle ekkhānā.
Beṭā yeman beṭi teman biṭir majāye jhulanā.

Due to long practice of *Kriyā* when the dynamism of *Prâṇá* becomes extinct at the confluence of His stillness, a state of enigma evolves; the dynamic *Prâṇá* proceeds towards His temple, the static state and on arriving becomes One. The stillness and dynamism of *Prâṇá* are equivalent but involvement in dynamism is certainly not desirable as it creates all types of earthly attachments.

Sureś uha bikhyāta jagatme suranke
Mālik ohi hoi.
Bisvādhār haye uha jagatme
Uha binā rahe na koi.
Gagan sadṛiśa ākār oyāko
Dekhat sthir ghar jāi.
Meghvarṇa rañj oyāko bhali lahe
Akshar jab dekhāi.
Subhāṅg isliye kahalāoe buddhi
Sumati le jāi.
Lakshmikānt ohi raṭnu haye
Dāridra sab nasāi.
Icchā hoye daridratā baḍhe icchāi
Ulta santosh hoi.
Kamal nayāna oyāke log kahat haye
Jekā sobhā varṇan na jāi.
Jogivirdhyāna agamrūpá haye
Paiho sab parivār thoi.
Bande bhaktā bhavabhaya haraṃ ajapā
Siddha jab hoi.
Sarvalo kaikanāth mile tab
Bajat ānand badhāi.

O God, You are the Master of each and every wonderful sound emanating from this great universe created by You. O still *Prâṇá*, Your Splendid Static Kingdom is the Master of the dynamic universe. This dynamic universe subsists upon the Static Kingdom, barring the Static Kingdom everything is absent. It is resemblant of the sky, constantly envisioning it the still state is reached. When it becomes perceptible as the Imperishable Form then it's cloudy colour can be realised. It is considered auspicious because the intellect or virtuous inclination can lead there. The Static Kingdom is regarded as fortunate because this state eliminates all types of life's deficiencies or shortcomings. This penury stems from desire, in this manner the more intense desire evolves the more this penury is experienced, but when desire is extirpated contentment accrues. This state is termed to be the Resplendent-Eye Whose splendour is indescribable. This state can be achieved through the medium of *yogi's dhyāna* which is inaccessible to non-*yogis*. In this manner when the state of emancipation is attained then a *yogi's* dread of earthly attachment and vital breath are seized, then the *yogi* himself invokes his own self. A *yogi* then achieving an all pervasive still state or *Śivá* state brims with bliss.

Bārto pakā abahu mánas leyā caraṇ Bhagavān
Sumirat yāhi ho jāi ebao chute abhimān
Tek pakaḍ sādhu vacana hoihe ómkāratān
Nāmdeva ehi nām leta hogae antardhyāna.

Continual practice of *Kriyā* leads to it's advancement and the mind can be settled at the Lotus Feet of God; in this state the moment God is remembered, all types of conceit are exterminated; abiding by the advice of *Gurú*, practising *Kriyā* properly, the *Ómkāra* sound is made accessible; if *Kriyā* is practised for progressing towards stillness, intra-*dhyāna* occurs.

Khete dibi sute dibi.
Karte dibi sakala karma.
Manasgata icchā cheḍe tushṭa haye,
Dekhe Ātmakarma..

Regularly practising *Ātmakarma* eliminates all desires and the mind attains contentment. In this state a *yogi* eats, sleeps, performs all actions by keeping himself in absolute detachment.

Aiming at this state God has expressed —

Prajahāti yadā kāmān sárvān Pārtha manogatān.
Ātmanyebātmanā tushṭaḥ sthitaprajñastadocayate.. (*Gītā* 2/55)

This denotes — Dear *Arjuna*, when a *yogi* becomes contented with the supremely blissful soul and abandons all mental aspirations, he is regarded to be having wisdom-equipoise. It infers when a *yogi* appeases himself by becoming rapt within the soul-bliss of his own self and forsakes all types of desires and aspirations or by the mind settling in the infinite soul's action-cessation state, the person in whom superlative knowledge or soul-knowledge dawns i.e. knowledge of the self by the self becomes nascent he only is termed to be having wisdom-equipoise.

Prâṇávāyuko bindume ṭhaharānese vāyu sthiti hojāye — vāyu bind bidhāraṇaṃ. — If *Prâṇá* air is stilled within the cynosure-like dot visualised in *Kūṭastha* by continual *Prâṇákarma*, all the fortynine airs lose their function and the state of *dhyāna* is thus achieved. That is withholding the air in a special manner within the dot. ***Nāda bedhnā — āoyāj sumār kare narike jihvá agrakar roke Ómkāra dhyāoe tab sthir hoye o netra nāsikā bic dhyāna kare nirāle baiṭke tab nirālamba prāpta hoye. Ānand śabdse dhun hotā haye — dhun se jyoti — jyotise mánas haye — tāhā mánas laulin hotā haye so Víshṇukā padá haye.*** — Surmounting the sound emanating from *Brahma*, remembering the *Ómkāra*, placing the tongue in the palate cavity and practising *Ómkārakriyā*, stillness is achieved and in between the eyebrows or in other words fixing the eyes on *Kūṭastha* practising *Prâṇákarma* in solitude, one can achieve supportlessness or settling in the void one can become supportless. From the blissful sound, sound evolves; effulgence evolves from sound and mind evolves from effulgence; if the mind merges in that Soul-Effulgence the still state which arrives is the state of *Víshṇu* or that sublimely still infinite void is the state of *Víshṇu*. ***Isi tarha dekhte dekhte oos dekhneko āpne ānkh oos jagahase na haṭāoye***

— āur dekhtehi jāye lekan jab utar āoye tab phir usi taraf āpnā ānkh na haṭāoye āur thoḍā nice damko choḍ phir acchi tarhase uṭhāoye isitarha dekhte dekhte phir ādhiyārā phir khyālse phāḍte phāḍte subahake māphik mālum hogā tab jyot bicme kariyā pahale āgke māphik o dhupke māphik jaradrañj dekhāye uske bic ātasbāji o gayeraha — phir sabuj rañj hogā tab lāl rañj — tab harā —tab nilā — tab kālā — adhiyārā sannāṭā — phāḍte jāye phir subh hoye — phir bhitarse jyot dekhlāye sāmne adhiyārā usiko dekhe. — That Soul-Effulgence or that sublimely still infinite void *Víshṇu* state being continually visualised, engrossment in it has to be achieved; the gaze towards it has to be stilled but do not remove your gaze from this; keep on visualising. Later again when you will descend from there or from *Kū́ṭastha* (descending from *Kū́ṭastha* implies visualising the world), then also keep a rapt attention on *Kū́ṭastha*, for then you will gain a state of detachment from all worldly actions, the bondage of action will no longer exist. In this manner placing a static vision on *Kū́ṭastha,* again ascend towards *Kū́ṭastha* through excellent *Prâṇákarma*. If *Ātmakarma* is executed for a prolonged period in this manner in the path of the six *cakrás*, the non-radiant, dim infinite void similar to the twilight sky will be envisioned. The effulgence which is visualised is sometimes black, sometimes fiery, sometimes like the sunbeam and sometimes firework sparks will flash. Again the effulgence will assume green, red, blue, black hues and subsequently become the infinite void twilight sky. If *Kriyā* continues, the non-radiant dim twilight sky state ensues. If further progress is made then again the effulgence from within can be visualised and eventually the twilight sky infinite void will visibly appear and visualising this should be continued. Neither light nor darkness, yet the self-manifested crystalline infinite void, this only is pure *Brahma*. ***Jo Brahma sei śūnyá soi sū́rya jyoti. Mahā́devá so a haye sū́ryake bhir.*** — What is *Brahma* is the infinite void and that is the Effulgence of the Soul-

Sun. The One existent amidst this *Atmasűrya* is *Mahădevá*. ***Sűryai nirākāra Parambrahma svárūpa Ómkāra rūpá.*** — That *Atmasűrya* is the form of Amorphous Absolute *Brahma* and *Ómkāra*. ***Sűryai Ómkāra Mālik*** —That *Atmasűrya* only is the *Ómkāra* and Master, in other words it is the place of origin and merging for everything.

1.	***Ulti oyāso jñānako lāgi isbidha devā sebu.***	***— Piche lejānā***
2.	***Gurgam bhitar japey ajapā.***	***— Prâṇâyāma***
3.	***Hṛidaya pustak kijiye.***	***— Hṛidaya dekhnā***
4.	***Anbhow kathā kichu bhāi sādho iha bidha pāṭh paḍhded.***	***— Bhabishyad.***
5.	***Anahad ghaṇṭā jhālar bājey.***	***— Anāhuta śabda***
6.	***Alakh púrushaki sevā.***	***— Purushôttama.***
7.	***Purādhā nirantar aysā sādho***	***— Rātdin sādho.***
8.	***Bom bom se devā.***	***— Sárvavyāpi***
9.	***Gáṅgā Jamnā rahey Sárasvatī.***	***— Iḍa Piṅgalā Sushumnā***
10.	***Janhā jāye dhyānakā dharijo.***	***— Bund karke dhyāna dhare***
11.	***Tríkūti mandir baiṭhā sādho.***	***— Dhyāna bhnouke***
12.	***Oanhā jāye dárśana kijiye.***	***— Kűṭastha***
13.	***Sahajá siṃhāsana nirbhay sebo.***	***— Sahajá samādhi***
14.	***Cit ki camar kijiye.***	***— Citta ki camar yāne mánase Prâṇâyāma.***

The serial numbers do not contain separate ideas, instead each of the hyphenated divisions run sequentially :—

1.	For acquiring knowledge reverse the ignorance and serve God in this manner.	—	Revert to spinal cord.
2.	Grave and solemn internal *Prâṇâyāma* should be practised	—	*Prâṇâyāma*
3.	*Anāhata* area should be converted into *śāstrá* knowledge.	—	Envision the *Anāhata cakrá*
4.	*Sādhana*-oriented realisation should be practised and this should be regarded as the study of one's life.	—	Future
5.	Ringing of *Anāhata* bell resembles an oscillating fringe.	—	*Anāhata* sound
6.	Serve the Imperceptible Primordial Being	—	Supreme Being
7.	Commence *sādhana* in quest of Indweller in this manner as early as possible.	—	Practise *sādhana* day and night
8.	Void-God	—	Omnipresent
9.	The rivers Ganges, Yamuna and Sarasvati are present	—	*Iḍā, Piṅgalá, Sushumná.*
10.	How you should remain engrossed in *dhyāna*	—	Engross yourself in *dhyāna* after ceasing the external air.
11.	Settle yourself in the *Kū́ṭastha* temple and practise *sādhana*	—	Practise *dhyāna* within *Kū́ṭastha*
12.	Visualise after reaching there	—	*Kū́ṭastha.*
13.	Serve the throne (*Kū́ṭastha*) fearlessly by *sahajákarma* (innate action)	—	*Sahajá samādhi.*

14. Metamorphose the mind into a brush used for fanning deities — Fanning deities signifies the practice of *Prâṇâyāma* attentively.

On 1st November 1873, Yogiraj chronicled — ***Ómkāra āur sthir baḍā gambhir. Jo Ómkāra so Merā Rūpá. Ómkāra sār ṡabd — Ómkāra ṡabd yeyādā soke sunne lage. Sthir ghar baḍā sukh.*** — *Ātmasúrya* is *Ómkāra*, this *Ómkāra* is now more still, solemn and with grave sound. What is *Ómkāra* or *Ātmasúrya* is My Form. That *Ómkāra* is the essence of all sounds because all sounds originate from that *Ātmasúrya*. Now on lying down, I can hear a great deal of the *Ómkāra* sound. This still state imparts immense bliss, such a bliss exists in nothing else.

Describing the four states of conscious, dream, dormant and transcendental of a living being, Yogiraj has stated —

JĀGRATA (conscious) — *Prâṇâyāma* should constantly be executed within the body or one should constantly visualise the Imperishable *Kúṭastha* and remain merged in *Brahma* incessantly .

SVAPANÁ (dreamful state of sleep) — Consider the world to be a dream, sometimes consider it to be true — be rapt in this truth.

SUSHUPTI (profound sleep) — The *Ómkāra* and *Anāhata* sounds should be slightly touched intermittently. The mind should merge in it.

TURĪYA (communion with the Absolute) — remaining divinely conscious but materialistically apathetic. *Brahma* and mind should be made one and attain oneness.

Regarding the place of settlement of a living being Yogiraj stipulates —

ÓMKĀRA — Imperishable *Kúṭastha* implies Dronacharya of *Mahábharata.*

Circular array of strength	Illusion	A living being
Circular array of nature	Action	dwells within
Circular array of prosperity	Deep attachment	this.

Ṡāntākār ṡāntākār kahe sab loi
Ṡ-ante bhayā jiskā ohi marma pāi
Gurúkṛipā binā bhaye kaise maṅgal hoi
Ṡ-ke ante āur kyā Kévala Ómkāra hoi
Ṡantākār dekhepar nayanme dui bindi hoi.
Oyāko dekhe ohirūpá naba phir hojāi
Bhujābal yo snāp calat gharāime opar nara soi.
Bhujag eysā banā haye sur nara muni sabe khāi.
Padmanābha sāntra oyāko kahat haye
Nābhkamal hardam āi o jāi.

Everyone raises a hue and cry about attaining peace, one who can reach beyond the breathing motion he only can comprehend the significance of peace. This is the true benefit but cannot be attained without the *Gurú*s grace. Nothing else but only *Ómkāra* exists beyond the breathing motion. At the end of the breathing motion or else in the still state, two dots signifying duality can be envisioned in the *Kúṭastha.* After visualisation of the dot, the self is transformed into the dot. The internal air which circulates within the body is the serpent and the human body exists atop the serpent. This serpent symbolises devilish propensities and how it devours, *devatás*, humans, sages etc. Since this serpentlike kinetic air exists at the root of the navel, it is termed as *Padmanābha* (*Víshṇu*). Through the medium of each inhalation He travels in the navel essence. This air has been compared to a serpent. If this kinetic air is controlled and made still then *Brahma*-knowledge is attained, similarly the venom of the serpent which is so poisonous has medicinal properties also; again on the contrary if the internal air is not controlled then an aberration of airs is inevitable resulting in death, similarly the serpent has power to kill with it's venom.

Balago bala āmāye bala
Tāre dekhe eli kothāye
Sakala jyotir jyot
Ānanderi śrot
Nāca Kālī komar neḍe
Āmār māthāye.

Still wind implores to know where the kinetic mind exists, because the source of all effulgences and eternal current of bliss is the still mind. Still mind commands the kinetic mind (Goddess *Kālī*) to prance about on it's head — this signifies that no matter how much of dynamism is instilled in the still mind, it is unchangeable or else remains still and static.

Kaṇṭhe baso tumi Hariramani
Ke jāne mā tumi kār ramani
Śibe śaibāni trilocanibāni
Kātyāyani kādambini Bhabāni
Śulapāni khaḍgapāni Sarvāni
Śi śi śabd bale karbe dhvani
Jagatpitā bharttā saṃhārini
Anāhuta haye Ómkāra dhvani
Dhvanirantar jyoti svetrūpini
Ke jāne ki Kālī kāl nāgini
Svarūpākhyāne se mánas ramani.

Hari connotes still *Prâṇá*, *ramani* connotes dynamic *Prâṇá*. Yogiraj advises the dynamic *Prâṇá* to settle at *Viśuddha Cakrá* (throat region) for then dynamic *Prâṇá* will attain stillness. None know with whom maternallike kinetic *Prâṇá* communes; sometimes she communes with *Hari*, sometimes with *Śivá*. Thus she bears many forms. Through the medium of dynamic *Prâṇá* while executing *Prâṇâyāma*, the whistling sound emanates. When kinetic *Prâṇá* is stilled it becomes the Universal Controllerlike Maintainer of the universe, again when she achieves kineticism she becomes the Destroyer. While the whistling sound emanates during *Prâṇâyāma*, the *Ómkāra* sound evolves unexpectedly. Within the *Ómkāra* sound a white effulgence can be visualised. This is the *Kālī* and cobra essence. This essence communes within evehryone in the form of separate minds.

Peye cheḍonā kona jana, se je biraler dhan
Svaprakāś mánas, balār thā pāynā mánas
Avarṇa varṇan āche Veder likhan
Śe je abhāberi bhāb—māthār tanakmaḍā bhāb,
Bhābte gele kul nā pāye munijan,
Kālīghāte calore mánas jethāi āche Haridhan,
Yekhāne Śrināther dhām ānandakānan.

After attaining *Ātmā* (soul) none should abandon Him, this wealth is a rare one. He cannot be described with the help of the manifested kinetic mind. Even the scriptural text Vedas cannot expatiate on Him. He is the non-engrossment state's engrossment—when *Prâṇávāyû* rises on the head only then knowledge about that engrossment dawns but endeavouring to know Him through the kinetic mind has made sages also fail to gain access to this knowledge. The kinetic mind has to be reposed on the head or at Kalighat where Divine bounty abounds. That is the Abode of *Śivá*, supreme beatitude, garden of bliss.

Kār sāddhi ṭhokar māre
E atal sparshe.
Yadi thāken Tripurāri
Tabeto bharsā kari
Natubā Prâṇemari
Sakala yāye bhese.

Who has the capability through *Ṭhokar Kriyā's* medium to experience the boundless state of *Ātmā* (soul). If *Śivá* or still *Prâṇa* is present then depending on Him, attainment is possible, otherwise habiting in dynamic *Prâṇá*, one will plummet to death and all will be swept away.

Ānkh munde tum kyā dekha
Baiṭhe Brāmaṇ Rāma
Ānkh āp munde tab
Dekho sahaje Ātmârāma.
Ātmâ kyā dekhāi paḍe
Jhuṭe dhyāna dharo mati
Tada lakshmaṇ ātmânaṃ
Jyotirūpaṃ prapaśyati
Ātmâ dekhe kyā phal
Aur kyaise kārya sadhāye
Paramātmā mánase mánas
Jayse biryya paḍ yāye.
Dure dur kabale soce
Yāme haye baḍa kashṭa
Bhaktise palme mile taba
Ek sarva bishishṭa.

O *Kriyābān*, what do you visualise sitting in *āsaná* with your eyes closed? If the eyes spontaneously close being steeped in *Kriyā* engrossment then *Ātmârāma* visualisation will be efortless. *Ātmâ* or soul is not perceptible but engrossment has to be initiated through the fictitious kinetic mind. The indication of the soul is the Effulgent Form. Endeavours should be made to know the consequence of *Ātmâ* visualisation; how all earthly actions can be accomplished through soul-visualisation. Regular practice of *Prâṇâyāma* entails the emplacement of kinetic mind upon the still mind, this is *Paramātmā* (Infinite Soul), just as coitus results in ejaculation, entailing emplacement of spermatozoa in the ovary—impregnation. Having deviated from stillness falling into the clutches of dynamism and being attached to thoughts being a victim to the onslaught of time; agony, afflictions, sufferings are caused.

But if *Kriyā* is practised with intense devotion, He can be attained quite fast, this Onc is the Supreme, the Absolute.

Ekjana āche paḍe
Balonā balonā tāre,
Seje antareri antar
Balbe keman kare.
Jaḍabad sthir seje
Ābār jiteche capalāre,
Mātālke matta karāye
Guṇa ke balte pāre.
Saguṇa nirguṇa seto
Āmā chāḍā baite nāre,
Mánas jeneśune keno nā
Cintā kara sadā tāre.
Ashṭasiddhi paḍe āche
Cintāmaṇir nāc dvāre.

Someone exists within you, repeatedly invoke Him. But how can you invoke Him; because He pervades in the innermost recesses, He is inanimatelike still, again He only has conquered dynamism, in other words He has stilled dynamism. He only makes a *yogi* inebriate with the headiness of *Kriyā,* who can speak about His attributes? He is both within attributes and beyond attributes, He pervades amidst one and all. O kinetic mind you know full well about Him, then why do you not cogitate on Him? Soul-wealth abounds at the portals of that thought-free state.

Mánas rājāko Bhagavānke taraph lagā
Pnāco indriko laḍāi kare
Sab icchāke sāth
Tab saicchāko dūr luregā.

Establish the mind-Regent towards God. Uniting with desire fight all the sensory dispositions, only then will the self-desire be removed.

Āndhi dekhe āndhi
Uce dhāye
Kichu nā dekhte paye
Kevala cokh ragḍāye.
Miche keno mánaske
Bhramaṇ karāye
Dekhto ghaṭer bhitar
Svarupá jaladhar kāye.

Multifaceted tempests or else life's various impediments cause mind's agony. But when nothing can be observed, in other words when in *Kriyā*'s transcendental state settlement is attained in the void then the Third Eye yearns to visualise the soul-effulgence. It is futile to make the kinetic mind wander amidst the falsities of the earth. If visualisation is at all important it is good to visualise the own amorphous form within one's own self.

Hey mánas deo tum sadā hājiri,
Āpasme kyā tum karo jāri.
Leo Rāmanāmkā tabildāri,
Rāmake dhanuā Rāma toḍdāri.
Iha kām haye atyanta bhāri,
Snāpke mārnese haye hunri.
Madan haye dusman baḍa bhāri,
Madankā agni haye hameśā jāri.
Nāgaras dekar usko māro,
Nāginke tab uspar jaro.
Ragaḍ ragaḍ tar usko jāro,
Eysekar param lābh karo.
Brahmapad kāñcan ekkar nihāro,
Atulya dhan haye tab tumāro.

O mind, always pay attendance to the soul. On your own why do you command yourself? Abandoning all these, sit with the boundless storehouse of chanting *Prâṇá*'s name. With *Ātmârāma*'s bow annihilate the dynamism of the corporeal *Rāma* but this is an immensely difficult task. The one who can exterminate the kinetic airlike serpent he is extremely dexterous. Carnal passion is the greatest enemy and is a difficult one. The fire of carnality is always latent in the mind. Destroy carnality through the medium of *Prâṇâyāma*. Again through *Prâṇâyāma* entwine the kinetic air or else the female serpent stemming from dynamic *Prâṇá* and confine it. After this cause it to metamorphose into still *Prâṇá*. In this manner strive for the supreme attainment. Have an equanimous vision concerning the *Brahma* state and material wealth, that is realise the all-pervasive *Brahma* in material objects also. You will then be the possessor of incomparable wealth.

Kshiti cakre jābi
Cār bindu dekhte pābi
Tārmadhye bij laṃ prathībi.

If settlement occurs at the *Mūlâdhāra cakrá* or *Mūlâdhāra* (earth) essence, visualisation of four dots occurs at *Kūṭastha*. Within this the seed of the *mántra*(laṃ) can be obtained, this is the essence of the earth.

In this regard through the medium of questions and answers Yogiraj has conferred an unique knowledge on yoga—

Praśna : ***Brahmā kise kahidehu Gurú mujhe batāye.***

Uttar : ***Khānese icchā upje uha coudiś dhāye.***

Praśna : ***Humto use dekhe nahi kyāsā uskā kāye.***

Uttar : ***Haṃsa uskā nām haye uspar icchā jāye.***

Praśna : ***Haṃsa kise kahe iskā kyā haye abhiprāye.***

Uttar : ***Svāsā haṃsakā rúpa haye baḍhe ultā calāye.***

Praśna : ***Ādmi kyā pānitare maṭṭi choḍeke jāye.***

Uttar : ***Garmi Prâṇâyāmase pāni śirdi āye.***

Praśna : ***Haṃsaki āoyaj dijiye ādmise milāye.***

Uttar : ***Yaṃ raṃ laṃ baṃ sakti bindu mildeta sunāye.***

Praśna :	***Iha sab kyā haye hume dijiye samjhāye.***
Uttar :	***Laṃ prathibi bij haye ehi sab karāye.***
Praśna :	***Laṃ kaise prathībiji dijiye batāye.***
Uttar :	***Dantabarṇa courañgi icchā mánasme dekhāye.***
Praśna :	***Nirākār kyā manuṡye rahe prathibi āye.***
Uttar :	***Svādrahita bhojaná nirāhār bolāye.***
Praśna :	***Āhār binā kaise jie pṛithvitala āye.***
Uttar :	***Niḥśabd icchārahit mánashi mánas jāye.***
Praśna :	***Baṃ bijkā kyā kārkhānā dijie dekhāye.***
Uttar :	***Uskākā śuklavarṇa jalárūpá darśāye.***
Praśna :	***Jaláse kyā icchā bhayā so dijie batāye.***
Uttar :	***Jihvāse jalá gire icchā mālum hojāye.***
Praśna :	***Lobhkā kyā rūpá haye kadhitai dekhāye.***
Uttar :	***Lalmu ākh āṭhaor uckā kahāye.***
Praśna :	***Raṃ raktavarṇa agnimaṇḍal kneyokar dekhāye.***
Uttar :	***Māre bān jab śabdkā bole bināś rahāye.***
Praśna :	***Yaṃ vāyumaṇḍal dhūmbavarṇá madanālāye.***
Uttar :	***Unhā bañchāti riktaphala kabhi na naśāye.***

Q. What is *Brahma*, O *Gurúdeva* please explain.

A. When pangs of hunger afflict the body, the mind wanders in different directions concerning the appeasement of hunger, similarly all-pervasiveness is *Brahma*. From this Omnipresent *Brahma* everything evolves.

Q. What is the form of that *Brahma*, I have never seen before.

A. Breathlike *Haṃsa* is His name, desire is oriented towards breath.

Q. Who is termed as *Haṃsa* and what is it's significance?

A. Breath is the form of *Haṃsa*, it misdirects man to proceed in the reverse direction, that is towards the sensory dispositions.

Q. When man proceeds towards water, then does he progress by going beyond the earth?

A. Water is the form of Amorphous *Brahma*. If perfect *Prâṇâyāma* is practised, waterlike Amorphous *Brahma* settles on the head.

Q. Expatiate on that *Haṃsa* which enables a *yogi* to reach the Primordial Being.

A. *Yaṃ*(यं) (air essence, smokish hue), *raṃ*(रं) fire essence, red colour) laṃ(लं) (earth essence, the universe) and *baṃ* (बं)(water essence, white) — when the power of these four essences through austere augmented *Prâṇâyāma* practice merge in the *Kűṭastha* dot, only then it's sound emanates (*Óṃkāra* sound).

Q. Could you please explain all these in an elaborate manner.

A. The word *laṃ*(लं) is the seed of the earth (earth essence) and is responsible for causing all earthly causations.

Q. How did *laṃ* become the earth essence, please explain.

A. The four-petalled lotus is stationed at *Mūlâdhāra,* it is here that the seed of the earth *laṃ* exists. Due to the force of exalted *Prâṇâyāma*, when settlement occurs at *Mūlâdhāra*, the ever-wandering kinetic mind can be envisioned in the still mind.

Q. Is Amorphous *Brahma*-knowledge possible for man habiting this earthly world, in other words for the *yogi* settled at *Mūlâdhāra* essence?

A. Just as the one who consumes food having no attention towards taste is referred to as the non-eater, similarly the *yogi* settled at *Mūlâdhāra* essence having no attention on the earth-essence, *Brahma*-knowledge is possible.

Q. By what means can a living being born in this earth subsist without food?

A. Through excellent *Prâṇâyāma* when a *yogi* goes beyond *Anahatā* or the *Ómkāra* sound then he is free from all aspirations. In this aspiration-free state, kinetic mind merges into the still mind. Then remaining in the state beyond body-consciousness, food intake becomes redundant.

Q. What is the function of the *baṃ* seed or else show me what evolves from the seed *baṃ*?

A. The seed *baṃ* is white in colour located at *Svadhisṭhāna*. It is the water essence, it's form is amorphous like water.

Q. How does desire evolve from the water essence, kindly explain.

A. Water evolves from the tongue. This purports the existence of desire.

Q. What is the form of greed and how does it look?

A. The mind hankers for this and that and frets in suppressed greed, in other words is oriented towards material objects.

Q. When can the red *raṃ* seed, ball of fire be visualised?

A. Through the power of intense *Prâṇâyāma* when a *yogi* can go beyond *Anāhata* and *Ómkāra* sounds, then he habits in the *Maṇipura Cakrá*.

Q. *Yaṃ* seed (*Mūlâdhāra*) is airlike and smokish in hue and is the place of the God of Love (*Bhagavān* Krishna).

A. Settlement at *Mūlâdhāra* entails going beyond desires, aspirations; going beyond consequences (non-producing results, dispassionate). This state is imperishable. In this state a *yogi* remaining in the state of non-volitional volition, attains everything. Then he visualises Amorphous *Brahma* akin to the formlessness of water and an all-pervasive red *Ātmasúrya* (Soul-Sun). He envisions Amorphous *Brahma* less opaque than smoke.

Therefore Yogiraj recounting His daily *sādhana* realizations had explained — ***Brahma jalkā rūpá haye. Raktavarṇa sūrya dekhā. Dhuyāse kuch patlā Brahmakā rūpá nirākār mālum huyā.*** *Brahma* is the form of water. I visualised the blood-red sun. I realised the Amorphous *Brahma* to be less denser than smoke.

Yogiraj would note almost every detail in His diary. From His diary an interesting information regarding the then market price can be deduced. On 31st December 1890, he paid Rs. 3.00 to a shopkeeper, Prankrishna Modak for price of 6 seers (13.1/2 lbs) sandesh and Rs. 2.50 for 1/2 maund (41lbs) milk. On the same day, He paid the following amount to Ramcharan, another sweetmeat shopkeeper of Kashi — Rupees two and six annas for 5.75 seers (12.95 lbs) of bundiya, rupees one and eleven annas one paise for two seers three poas (6.30 lbs) of kachoris, rupees two and three annas for five seers (11.25 lbs) of jilebis and rupees two and seven annas for eight and half seers (19 lbs) of buttermilk.

* * * * * *

The *yogic* or intrinsic explanation through allegories made by Yogiraj in His diary regarding Bhagavan Krishna and His Divine Abstruse Causations through the medium of questions and answers have been rendered here precisely without any distortions —

Q. — Bhagavan Krishna was born as a son of *Devakī* and *Vāsudeva* at Mathura, later due to the dread of King *Kaṃsa*, He had to be removed by *Vāsudeva* to a safe place in the house of *Nanda* at *Gokul*. Renowned as the son of *Nanda* and *Yasodā* He visited *Vrajá* (*Vrindāvana*) from *Gokul* with *Gopes* and *Gopinis*. He accompanied by *Valarāma* and all the *Gopes* would make the cows graze; caper in a holy manner; His mother bound him to a husking machine as He stole butter; He uprooted two Arjuna trees by hand; with the help of *Valarāma* He killed demons sent to Him by *Kaṃsa*; subjugated the monstrous serpent in River Yamuna; consumed fire; when *Nanda* decided to perform *Indrayajñá* Bhagavan Krishna persuaded him not to do so, instead He demonstrated His own *yajñá* and proved the supremacy of it; on being offended *Indra* caused torrential downpour, Bhagavan Krishna upheaved a hillock and held it as an umbrella to protect the *Gopes* and *Gopinis* of *Vrajá* from the rain; during childhood He overturned a bed by His legs; on the pretext of sucking breast milk of *Pūtnā*, a female demon, Krishna killed her; the notes of His flute effected raptness, subjugation and submissiveness from *Brahmā* and the lesser gods to animate and inanimate objects to the extent that on the night of the full moon, married women eloped abandoning their homes, husbands, sons, relatives; while they were away bathing in a pond, He took possession of their clothes surreptitiously, communed with each of them by taking shape of many Krishnas and observed *Rāsa* festival; later He went to Mathura alongwith *Valarāma* and killed the demons — an elephant ran amuck, *Cāṇur, Mushṭik* etc. and subsequently *Kaṃsa*; eventually constructed the city of *Dvārakā* and resided there.

Afferent answer :

Srikrishna	*Kúṭastha*
Mathurā	Head
Devakī	Body
Vāsudeva	Soul
Kaṃsa	Illusion
Gokul	Tongue to be placed on the upper palate.
Nanda abode	State of settlement.
Gope / Gopini (Milkman/Milkwoman)	Practising *Ómkāra Kriyā* with the help of soul and body.
Yasodā	Renown occurs when settlement is achieved.
Vrajá	Passing away.
Vṛindāvana	Visualising forests within *Kúṭastha*.
Valarāma	Application of strength during internal

		inhalation whereby stillness is achieved.
Milkman(*Gopi*)		Different types of *Kriyā* such as *Tríkuṭa* (triangle within *Kűṭastha*) *Brahmarekhā* (the sign of *Brahma*), *Pañcasrotā* (the five streams) etc. are located at various places on the tongue.
Grazing		Lifting the tongue to the palate cavity.
Holy caper	a)	Raising the tongue by springing.
	b)	Proper raising of tongue.
Stealing of butter		Merging of Soul-Moon in *Kűṭastha*.
By *Yasodā*		Being settled, yogic renown occurs.
Husking machine		Head.
Bound		Affix.
By hands		*Sushumná*.
Two *Arjuna* trees		*Iḍā* and *Piṅgalá*.
Uprooted		Remaining in *Sushumná* after abandoning *Iḍā* and *Piṅgalá*.
Various demons		Digression of mind.
Killed		Destroyed.
Yamuna		*Piṅgalá*
In Yamuna (between *Iḍā* and *Piṅgalá*)		*Sushumná*
Monstrous serpent		Passage of time, material attachment.
Subjugated		Settlement occurs after material detachment.
Consumption of fire		Water and fire being purified by air, fire evolves in the body; that air attaining stillness consumption of fire occurs.
Indrayajñá		Affixing unitedly at *Kűṭastha Brahma*.
Persuade		Persuading the mind not to digress.
Own *yajñá*		Transcendental state of *Kriyā*.

On being offended *Indra* caused torrential downpour	Due to material attachment existing in a different essence through the medium of eyes, conjecture of mind, the waves of thought termed as torrential downpour emanate.
Hillock upheaval	Raising the tongue and holding it for *Ómkāra Kriyā*.
During childhood He overturned a bed by His legs	During internal *Prâṇâyāma* the air is raised from the *Mūlādhāra cakrá* to the *Ājñācakrá*, this is overturning of the bed.
On the pretext of sucking breast milk of *Pūtṇā*, a female demon, He killed her.	Stilling of air in the *Anāhata cakrá* eliminates ignorance.
Notes of flute	The *ṡi ṡi* sound of *Prâṇâyāma*.
From *Brahmā* and lesser gods	All desires.
From lesser gods till animate and inanimate objects are enamoured	At the time of practising *Kriyā* all the senses are enamoured and thereby results in fulfilment of all desires.
Married women	Illusion.
At night	When there is darkness (ignorance).
Abandoning homes	Engrossment of the mind in the five senses instead of communing with the soul.
Their husbands	Self-conceit.
Sons, relatives	Illusion.
Taking possession of clothes surreptitiously.	Spontaneous evocation of impediment-free state this infers *Brahma*-pervaded universe.
Rāsa festival on full moon night	Envisioning *Brahma* in everything.

Elephant ran amuck, *Cāṇur, Mustịk*, other demons and *Kaṃsa*	Everything is illusion.
Dvārakā city	*Kūṭastha*

* * * * * *

Seoyāye Bhagavānko jo koi kām kare so baḍā kharāb ādmi haye — sab mánas luṭ jāye par oospar najar na kare — jo Bhagavānko hāmesā dhyāna kare oosko kām uha kartā hyāye. — The person who performs all actions other than remembering God is not good. When the existence of the present kinetic mind is obliterated, the kinetic mind settles in the still mind, a state of mindlessness is achieved, in other words when the present kinetic mind does not harbour an iota of mindfulness any longer — while practising *Prâṇákarma* when this type of mindless state evolves, it is the actual state of *dhyāna*. The one who constantly practises this type of mindless *dhyāna* towards God all his actions are then performed by God Himself, he performs nothing since he is beyond actions. Hence, in this state all his actions are executed by God. Thus on 26th March, 1873 Yogiraj has stated — ***Āhaste āhaste bemālum sab kām hotā haye.*** — Slowly or gradually without being aware of anything, without desiring or thinking, all actions are spontaneously occurring, by My Soul-Self, the endeavour to perform anything no longer exists. When does this state arrive for a *yogi*? Yogiraj has defined — ***Binā icchār lābh baḍā lābh bodh haye tadbad binā Kumbhake Kumbhaka baḍā ānanda.*** —The object which was never desired to be gained even then if the object is acquired by fluke it is regarded as an immense gain, similarly even if *Kumbhaka* is not wilfully practised, still it spontaneously occurs, this is extremely blissful. A *yogi* invested with this type of state attains all forms of Divine powers. Therefore He has elucidated — ***Sárvaśaktivānkā honekā āgam mālum huyā jo sakas sab cij jāntā***

haye so sakas sab cij kar sektā haye. Jab sab aihi haye to Humbhi aihi haye to Hum sab kuch kar sektā haye — I comprehended the esotericism of becoming Omnipotent, the person Who is Omniscient can perform everything. When everything is pervaded by His Ubiquitous Being then I also am Him, therefore now I also can perform everything. Yogiraj has expounded on 13th May, 1873 — ***Iha sűryahi Ādipuŕusha ho jātā haye phir ehi Brahmakā liṅgarūpá lambā mālum hotā haye soi Hum haye. Usse ek jyot nikaltā haye jo na din na rāt — usse mil yānekā nām huyā laya tabhi śarīrse budā hotā haye — āur yo kuch irādā kare so kar saktā haye — das roj rātdin ekāgracitta binā khāye piye soye premlagāoye tab iha bāt siddha hoye binā sab āśā choḍnese iha bāt kayse hogā — āge marji Mālik ki*** — This *Ātmasűrya* I am visualising became the Primordial Male Energy, again He was converted into the extended phallus of *Brahma*, that only is Myself. From that phallus of *Brahma* a certain resplendence is emanating where there is no day or night, only self-manifestation, becoming confluent there, is known as mergence. When this type of mergence occurred, then the body became non-vibratory, in this state I could perform anything I wished; without food, water and sleep for ten days and ten nights, if *Ātmakarma* is practised in the same *āsaná* with deep abosorption only then can this state be attained but until all types of aspirations are relinquished, how is this possible? Thus aspirations evolve from vibrations of the mind. As long as vibrations of the mind persist, aspirations will also persist. While continually practising *Ātmakarma* when all types of vibrations being exterminated complete stillness arrives, then aspirations are non-existent, deriving this state entitles spontaneous fulfilment in all aspects, therefore the state of permanent settlement is attained. Thus offering all cares to the Master, totally surrendering His Self He remarked — now the difficult *sādhana* which lies ahead or else the difficult step of *sādhana* which I am perceiving, let that occur which the Master so desires. The complexities of this step of *sādhana* has been detailed by Him on 16th July 1873 — ***Svabhāv Brahma haye — isse pār jānā muskil āj indriyone satāyā sabko mārke āśā tyāgke āpne āp laya honā kām haye — lekan magan rahanese ānandá rahat haye — par bishay caitanya nahi rahatā haye — rātke ab ehi erādā kartā haye ki rātbhar baiṭhke magan kaṭāoye — tākat kuch baḍānā cāhiye***— It is specious that the soul-consciousness only is *Brahma* and it is difficult to overcome this. Therefore now My function is to control all the senses, relinquish all desires and merge Myself totally with *Brahma*. Bliss exists if one is uninterruptedly engrossed in *Brahmadhyāna*, in that state material consciousness or material intelligence does not persist. Thus the wish is to spend the whole night in the state of *samādhi* by being engrossed in *Brahamadhyāna* but for this I have to acquire some more extra energy. Before this He has made a statement on 29th June 1873 — ***Ab bhitar bhitar kuch kuch jāne lāgā — baḍā kaṭhin kabārā — inhā koi haye nahi ki jisko pakaḍke hosme ādmi rahe — jayse nid — lekan ṭhik nid nahi haye — hamesā Ómkāra dhvani — Rājā Purushôttama sāmne khaḍe — santoshāmṛita pān — is majeke āge koi majā jo kare so cākhe nahito rahe gotā khāte*** — Now I have entered somewhat within, it is an abstruse access. To traverse this abstruse access is difficult. In this state there is none who can provide support to enable one to remain in consciousness or else while regularly practising *Prāṇákarma* when the totality mingles and merges into one, then duality being non-existent who will lend support to whom ? This implies a material mindlessness evoking a state of impassivity. It resembles sleep but it is not exactly sleep. In this state the *Ómkāra* sound can be perpetually heard. The Paramount Ruler, the Supreme Being is standing ahead, that is drinking of the ambrosial bliss. Before gaining this type of ecstasy the other types of material happiness become insignificant the moment they are tasted, a person remaining contented with this type of happiness suffers blows and counterblows. He has repeated — ***Piche merādaṇḍme śvāsā majese calne lagā — āb gharme āoye — āb baḍā ānandá — murdā jitā haye jabtaome laya hoye — jiskā ki Brahmamay dṛishti haye unke icchā karneke pahile manokāmanā siddha hoye — ab sthir honekā lakshmaṇ pak āyā haye.*** — Fluid breathing continues within *Sushumná*, now I entered the still state and am feeling extremely ecstatic. After this when the totality merged then body-consciousness became extinct, in other words all types of vibrations within the body being annihilated, the state beyond body-consciousness was conquered which signified the acquisition of the permanent habit of remaining for a long period of time in the state beyond body-consciousness. In other words the true *Śabsādhana* (a mystical rite or contemplation on a dead body) is to convert this conscious body into a deadlike still body and dwell within it. Pulling any dead body and squatting atop it is not the actual *Śabsādhana*. This type of *yogi* who has settled himself beyond body-consciousness constantly perceives the pervasive *Brahma*, before he wishes anything his desire is automatically fulfilled. Achieving this state, Yogiraj thus remarked — now there has been a permanent indication of that type of still state. It is an exalted state of a *yogi*. Attaining this state on 6th August 1873 Yogiraj comments — ***Brahmai asal haye — sūryarūpá haye phir uha rūpá nahi haye kévala Brahma — ab ek jagai baiṭhkā erādā kare — sāhas karke jo kare so hoye eysā mālum hotā haye — stṛímātāri Purúsharūpá laḍki mākārūpá — laḍkā bāpkārūpá — bāpmātāri sab jātā haye — āpnā sab dono rūpá rukh jātā haye — Púrusha Prakṛiti choḍāye āur kuch nahi iha anādi banā haye — uskā bahut rūpá haye isliye uha anantarūpá haye — lekan ekhī rūpákā sakala pasarā haye.*** —*Brahma* only is the Origin and Primordial. This assumed the form of *Ātmasúrya*, again it did not exist for it merged with the infinite void, only the still *Brahma* remained. Now I feel like sitting in *āsaná* at a stretch and I also realised that if I cause anything to be performed with courage, it will be performed. The essence of wife and mother assumed the form of Primordial Male Energy; the essence of daughter and son assumed the forms of mother and father respectively. In this manner the essence of each and everything alongwith that of father and mother merged into that infinite void, even this Self of Mine which was being perceived as separate, dual, that also became stilled and attained oneness. Thus barring the Primordial Male Energy, I cannot perceive anything else in totality, the Primordial Male and Female Energy are eternal. That Energy has assumed many Forms, for that reason this Energy possesses Infinite Forms, but I realise that from that sole Amorphous *Brahma* everything is being expanded or extended. Therefore He would advise His devotees thus — ***Āineme dui dekhnese ahaṃkār ek dekhnese kuch nahi.*** — As long as reflection is noticed on the mirror duality and self-conceit exist, but when the entirety merges into one then nothing is present because duality being absent, who will feel conceited ?

Where there is no duality, there is no evidence. As long as the body-consciousness exists, till then evidence exists. When there is no body-consciousness, there is no duality. For instance, silver is an element. Anything possessing the virtue of the silver element is silver also. Where these two (object and virtue) are non-existent, it is beyond evidence. Practising *Kriyā* of the essences, the *Kriyā's* transcendental state which arrives is the state beyond essences. Duality results in misery and if one desires to go beyond all miseries it is imperative to constantly exist, but *Brahma* is beyond conflicts. It is for this reason that by proof or by being provable *Brahma* cannot be ascertained. All the forms which can be visualised while practising *Kriyā*, what those forms are, from where they emanate and in what manner they can be visualised, all these thoughts give rise to malice (antipathy towards the self) and for visualising this attachment evolves. A perceptible object is destructible. *Kriyā's* transcendental state which is beyond the *Brahma* Who exists within all shapes in the form of *aṇu*, is the knowledge of essence. Visualising all the forms, many arguments appear in the mind—whether these are real or fallacious? This argument appearing in the mind evokes malice on ascertainment of it's form; *Brahma* does not exist here also. Ultimately it was resolved through the medium of arguments and deliberations that all these were actions of the kinetic mind. The static mind is *Brahma*. All those forms which seemed subtle could not be perceived. Ascertaining likewise is the function of malice, but *Brahma* is absent in it because He is beyond essence. In *Kriyā's* transcendental state when self is non-existent, duality is non existent. Thus duality being extinct, malice, arguments etc. are all non-existent. Only by constantly abiding in this state, the knowledge of essence dawns. Then the void essence exists beyond speculations and sophistry. That void essence is *Brahma* because *Brahma* is beyond the essences. Where there is duality there is evidence, but beyond evidence is *Kriyā's* transcendental state; duality being non-existent there, evidence is absent. Then is 'one' prevalent ? That existence or non-existence of that 'one' is the same because if the person who will denote oneness becomes 'one' himself, then there is no difference whether 'one' exists or not. Thus *Brahma* is beyond proof, for He himself is His only proof. This proof is executed through the medium of sense-oriented perception, conjecture, analogy and mystic sound. Just as forms can be perceived by the eyes; eyes exist in the dead body, but why cannot these eyes perceive? Perception through the eyes by the medium of a particular power is *Brahma*-Power or *Brahma*-Energy. *Brahma* is the Principal Source of all Energy. In the transcendental state of *Kriyā*, there is no energy yet it is replete with energy. Practising *Kriyā* evokes *Kriyā's* transcendental state. Then the *Prâṇá* air becoming still merges in *Brahma* evoking *Kriyā's* transcendental state, in other words the transcendental state of *Kriyā* which did not exist before, now exists, it only is knowledge, this is self-consciousness. But what stands in comparision with this *Brahma*? *Sādhya, sādhanā* and *sādhárma. Sādhya* — The One Who can be attained by austere endeavours or else *Brahma. Sādhana* — the medium by which the object of austere endeavours can be attained i.e. *Kriyā. Sādhárma* —transcendental state of *Kriyā*. By not abiding in *Kriyā's* transcendental state the mind wanders elsewhere, if the mind wanders it observes and observation causes suffering. Digression of the mind entails earthly action. Thus it is erroneous not to exist in *Kriyā's* transcendental state. If one remains in material attachment, birth continues. The error which stems from non-abidance in *Kriyā's* transcendental state is the result, in other words various desires evolve in the mind due to the non-existence in *Kriyā's* transcendental state; in accordance with all those desires various actions are being accomplished. To suffer the consequences of those past actions birth is inevitable. Thus remaining in *Kriyā's* transcendental state desires are extinct; when desires are extinct, actions are absent; when actions are absent results or material attachment are non-existent thereby eliminating births. Therefore to cause a cessation of the cycle of births and deaths, instead of arguments and deliberations or wasting unnecessary time it is imperative to practise *Kriyā*. Practising *Kriyā* in this manner is referred to as *sādhana*. By practising this *sādhana*, the Supreme Energy or *Brahma* Energy evolves, dwelling in it is *Pañcatapa* (five mystic fires present in the body).

If the present does not exist, past and future also do not exist. Therefore the past and future subsist on the present. Abandoning the present does not bring forth direct perception. The direct perception is within the fold of time; without time there cannot be direct perception. When direct perception occurs, then present exists, thus due to dearth of the present or of time, direct perception becomes a non-entity. Again when direct perception is absent, then past, future, present and the continual flow of time, nothing exist. Similarly in

Kriyā's transcendental state all these are absent. This *Kriyā's* transcendental state is exclusively dependant on *Kriyā*. This *Kriyā* is the *yajñá* of sacred fire and the latent laudation. If anyone develops a disinterest towards *Kriyā* then it's virtues should be extolled; through the medium of direct realisations and examples his inspiration in *Kriyā* should be augmented, this is the external laudation, in other words it is the foremost duty of a good *Kriyāban* to explain to the disinterested one that practising *Kriyā* imparts welfare and benefits and many have attained spiritual upliftment through this. Again those who fail to practise *Kriyā* and abandon it after obtaining initiation should be condemned. Practising this *Kriyā* all types of benefits accrue and this should be repeatedly explained to the erring one. Administration of a particular medicine alleviating a particular disease has been stipulated in the books on Ayurvedic treatment. When alleviation of the affliction by administering the relative medicine is noticed, then it is authentic. Similarly when practice of *Kriyā* causes mental deliverance and acts as a panacea, then this *Kriyā* is also authentic. If the right medicine is not administered at the right moment the disease will not be allayed, similarly if the method of mental deliverance from the right *Gurú* is not derived, the *mántra* is rendered futile. The state of deliverance of mind is known as *mántra*. Those who have achieved the state of union are knowledgeable about the God-essence and they being moved by the misery of others impart advice pertaining to *Kriyā*. If the mind is wholly offered, *Kriyā's* transcendental state evolves. That is oblation and if the mind is offered in an excellent fashion it never remains disconnected with the one offered to, thus when it perpetually remains united it is positively permanent. A deep engrossment occurs in the transcendental state of *Kriyā*, when this depth of engrossment lessens, it is referred to as the pre-transcendental state of *Kriyā*. A *yogi* by existing in this state performs all actions, and though performing all actions does not perform anything at all. Of course immediately after initiation *Kriyā's* transcendental state cannot be realised because it is dependant on prolonged practice. Thus merely obtaining *Kriyā* initiation does not effect *Kriyā's* transcendental state, and it's repeated execution becomes the habitual action. Whenever *Kriyā* is practised *Kriyā's* transcendental state of *samādhi* occurs, therefore the act of self-reformation or habitual action resulting in *Kriyā's* transcendental state is imperative and is beyond being forsaken. In *Kriyā's* transcendental state (*samādhi*) which is beyond the senses, where one existed, in what manner or in what bliss one existed cannot be ascertained as the ascertainable mind has become extinct. Being beyond all types of essences, attributes, entities and the sense of touch, it has no impediments regarding it's permanance and it has no means by which it can be expressed. Types of essence being latent in a human in a special manner is termed to be the human shape. In the idol of Krishna which is worshipped, the inherent essence of *Bhagavān* is totally absent, even the most common attributes of *Sattva, Rájas, Támas* are non-existent. The Supreme Being *Nārāyaṇá* invested with the inherent essence or the infinite essence, Whose Form exists within all of us, knowing this *Nārāyaṇá* tantamounts to be knowledge of the *Satya-Nārāyaṇá (true Nārāyaṇá)* failing which entails lack of knowledge about the *Satya-Nārāyaṇá*.

For soul, intellect is not necessary. All the elements for intellect pertain to the kinetic mind, the still mind is vacant because *Brahma* is eternally Omnipresent in the same manner, He is unchangeable. The mind, soul etc. are merely variances in definition. When the mind is rapt in the soul, then this rapt-mind is referred to be the soul; again when the mind is rapt within the essence, this only is termed to be the mind. All the senses are subject to the mind, the mind is subject to the soul, the soul in turn is subject to the Infinite Soul. The One *Brahma* only is the eternal totality. Habits of previous births continue well into subsequent births thus mirth, fear, grief, anger, etc., occur. One who has performed function of *Sattva* attribute in previous birth, will in this birth and the next birth perform same function of the same attribute. The one who was in *Sattva* attribute in the previous birth, will in this birth be religious from childhood and the one who belonged to *Támas* attribute will naturally be oriented towards cruelty or evil in this birth. All the indications can be noticed from childhood. For instance certain children are fond of frogs, whilst some are cruel towards them. Some are extremely grief-stricken at the loss of their son while some are not affected even a little. But mirth, sorrow, fear, grief, anger, etc., are all absent to the soul. Desire itself is a possession of the mind; achieving cessation of desires entails the birth-free state. When the soul is free from desire, when desire dissolves, then how is rebirth of the soul possible ? But the soul being invested with virtues, birth accrues. Just as when the virtue of a tree is lost, the tree withers away, similarly the moment the soul becomes attributeless, it merges with *Brahma*. *Brahma* is Infinite and from this Absolute *Brahma* everything emanates. For this reason *Brahma* is Omnipotent. One who is conversant with *Brahma* possesses unlimited power. The three worlds are in proximity to *Brahma-aṇu*, therefore the *Brahma*-conversant person can visualise the three worlds within the *aṇu* of *Brahma*. But due to the disparity of stillness and due to the proximity of the mind or virtue a different state arises and this entails a difference in perception, for instance the deities of *Jagadhāṭri, Sárasvatī, Ganeśa* and *Brahmā* prevail in the *Mūlâdhāra cakrá*, Radha-Krishna in the *Svâdhishṭhāna cakrá* etc. The action of visualisation also is the disposition of the elements but nothing can be envisioned in *Kriyā's* transcendental state. Then if non-visualisation becomes the disposition, why does visualisation occur? The respective divisions of *Brahma-aṇu* brings about the respective forms of manifestation, then those types of forms can be visualised because each and every *aṇu* of *Brahma* comprises three worlds. That state in a subtle form reacting on the elements appears to be different, thus envisioning this also is the elemental propensity. The Effulgence of *Kūṭastha* is so intense that this shades all other earthly effulgences thus rendering them imperceptible, likewise daylight being intenser than the shooting of a meteor renders the latter to be imperceptible. However the gods and spiritually attained beings characterised by Br*ahma*-Effulgence can be visualised within *Kūṭastha* (in *Yónimudrā*). When one is characterised by *Brahma*-Efflugence or spontaneously settling in *Brahma* everything can be perceived then, because in the one part of a *Brahma-aṇu* the world exists — *Gītā* proves this — ***Ekāṃśena sthito jagad.*** — After the augmented practice of *Prâṇákarma* and *Ómkāra Kriyā* when an equally replete intensity of resplendence occurs then the demarcation between small and great is obliterated and going beyond the elemental propensity none can elude the other thus it is impediment-free. *Yogis* being characterised by this type of intense resplendence and achieving the non-illusory state do not visualise anything yet can visualise everything. This intense resplendence of *Brahma* is all pervasive but does not manifest by being unequal and being equal brings forth manifestation. Being manifested by *Brahma*-Effulgence, all internal images can be envisioned through insight, again entering the *Brahma*-Effulgence or *Brahma* or achieving mergence, all functions of hearing, seeing etc. attain dissolution just as salt dissolves in water. Then the manifestable, clarified attribute of ignorance not existing *Kūṭastha* also cannot be visualised. Attaining stillness through *Kriyā* is intelligence, constantly abiding in this state is settlement, remaining in stillness a *yogi* can move anywhere in a subtle form and if movement is present forms can be viewed; but when *Kriyā's* transcendental state is Void *Brahma*, then there is nothing, it's reverse entails intra-visualisations and intra-sounds. But these visualisations and sounds also are perishable thus transient because visualisation and non-visualisation not co-existing, it is impermanent. Thus not settling in *Brahma* one is within the ambit of form, or concentrating on extraneities the appellations of householder, *saṃnyāsin*, **Brahmin, Kshatriya** etc. evolve. These appellations are untrue, because not abiding in *Brahma*, but abiding in attributes these appellations ensue. Both mind and soul are the same. In *Kriyā's* transcendental state soul is free from attachment; again when it acknowledges happiness and misery it is mind. Origination of universality is the domain of the Master, not of mind. Why? When the kinetic mind becomes Master after attaining stillness, the soul is capable of visualising both. As long as the mind is externally oriented it is restless but when it becomes still and enters the still mind then it is Master. Master means *Brahma*. Universal unison and universal consciousness originate in *Brahma*. This irradiance occurs in the transcendental state of *Kriyā*, it does not pertain to the kinetic mind. When the mind becomes tranquil it becomes the intellect because then visualisation, non-visualisation, knowledge, ignorance are all extinct, thus there is no conflict and conflict being absent when everything attains permanence, then intellect also becomes permanent. Thus *Kriyā's* transcendental state or the cessation of desire is knowledge. That state or knowledge occurs through *Ātmakriyā*. The *sādhana* by which knowledge accrues, executing that *sādhana* wholly is termed also as knowledge; knowledge ensues in *Kriyā's* transcendental state. The *sādhana* for acquiring that state is *Kriyā* and if this is practised wholly or excellently, knowledge dawns or *Kriyā's* transcendental state can be realised. Practising *Kriyā* wholly pertains to the soul, for who can practise *Kriyā* if the soul is absent? Since reformation is caused by the soul, the mind's proximity is effected in the soul, then the desire to practise *Kriyā* is enkindled and practising continual *Kriyā* causes the mind to merge in the soul, this manner of the soul and mind's proximity results in memory. For instance, a necessity to go somewhere the next morning occurred to the mind. On the previous day's recollection the next morning's visit was made to the place concerned, similarly certain events of previous birth are called to mind in subsequent births also. When the soul and mind of this birth come in contact and are united, then events co-relating to the previous birth impinge upon the mind and actions in this birth are executed in accordance to them. The attribute of soul is mind, for this reason both the attributive quality of soul and kinetic mind are same. When that mind becoming still enters the soul, *Kriyā's* transcendental state occurs, then the simultaneous evolvement of the soul and mind do not occur for the non-existence of duality; just as when curd and milk are mixed together, it being one and same none can know the other. The conjunction of body, mind and soul is life. This life by the union of soul and mind abiding in the shelter of action gathers experience, on the reverse this life itself is capable of achieving *Kriyā's* transcendental state (Master) by practising *Kriyā*. Mind only develops external knowledge, in other words the mind conceives externalities through senses. But the soul is not involved in it because it is devoid of attachment. Since soul is devoid of attachment, visualisation and the faculty of sound are all products of the mind. All these are executed by the body and mind's development of external knowledge. Body being the field of enjoyment and suffering, weal and woe pertain to the body but are sensed by the mind. It is not always necessary that the moment recollection is made visualisation will occur in the mind, again solely mind is not the agent for whatever is being visualised but the coalescence of soul and mind brings about visualisation. Thus *Brahma*-realisation is not the mind's domain, when impediments are exterminated or else the impediment-free state brings about realisation, the mind attaining conjunction with the soul causes memory, which occurs due to the propensity of previous births. In other words, the mind on entering the soul repeatedly strives to gradually memorise memorable objects, just as the moment mind conceives about milk, it's form, virtue and taste do not evolve in the mind at once and the same time or simultaneously. If the symptoms of all objects could be conceived at one and the same time then memory also would have evolved simultaneously. Again practising enhanced *Ātmakarma* when totality can be envisioned then the origination of universality and it's non-origination are absent, in other words the soul's attachment and detachment are absent because *Brahma* is all-pervasive; in one *aṇu* of *Brahma* the five essences are prevalent. Remaining afar from *Brahma* is called misery. One who does not possess desire to obtain anything is devoid of happiness or misery because happiness or misery pertains to the mind. Soul is Omnipresent and Infinite, exists in the form of a living being, in this manner *Śivá* (soul) in the form of a living being exists in universal pervasion, therefore He is Master of Universe. *Brahma* abides as the Void in all elements animate and inanimate. All elements are framed by the five essences and life exists in all essences. Animate within inanimate is comprehensible to *yogis* only. For this reason *yogis* (whose actions have ended; who have achieved the state of union) do not practise *dhyāna* because engrossment, engrosser and engrossed have attained oneness for them, they are visualising *Brahma* universally. Though he does not perceive anything through senses, he has no impediment to realise it through knowledge.

If *Kriyā* is practised attentively only then it is *Kriyā*, otherwise it is not *Kriyā* at all. Likewise attentive habitation in the material world entails actual habitation, otherwise it becomes habitation being non-habitant. As long as mind and desire are present till then material attachment exists, when mind and desire are absent then material attachment is also absent. If mind and desire are absent, rules and actions are also absent, thus *dhāraṇā* (realisation), *dhyāna* and *sāmadhi* are all non-existent. Many a time it so happens that a memorable object failing to be remembered is entered upon deeply by the mind which gradually loses it's entity, in other words the recollection occurring in the mind's state of non-kineticism or detachment is termed as profound *dhyāna*. Again reflecting upon the symbol, shape, virtue etc. of an object which has been lost, memory results in the mind's complete fastening into it which is referred to as fixation of the mind. Such an object capable of being recalled once appears in the mind, this object can be well remembered by the mind, repeatedly concentrating upon it the appellation of this repeated concentration is practice. This is the function of soul, for this reason soul is the cause for recollection as nothing would have occurred or will occur if the soul is absent. But when the quest for the signs of recollection is made then it infers absence of the perpetual existence of recollection, again recollection is not possible without symptoms, because it is symptom-dependant. Thoughts can never evolve if an object which may be called to mind is absent or it's indications are absent. In this manner recollection being termed once as permanent, again as impermanent infers the soul also to be permanent and impermanent. But this is not so because by the actuation of intellect and transcendental intellect, the soul merges in the Infinite Soul and remains static, it's recollection implies the existence of duality, thus recollection is actuated by the intellect, for this reason intellect acts as a stimulus for recollection. But recollection, intellect are all non-existent in *Kriyā's* transcendental state. Again when there is a descension to the pre-transcendental state of *Kriyā,* then recollection on mind and *Kriyā's* transcendental state are effected; due to this, recollection attains duality.

The continuum of this sequel of previous births results in the present body-origination. Propensities of the previous body can be observed at the inception of the present body, for instance immediately after nascence a newborn wails, looks, stirs etc. This is the continuum. As an effect of previous births the virtues and vices of this birth result; for the sake of suffering and enjoyment the soul dwells in this body but the independent *Brahma* remains detached which He always is since eternity. To suffer and enjoy the sequel of preceding births, the soul presides in this body in the form of bubbles which is referred to by people as 'myself'. Since all the actions of preceding births remain attached to the soul in a special manner, these unnecessary sufferings and enjoyments occur. But in

Kriyā's transcendental state when a decrement in actions can be noticed then how is body-origination for the purpose of action possible ? For the purpose of action, body-origination alongwith the soul, happiness and misery are sensed. But when there is a decrement in actions, abstraction of the soul occurs which in turn results in abstraction of the body; the soul then becomes confluent in *Brahma*. The moment there is an action declension, stoicism arrives and when this is effected there is a cessation of attachment-oriented thus physical mental-verbal-oriented action. In this manner there being an action declension the Primordial Soul attains passivity, then the cause for action not existing in the passive state body-origination does not recur. Here body-origination signifies origination of all three bodies—gross, subtle and causal. Then that passive state becomes the origin. Essence of the Supreme Being is *Kűṭastha*, the essence of *Kűṭastha* is soul, soul's essence in turn is the mind and mind's essence is the senses. Action of all elements are executed by these sensory faculties and in the state beyond action or in *Kriyā's* transcendental state all attain the state of mergence in *Brahma*, therefore then the body no longer exists, this implies that the body-consciousness is absent. Therefore then both the body and visualisation are non-existent. Again in the pre-transcendental state of *Kriyā*, a gradual body-consciousness emerges. Thus the type of visualisations, intra-sound faculty and finally the confluence depend upon the quality of *Kriyā* one practises. This infers that visualisation, intra-sound faculty and ultimately the attainment of Divine Confluence are relative to the level of excellence in *Kriyā* practised by an individual. Being detached by remaining in *Kriyā's* transcendental state all actions can be performed because then all the senses merge in the mind, the mind in the soul and soul in *Brahma*. Again when *Brahma* coalesces in the soul, the soul in the mind, the mind in the senses and senses in the five elements then alongwith body-consciousness all attachments are evoked, signifying that the one and only *Brahma* sometimes prevails in *Kriyā's* transcendental state and sometimes within the five body essences. This is life, in other words the union of senses, mind and soul is life and it's reverse which is the imperceptible *Kriyā's* transcendental state only is *Brahma*. Thus not practising *Kriyā* when that state or *Kriyā's* transcendental state which is the mainspring does not evolve, then it is the duty of all to practise *Kriyā*. The person who is unfailingly constant in *Kriyā sādhana* and whose intellect is perpetually rapt in *Brahma* achieves *Brahma*, there cannot be any deviation from this. Conversely the person who being initiated in *Kriyā* forsakes it considering it's practice to be endeavoursome and the result for relinquishing *sādhana* is that he remains in extreme misery. It is infallible that shirking from *Kriyā* will inevitably produce misery while practising *Kriyā* happiness will inevitably accrue. If the intellect and transcendental intellect can be completely comprehended, salvation results, that is esoteric *śāstrá*. The great sages have resolved by settling in *Kūṭastha* that the persons who concentrate on extraneous matters or whose minds are affixed on the five essences, this vision does not represent the truth, i.e. not abiding in *Kriyā's* transcendental state they undergo body-origination and subsequent happiness and misery.

Any visualisation infers attachment. Even in the visualisation of Bhagavan Krishna attachment is inherent but in the non-visualisation detachment inheres. Continuum of motion is the material world. This motion is continuing incessantly, for this reason it has no beginning or end. When attachment is directed towards that motion, it appears to be true. This apparent truth gains detachment by the knowledge of essence or by practising *Kriyā* and abiding in *Kriyā's* transcendental state or by the cessation of motion. Thus remaining in union in *Kriyā's* transcendental state is *dhárma* and this resultant union is detachment, because of this there is no fault but the attachment accruing from the non-union is fault. Because not being united in *Kriyā's* transcendental state, body-consciousness is aroused and body-consciousness arising; mind, intellect, intelligence, anger, malice, attachment etc. originate and that is the fault. Remaining united in *Kriyā's* transcendental state is the state of oneness or the state of *Brahma*. The one who constantly abides in this state has profound wisdom because the aforementioned anger, malice, attachment etc. all become one in that state, therefore *Kriyā's* transcendental state is the exterminator of all. Remaining within the soul in *Kriyā's* transcendental state detachment of attachment etc. being effected there is a total cessation of origination, then a singular thought origination being caused the mind does not wander elsewhere, thus the mind not wandering elsewhere a cessation of births ensues. Birth signifies the affixation of the mind in it's alien placement. That affixation, in other words attachment is the tenacious adherence to the five essences in this birth, existing in this attachment produces afflictions. The transcendental state of *Kriyā* is abstruse, from this abstruseness everything becomes explicit in the pre-transcendental state of *Kriyā*. The concept of visualisation cannot effect the process of visualisation, in other words omnipercipience occurs through *Brahma* but abiding in that *Brahma* there is an absence of visualisation, just as an object cannot visualise itself, the self metamorphoses into the object being envisioned then who will be the viewer ? Prior to *Kriyā* practice the state of illusion prevails and after *Kriyā* practice the state of truth which is *Kûṭastha*-visualisation prevails. By practising unfructuous action or *Prâṇákarma* whatever occurs in *Kriyā's* transcendental state though occurring is within the ambit of non-occurrence. All the consequences of action occur due to one's innate disposition, God is not causative. Supreme Being has no fructuous action, the soul being invested with attributes (*Sattva, Rájas* and *Támas*) existing in this body causes evolvement of the untrue self which undergoes everything; God is immanent in the state of non-attachment just as Infinite Soul *Kûṭastha Brahma* is. The appellation Godhood is ascribed to the achievement of *Kriyā's* transcendental state; soul and God are one and the same, there being a mere difference in essence only. If the mind pays attention to anything else other than the soul it implies non-endeavour of *dhárma*, practising *Kriyā* is *dhárma* and realising God through the practice of *Kriyā* is termed as knowledge, practising *Kriyā* and enhancing engrossment is referred to as preservation of *dhárma*. If *Kriyā* is practised in this manner the moment oneness is attained *samādhi* results that is concordantly being poised in *Brahma*. Then the *Brahma*-pervaded universe becoming absolute, duality is extinct. The existence of duality can never synchronize with the existence of God or in other words where there is duality, God is non-existent thus God is beyond perception, conjecture and abrupt apperception. All these connotations purport the intra-aspect i.e. intra-perception, intra-conjecture and abrupt intra-apperception. Intra-perception entails two, if duality is absent who will perceive whom ? Presumption of God is conjecture, duality exists there also. Abrupt apperception also entails duality. Duality cannot be concurrent with God, it is for this reason God is beyond perception, conjecture and abrupt apperception. Intra-*sādhana* on God can be exercised but gross *sādhana* (superficial mode of worship) cannot be because the power of *Brahma-aṇu* is a million times more potential than the power of the earthly *aṇu*. 1,00,000 *Brahma-aṇus* compose an *aṇu* of the earth, 10,000 Brahma-*aṇus* compose an *aṇu* of water; for this reason water is more potent than the earth. 1,000 Brahma-*aṇus* form one *aṇu* of heat, 100 Brahma-*aṇus* one *aṇu* of air and 10 Brahma-*aṇus* one *aṇu* of the void. Hence fire is potential than water, air than fire and void than air. When the aforementioned 1,00,000 *Brahma-aṇus* accumulate in one, then that one attains 1,00,000 times potency. Since *yogis* remain engrossed in *Brahma-aṇu* in this manner they gain supremacy over the five essences and time, becoming all-powerful. A *yogi* then wandering in the realm of *Brahma* becomes a Brahmin. Being born in a Brahmin family does not necessitate one to become a Brahmin. Since everything originates from *Brahma* everyone can be termed as Brahmin, nevertheless not abiding in *Brahma* but in the body-abode ascribes him to be a householder. Just as a warm object possesses the quality of fire but is not fire which is untrue, similarly though being born in Brahmin families all are untrue Brahmins. In accordance with the consequence of actions of previous births when a living being takes birth then each and every living being is a householder because at that moment the soul manifests in an explicit manner as it enters into the body-abode. Later human beings by repeated practice of *Kriyā* exterminate body-consciousness, then non-abidance in the body-abode ascribes one to be a Brahmin; then body-origination does not recur. One who has amassed virtuous deeds he only receives *Kriyā* initiation and practising *Kriyā* perceives *Brahma* in all objects, only he is designated to be a *ṛishi*. *Ṛishi* implies the one who perpetually is settled in *Kūṭastha*. Who, where and when terms a *Brahma* non-conversant person to be a *ṛishi*? This type of *ṛishi* imparts advice pertaining to *Kūṭastha*-visualisation, who, where and when dances to exhibit dancing to a blind man ? Similarly who would impart initiation to one devoid of good deeds, inclination and fortitude? Inclination and advice are necessary for the attainment of *Kriyā's* transcendental state. *Mántra* signifies that which causes mind's deliverance or else the process by which kinetic mind is stilled, that is *Kriyā*. Stillness only brings forth salvation and attaining stillness one who becomes an inhabitant of stillness he only is termed to be a Brahmin; this action only is the true action. One who designates this action to be action is not kinetic, hence he is not a householder, in other words not habitant within the dynamic *Prâṇá* by being devoid of the breathing motion, he is not a householder; thus householder is nascent implying one who is being born in a cyclical manner, this purports the continuum. This householder practising *Kriyā* abiding in *Kūṭastha* in *Kriyā's* transcendental state, becomes a *ṛishi*. Again those who do not engage their minds in extraneous affairs, perpetually engross their minds in *Kriyā's* transcendental state and attain immortality, again the thought to attain immortality does not appear, by constant habitation in the cavern or the source or origin achieves total relinquishment and to those the realisation "I only am the Primordial Male Energy occurs" causes evolvement of the *Brahma*-pervaded universe and the comprehension that nothingness exists after this dawns, such a person is a *manishī*. Thus the first step of discipline is remaining stationed in *Kūṭastha*, the second step of discipline is abiding near *Brahma* or existing in *Brahma* being stationed at *Kuṇḍalinī*like (latent Female Energy of the microcosm) soul and the third step of discipline is reposing soul within *Kūṭastha* and remaining united which denotes *Kriyā's* transcendental state. These actions produce men possessing superlative qualities. One who performs this passive action or *Ātmakarma*, his *Prâṇá* does not deviate or disunite from the union with *Brahma*; he then attaining an equivalence with *Brahma* achieves confluence in Him or he himself becomes *Brahma*.

Extraneous application of mind causes evolvement of materialism, that is conceit, in other words the knowledge of the self arising makes the mind concentrate on worldly pleasures and this conceit impedes settlement in the soul. In transcendental state of *Kriyā* settlement in the soul implies non-settlement in attachment and settlement in attachment implies non-settlement in the soul. By continually abiding in the transcendental state of *Kriyā*, conceit, birth, material attachment all cease, the obliteration of all these produces salvation, this is aimed at by all the *śāstrás*. When all these untrue volitions non-exist, then the mind is reposed in the soul, this state is termed as the state of emancipation. This is desirable by all. Material objects appear to be pleasant but are inherently bitter, the mind is fascinated by superficialities, this is illusion and the mani-festation of vibration and it's intra-orientation results in relinquish-ment. Knowledge signifies *Brahma*-knowledge which is *Kriyā's* transcendental state and ignorance infers mind's orientation towards everything barring *Kriyā's* transcendental state. This digression of the mind or not abiding in transcendental state of *Kriyā* signifies disunion. Then the mind encompassing material facts through the sensory faculties, *Kriyā's* transcendental state cannot be realised. Application of the mind towards attachment makes the sensory faculties effete and this effete mind fails to realise *Kriyā's* transcen-dental state. In this state kinetic mind being settled in still mind, senses are rendered incapable of being directed towards attachment, thus sensory intake like olfaction etc., does not occur. *Kriyā's* transcendental state is synonymous with dissolution of what one is. This transcendental state of *Kriyā* is beyond the three attributes. When the mental state dawns, duality occurs. Conversely when the mental state is devoid in a superior manner or *Kriyā's* transcendental state dawns then there is amorphousness, when amorphousness prevails there is void, then being merged in *Brahma* material detachment evolves or all sorts of propensities become extinct. Therefore the conception of all objects merging cannot occur, because then it is you only who has merged and other objects remain as they are. When amorphousness arrives then *paramāṇu* (atom) of all objects disintegrating in a special manner mingles in *Brahma*, thus *aṇu* (molecule) of the earth mingles in water, *aṇu* of water in heat, *aṇu* of heat in air, *aṇu* of air in void, *aṇu* of void in *Brahma*; thus what was expansive achieved contraction in this manner, later remained united in the region where even *Brahma-aṇu* was absent. This is the transcendental state of *Kriyā*. The sky being extremely subtle it is intangible yet that something exists is experienced, similarly Amorphous *Brahma-aṇu* being much more subtler than the sky cannot be realised though there is consciousness of something existing. Therefore *Kriyā's* transcendental state is the state of nothingness, this state of nothingness is *Brahma*, everyone has to merge here. No forms are visualised in *Kriyā's* transcendental state, it is all pervasive. When the mind is attached to any object it is illusion, conversely when it is non-attached with any object it is sans illusion. The void in *Kriyā's* transcendental state is all pervasive and sans illusion. Therefore barring the transcendental state of *Kriyā*, none else is the benefactor in this world. He only is the Fearless State, Almighty, Holy and Sublime. He is Primordial and Abode of all, He is the *Kūṭastha*-Boundless Eye and the Soul-Moon, Soul-Sun and Soul-Star. This transcendental state of *Kriyā* appears suddenly, but when it does appear a prolonged habitation in that state is beneficial or it is imperative to remain in that state. To break this state tantamounts to self-annihilation.

* * * * * *

Can Yogiraj be ascribed to be a *Vaishṇavá* (worshipper of *Víshṇu*) ? Is He a *Ṡaiva* (worshipper of *Ṡivá*), *Ṡākta* (worshipper of *Ṡakti*), *Saűrya* (worshipper of Sun God) or a *Gắṇapatya* (worshipper of *Ganeṡa*)? *Víshṇu* is Omnipresence, *Ṡivá* is still *Prâṇá, Ṡākta* is kinetic *Prâṇá,* Sun God is *Atmasűrya, Ganeṡa* is *Prâṇâyāma.* Shama Churn is nought yet He is All. In this regard He Himself has borne testimony to this in His diaries. He has visualised all types of Krishnas and *Víshṇus*, all types of *Ṡivás* and *Mahắdevas*, all types of *Kālīs* alongwith various goddesses; in accordance with the *Saűrya* philosophy, He has visualised manifold Soul-Suns. He has also envisioned various *Ganeṡas*. He was not a Sadhaka of any particular discipline or path, the union of all disciplines and paths coalesced in Him.He only is at one and the same time a Supreme Vaishnava, a Supreme Saiva, a Supreme Sakta, a Supreme Saurya and Supreme Ganapatya. These five divergent paths of *sādhana* converged in Him, because He is Omneity.

While effecting progression in His path of *sādhana* whatever visualisation He has caused to occur in Him has been penned in His daily notes for the proper orientation of aspirant *yogis* which are enumerated below :—

1. ***Ihnā Kāliji birājmān — khāli Kālī nahi sabkoi yāne kuch nāhi āur sab kuch — āhā kyā majā haye.*** — *Kālī* is prevalent here, not only *Kālī* but all deities pervade. Though this state is nothing conversely it is everything. He conferred effusion upon Himself to express this visualisation — What an extreme delight!

2. ***Lol jihvā́ mālum huyā Kālīkā. Iha jihvā́ jab talumulme lapaṭ jatā hyāye. Jihvā́ āur uṭhā āur iha mālum hotā hāye ki nid choḍ denā. Āur baḍā majā mālum huyā āur basulikā āoyāz āur sāf bajne lagā.*** — Comprehension of the desire-ridden lolling tongue of *Kālī* was beckoned by Me. Only when I bestowed realisation upon Me I made My tongue attain fixation in the palatal cavity. This state has been symbolised externally by the lolling tongue of Goddess *Kālī*. My tongue was raised further upwards and the realisation that I have to relinquish sleep in this state served Me. Then I showered immense delight upon Myself and the flutelike sound during *Prâṇâyāma* similar to the sound of the flute of Krishna was being piped more distinctly.

3. ***Mahā́devá o Kālī dárśana huyā — aj thoḍā safā Brahma dekhā*** —*Mahā́devá* and *Kālī* acquiesced to occur in My visualisation and today a slightly clear *Brahma*-visualisation was effected in Me.

4. ***Hāḍkā Kālī dekhā, phaṭikkā āur jyotikā Kālī dekhā*** — The skeletal frame of Goddess *Kālī* was caused to create My envisionment, a crystalline and resplendent *Kālī* perception was occasioned to be in service.

5. ***Sū́ryahi Kālīkā rūpá*** — Soul-Sun only is the form of *Kālī*.

6. ***Nīlvarṇa Kālījikā śirkā upar dekhā*** — A bluish *Kālī* perception was caused to dawn in My sinciput.

7. Delineating the image of a Goddess atop a lion, He has written beside it — ***Ādhār cakráme jo devī́ svetavarṇa svetavastra paridhān siṃhabāhiniko dekhā — Kulakuṇḍalinī Śakti*** — A white complexioned, white-attired Goddess mounted on a lion in the *Mūlâdhāra cakrá* was caused to occur in My vision. She is *Kuṇḍalinī Śakti* (female vital force) *Jagaddhātṛi*, Who bears this body-universe.

8. ***Kālīkā caraṇ dekhā*** — I occasioned the perception of Goddess *Kālī's* feet in Me. ***Kālīr nām arthād sűryer dhyāna o Prâṇâyāma Kālīr pā ek ai pā dui haiyāche bnā pā o dān pā arthād candra o sűrya arthād Iḍā o Piṅgalā.*** — *Dhyāna* of *Ātmasűrya* is the appellation of Goddess *Kālī*. The *Prâṇâyāma* within *Sushumná* is the foot of *Kālī*, but that foot has acquired duality i.e. attaining vibration, motion in *Iḍā* and *Piṅgalá* has been formed and this has resulted in the occurrence of two feet. *Iḍā* is moon and *Piṅgalá* is sun. Similarly *Iḍā* is the left foot and *Piṅgalá* the right foot. If one can hold these *Iḍā* and *Piṅgalá* feet, *Kālī* can be achieved. The gross feet of flesh and bones have no capacity to move on their own. The existence of *Iḍā-Piṅgalá* feet causes the existence of gross feet. Feet here signifies that which wanders. Since breath wanders in *Iḍā* and *Piṅgalā* the body exists. Thus Yogiraj has expressed — ***Caraṇ yāne dono śvāsā yaisā caraṇ e sthān choḍke jātā haye oyesāhi śakti śvāsākā*** — *Caraṇ* (feet) implies the flow of breath in both nostrils just as the gross feet move from one place to another, similarly breath also abandoning this present body moves into a new body.

9. Sketching a human face with a sun on it's forehead, He has inscribed beside it — ***Sűrya ohi Kālī — Sűryakā Rūpá āur Humārā Rūpá ek haye.*** — The *Ātmasűrya* is *Kālī*. Both *Ātmasűrya's* Form and My Form are the same, in other words what is *Kālī's* form is My Form, inseparable. A few days later He has again remarked —

Súryai Kālī soi Kālī Hum soi Hum — implying what is the *Ātmasúrya* is *Kālī* is Myself, I Myself am *Kālī*. Exactly a couple of days after this He has written — ***Súryai Brahmarūpá haye ebaṃ Súryai jagat ādhār haye ohi aṭal chatra — ohi Súrya phir Hum nirākār Brahma hote haye — ab śvāsākā calnā o na calnā mālum na hoye — baḍā majā.*** — *Ātmasúrya* only is the Form of *Brahma* and the Sustainer for the universe. Everything originates and merges there. *Ātmasúrya* is the Eternal Protector for everything. In this *Ātmasúrya* visualisation whether the inhalant-exhalant breath continues or does not continue cannot be understood at all, in other words it is the *Kévala-Kumbhaka* state. This state imparts immense delight or bliss. I am that *Ātmasúrya*, again I am Amorphous *Brahma*.

10. ***Kabhi kabhi nilā yoki ṭhāṇḍi Kālīkā raṅg haye raṭanti nām unkā esā vyāpt huyā ki jab praṇāmko baṭte hāye tadya bic bicme aihi raṅgkā súrya najaḍ paḍātā haye, Kālīta ek haye lekin raṅgme parbhed haye.*** — I caused a placid blue *Kālī* known as *Raṭanti Kālī* to occur in My vision at times. When *Prâṇâyāma* is practised then that *Kālī* manifests in such a manner that sometimes *Ātmasúrya* of this *Kālī's* hue can be visualised. *Kālī* is one but since different colours are perceived, she appears to be different.

11. ***Śakti o Mahādevákā liṅga dekhā*** — Primordial Female Energy and the phallus of *Mahādevá* were visualised.

12. ***Kālīkā khaḍga dekhā*** — The falchion of *Kālī* was occurred to come in vision.

13. ***Śaktirūpá Bhagavatī dekhā*** — The female vital force Goddess *Durgā* was occasioned to appear in vision.

14. ***Chinnamastā rūpá dekhā*** — The form of beheaded Goddess was envisioned.

15. ***Ādyāśakti dekhā*** — *Ādyāśakti* in other words, the primordial divine eternal Goddess *Durgā* was perceived.

16. ***Āj sonekā Kālīse bheṭ huyā*** — Today golden-hued *Kālī* met Me.

17. ***Sūryake jhālar yāne kirīṭ. Sūryase Kālīkā khaḍga haye. Sūryai Mālik. Ohi uttamrūpá Sūryakā haye*** — *Ātmasūrya's* fringe is the diadem. Falchion of *Kālī* is derived from *Ātmasūrya*, that *Ātmasūrya* is the Master or the Principal One. That is *Ātmasūrya*'s excellent form.

18. ***Dui cnād — Mahādevá Kālī dárśana huyā*** — Two moons *Mahādevá* and *Kālī* were effected in vision.

19. Drawing a sketch of Goddess *Śyāmā*, He inscribed beside it — ***Śyāmāsundarī rūpá Kālīrūpá dekhā bahut dertak*** — Perception of splendid Goddess *Śyāmā's* form, also *Kālī's* form were effected for a long period. On 13th August, 1873, He delineated the garland of *Kālī* and remarked beside it — ***Mahākāla — ehi āpnā rūpá — ehi ghaṭākāś — ehi Kālījike mālā galeme — iha mālā galjāye yāne nahi rahe to sabke upar ajar amar ghar haye — onhā jānese sthir gharkā tha miltā haye — usi sthirme āj dominiṭ rahe — sabere, hnui hameśā rahanā cāhi. Humhi Sūrya haye phir ulaṭke Sūrya Humhi — Humhi nirākār Brahma*** — This is the eternal dynamic void; this is the own form — the origin; the confined space; again this is Goddess *Kālī's* garland of demon-heads. This garland becomes void or extinct, that is the ageless immortal state; arriving there a static station can be acquired, today morning settlement occurred in that still state for a couple of minutes. It is imperative to perpetually remain in this still state. I only am *Ātmasūrya*, again conversely *Ātmasūrya* is Me only, I only am Amorphous *Brahma*.

20. ***Iḍā Piṅgalā shaṭcakrá yokī Sushumnāme milke paduke rūpá sāf mālum hotā haye uhike upar Sárasvatī haye dekhā*** — That *Iḍā, Piṅgalā* and the six *cakrás* mingling in the *Sushumná* formed the lotus which could be clearly realised and vision of Goddess *Sárasvatī* atop this was caused.

21. ***Sűryake bhitar padmakā vána vīṇāpāṇike dekhā*** — Within *Ātmasűrya* in the clump of lotus, visualisation of Goddess *Sárasvatī* was effected.

22. ***Vidyudprabhā pushpa sadṛiśa raktavarṇa kāmbīj Bāgdevī dekhā*** — *Bāgdevī* (goddess *Sárasvatī*) characterised by the radiance of lightning, flower-semblant and resembling the blood-red seed of indelible passion was effected to be envisioned.

23. Delineating the icons of *Sāvitṛī* and *Brahmā* on the dorsum of an elephant He remarked beside it — ***Sárasvatī vināyak arthād Sāvitṛī saha Brahmā hastibāhan dekhā*** — The deities of *Sárasvatī* and *Gaṇeśa* or *Brahmā* and His wife *Sāvitṛī* atop their mount, the elephant was caused to be perceived.

24. ***Gaṇeśa Kűṭastha aksharke bhitar yāne caturmukh Brahmā dekhā*** — *Gaṇeśa*, in other words the quadri-headed *Brahmā* within the imperishable *Kűṭastha* was caused to be envisioned.

25. ***Ab dhvani mune Rādhājikā dárśana bhayā*** — Now within the *Ómkāra* sound the visualisation of *Rādhā* was effected.

26. ***Sűryake bhitar Gaṇeśakā mūrti sāf dekhā*** — The image of *Gaṇeśa* within the *Ātmasűrya* could be clearly perceived.

27. ***Baiśuṇḍkā Gaṇeśa Nārāyaṇáse nikile dekhā*** — The trunkless *Gaṇeśa* emanating from *Nārāyaṇá* could be envisioned.

28. Delineating a picture of serpentine *Kuṇḍalini* (female vital force) He commented — ***Ehi kulakuṇḍalinī sārdhatribalayākārā sayambhuliṅga beshtinīṃ bhujagākār rūpiniṃ — eysā dekhneme ātā haye*** — That is *Kuṇḍalinī*, it surrounds the phallus emanating from esse conforming to the three and one-half serpentine coils, which can be visualised. Later drawing a sketch of *Ómkāra Kriyā* He has remarked thus — ***Śarīrke īśān konme śayambhu Kuṇḍalinī beshṭita jvalanta gandhakkā raṃmaśālke māphik lekan sthir***

svetvarṇa sarpākār dekhā — That *Kuṇḍalinī* serpentiningly entwines the eternal self-generative energy in the mid-point of the north-eastern side of the body which resembles a resplendent flambeau but in actuality it is stillness and neutral whiteness.

29. On 22nd January 1873, He has recounted thus — ***Candra Sũrya jyoti dono taraf dekhā — Vísvanāthkā liṅga Sushumnārūpá bicme dekhā — Tántrapramāṇaṃ — Yoni Brahma hṛidākāraṃ antarātmani cintayed.*** — Effulgence of Soul-Moon and *Ātmasũrya* occupied the vision of both sides of *Kũṭastha* and within focal point of *Kũṭastha*, phallus of *Vísvanāth* resembling *Sushumná* was perceived. The *Tántra śāstrás* have given evidence to this fact that this is that *Brahmayóni*, the source or origin of the entire creation which is realisable in intra-oriented *dhyana*. Later sketching a two petalled lotus He has directed — ***Dvidalpadma koṭi candraprabhā jasā dekhā.*** — The two-petalled lotus *Ājñācakrá* ten million times more resplendent than the planet moon was effected to be envisioned. On 12th August 1873, He remarked — ***Pnāc Sũryaka uday Sũryahi haye svet dhvajā. Sũrya Nārāyaṇá Mālik — Ohi Sũrya Mālik — Ohi Sahasrâṇśu haye.*** — Quinary suns evolved from *Ātmasũrya* that *Ātmasũrya* only is the neutral power of generation. *Ātmasũrya* is *Nārāyaṇá,* that *Ātmasũrya* is the Master, He is *Sahasrâṇśu* (power of thousand suns). Sanjay has stated denoting this —

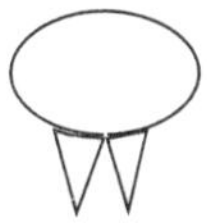

Divi Sũryasahasrasya bhaved yugapadutthitā.
Yadi bhāḥ sadṛiśī sā syādbhāsastasya Mahātmanaḥ. (*Gītā* 11/12)

After the sensory inclinations are equally conquered, the one who manifests the transcendental vision signifies Sanjay. That Sanjay or transcendental vision confers an exegesis to the mind. *Divi* connotes the sky, then this radiance may be similar to that

Mahắtmanaḥ's (*Sahasrâṉśu*'s) influence. In other words, that resplendent sublime form is incomparable, that only is the immense form of *Kűṭastha Brahma*. Therefore Sanjay stipulates that if the resplendence of thousand suns accumulates then this can resemble that sublime soul[1].

Visualising this *Sahasrâṉśu* (thousand suns) Arjuna has commented —

Tvamaksharaṃ paramaṃ beditabyaṃ
Tvamasya víśvasya paraṃ nidhānam.
Tvamavyaḥ śāśvatadhármagoptā
Sanātánastvaṃ púrusho mato me. (*Gītā* 11/18)

---

1. The sages have rendered various explanations about this Sun and the Infinite Void in different parts of the *śāstrás*. Regarding the exactness of the Sun and Infinite Void, the *paṇḍitas* (erudites) and exegetists at a later date have specified them to be the planet sun and perceptible sky respectively. But Yogiraj has expounded that the planet sun is transitory, thus the sun referred to in the *śāstrás* is *Ātmasűrya* Who is permanent, eternal and indestructible. Only *yogis* are capable of visualising this. Arjuna also referring to this *Ātmasűrya* in the *Gītā* has commented that if thousand planet suns rise together, then the collective brilliance may resemble the sublime *Ātmasűrya*. From this it can be deduced that in *Gītā* it is not the planet sun which has been referred to but *Ātmasűrya*. This exegesis has been exclusively rendered by Yogiraj as He Himself is *Ātmasűrya*.

Again regarding Infinite Void mentioned in the *śāstrás* all the aforementioned *paṇḍitas* and exegetists have explained it to be the perceptible sky or the infinite expanse. But Yogiraj has stipulated that this infinite expanse or space is the last of the five elements which gradually has attained subtlety from grossness; it is the last great subtle element. Thus this perceptible space being gross is not the infinite void. This space is transient in it's constituent-transience; but it being limitless cannot be measured. Since space is last of the five great elements, it is invested with attributes and is not beyond attributes. Therefore regarding the Infinite Void Yogiraj has explained that this space within the void, or in other words, the existence of that void upon which the existence of this space originates, pervades and merges, He only is Infinite Void and this Infinite Void inherent within this space is *Brahma*. The Infinite Absolute Void inextricably pervades within this space. He Himself being Infinite Absolute Amorphous Void *Brahma*, He conferred His exegesis on this to His superlative creation — mankind to effect their fulfilment. Merging and fusing into oneness with that crystalline, imperishable,

This verse signifies thus — Only You are the Imperishable Supreme *Brahma*, only You are worth knowing, only You are the True Haven for this universe, only You are the Immortal and Esoteric Custodian of *dhárma* and You only are the Eternal Being, this is my belief. In other words, You only are *Kúṭastha*- Consciousness and the Still *Prâṇá*like Imperishable Being, for You are beyond destruction. Above *Kúṭastha* in the *Sahasrâra* You only are the Inexpressible Sublime *Prâṇá* Absolute *Brahma*; the Only One worth knowing, realising You is self-knowledge which is the true knowledge. Thus after realising You, nothing remains to be realised. Therefore You are worth knowing exclusively. You are the Principal Haven for the universe because the still state of the Inexpressible *Brahma* having no finitude is the shelter for the universe, Supreme Haven, hence perpetual still *Prâṇá*. You only are the Eternal Esoteric Custodian of *dhárma* or the Protector of *Sanatána dhárma* (eternal religion) because You only are abstruselylatent in the *yógakarma* of *Sanātána dhárma*, this esotericism can be unravelled exclusively by the *Gurú*. You only are the *Sanātána* Primordial Being because it is my firm belief that there is none preceding and succeeding You.

Sahasrâṉśu visualisation occurs to a *yogi* when he is settled in *Kúṭastha*, this only is visualisation of the universe in it's universality in accordance with the *Gītā*. Implicitly this is the all-Pervasive Universal Eye, Soul-Sun, Soul-Moon. *Sahasrâṉśu* is the eternal apogean abode of the universe.

---

attributeless, Absolute Void *Brahma* is the last and ultimate state of *sādhana*. This is ascertained by *Vedānta*. Merging with that Absolute Void *Brahma* results in loss of entity because in this state there is none to specify about duality, this only is non-dual nothingness, stateless state. Prior to this everyone is within ambit of the dual state. Knowing about this *Ātmasúrya* and Absolute Void is knowledge substantiated by *Gītā* and *Vedānta* which is the zenith of all states. Here *Divá* signifies void or else that crystalline, indestructible Absolute Void. Originating from that Absolute Void or the initial manifestation is god. Therefore Yogiraj has expressed that the Krishna state also attained confluence into Absolute Void because this Krishna state also is transient. Only Absolute Void *Brahma* is eternal; this is the dictum of Yogiraj.

Visualising the universal visualisation, a great *sādhaka* like Arjuna was also petrified, but Yogiraj comments — ***Āditya serā Púrusha haye — ab sahaje āoye jāye.*** — That *Sahasrâṇśu* is the Supreme and Fundamental Being, He appears in and disappears from vision easily. A few days later He delineated a thousand petalled lotus and wrote beside it — ***Aysā hajāro cakrá maye haraph samet mālum hotā haye sahasrârame.*** —

Sahasrâra is characterised by the thousand petalled *cakrá*, every petal alongwith their mystic syllable was beckoned to occur in My vision.

30. ***Svet dvīpavāsi Nārāyaṇá dekhā.*** — The white island implies the island of the Soul-Moon which is the Abode of *Víshṇu*. *Nārāyaṇá* within the Abode of *Víshṇu* was caused to be envisioned in *Kúṭastha*. He has again remarked — ***Súrya Nārāyaṇá rūpá dekhā*** — The Form of *Ātmasúrya-Nārāyaṇá* was effected into visualisation. Again He has commented — ***Jyotirmoy svetvarṇa Mahādever rūpá dekhā, baḍā ānand huyā*** — Envisionment of resplendent white form of *Mahādevá* was caused to occur. Solicitation of an extreme delight was effected. After this He has noted — ***Jyotirūpá lāl dorā sushumnāko kināre mehin dekhā — pahale jyotirmoy liṅga dekhā phir śūnyame samāye gayā.*** — By the side of *Sushumná* a red-striped fine effulgent form was beckoned into vision. Before this the Resplendent Phallus appeared but it merged in the void within the void, i.e. the infinite void. Further to this, He stated — ***Nákshatra loka dekhā*** —This is the state where activity of the perceptible sun and moon evanesces and a perpetual illuminative state pervades. *Nákshatra* = *Ná Kshayaḥ atra* = where on settling destruction is extinct, or the still state is semblant of *Kriyā's* transcendental state. In this type of still state within *Kúṭastha* the static true brilliant star can be visualised.

31. ***Jyotrūpá aṅgusṭha pramāṇ Púrusha dekhā*** — The effulgent thumbesque Primordial Being was effected to be perceived.

32. Drawing two dark forms He noted — ***Rādhākṛishṇa Svâdhis-hṭhāna padme Kṛishnavarṇa dekhā*** — The dark *Rādhākṛishṇa* in *Svâdhishṭhāna cakrá* could be visualised.

33. Yogiraj penned on 21st September 1873 — ***Mahādevákā triśul — Víshṇukā Sudarśaná cakrá — Brahmākā daṇḍa pañcadevátā dekhā — satya heye Bhagavān.*** — Trident of *Mahādevá*, the *Sudarśaná cakrá* (holy discus) of *Víshṇu*, the staff (powerful holy weapon) of *Brahmā* and the five deities (*Ganeśa, Sūrya, Víshṇu, Śivá* and *Durgā*) acquiescingly appeared in vision. Paying obeisance to His Own Esse, He conferred the dictum — O God, You are the only Truth.

34. ***Saptaṛishi o cār Mánu dekhā*** — The seven sages and four *Mánus* occurred in vision to appease. The seven sages are *Vṛigu, Attri, Aṅgirā, Marīci, Pulastya, Pulaha* and *Kratu. Mánu* is the son of *Brahmā*, the first progenitor of the human race. The names of fourteen *Mánus* have been referred to in the *śāstrás* — *Svāyambhuv, Svārocish, Uttama, Tāmas, Raivata, Cākshush, Vaivasvata, Sāvarṇi, Dakshasāvarṇi, Brahmasāvarṇi, Dhármasāvarṇi, Rudrásāvarṇi, Devásāvarṇi* and *Indrasāvarṇi*, but only four *Mánus* appeared before Yogiraj.

God in this regard has commented —

Maharshayaḥ sapta pūrve catvāro manabastathā.
Madvābā mānasā jātā yeshāṃ loka imāḥ prajāḥ. (*Gītā* 10/6)

This denotes that the four *Mánus* — *Sanaka, Sananda, Sanātána* and *Sanadkumār* who existed even before these seven sages, alongwith the fourteen *Mánus*, all of them have originated from My potent, eternally pure, generative non-volitional volition and the ever-increasing human race is My progeny. Thus here, these four *Mánus* appeared before Yogiraj.

35. ***Śrīnāthkā dárśana huyā.*** — *Śrīnāth* or else *Śrīvíshṇu*, *Swāmi* (husband) of Goddess *Lakshmí* appeared in vision to Yogiraj.

36 ***Śeshanāgpar Hari sayan kiye haye hṛidayme dekhātā haye.*** — It can be visualised in the *Anāhata cakrá* that *Hari* lies on the infinite coil of the King of serpents, in other words the infinite coils of the serpent form the couch and canopy of *Nārāyaṇá*.

37. ***,Kṛishṇakā śeshanāgpar sayan — eysā rūpá ānkhose dekhā.*** — Krishna lying atop the King of serpents was envisioned through open eyes. Yogiraj has sketched this form in His diary.

38. ***Anantadevá dekhā.*** — Visualisation of the Eternal Being *Nārāyaṇá* was effected.

39. ***Rudrárājá dekhā.*** — *Rudrá*, the destructive form of *Śivá* was caused to occur in vision.

40. ***Matsyāvatāra dekhā.*** — Amongst the ten incarnations of *Víshṇu,* the piscine incarnation appeared in vision. The ten incarnations are *Matsya* (fish), *Kūrma* (tortoise), *Barāha* (boar), *Nṛisiṃha* (lion-headed human shape), *Vāmaná* (dwarf), *Paraśurāma* (he carried a battle axe with which he exterminated *Kshatriyas* twenty one-times from the earth) *Rāmacandra* (*Rāma*), *Valarāma* (elder brother of Bhagavan Krishna), Buddha (the beacon of consciousness, enlightenment and knowledge) and *Kalkī* (last incarnation).

41. ***Barāhamvatāra dekhā.*** — *Barāhamvatāra*, the third amongst the ten incarnations of *Víshṇu* came into vision.

42. ***Śivá Sanaka Śakti — Rāmacandrakā dhanuka dekhā.*** — Visualisation of *Śivá, Sanaka* (the son emanating from the non-

volitional volition of *Brahmā*), *Śakti* (the female vital force by which the creation is borne) and the bow of *Rāma* was occasioned.

43. ***Nāradkā vin dekhā.*** — The *viṇā* (musical heptachord) of *Nārada* was summoned into vision.

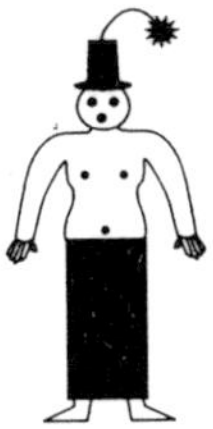

44. ***Mogul durvān Bhagavānkā dekhā.*** — The Mughul form of God's sentinel was beckoned to appear in vision. Here Yogiraj has sketched the picture of a human wearing a conical cap and lungi in His diary.

45. ***Víshṇujikā padam dekhā.*** — The holy state of *Víshṇu* was brought into vision.

46. ***Nārāyaṇá dekhā.*** — Visualisation of *Nārāyaṇá* was brought into occurrence.

47. ***Pañcānan śaktirūpá dekhā.*** — *Pañcānan* (the pentaheaded) infers the potential form of *Śivá* occurred in vision. Here Yogiraj has noted that *Śivá* and *Śivá's* power are inseparable.

48. ***Lakshmínārāyaṇá dekhā*** — Goddess *Lakshmí* and *Nārāyaṇá* were occasioned in vision.

49. ***Tríśul Mahādevákā dekhā*** — Visualisation of the Trident of *Mahādevá* was made to occur.

50. ***Kṛishṇa Kālīji bhaye rāha dekhā lekin kuch bole nehi.*** — *Bhagavān Kṛishṇa* became Goddess *Kālī*, in other words *Kṛishṇa* assumed the form of Goddess *Kālī* but said nothing. This was effected into vision.

51. ***Kṛishṇakā rūpá — Ómkāra Harikā rūpá dekhā.*** — The form of *Bhagavān Kṛishṇa* and the *Ómkāra* form of *Hari* were made to appear in vision.

52. ***Sárvaghaṭ virājmān Ómkārase pare Purushôtama Nārāyaṇákā rūpá isi ghaṭme Sūryako dekhat dekhat mālum hotā haye.***

— Delineating the form of the Supreme Being *Nārāyaṇá* here, He has recounted in His diary — attaining settlement at *Kūṭastha* within the body-temple the *Ātmasūrya* is envisioned by constantly visualising, the realisation that the Omnipresent Supreme Being beyond *Ómkāra* is *Nārāyaṇá*, occurs.

53. ***Brahmā, Víshṇu, Mahêśa dekhā*** —The three principal deities — *Brahmā, Víshṇu* and *Mahêśvara* were effected to be envisioned at the same time.

54. ***Daśamahā́vidyā dekhā*** —The ten principal goddesses viz. *Kālī, Tārā, Shoḍaśī, Bhuvanesvarī, Bhairavī, Chinnamastā, Dhūmāvatī, Bagalā, Mātaṅgī* and *Kamalā* were caused to be envisioned.

55. ***Kalpa bṛiksha nāl — Brahmā, Víshṇu, Mahêśa Pañcadevátā dekhā. Kalpabṛiksha asal.***—Root of the Cornucopian Tree, *Brahmā, Víshṇu, Mahêśa* alongwith five deities were effected into vision. That Cornucopian Tree is real. ***Bhāri pardā bickā jisme lakhān jāye uha Parampúrusha yo anādi nirākāra āpne me haye yāne ānkh ek yo haye kalpabṛiksha. Uske bād phir ek lambā dekhā yo lejātā abhaypadko uha Sūryase paydā haye yo Sūrya śūnyáme milā haye. Ehi haye Śiváliṅga iskā varṇanko karsake ehi tumho iha choḍāike dusrā koi nahi.*** — What is visualised within the grave sublime *Kūṭastha* is the Supreme Being, Who is Self-Nascent, therefore has no beginning and is Amorphous, this infers the *Kūṭastha*-Eye to be the Cornucopian Tree. After this a length was brought into vision which guides one to the fearless state, this length has emanated from *Ātmasūrya* and the *Ātmasūrya* merges in the Infinite Void. The length is the phallus of *Śivá*, this description can be conferred by Me only, this is omneity, barring this there is nothing.

56. ***Kisor mūrti dekhā*** — Visualisation of the adolescent form of God was effected.

57. ***Jyotirmoy svetvarṇa Mahâdever rūpá dekhā — baḍā ānand huyā.*** — Visualisation of the resplendent white form of *Mahâdeva* was caused and immense delight beckoned.

58. He sketched a form of *Gurú* Nanak and wrote beside it — ***Nānaksāb Sûryakā mūrta haye.*** — *Nānaksāheb* is the direct symbol of *Ātmasûrya*.

59. ***Dvidal padma (Ājñācakrá) jaisā dekhnā cāhiye*** — The bipetalled lotus *Ājñācakrá* as it should be visualised.

* * * * * *

Without enhancing the contents of the book it should be remarked that the different states of *Brahma*-conversant persons described by *ṛishis* sequentially in the *śāstrás* viz. *Vedas, Vedānta, Upanishâds, Gītā* etc; have all been caused by Yogiraj to be completely realised by Him as is clearly indicated in His diaries.

Surrounded by devotees the Sublime Yogi being seated, imparted advice. A devotee prayed to know — "What is God?"

Yogiraj enlightened thus — "Do you know Who God is ? The power by which you asked 'What is God', He only is God. If He does not exist, you would not have been able to say the words 'What is God' also. Since He perpetually bears the Creation, this state is *Jagaddhāttṛī*. Since a living being is borne by Him, this state is *Rādhā*. Here *Rā* implies living being and *dhā* the act of bearing.

Another devotee prayed — "What is death?"

Yogiraj elucidated — Due to natural causes when the vibratory *Prâṇá* is stilled, it is termed to be death. In that state consequences of previous deeds persist. But the still state in *samādhi* is also akin to death, consequences of previous deeds do not exist then. One subtle observation is noticed that inhalation is the living condition of a being and exhalation is death because after exhalation if a living being cannot further inhale, then death occurs. If inhalation and exhalation are the living and death conditions respectively, then these conditions constantly occur within a living being. Birth-death is a cycle. None notice this. Thus it is not real death. It is just like the casting of a slough because in this type of death, recurrence of birth is inevitable. This cycle is continual. The actual death is merging in *Brahma*, returning to the source or origin where on arrival there is no recurrence.

Ābrahmabhuvanāllokāḥ punarāvartinoarjuna.

Māmupetya tu Kaunteya punarjanma na vidyate. (*Gītā* 8/16)

O Arjuna, even from the Abode of *Brahma* there is return but attaining Me (Soul), the return ceases. In other words, impermanent settlement in the *Brahma*-Abode being achieved at *Ājñācakrá* return occurs but when permanent settlement occurs there then there is salvation. Due to the impermanence in settlement it ceases to exist and then the mind retrogresses from *Ājñācakrá* to *Mūlâdhāra cakrá* and *Prâṇá* on resuming dynamism there is a resumption of inhalation, hence rebirth. But when there is a permanent settlement above the impermanent state or when the mind merges that settlement is boundless, this is the permanent settlement. Before death this type of settlement being attained rebirth does not occur.

Yogiraj has recounted in 1886 (date not mentioned) in His diary ***Kathopakathan Navahādhar sahit.*** —Alongwith *Navahādhar* implies that the immensely powerful *Ātmasúrya's* oracle or Divine Message was caused by Him to be the intrinsic audition or in other words He effected the progress of a conversation with the *Ātmasúrya*-Master (Who is His *Brahma*-Self) pertaining to the moment of His Mortal Frame cessation. Clarification not mentioned. Next query — Where cessation of Mortal Frame will occur?

Clarification —At Kashi. Last query — The path being proceeded is it correct ? Clarification — *Yogasādhana* rite.

Jiva-Shama Churn queries Krishna Shama Churn whether the Former Self will cease His Mortal Frame, where this cessation will be effected and whether after descending in the Form of Jiva Shama Churn, the *yogasādhana* He revived for the masses is apt or not ?

To enable us to have a lucid comprehension of the Yogiraj concept, three facets of this concept should be taken into consideration — Jiva Shama Churn, Krishna-Shama Churn and Brahma-Shama Churn. Brahm*a*-Shama Churn is perpetually Still and Static, Krishna-Shama Churn is Kutastha-Shama Churn and Jiva-Shama Churn is when He causes Himself to enter the domain of one lac vibrations in accordance with the discipline of Brahma-Shama Churn.

Yogiraj has reiterated that this immensely powerful *Ātmasūrya* is the Master, is for omneity the Source or Origin, the Abode of Settlement and the Haven of Mergence. This is God, eventually this is Sūrya-Brahma-Shama Churn. Nothing exists barring this *Ātmasūrya*. He has no second. This *Ātmasūrya* is all-pervasive and is eternally True Immaculate Pure Absolute Void *Brahma*. All creation is the manifestation of that perpetually Immaculate, *Ātmasūrya's* dynamism, which is spiritual ignorance and illusion; through all these the *Ātmasūrya*-like Absolute *Brahma* is resplendent. One who directly visualises this *Ātmasūrya* and eventually fuses and merges within Him attaining oneness, that *yogi* only is a non-dualist and before this everyone is a dualist. Thus Yogiraj would comment —"Where *sādhaka's sādhanā* ends, *yogi's sādhanā* begins," this infers, where a devoted disciple's ritual practice ends, a *yogi*'s spiritual practice begins.

Chapter X

MAHASAMADHI

Three images of *Śivá* were already installed in the house of Garureswar before Yogiraj had purchased it and commenced residing. Kashimani Devi would worship that *Śivá* daily. But she harboured an intense desire to instal an idol of *Śivá* herself. In the chapter on Kashi in *Skandapurāṇá*, it has been mentioned that installing an idol of *Śivá* in Kashi is a highly virtuous feat. For this reason at Kashi the Abode of *Śivá*, many would instal images of *Śivá* in their houses. One day Kashimani Devi expressed this desire to her father (Devnarayan Vacaspati) to which he explained that it was not desirable to instal an image of *Śivá in* the house because with the passage of time, that *Śivá* would not be worshipped properly. Instead, he asked her to regard the *Śivá* she was worshipping as her own installed image and duly worship Him. From this time onwards, Kashimani Devi devotedly worshipped that *Śivá* throughout her life.

One day, as usual in the morning Kashimani Devi was worshipping *Śivá*, when Yogiraj arrived and stood in front of the door. Kashimani Devi pondered that as Yogiraj normally never came to that spot at that time, what could be the reason for His coming there suddenly that day? Kashimani Devi turned back and looked.

Yogiraj smiled gently and in a pacific tone stated to Kashimani Devi — "Look the purpose of My Advent has been completed. It is time for Me to depart now, I shall be in Mortal Frame for another six months only and then depart. None of you should grieve over this, I am making only you aware of this." He further continued — "After My Departure, keep My Mortal Frame in the room I stay for I shall mark My Readvent. And if this is not possible bury Me in that room."

Kashimani Devi did not pay any importance to these statements. She had thought her Brahma-conversant husband said these words remaining in transcendence.

The Sublime Yogi had decided the day and time of His Sublime Departure and was preparing to dissolve His worldly activities. The devotees also had to be prepared, therefore nearly three months in advance He had declared this to a few of his advanced devotees. Gradually, the appointed day started approaching. A month before the completion of six months, He effected the origination of a carbuncle on His dorsal area. Using this carbuncle as a pretext, the Sublime *Yogi* commenced arrangements for Departure. Receiving the news, His eldest son Tinkari Lahiri *Mahāśaya* who was employed in Delhi, shortly reached home.

Devotees continued serving Yogiraj toilsomely. Purnachandra Bandopadhyaya, the family physician was treating Him. But the carbuncle was not being alleviated. Hemchandera Sen, His devotee, an eminent physician of Calcutta Medical College, on receiving the news came to Kashi and began treatment on Yogiraj. But no sign of recovery could be noticed. Hembabu decided for an operation and begged the consent of Yogiraj. Yogiraj mildly smiled and stated — "It is better to stay within the rules of nature." The doctor understood that Yogiraj was not agreeable to an operation therefore he abandoned the idea and cleaned and bandaged the wound. But the One Who is free from all bondages, can He be bound ? The Great Yogi disapproving of this, compelled the helpless doctor to unfasten the bandage. Yogiraj Himself used to prepare neem oil and administer this for the various afflictions of His devotees. This oil was now applied on the wound of Yogiraj. But there was no alleviation of the carbuncle. The doctor, Hembabu returned to Calcutta.

Yogiraj would engage himself in daily discussions with His devotees in the parlour downstairs. Sitting on His bedstead He would make His devotees replete with the flood of *Brahma*-knowledge and it was on this bedstead He was now lying. The devotees constantly kept coming and going and rendering service. People from all sections of society came and enquired about the condition of Yogiraj for everyone was anxious. Krishnaram, a Rajput Brahmin devotee was perpetually serving Yogiraj and remained with Him like a shadow. He served Yogiraj intently. His endeavour was for the recuperation of Yogiraj only. But the carbuncle gradually exacerbated. The doctors were trying all types of treatment. Despite the incessant toil, tears streamed down Krishnaram's cheeks. Everyone desired to serve Yogiraj. The ladies of the house also wished so. In the conservative society of those days, generally the ladies would not appear before men who were not their own kith and kin. Due to constant service of Krishnaram and the continuous flow of devotees, the ladies were impeded from the opportunity of serving Yogiraj. Krishnaram alone was enough, he himself only intended to serve. His conception was that if he himself did not serve Yogiraj, the service rendered to his Guru Maharaj perhaps, would not be proper. As a result, none derived the opportunity to serve Yogiraj.

Yogiraj was immensely appeased by the tireless efforts of Krishnaram. The day before the Sublime Departure He affectionately called Krishnaram and said — "Krishnaram, I am well pleased by your service. Tell Me what you want. You will get what you want."

Krishnaram was standing with folded hands. Torrents of tears streamed down his eyes, his throat became parched and legs started quivering.

In a solemnly affectionate tone, the voice resounded — "Tell Me Krishnaram, what you want ? I am extremely pleased with you."

With tearful eyes, quivering voice and with a mind steeped in devotion, Krishnaram replied — "I have nothing to ask for. I have only one prayer, to obtain a place at your Lotus Feet."

Yogiraj smiled gently and remarked — "It will be so, Krishnaram."

Krishnaram then lay prostrate at the Lotus Feet of Yogiraj.

The fact that Krishnaramji did not have any greed can be learnt from another instance as provided by Bhupendranath Sanyal *Mahāśaya* himself, one of the principal disciples of Yogiraj who had come to Kashi alongwith Rabindranath Tagore. After visiting all the notable places, Rabindranath stated — "Sanyal *Mahāśaya*, I have heard Kashi to be a place of ascetics. Can you show me a genuine ascetic ?"

Sanyal *Mahāśaya* remarked — "Do you want to see the renowned ascetic who assumes a garb or do you want to see the ascetic whom I know to be the true one ?"

Rabindranath replied — "Show me the ascetic whom you regard as the true one."

Both of them went to the bank of the Ganges at Kashi in the locality of Ranamahal, the place where Krishnaram used to live. He would reside in a room at Udaipur estate adjoining the Radha-Krishna temple. Krishnaram was seated with closed eyes fixed upwardly in engrossment. A look at him would indicate that he was free from all the bondages of the material world. He was oblivious about who came and went. Both of them stealthily sat down. Krishnaram was sitting quietly.

After a few moments Sanyal *Mahāśaya* said — "Krishnaramji,

we have come."

Krishnaram descended to the transient abode.

Sanyal *Mahâśaya* introduced him to Rabindranath. Rabindranath was contented after discussing *dhárma* with him for a long period. While leaving Rabindranath gave ten rupees to Krishnaramji and said — "I will be happy if this sum can be used for your service."

Krishnaram stated — "I have no necessity for money now."

Rabindranath humbly entreated again — "It is my ardent desire that this money be used for your purpose."

Krishnaram replied in a placid tone — "Alright, consider that money to be mine. Now keep it with you. I shall ask you for it when it will be required."

* * * * * *

Alongwith *paṇḍitá* Panchanan Bhattacharya[1] of Deoghar, many other devotees had arrived. Another of his favourite disciple, Swami Pranabananda was staying in Udaipur then. Hearing about the Final

---

1. Bhattacharya *Mahâśaya* later returned to Calcutta on account of some work. He was not present at Kashi at the time of the Departure of Yogiraj. The next day after the Sublime Departure i.e. 27th September 1895, Friday, Tinkari Lahiri *Mahâśaya* the eldest son of Yogiraj had written a postcard addressed to Panchanan Bhattacharya *Mahâśaya's* Calcutta address at Brindaban Bose Lane — "Yesterday at 5.25 in the evening, my Revered Father has departed. *Mahâśaya*, inform the devotees of Calcutta and other places whom you consider necessary. It is your responsibility to see that the task is accomplished properly. Through the medium of this letter, I have entrusted you with the charge."

Previously, in many books it has been mentioned that at the time of the Sublime Departure of Yogiraj, Bhattacharya *Mahâśaya* was present in Kashi. But this is not correct. However he was aware of the Departure of his Gurudeva from before.

(In accordance with the rightful consent a copy of the letter has been given above).

Moment of his Gurudeva, he started making arrangements to reach Kashi soon. Suddenly Pranabanada saw that his Gurudeva assuming a Subtle Form appeared before him and said — "Pranabananda, there is no use for haste. I shall depart before you reach."

Pranabananda began crying. Yogiraj comforted him saying — "Why are you crying? Though the body departs, the Esse of Sadguru remains. I am always present."

Another devotee of Yogiraj, Panchkori Bandopadhyay[1] was residing at Hardwar then. A few days before the Departure of Yogiraj, Bandopadhyay *Mahāśaya* saw the Resplendent Image of Yogiraj appear before him and say — "Come to Kashi immediately."

Bandopadhyay *Mahāśaya* arrived at Kashi immediately and noticed his Gurudeva deciding to leave His Mortal Frame.

Yogiraj in this manner made many of His devotees aware before His Sublime Departure.

Only a small amount of light would enter the room Yogiraj would inhabit as it did not have sufficient windows and doors. The Sublime Yogi was lying extremely indisposed in the afternoon, a day before His Departure. His eldest son, Tinkari Lahiri *Mahāśaya* was engaged in keeping a close watch upon his father, from the parlour adjoining the room. Suddenly he noticed his father leave His bed, walk up to a bookcase fixed on the wall of the room, go through some books, eventually walk back to the bed in a healthy and able manner and lie down.

Noticing this astounded him and entering the room he enquired his father — "If You are so well, then lying in bed why do You defecate and micturate in the bed pan? At least You can do this near the drain ?"

1. He later became famous as Keshabananda Brahmachari.

Benares

The Treasury officer
of
Benares

Sir

I request the favour of forwarding the accompanying Pension Roll for renewal.

Inspector General of Military Works No. 4642 d/ 6th Octr 1880, & Offg Assistant Ac to Accountant General Mil and Audit No 5678 d/ Allahabad 9th October 1880 ~~Last payment~~ drawn upto ~~Decr 1890~~ April 1891 I am in caste Brahmin. Date of my birth is May 1826.

Benares
9th May 1891

I have the honor to be,
Sir
Your most Obedient Servant
Shama Churn Sahioi
Garwodeshwar
Benares City

Benaras

To

The Treasury Officer of Benaras,

Sir,

I request the favour of forwarding the accompanying Pension Roll for renewal.

Inspector General of Military works No. 4662 dt. 6th October 1880 and offg. Assistant to Accountant General NNP and audh No. 5678 dt. Allahabad 9th October 1880 for Rs. 29/4/6 four months drawn upto April 1891. I am in caste Brahmin. Date of my birth is May 1826.*

I have the honour to be
Sir
Your most obedient servant,
Shama Churn Lahiree
Guroodeshwar
Benaras city.

Benaras
7th May 1891

---

* The month and year of His birth as stipulated by Yogiraj in this letter is not correct, though specifically this had been mentioned in His service record. The horoscope of Yogiraj detailing the date and time of His birth which has been noted by Him in His diary has been regarded by us as authentic. The self-written horoscope of Yogiraj has been presented in Appendix - C.

Yogiraj asked — "Where were you?"

Tinkari replied — "I was observing everything from the next room."

The Sublime Yogi pleasantly smiling said — "Everyone desires to serve Me, therefore I am lying on bed. If I don't lie down, how will their desires be fulfilled?"

At last, 26th September 1895, a Thursday, *Mahâshtami*, arrived at the portals of Garureswar house.[1] Though Yogiraj was lying ill in bed, like other days when he would impart religious advice to His devotees either lying or sitting down, on that day also although extremely unwell. He was explaining a few *ślókas* from the *Bhagavadgītā i*n a low voice. Many devotees were listening amidst grave silence. Everyone was grief-stricken and tearful. The *Mahâshtami* festive melody was being wafted by the breeze. The sun was about to set beneath the horizon for that day.

The devotees asked with tearful eyes and quivering voices — "In Your absence we will become helpless, what will be our alternative then?"

Yogiraj assured them — "This immortal *yógasādhana* has been fostered by sages and the ones who practise this will never become helpless. This *Prâṇákarma* will never become extinct. It was existent always and will always exist. The more a man will advance

1. The present address of the Abode where Yogiraj resided is D/31/58, Madanpura, Varanasi, U.P., India. The then Garureswar now is within Madanpura locality. At present His descendants reside there. This Abode is a pilgrimage for innumerable devotees. Normally the habitat of departed *Mahâpurushas* being a personal domain, is very rarely noticed but the Holy Abode of Bhagavan Krishna-Shama Churn where He effected His Divine Abstruse Causations, unfortunately being personal property, many ardent devotees particularly distant ones are deprived of free access to pay their devotional tributes, if they fail to arrive at the stipulated hour. Moreover sometimes the Holy Abode remains closed. Devotees regard Ghurni as Mathura since God Himself marked His Advent here and regard Varanasi His Mortal Abode and the field of His Divine Play as Vrindavan. But alas! The nation today is heedless in this regard.

towards spiritual fulfilment the more interest towards *Prâṇákarma* will increase, because it is a scientific *sādhana*."

Eyes half closed fixed upwardly in transcendence; the devotees were addressed — "The sublime and immortal *yóga* which has been obtained from *Gurúdeva* and revived will be practised in every household in future and gradually man will proceed towards the path of salvation. As in the past the path of salvation will become widened."

Yogiraj seated Himself in *padmâsana*. Looking towards His tearful devotees He remarked — "The time for My Departure has arrived. Do not grieve. Though the mortal body disappears, the Esse of the Sadguru remains. I am always amidst you."

At the auspicious juncture of *Mahắshṭamī* and *Mahắnavamī* sitting on the same bed, Yogiraj effected His Sublime Departure in *Mahắsamādhi*. It was 5.25 in the evening then.

His Mortal Frame after Departure abstained from the natural discipline. The devotees adorned the Mortal Frame with flowers and sandalwood paste. Many ladies and gentlemen started offering their respectful obeisance.

Many expressed the opinion that the Mortal Frame be buried. But the *paṇḍitás* reasoned that although Yogiraj was a Brahma-Rapt Yogi, He maintained a family existence. Thus keeping in accordance with the domestic norms it was necessary to cremate the Mortal Frame. Eventually, a large procession amidst the chanting of hymns brought the Mortal Frame to Manikarnika Ghat. Here also many hermits, *saṃnyāsins*, ladies and gentlemen came to offer their last Reverential Obeisance. According to the *śāstrás*, His eldest son lit the sacred fire and gradually the consecrated Funeral Pyre was set afire. Thus the Mortal Frame of Divine Ábstruse Causations was aflame. The all-devouring flame started blazing. The chant of hermits, *saṃnyāsins* and other ladies and gentlemen in unison sounded. — ***Hara hara Mahādevá Śambhú***. Torrents of tears rolled down the eyes of devotees. The bell of worship at the temple of *Vísvanāth* began ringing.

Overwhelmed with grief, Kashimani Devi had forgotten about the declaration, Yogiraj made six months before. A few ladies alongwith Kashimani Devi were in the house. Everyone was benumbed with grief. Suddenly Kashimani Devi remembered the declaration Yogiraj made six months back. Immediately calling her brother Rajchandra Sanyal, she sent him to the burningghat. But arriving there, he saw the blazing Funeral Pyre.

The grief-stricken Kashimani Devi kept on lamenting as to why she made this great mistake.

The congregation who participated in His Obsequies returned shortly. Another brother of Kashimani Devi *paṇḍitá* Bhagwan Sanyal hearing everything commented — "This mistake was ordained by Him. The Great Yogi would not always remain attached in earthly matters. Perhaps He had stated it remaining in non-attached state. Later he decided that as He existed in the family precincts, keeping in accordance with the domestic norms it would be proper to cremate His Mortal Frame. Therefore it is He Who caused the mistake to have been committed. For this, one should not grieve."

The fact that He made a prior decision to leave His Mortal Frame through *samādhi* has been proved in His self-written diary which is similar to the declaration He conferred to Kashimani Devi. In one instance, He has written — ***Āj erādā haye ki anahad dhvani me dhyāna sāmse kal sām tak lagāoye agar Hum mar jāye to koi Humko na pheke — yehoi gāḍke rakhe yā oyesehi baiṭhāyeke rakhe — Hum phir jāgeṅge.*** — In other words I have decided to engross Myself on the *Anāhata* sound from today evening till tomorrow evening; if I depart in this state, none should cast Me but should bury Me in this room or make Me sit in this posture — I shall appear[1] again.

After His Departure, His dear disciple *paṇḍitá* Panchanan Bhattacharya *Mahá́saya* of Deoghar in an elaborate letter to a *Kriyā bān* had given a detailed description about the sublimity of his Guru[2] :—

Dear.....

"If the *Gurú* who imparts initiation is not spiritually fulfilled then medicine may be necessary to be administered to him. A spiritually fulfilled or emancipated being does not require anything. Due to an aberration and vibration of internal airs, various types of afflictions occur; a spiritually fulfilled or emancipated person perpetually remains in still air. Are there afflictions, where still air is present? But ignorant persons who constantly exist within the ambit of body-consciousness consider the emancipated and spiritually attained persons to be like themselves and are engaged in relieving these persons from afflictions with the application of medicines. This is merely a result of their lack of foresight. Without realising they

---

1. Here 'appear' may or may not infer the Same Form. God in this regard has expressed in the *Gītā* —

> ***Yadā yadā hi dhármasya glānirbhabati Bhārata.***
> ***Abhuthānamdhármasya tadātmānaṃ śrījāmahyam.***
> ***Paritrāṇāya sādhunāṃ bināśāya ca duskṛitām.***
> ***Dhármasaṃsthāpanārthāya sambhavāmi yuge yuge.*** — (4/7-8)

O *Bhārata* (Arjuna), I Myself manifest Myself from My Ownself whenever there is a religious decadence. To cause salvation to virtuous souls, to terminate evil and to effect a revival of *dhárma* whenever necessity demands, I mark My Advent.

2. In accordance with the consent of the person concerned, a facsimile of the aforesaid letter is being given. Panchanan Bhattacharya was the affectionate disciple of Yogiraj and attaining an elevated state in *sādhanā* had shown many men the path of soul-seeking. Several yogic aspirants of Bengal and Bihar would many a time be sent to Bhattacharya *Mahá́saya* by Yogiraj. The printing and publishing of most of the books of Yogiraj would be accomplished under the supervision of Bhattacharya *Mahá́saya*.

disrespect these emancipated persons by regarding them to be afflicted, this is done for the fulfilment of their own self interests or those who pretend to be hermits are desirous of being one; it is they who circulate the notion that spiritually attached persons suffer from afflictions and medicines are administered to them, because if these statements are not made in what manner can their renown spread? Because when they themselves suffer from afflictions they have to take medicines as the fear of death exists for them. Thus the ignorant ones state that the spiritually attained persons take medicines and the latter should be administered and if not administered, it is sinful. Is it not immensely sinful to regard a spiritually attained or emancipated being as an ordinary person? Spiritually attained or emancipated beings in order to avoid being exposed behave like ordinary human beings and this only impels the common man to say that those spiritually attained persons administer medicines for themselves, that they are afflicted by diseases and that they perform good and evil actions. But common people are unaware of the fact that the spiritually fulfilled persons do not perform anything and are not afflicted by diseases. This had occurred to Gurudeva at the moment of His Departure. One of the devotees of Gurudeva who used to acknowledge his Gurudeva as Guru in society, had considered Him to be a patient and by arranging for His treatment had shown outward concern, but Gurudeva had told His son, Tinkaribabu — 'It is not advisable to make Me undergo any treatment, it is always better to depend upon the law of nature'. I can understand how the type of people who interfere in God's actions are. Just think of the fact that if He at all was affected by disease then why did not His faeces and urine have the foul odour stemming from disease? The pus of the so-called wound He was suffering from should have at least had the foul smell, but this also did not exist. Observing all these also is not the consciousness of men aroused? Alas, have they thought, that He was a mere Sadhu Who had assumed a garb or merely a Great Soul?

What was the reason for His Departure ? Why He appeared and why He departed it is beyond their knowledge. Who will execute treatment on Him? Ordinary man should be conscious that the proud living being driven into a frenzy by vanity and arrogance continues raving and this brings no harm to the great souls. He had enlightened me last August about His wish to depart and I had conveyed this to eight or ten persons.........."

(The concluding portion was not available)

*　　*　　*　　*　　*　　*

Observing this Sublime Yogi would indicate that a Divine Child was seated in supreme peace on the fearless lap of the universal mother. Senility could not affect this Sublime Yogi replete with spiritual power. Only His hairs had turned grey, but His Mortal Frame did not have a single wrinkle anywhere. This Sublime Yogi could metamorphose His Gross Frame.[1] But He did not execute this, instead He would say what has imperatively to be cast off one day, the moment it's necessity ends, it is best to cast it off.

Though He has departed from this phenomenal world, He is constantly pervasive to His devotees. The effectiveness of the blessings of this Sublime Yogi on the lives of His innumerable disciples can be comprehended by taking a few of His devotees into consideration.

This Sublime Yogi at the moment of Departure being appeased by Krishnaram's dedication had instructed him to seek his desired prayer. Krishnaram was above material desires and aspirations. He had appealed with folded hands that barring the shelter at the Lotus Feet of his Guru he desired nothing.

---

1. The exact *sādhana* technique by which the body can be rejuvenated and a new body acquired has been recounted in His diary. But it being an extremely esoteric *sādhana* essence, has not been published.

It has been previously mentioned that Krishnaram used to stay at Ranamahal Ghat on the lap of the north-bound Ganges, in a room adjoining the Radhakrishna temple of Udaipur estate. When his end drew near, the eldest son of Yogiraj, Tinkari Lahiri *Mahâsaya* was seated on one side of him and on the other side was seated the greatest devotee and worshipper of Yogiraj, Bansidharji. The last moment had arrived, the breathing motion was oriented upwards but Krishnaramji in a steady, calm and unquivering voice was reciting by heart, the *Gītā* from beginning to end. The very moment the last sloka of *Purushôttama Yoga* — ***Etadbuddhā buddhimān syād kṛitakṛityasca Bhārata*** was uttered, his *Prâṇá* air merged in the infinite void. Tears streamed down the cheeks of the ever-grave and steady Tinkari Lahiri *Mahâsaya* and Bansidharji.

* * * * * *

Kashimani Devi was lying on bed in respect of her departure. She was not plagued by any disease, decrepitude was the cause of her death. Suddenly calling her grandson, she remarked — "Your Grandfather will arrive, provide a seat for Him."

The grandson asked — "Where is Grandfather now?"

With a gentle smile, Kashimani Devi replied — "He is in the Abode of Lord *Vísvanāth*."

The grandson jokingly inquired — "Does He come to you everyday?"

Again with a mild smile Kashimani Devi answered — "Yes, He comes to see me everyday. He sits here and discusses with me. Today also He will come, that is why I am asking you to provide the seat."

The grandson laid out the seat. A few days after this, Kashimani Devi departed with full consciousness.

*   *   *   *   *   *

His favourite disciple Rampadarathji would regularly visit the Holy Room used by Yogiraj and sitting here would practise *dhyāna*. Due to old age he became physically unfit, his vision was impaired, nevertheless he would with the help of a walking stick visit the Abode daily. One day while coming in this manner Rampadarathji fell down on the road. The youngest grandson of Yogiraj, Satyacharan Lahiri *Mahāśaya* was passing by at that time. Seeing this, he rushed to the spot, helped him get up and asked him — "What is the use of coming regularly in this old age taking immense pains ?"

Though his feet was wounded, Rampadarathji smiling a little stated — "Guru Maharaja has showered innumerable graces on me, but I am so useless that I could not make my life fruitful. Therefore I give regular attendance to His Durbar. It is the Durbar of His holiness. The day He will take mercy on me, I will gain deliverance."

Gradually, devotee Rampadarathji due to old age could not frequent the Holy Abode of his Guru. Eventually, his last moments had arrived. Calling his nephew (brother's son) he said — "Guru Maharaja has come and is standing, place a seat for Him to sit."

The nephew asked — "Where is your Guru Maharaja?"

Rampadarathji whose end was near, making an indicative gesture smilingly said — "Can't you see Guru Maharaja standing there? Place a seat for Him."

The nephew acted likewise. After a few moments, concentrating fixedly on his Guru Maharaja Who was much more dearer to him than his life, the lamp of Rampadarathji's life was extinguished.

Harimati Devi, the eldest daughter of Yogiraj, being widowed shortly after marriage would reside at her Father's house. She was alive for almost 85 years.

The evening before her departure from this Earthly Abode, hymns dedicated to Bhagavan Krishna were being chanted and she was listening to this sitting on the first floor verandah. She felt indisposed due to old age therefore went to her room, lay down on the bed and called for her nephew Satyacharan. When he arrived, she remarked —"Place a seat here, for Father has come to take me."

Satyacharan Lahiri *Mahấsaya* was astounded by her words and laid down the *āsaná* which was exclusively placed for Yogiraj, at the moment of the departure of Kashimani Devi. That day in the early dawn, by reciting her favourite morning eulogistic verses her *Prâṇá* air merged in the infinite *Prâṇá*.

Bansidhar Khanna, the earnest devotee of Yogiraj at a later date was employed as a rent-collector in the estate of the descendants of Yogiraj, twenty miles away from Kashi. Since he was extremely reliable, he was given the responsibility of managing all the affairs of the estate. Therefore he would guard the property of his Guru sincerely.

On becoming old, Beniprasad Khettry one of his relatives told him one day — "Now you should live in Kashi, otherwise do you want to die in this uninhabited place?"

Bansidharji replied — "Guru Maharaja has been extremely merciful to me, but I could not serve Him. Therefore all the actions which can be performed by this body are all His actions, thus I have offered this body at His Lotus Feet. If He so desires He will throw this body in the jungle or place it at His Lotus Feet. I do not worry about that. "

One day Satyacharan Lahiri *Mahāśaya*, grandson of Yogiraj went to the estate and told Bansidharji — "You have become old, now you need to be tended. Go and stay with your son and daughter-in-law, I shall send you some monthly expenses."

Bansidharji remarked — "Kindly do not say like this. As long as I can hold my pen for your service, I wish to eat your bread till then. The day I will fail to hold the pen, I pray to Guru Maharaja, that day He give me place at His Lotus Feet. I do not want to place my burden on you or on my son. After my death, do not take this body to Kashi. I do not want the wealth of my Guru to be spent on this account. Throw this body in the jungle, it will be of use to the wild beasts there."

After a short period, while still being employed in the estate he suddenly became ill and was brought to Kashi for proper treatment. The next afternoon, Bansidharji who was about to leave this earthly world was lying on the verandah in front of the room of Yogiraj. Alongwith Satyacharan Lahiri *Mahāśaya*, grandson of Yogiraj, Bhupendranath Sanyal *Mahāśaya*, one of the principal disciples of Yogiraj; many other devotees were present. Sitting near the head of Bansidharji, Sanyal *Mahāśaya* was reciting the *Gītā* in a dulcet tone. Keeping on remembering his Guru who was dear to him, Bansidharji attained eternal *samādhi*.

Ceaselessly rendering service towards his Gurudeva for a long period of thirty eight years an advanced *Kriyābān's* life was merged at the Guru's Holy feet.

The benefits conferred in the worldly context on taking recourse to the Lotus Feet of Guru is long-standing as has been substantiated by Rammohan De and his sister Manomohini previously. The immense faith and devotion towards the Lotus Feet of the Guru which Manomohini possessed could be noticed at the time of her death.

At the head of her bed, a photograph of her adorable Gurudeva would be kept. The day before her death, she called her son and asked him to place the photograph in front of her. The next day, in the early morning she remembered Satyacharan Lahiri *Mahāśaya*, the youngest grandson of her Gurudeva and prayed to him to bring the water with which the feet of her revered Gurudeva had been washed. After this was brought, she drank it with deep reverence from the hands of her Guru's grandson and other dear ones and placed the photograph of her adorable Bhagavan on her chest with intense devotion. She placed both her hands on the Lotus Feet of her Guru : with unblinking eyes and steadfast gaze observed the photograph and within a short while an existence so long sheltered by the Guru merged in His Lotus Feet.

* * * * * * *

Yogiraj has departed into the Ambrosial Effulgent Abode of Effulgence. but the ideals He has set and the quest for the path of salvation He has unravelled will never be forgotten by householders. In the path revived by him, millions of men till today are practising *sādhanā* secretly within the precincts of their homes and are progressing towards the path of salvation. Till today, His innumerable devotees many of whom are renowned are present throughout India and the Orient and Occident.

Like many incidents in His personal life, His life of *sādhana* is unknown to the common men. Most of His *sādhanās* have been performed secretly. *Sādhanā* is practised by ordinary men for their own salvation, but *sādhanā* for such a Divine Soul is for the salvation of each individual and for the establishment of ideals. So far as the concept of *sādhanā* is concerned, both *sādhanās* are the same but objectives are different.

He did not proceed towards oneness through the medium of many types of *sādhanās*, instead by remaining established in oneness, He caused several *sādhanā* realisations. By not practising *sādhanā* of any god or goddess separately, but by firmly existing in the fundamental soul-essence, all the deities have been effected to be visualised by Him automatically in *sādhanā* which He has practised. He effected *sādhana* of the pervasive and omniscient soul. His soul-*sādhana* is *sādhana* on the One Who exists within all gods and goddesses. He did not develop a relationship with God in the form of mother, father or friend. He had regarded the soul as a soul or as a self-soul. He advised — "Just as, if day exists night also has to exist; if happiness exists misery also has to exist; similarly if the propitious deity exists, the unpropitious deity also exists. Nurse *Prâṇá*, for by tending *Prâṇá*, you will reap benefits and not nursing *Prâṇá* will bring harm upon yourself. *Prâṇá* is served by practising *Prâṇákarma*. The dynamism of *Prâṇá* is harmful, stillness is beneficial."

Soul-introspection is the principal aim of life. If soul visualisation does not occur, then being born as a human being, human existence becomes fruitless. This was the basic philosophy of His life. He would state — The objective of human existence is not how well one has eaten, how well one has maintained one's existence or how much of worldly pleasures one has enjoyed. He used to comment, by reading different *śāstrás* what was the use of acquiring erudition or what was the use of rendering lectures for propagation of religion if soul-visualisation does not occur? He would remark that what was the use of being busy for imparting welfare to the world? How much of permanent welfare can be imparted? What can be done is impermanent. Showing the path for soul-visualisation is the permanent welfare by which miseries of all births are eliminated and worldly afflictions disappear. If birth does not occur, then where is sorrow? Therefore He has warned man not to involve himself in a great deal of actions. He would note that the mind when perpetually engrossed in soul-introspection can attain

God, if that mind is constantly busy in imparting welfare to others or is busy in selfish thoughts, then it should be understood that the mind is being misused and vibration is augmented. It is true that those who are benevolent are good people but soul-attainment is not possible for them. These are external facets in the path of *sādhanā*. If it has been decided that the principal aim of life is soul-attainment then *Prâṇá* should be nursed constantly by practising *Prâṇákarma* and engrossing in soul-introspection. If there is slackness and dearth of endeavour in *Prâṇákarma*, that valuable treasure cannot be derived. For this, conscience, apathy and fortitude are required. But He never gave indulgence to absurd apathies. He would state that absurd apathy is equivalent to brashness. He did not totally forbid giving lectures, but would ask to first attain soul-visualisaiton and a permanent settlement, then give lectures or do anything else. He disliked lectures by people who were not conversant with the practice of *sādhana* and who by studying books assumed the garb of *paṇḍitás*.

He was an innate Yogi and a true Yogi. Thus His axioms touched the innermost recesses of the minds of people and created ripples. He vehemently opposed the use of trickery, pretentiousness, hypocrisy, deception, bigotry regarding *dhárma* or *sādhanā*. He would never give indulgence to any of these. Therefore He used to tersely remark to everyone — by applying deceitful stratagem all material benefits can be acquired, but not soul-attainment.

His Advent in the Indian sky emitted an intense radiance in the minds of men and dazed them. Therefore the Indian people to appease their indomitable thirst for Bhagavan made Yogiraj exclusively their own. Yogiraj used to pay genuine honour to Divine Truth. Therefore He is the Indian Yogi in it's true aspect. He did not harbour any discrimination towards, Hindus, Muslims, Christians and those of other faiths. He would express — all human beings are progenies of the same God, everyone can practise *Ātmasādhanā*, all men have the right to acquire this *yógasādhanā*. Therefore He would impart assurance to all sinners of the earth and say — none is a sinner or a saint. There is no sin if the mind is placed on *Kūṭastha*, but if it is not placed, it is sinful. Since He made such positive declarations, He is the Yogi Who effected an equipoise amongst all faiths. This is not merely an incidental talk — practising *sādhanā* Himself He set an example for mankind. He visualised all the Hindu gods and goddesses alongwith *Khodā* and *Āllāh* and progressing further in the path of *sādhanā*, He expounded Who God is in actuality. How many *yogis* could elucidate likewise? Therefore His Divine-Maxim has instilled an unflinching and irrevocable faith in the hearts of men towards *sādhanā*.

Yogiraj directed to bring about a change in the prevalent religious systems and beliefs of human society. In many an instance, these have been converted to superstitions. The ancient *śāstrás* should be regarded to be the only basis. He initiated the liberal discussion of ancient *śāstrás* and thereby the gleaning of *sādhanā*-derived true esoteric essence. He did not stop at mere comments; instead He has rendered explanations replete with the esoteric *sādhanā* essence to many ancient *śāstrás* which are most essential for *sādhakas*. He imparted *yogic* explanations to the *Gītā*. One of His devotees published hundreds of copies and distributed these amongst the other devotees. In this manner, by abandoning religious conservatism, He effected it's reformation. By making His Advent on the Indian soil, He advised everyone to follow the tenets of *śāstrás*. Effecting the causation of these tenets and the concord between domestic and spiritual lives in this very Advent He expounded these in a simple and facile manner thus unravelling a new world for humanity. He has instilled the precepts as to how one can easily abide by the ancient *yogic śāstrás* and their exalted ideals in life. This Advent of Him is an ennobling illustration of how man though by remaining in the vortex of material actions can direct his life towards the exalted ideals of the spiritual world and gradually reach the pinnacle of spiritualdom. Yogiraj caused the reviviscence of the novel, pure, dispassionate path for the mass blinded by covetousness and greed. This will never become evanescent to the householders. An intense fervour is noticed in the present human society to become acquainted with the abstruse subject of *dhárma*. Present day *dhárma* being based exclusively on propaganda, the Divine Apophthegms and Precepts of this Sublime Spiritual Fountain-Head deserve special study during this stage of decadence. Temples in His memory are located at many places like Kashi, Hardwar, Bankura, Bishnupur, Ranchi, Mandar, Malipur of Faizabad, Jhargram, Deoghar, Howrah, Calcutta and the stately one at Kakdwip in West Bengal and at Neuvy-En-Champagne, France where His devotees till today by offering prayers and reverence daily, take care to preserve His Consecrated Memorial. The *Brahmasādhana* which He bestowed upon mankind is being reverentially adhered to in India as well as throughout the world.

If Yogiraj is conceived to be a Hindu merely, it is a cardinal error. He is the Divine Insignia of a human life's fulfilment. He would remark that the two requisites to practise this immortal *yógasādhana* are a human body and a true desire. One who possesses these two attributes, can easily practise this *sādhana*. No matter whatever apparent religion one may belong to, that eternal soul is Omnipresent; thus causing a revival of the glorious maxim underlying *Vedas, Upanisháds* and *Gītā* He has portrayed the avenue for arriving at the sole and ultimate destination. Thus it can be noticed that men irrespective of the apparently different faiths or beliefs or creeds took recourse in Him. Therefore in today's discordant world, His ideals are the exclusive mainstay for mankind.

In this era of materialism, He has placed the exalted and living ideals of spiritual knowledge before us. Apart from worldly possessions and wealth, man has an ultimate and deep aspiration, i.e. salvation; Yogiraj has drawn the attention of all towards the perennial truth as to how family men can achieve that eternal immortal state. So He is the **'God of Householders'.**

There are many exalted ideals which only a handful of spirited men can execute in their lives. These ideals are not applicable to all.

But we term those ideals to be the greatest which can be executed by everyone in their lives, if they make the smallest endeavour. Shama Churn Lahiree Mahasaya has set forth such an ideal. He merely did not stop at expressing these ideals verbally to everyone but completely executing this in His Own life, He set an example. He would stipulate that through the medium of proper action, the respective life of each man will have to be established. The world is a place of action, there is no alternative other than action. Nothing can be abandoned while habiting the material world. It is not advisable to forsake the domestic existence, because it is here that everyone is born and leads an existence. Thus to remain amidst everything, not relinquish anything, constitute one's life gradually through proper action and attain the ultimate in spiritual fulfilment, Yogiraj has expounded the specific, proper and scientifically approved path which today is imperative for all.

Bharata is a land of *yogis* because *yóga* has taken it's root here. *Yóga* is the mainstay of *Sanātána Dhárma*. Barring *yóga*, *Sanātána Dhárma* cannot be known and not knowing *Sanātána Dhárma* one cannot be acquainted with spiritual India. Therefore to become acquainted with spiritual India one should know about Indian *yogis* first and to comprehend the *yogis* one has to follow the path demonstrated by them. Therefore God advised humanity through Arjuna to become *yogis*. He declared that *yogis* are greater than hermits, the wise and the active. If people belonging to *Sanātána* Bharata, do not learn about Indian *yogis* and follow the path related by them then though by birth they are Indians they cannot be termed to be true Indians. Therefore without *yóga*, there is no India and without India there is no *yóga*.

Each nation has it's respective trend of thought, by which the respective nation's welfare is accomplished. The Indian trend of thought is spiritual knowledge, soul-knowledge, knowledge about *Brahma* or *yóga* knowledge. That soul-knowledge or *yóga*-knowledge which has been nurtured and demonstrated by *ṛishis*, though for a while seems unapparent perennially inheres as an undercurrent in Indians. That extinct soul-knowledge was accessible only to a select few conversant in *yóga*. It was evident to Yogiraj that barring this noble, immortal, soul-knowledge *yógasādhana*, lives of Indians would not be fulfilled. Therefore He caused it's reviviscence by unravelling this invaluable treasure of *Sanātána* Bharata (eternal India) from mountain caverns thus leading to it's expansion irrespectively amongst all castes, creeds and sects. Previously for the hope of gaining this soul-knowledge many had forsaken their household lives and pursued ascetics and *Mahấtmās* in mountain caverns. Initially it is Yogiraj only Who has caused an awakening of the soul essence immortal *yógasādhana* nurtured by sages amidst family men plagued by problems and by doing this infused life into the masses. Today, by the Grace of Krishna Shamachurn this knowledge has become easily obtainable. Indians are blessed reobtaining that sage-demonstrated path by the Providence of Brahma-Shamachurn. The spiritual lamp which He has lit is glowing luminously in the hearts of millions.

Bhagavān has decreed in the *Gītā* that whenever there is decadence of this *yógadhárma* in the world it is only then that He Himself will mark His Advent to resuscitate the waning glory of eternal *yógadhárma*. Abiding by His Own decree He effected His Re-Advent in the Guise of Bhagavan Shamachurn and again portrayed to erring mankind the Royal Avenue for attainment of Ambrosial Essence. He has showered a Divine Assurance — ***Jiskā bojh Woh khud utār legā. Jo Bhagavān ko hāmesā dhyāna kare usko kām Uha kartā hāye.*** —If one is saddled by any impediment, the One Whose burden it is, will Himself release it. The one who perpetually cogitates on *Bhagavān*, all actions are executed by Him.

F I N I S

APPENDIX

APPENDIX - A

NATAL CHART OF YOGIRAJ

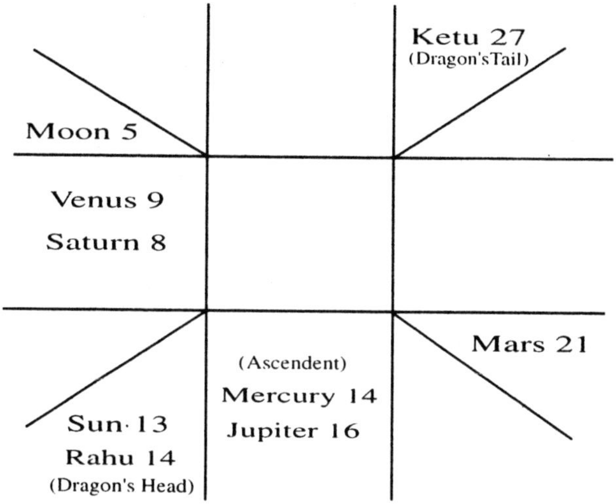

From times immemorial till the present day the soil of India is pregnant with the remarkable silence regarding the play of the imperceptible power. The name of this unseen force is the power of dharma, the knowledge of dharma, soul-knowledge or in other words the endeavour to bring the Infinite within the bounds of man's small realm. This is why perhaps the other name for Bharata (India) is Dharmakshetra (the realm of religion). Bhagavan has imparted an ultimate assurance in the Gita — ***'Sambhavami yuge yuge'*** — I shall mark My Advent at the transition of each yuga — this is the precise reason why He manifests Himself time and again —the sky, air, speck of dust, water, land, atmosphere of India through aeons will stand testimony to this.

Bearing resemblance to the above, a Sublime Soul marked His Advent in Ghurni beside Krishnagar, District Nadia, West Bengal, India on 30th September 1828 (Tuesday). It was the seventh day of the dark lunar fortnight to Gourmohan Lahiri (father) and Smt. Muktakeshi Devi (mother). It seemed that the eternal axiom of the

Gita gained a reviviscence :-

> ***Tapasvibhyoadhiko yogi jñānibhyoapi matoadhdhikah***
> ***Karmibhyascādhiko yogi tāsmdyogi bhavārjuna.***

Shama Churn was initiated in the domain of yogasadhana. He had dedicated His Whole Being to the pedestal of yogasadhana. He came to be known as Yogiraj Sri Shama Churn Lahiree. His spiritual Esse and Effulgent Form manifest even in the astrological calculations.

In accordance with Indian astrology Lahiree Mahasaya's ascendent is Libra, sun sign is Gemini and planet is Mars. The disposition of Mars is to probe, explore. The one who is such born tends to explore something, he seems to aspire for someone, to make the quest for something. The latent joy of Gemini is the power of creation and manifestation. It's predisposition is to express any conception, any abstract idea in a concrete manner. Alan Leo states — "Gemini, the synthesiser manifests the combination of the two — adaptability and intellect—. So Gemini produces enthusiastic, impressionable, sympathetic and versatile men and women —." Gemini's propensity is to provide stimulus. Once it abides by the rule of expansion, again it is pervaded by the rule of contraction. It infinitely manifests both man's power of impregnation and women's power of retention alike. It is extremely alert regarding the minor details surrounding it. It is the symbol of an ever-conscious sense of discernment, perception, intellect, contemplation, realisation and above all will-power (determination).

The ascendent is Libra. It reminds us of the aerial motion which is infinitely continuing even in the infinite dot of time. It is the quintessence of placidity, tenderness, gentleness and rationalism. It commences it's journey after establishing it's veracity on the touchstone of reason. The ascendent lord is Venus, exponent of life's restoration — whose contact enlivens even the inanimate unconscious (one who restores the dead to life).

The one who is successful in elucidating the esoteric abstruse scriptural knowledge and invaluable realisations into simple lucid crystalline prose through dexterity, the one who is aware of the material gross objects, the one who is loyal and energetic as well, such a Being is Yogiraj who by the influence of Venus was hemmed in within the family ambit, was a service holder and an epitome of fulfilment. Jupiter's location in the ninth house hence in the moon (fortune) forming a good aspect made Yogiraj family oriented yet apathetical, active yet passive, aware of earthly joys and aspirations yet stoic, the author of earthly happiness yet extra-mundane bliss. The ascendent lord of the fourth and fifth houses, Saturn is the most principal planet located in the water sign Cancer. Saturn connotes death, sorrow; is a symbol of austerity —practising sadhana irrespective of the body being incinerated in the sadhana-fire; Saturn confers profound concentration, holiness, loyalty, devotion, fathomless philosophical knowledge, wisdom, intellect, soul-realised state, strict discipline. Without Saturn's grace visualisation of the Lotus Feet is impossible. The connection between cardinal house (kendra) and angular house (kona) is named Rajayoga.

The location of Venus and Saturn alongwith the conjunction of Jupiter, Mercury and Moon confers the native with the highest pinnacle of yogasadhana and strengthens this position. Venus and Saturn are both centred on aspirations. Therefore Yogiraj throughout His existence has made the quest for deep engrossment. This is why Shama Churn is eternally afloat in the sublime realm, the epitome of Divine bliss.

APPENDIX B

GENEALOGICAL TABLE OF YOGIRAJ

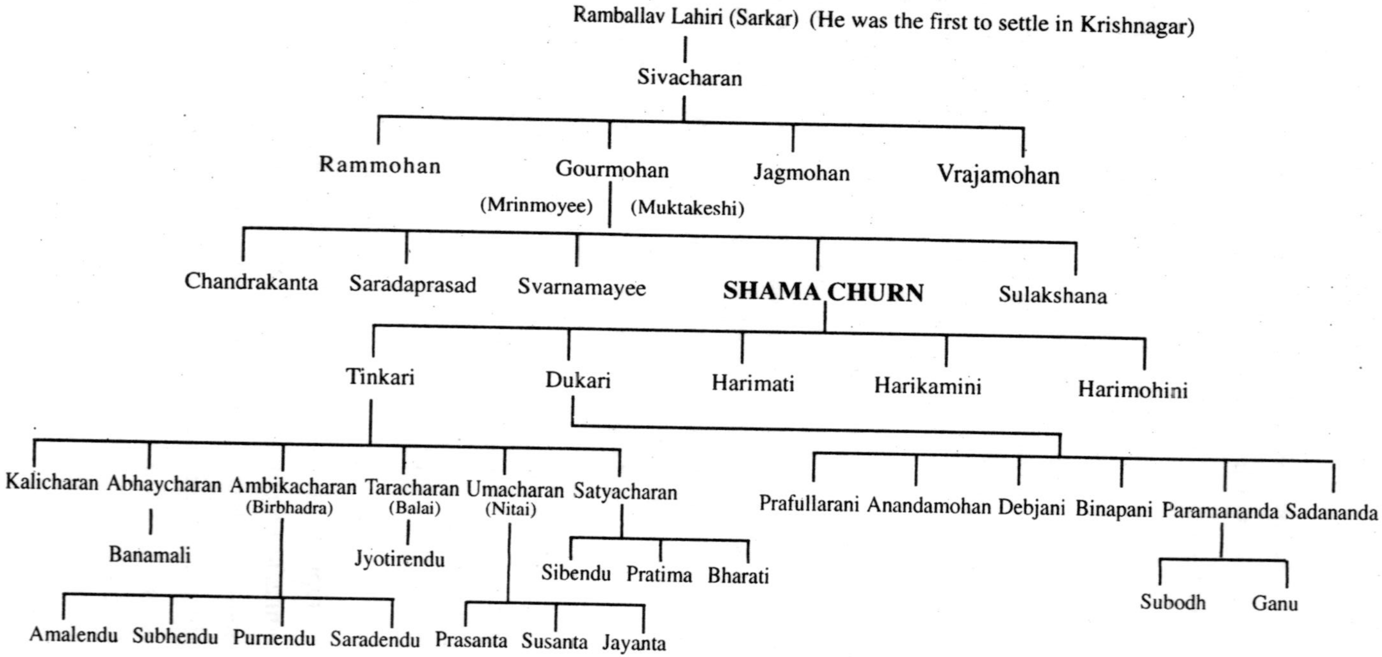

APPENDIX C

GENEALOGICAL TABLE OF KASHIMANI DEVI

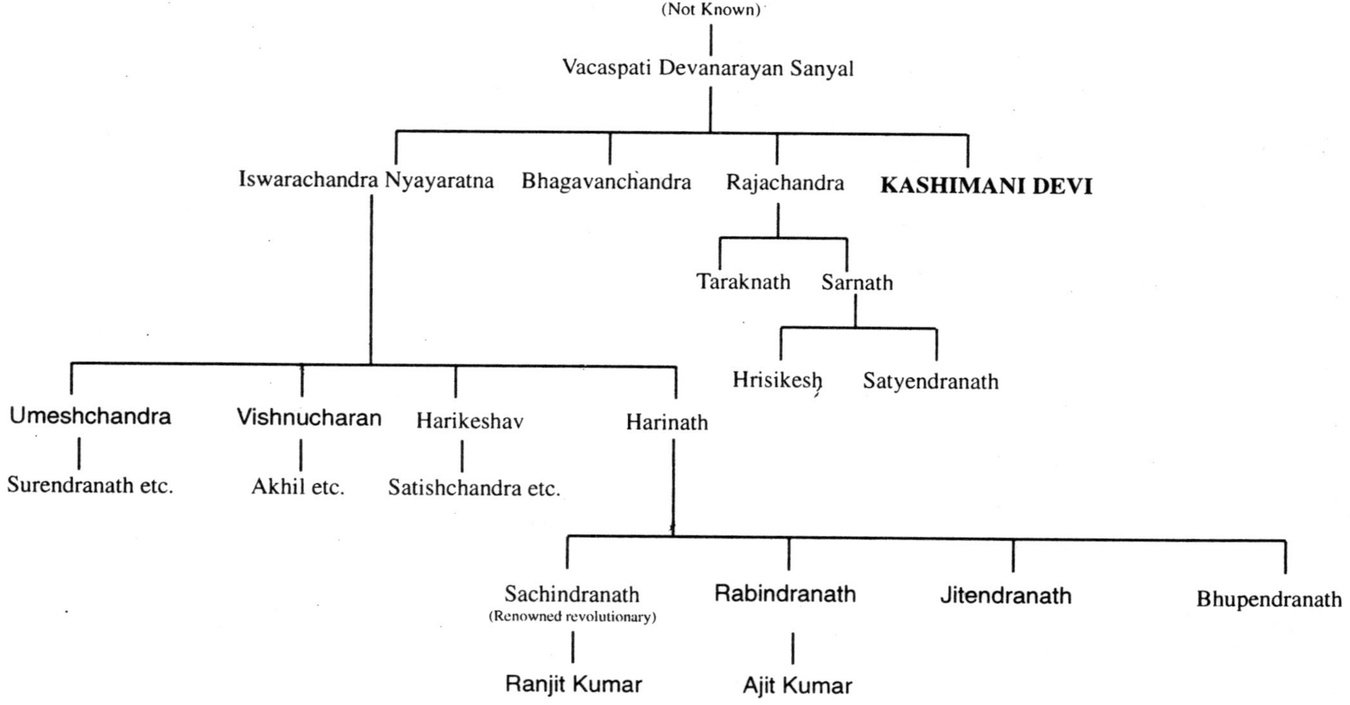

(Information provided as much as has been obtained)

Appendix - D

English phonetic scripts of Indian alphabets which have been meticulously abided by in the book to facilitate correct pronunciation of Indian words.

VOWELS

a	as	in	a
ā	”	”	father, mar. (fāther, mār)
i	”	”	sill, daffodil.
ī	”	”	sardine (sardīne).
u	”	”	pull, cushion.
ū	”	”	suit. (sūit).
ṛi	”	”	horrid, herring (horṛid, herṛing).
e	”	”	grey, fete.
ai	”	”	to be pronounced as o+e together. No English example available.
o	”	”	ocean, rope
au	”	”	auld (Old English Anglian = old).
n̲ or ṃ	as	in	plonk, monk (plon̲k, mon̲k).
ḥ	as	in	ah! hah! hah! (aḥ! haḥ! haḥ!).

CONSONANTS

k	as	in	neck, keg.
kh	”	”	kharif, Khyber.
g	”	”	God, fog.
gh	”	”	gherkin, ghetto.
ṅ	”	”	aṅkle, aṅgle.
c	”	”	chant, check.
ch	”	”	hatch, hunch.
j	”	”	jug. jig.
jh	”	”	hedgehog, gendarme (as in French).
ñ	”	”	binge (biñg).
ṭ	”	”	but, tell (buṭ, ṭell).
ṭh	”	”	penthouse, (penṭhouse).
ḍ	”	”	nod, doll (noḍ, ḍoll).
ḍh	”	”	redhead (reḍhead).
ṇ	”	”	mandolin (maṇḍolin).
t	”	”	mouton (as in French meaning sheep).

th	”	”	thank, think.
d	”	”	douce (as in French).
dh	”	”	dhyana, adhere.
n	”	”	net, nail.
p	”	”	pet, cup.
ph	”	”	philanthropy, philosophy.
b	”	”	box, cub.
bh	”	”	abhorrence.
m	”	”	mug, chum.
y	”	”	yarn, yacht.
r	”	”	ear, rock.
l	”	”	dale, sulk.
w	”	”	won, Antwerp.
ś	”	”	assure (asśure).
sh	”	”	shoal, should.
s	”	”	miss, sun.
h	”	”	help, horse.

GLOSSARY

Abhaypada — Lit. fearless state. For a *yogi* this state arrives only when the realisation dawns that the original still state is the only true state and everything else is a hoax. This realisation occurs only when the *yogi* through austere ardent *Kriyāyoga* practice reverts to the original still state. It is now that the greatest mortal fear — fear of death cannot touch him for he has mastered death and can beckon it at his will, therefore he has now arrived at *abhaypada*.

Ādideva — *See Purāṇá Púrusha.*

Ādi Purāṇá Kishuṇ — *See Purāṇá Púrusha.*

Ādi Púrusha — *See Purāṇá Púrusha.*

Āditya — *Ātmasūrya.*

Advaita — Lit. non-duality. For a *yogi* non-duality infers the state of mergence of the individual soul with the Absolute i.e. when dynamic *Prâṇá* merges in the still *Prâṇá* — the dual state disappears thus the gross aspects of life (both positive and negative) evanesce and a *yogi* then attains true eternal bliss.

Ādyāśakti — *See Kuṇḍalini.*

Agam ghar — See *ghar.*

Agamsthān — The unfathomable inaccessible static place *Kūṭastha*, where only *yogis* can reach.

Ahaṃkār — Lit. pride, self-conceit. A *yogi* before becoming a *Kriyāyoga* practisant is steeped in *ahaṃkār* but gradual *Kriyāyoga* practice eliminates this self-conceit or pride. A *yogi* only can go beyond this pride which originates from kinetic *Prâṇá* which in turn deters man from soul-orientation.

Áhiṃsā — Lit. non-violence, freedom from malice. Yogic interpretation is that a *yogi* goes far beyond malice as he endeavours to wean himself from kinetic *Prâṇá* which he has entered after birth and revert to the original still state. Since he goes through the stilling process; malice, violence is non-existent in him. He then cannot act maliciously or violently as these are products of dynamic *Prâṇá,* the kinetic mind.

Ajapā — Lit. respiration. Yogical implication is the incessant breathing motion which continues sans effort. In actuality none pay heed to this. But for a *yogi* this type of breathing is not acceptable, because austere *Kriyā-yogasādhana* infers the practice of internal breathing motion, thus this spontaneous motion has no connection with *iḍā* and *pingalá,* the external breathing motion. This internal breathing motion is *sushumná-*oriented. When a baby remains in his mother's womb, he abides in this *ajapā* state, a *yogi* through *Kriyāyogasādhana* practice endeavours to revert to this original still state — the *ajapā* state.

Ajar ghar — See *ghar*.

Ājñācakrá — *Ājñācakrá* is the sixth *cakrá* which is termed as the occipital bone. It is located exactly opposite *Kūṭastha* which is the glabella i.e. between the eyebrows. *Ājñācakrá* is the root of *Kūṭastha*. Since amalgam is present behind a mirror, it's property causes reflection, similarly since *ajñācakrá* is occipital, *Kūṭastha* is reflected. Therefore a *yogi* through *Kūṭastha* medium visualises the macrocosm, thus *Kūṭastha* is the mirror and *Ājñācakrá* is the amalgam. To a *yogi Kūṭastha* is the highest holy place, beatitude; *Kūṭastha is Dvārakā* (capital place) i.e. the origin of breath, *Kūṭastha* is *Bhagavān,* initial Form of Amorphous *Brahma* originated from here, Amorphous *Brahma* is above *Kūṭastha*. When *yogi* is settled at *Kūṭastha,* Soul-Sun, Soul-Moon are envisioned. *Kūṭastha* is the Third Eye, Transcendental Eye, Eye of wisdom which only a *Sadguru* unfolds at the time of initiation and it's effect is permanent unlike the transient instant self-awakenings prevalent now. Also see *cakrá*.

Akālmṛityú — See *kāl*.

Akshar — See *Purāṇá Púrusha*.

Akās — See *āsmān*.

Alakh/Alakh Nirañjana — Lit. One Who is imperceptible and immaculate. Yogically it infers the Supreme Being. A *yogi* envisions the imperceptible immaculate Supreme Being after austere *sādhana* practice.

Āllāh — The Supreme Being in Islam. Yogic connotation of *Āllāh* or *Khodā* is the root i.e. the original still state or still *Prâṇá* which a *yogi* endeavours to revert to through the medium of dynamic *Prâṇá*.

Amar Ghar — See *ghar*.

Amarpur — The immortal indestructible abode; the still state; *Kūṭastha*.

Anādi — Lit. eternal, endless. Yogically it refers the infinite *Kūṭastha*. A *yogi* seeks mergence with the Absolute and arrives at it through austere *Kriyā* practice —thus he then is at one with *Anādi* — the Absolute or Supreme Being.

Anāhata Cakrá — See *cakrá*.

Anāhata — It is the sound emanating without any friction. It is an internal sound originating from kinetic *Prâṇá*. This is the first internal sound a *yogi* hears. It is a constant sound akin to the chirping of a cricket. When a *yogi* enters this sound he is engrossed in it.

Ānanda — Lit. joy. Yogic significance is the divine bliss a *yogi* attains through *Kriyāyogasādhana* because he annihilates his inherent dynamism and arrives at the original still state. Since he reverts to his original state he is suffused in the supreme bliss inhering this state.

Anantadeva — Lit. the Eternal Being. *Nārāyaṇá, Víshṇu, Jagadīśvará* Who are intrinsically the same is termed *Anantadeva.* Yogic connotation is the Eternal Form as well as the eternal flow or motion flowing through the creation. A *yogi's* gradual progression in *Kriyāyogasādhana* entails him to have a visualisation of the Eternal Being after which he strives to merge therein.

Anantarūpá — See *rūpá* .

Aṅgusṭha pramaṇā Púrusha — See *Purāṇá Púrusha.*

Antardhyāna — See *dhyāna.*

Aṇu — Lit. molecule. Yogic interpretation is the *Kūṭastha* dot (*bindi/bindu*). When a *yogi* disciplinedly practises austere *Kriyāyogasādhana* he attains settlement at the *Kūṭastha* dot which is the subtlest of the subtle. He then loses his entity and becomes pervaded by the dot. Thus he spontaneously is detracted by the gross expansiveness surrounding him and settling in the dot he achieves contraction. *Brahmāṇu* is beyond this *aṇu* which a *yogi* attains after further austere endeavours for this is the state of nothingness, it exists yet is not definable, this is *Kriyā*'s transcendental state where a *yogi* ultimately achieves mergence and fulfils his human life.

Anubhab/anubhav — Lit. feeling or gross realization. Yogically it is the divine realization. A *yogi* ardently practising *Kriyāyogasādhana* goes beyond the gross senses and arrives at a state when he envisions the soul and attains yogic realization of the same. This is possible after the dynamic state of *Prâṇá* is ceased.

Apâná — See *Prâṇá vāyú.*

Aparūpá — See *rūpá* .

Ārādhanā — Lit. worship. Yogically it infers the *Prâṇá*-worship a *yogi* executes. Practice of *Kriyāyogasādhana* is *Prâṇá*-worship — through dynamic *Prâṇá* a *yogi* arrives at the still *Prâṇá*. This process is the *Prâṇá* worship.

Ārati — See *Ómkāra.*

Arpan — Lit. offering. Yogically it implies not the gross offerings people make to their deities but the offering of the dynamism attained at birth to the original still state — this occurs when a *yogi* attains the still state.

Āsaná — Lit. posture; a seat or mat in which one sits for meditation; the third stage of eightfold *yóga*. This posture makes the body still facilitating practice of *yógasādhana*, hence effecting a gradual engrossment within the body and mind, eventually within the soul. See *samādhi*.

Āsmān — Lit. the sky or space. It is also termed as *gagan*, *ākāś*, *sűrya*. The space within any container is *ghatākāś*. This sky or space has attributes but yogically *sūṇya*, *āsmān* etc. or the void within the void which is *Prâṇá* is beyond attributes. For this reason *Prâṇá* is Omnipresent and is the Controller or Master of the five elements. A *yogi* practising austere *Kriyāyogasādhana* ardently settles in the *gagan* or *āsmān* or *sűrya* - i.e. *Kűṭastha* or the cavern of divinity. Permanent settlement here enables a *yogi* to eventually merge with the Absolute.

Āśrama — Lit. a place of religious retreat where any retreatist group who has passively or hurting own kith and kin withdrawn from society induced by a sense of inability to attain or resist it's norms live together with shared spiritual or social aims.

Another literal connotation is the fourfold life of Indian tradition. All scriptures of *Sanātána Dhárma* mention this for barring this fourfold life, human existence is incomplete. They are *Brahmacarya,* the stage of celibacy which purports maintaining sound health, building character, obtaining education etc. The spiritual significance for this is to wander in the realm of *Brahma* and to attain this both the body and mind have to be conditioned by abiding the aforesaid discipline.

The prevailing concept for the second stage *gārhastya* is that it is the stage of a householder i.e. earning one's livelihood, marriage and procreation, acquiring *śāstrá* knowledge, caring for old parents, executing social and family responsibilities etc. but the spiritual significance denotes habiting in the body-abode and acquiring scientific knowledge thereby through *sādhanā's* medium bid farewell to the sensory faculties and vices by conquering them. A special feature of this stage is marriage, the system to maintain procreation. Marriage infers knowledge of the union between Primordial Female Energy (dynamic *Prâṇá*) and Primordial Male Energy (still *Prâṇá*). Maintaining procreation implies maintaining the creation i.e. the continuity of *Prâṇá* or *Prâṇá* in continuum.

Vānaprastha the third stage indicates executing *sādhana* retiring from life's turmoils. but the prevailing notion bears no relationship with it's spiritual significance. It is a state when continual practice of *Prâṇá-sādhana* completely ceases the breathing motion and the necessity to draw external breath becomes absent. A *yogi* settled in this state automatically becomes devoid of material attachment. It does not infer abandoning the material world in the gross sense.

The last stage is *Saṃnyāsa*. It indicates the life of a renunciate but not in it's gross sense. External breathing motion compels man to be ensnared with material objects, happiness, sorrow, emotions in other words the material world. Yogically it infers the cessation of external breath for then attachment also ceases thus a *yogi* becomes a renunciate. (See Gl. *saṃnyāsīn*).

Asura — Lit. devil or monster. Yogic inference is the devilish propensities in man which are kindled in accordance with the rate of dynamism of *Prâṇá* varying in each individual. These devilish or bestial proclivities in man abet him to be steeped in the gross senses, hence remain far removed from soul-orientation or the quest or endeavour to pursue the path of *sādhana* to attain God and eventually salvation. Thus such a person is the epitome of soul-negation hence *asura*.

Ātmadhárma — See *Kriyāyoga*.

Ātmajyoti — See *Ātmasúrya*.

Ātmakarma — See *Kriyāyoga*.

Ātmaprasād — See *prasād*.

Ātmârāma — See *Rāma*.

Ātmasādhana —See *Kriyāyoga*.

Ātmasúrya — *Súrya*, *súraj*, *adityā* all infer the sun. *Ātmasúrya* signifies the all-pervasive Soul-sun; total creation emanates from here and also merges here. Soul-sun is the Master of all creation; the Omni-effulgence, first form of Formless *Brahma*. when a *yogi* is engrossed in austere *sādhana*, he envisions *jyoti* i.e. *Ātmajyoti* — the soul-effulgence which is immensely resplendent surpassing all gross radiance and is semblant of *Sahasrânsu* i.e. the effulgence of thousand planetary suns. Envisioning *Ātmasúrya* a *yogi* is enabled to expiate his sins because this envisionment harbours a stupendous effect as all sins are incinerated by the intensity of the soul-effulgence, the *yogi* then attains true knowledge and omnipotence.

Ātmayajñá — See *yajñá*.

Bābā — A reverential term for father, a holy man or a spiritual Master.

Bājā — Lit. melody. It's yogic connotation is when a *yogi* is engrossed in *Kriyā-yógasādhana* then he can intrinsically hear his internal melody. Ten melodious sounds emanate within and a *yogi* is capable of hearing all of them. They transcend even the most incomparable gross melody.

Bandhu — Lit. friend. The Sole One whom one can rely upon, confide in, the only one who shows the path of actual bliss thereby weaning away one's apparent sorrows. Dynamic *Prâṇá* fosters kineticism hence enmity, therefore he is the arch enemy and if this dynamic *Prâṇá* is stilled through *Kriyāyoga*, then the still *Prâṇá* is the friend in actuality.

Bemánas — Lit. unmindful. Yogic interpretation is mindlessness. This occurs in a *yogi* when the kinetictism of his mind, the principal sensory faculty is annihilated through ardent *Kriyāyoga* practice. A *yogi* then remains materially detached and performs all actions without remaining attached to them.

Betā — Lit. an affectionate term for son. Spiritually it implies the still *Prâṇá*, which is the fundamental and origin for every being. Man after being born on gaining 100,000 *Prâṇá* vibrations forgets his essentially still state and is both confounded and absorbed in the state of *beti* or *biti* (lit. affectionate term for daughter) i.e. the dynamic *Prâṇá*, hence is constantly buffetted with sorrows.

Beti/Biti — See *betā*.

Bhāg — Lit. fortune, consequences of past actions. It's spiritual connotation is that when a *yogi's* external breathing motion completely ceases through continual *Kriyāyoga* practice, he attains stillness within and without. This is the true fortune for it transcends materialism, hence a *yogi* can shape his destiny by accelerating his spirituality.

Bhagavān/Īśvará — Lit. God. Yogically *bhag* infers *yoni*, the source or origin, *vān*=breath. By practising *Kriyāyogasādhana* when breathing ceases at *Kūṭastha*, that state is *Bhagavān*. *Kūṭastha* is compared to a *yoni* because it is triangular in shape and everything originates from there. *Bhagavān* is the Possessor of all since totality has originated from him yet is beyond the state of possessions. He is Omnifunctional yet is beyond all actions. *Prâṇá* only is *Bhagavān*. the word *Bhagavān* is an exclusively *Bhāratiya* term. He is the Almighty, Omnipresent, Master of the universe, the Creator, Preserver and Destroyer, Omnipotent, Who is beyond birth and death, from Whom everything has been created; barring Him nothing can exist; He is Indefinable, Unquestionable, Non-answerable, Incomparable, Non-debatable, Inconfinable, Indivisible, Immeasurable, the only and Eternal Truth, the Absolute knowledge. He is Omneity, the Omnitude; He is nothingness yet allness.

For the purpose of better comprehension we ascribe pronouns to Him and try to fathom the unfathomable within the parameters of language. In actuality no pronouns should be ascribed to Him, He is Omnigender and there is no language in the world which can express about *Bhagavān* because this subject transcends the sensory faculties i.e. the concept of *Bhagavān* is inaccessible to the intellect.

Science essentially researches on the gross, is researched by the gross, therefore can never reach or analyse or comprehend the state of *Bhagavān*, the stateless state.

Below are cited two tables — one of retrogression above and from the *Bhagavān* state; the other of progression towards and above the *Bhagavān* state —one is the elaborate table and the one beside it is it's shortened form.

1. ***Brahma (Paramātmā)*** — The Absolute (Infinite Soul)— non-dual
2. ***Ātmâ*** — Soul— non-dual
3. ***Prâṇá (Bhagavān/Īśvará)*** - The Supreme Being (kinetic state of the soul)— dual
4. ***Jīvana*** — Life
5. ***Jīva*** — Living Being
6. ***Buddhi*** — Intelligence
7. ***Vivek*** — Conscience
8. ***Cittá*** — Intellect
9. ***Mánas*** — Mind
10. ***Iccha*** — Wish
11. ***Cintā*** —Thought
12. ***Ahaṃ*** — Pride
13. ***Vāvanā*** — Cogitation
14. ***Kalpanā*** — Imagination
15. ***Kāmanā*** — Desire
16. ***Vāsanā*** — Aspiration
17. ***Lova*** — Greed
18. ***Krodh*** — Anger
19. ***Hiṃsā*** — Malice
20. ***Paraśrīkātaratā*** —Covetousness.

(Retrogression ↓ 7–15; Progression ↑)

Retrogression ↓ / Progression ↑

1. ***Brahma***
2. ***Ātmâ***
3. ***Prâṇá***
4. ***Jîvana***
5. ***Jīva***

Bhajan – Lit. devotional song. For a *yogi* this is not the superficial sensory chanting of devotion. This is intrinsic chanting — internal *Prâṇâyāma* through which devotion towards the One ensues and is a permanent one.

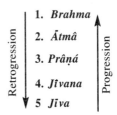

Bhakti — See *bhaktiyóga.*

Bhaktiyóga — *Bhakti* is devotion and *yóga* is union. Therefore *bhaktiyóga* is the union with the Absolute through the medium of devotion. Those abiding in the path of *bhakti* believe that this is possible but it is an irrational belief to a *yogi* because without *yóga*, *bhakti* cannot be derived. *Bhaktiyóga* in the *Gītā* has been mentioned as a compound word. Through *bhakti*, faith ensues which is a product of the kinetic mind. This type of faith is vacillating and transitory. Due to the religious decadence *yóga* became obsolescent, so that people depend now exclusively on devotion, faith, faculties of the mind. These transitory faculties are unable to settle one in the permanent devotion and faith. For this reason the world at present is hankering for love, peace and solidarity. The present world pivots around devotion and faith without paying regard to *yóga* (union). Thus everyone fails to achieve union with the Absolute which is possible only through the path of *yóga*. Therefore the world now is steeped in restlessness, rancour and discord; because devotion is dependant on kineticism, the concept and method of uniting with the Absolute is unknown to them. This purports that if the transitory devotion and faith could propagate and establish peace barring *yóga* then why is the world still hankering for love and peace?

Bhārata — Ancient name of the Republic of India. The country was named India during British rule. Before that it was *Bhārata*. *Bhārata* is a hallowed name. It has been noticed that the word *'Bhārata'* has a threefold application; this nation has been named *Bhārata*; this word finds mention in the religious epic *Mahábhārata* and is also applied to the most exalted *yogi* Arjuna. The map of *Bhārata* resembles a human shape, that is the posture of a human being standing with arms outstretched on either side. The nation is surrounded by Himalayas on the northern side and oceans on the other three sides. It's inaccessible upper portion is the north of the human frame. The Himalayas are an allegory of this part denoting calmness hence Static *Prâṇá* of an individual whereas the lower portion of the human frame is the south. Oceans on the other three sides are an allegory of dynamism hence dynamic *Prâṇá* in an individual.

This purports that without human shape this *yógasādhana* cannot be practised, excepting *Bhārata* this *yógasādhana* cannot be obtained.

Bhārata being an eternally peace loving country was never goaded by the ambition of territorial expansion by acquisition of other countries. *Mahádevá* the most revered deity Who is Primordial is the apex symbol of non-violence. He transcends the birth-death cycle. Rest of the world could not produce such a symbol. *Bhārata* is the capital of *Sanātaná*

Dhárma (eternal religion). This holy land yielded the supreme knowledge — the scripture *Gītā* where *Bhagavān* assured mankind that He Himself will appear when there is a religious decadence particularly at the juncture of two *yugas*. It is the only country where *Bhagavān* Himself repeatedly appeared in the Form of a Human. Historians state that the name *Bharata* has been acquired from the name of the legendary monarch *Bharat*. But this is not true. The reverse that the name *Bharat* of the legendary monarch has been gleaned from the name of this holy land, is the truth.

As *Bhārata* is a spiritual country it is quite befitting if we desire to make the inherent quest to realize the esoteric spiritual significance of the term *Bhārata*. '*Bhā*'=radiance, effulgence, resplendence, spiritual enlightement; *ra*=spiritual source, spiritual essence, spiritual fortitude, spiritual favour, spiritual halcyon. *ta*=deliverance, attainment of spiritual bliss through the yogic boat. Thus the intrinsic significance of the term *Bhārata* is that when a *yogi* gradually practising internal *Prâṇáyāma* through the heat essence latent in the navel settles at *Kū́ṭastha* envisioning the intensely resplendent soul-effulgence then he achieves salvation and soul-enlightenment. This state of a *yogi* is termed as *Bhārata*. (See *Gīta*.)

Therefore such inherent beauty and soul-knowledge pervades this holy soil and this pervasion has been caused by haloed *munis, ṛishis, yogis* and even by God Himself.

For this reason, this part of the world has been adorned with the name *Bhārata* and this country is oriented towards *Sanātána Dhárma* eternally. *Sanātána Dhárma* continues in this land since aeons which will never become extinct, hence this nation is called *Sanātána Bhārata*. Origin of *yóga* is *Bhārata* hence map of *Bhārata* as a symbol of the human body is it's yogic connotation. Since *yóga* is eternal, it's hallowed wings have spread outside *Bhārata* as well. Thus the Holy Cross worshipped by Christians also resembles the human frame.

Bhāvana — Lit. house. Yogically Immortal Abode. This occurs when a *yogi* achieves mergence with the state of void *Brahma*.

Bindi/bindu — See *aṇu*.

Bojh — Lit. burden. Man is saddled with problems after being born. He attains dynamism hence these impediments. But one who perpetually cogitates through *Kriyāyogasādhana* on the Absolute, his dynamism hence impediments are all removed by Him.

Brahma — The ultimate truth underlying and transcending universality; the ubiquitous reality within creation and beyond creation; void within the void; eternal statice; the unfathomable boundless profundity, this transcendent predicate is *Parambrahma*.

Brahma is permanently unchangeable, is devoid of decrease or augmentation, is ever-solemn, ever pure, always uniform; *Brahma* is the state where there are no impediments, distant-near relationships, origination, mergence, yet everything exists because of *Brahma*-existence; nothing can be present sans *Brahma*; existence of the whole creation depends upon *Brahma*-existence; *Brahma* is perpetually crystalline: is beyond being affected by birth-death; *Brahma* is where there is absence of sound, light, darkness, knowledge, ignorance, devotee, God, duality; in other words where there is nothingness yet allness; where none remains to express this nothingness, such a perpetual static state is *Brahma*, the Primordial cause, source or origin. *Brahma* is Non-Dual, Univocal.

Brahmā — The Creator. The first deity of the Hindu Triad responsible for the creation of the world.

Brahma-Aṇu — See *aṇu*.

Brahmacarya — See *āśrama*.

Brahmajñāna/Brahmajñānī — See *buddhi*.

Buddhi — This is the gross intelligence or intellect or the sensory knowledge. But *buddhi* for a *yogi* connotes otherwise, i.e. *Brahma-jñāna* (*Brahma*-knowledge), for only this is the true knowledge. All other worldly knowledge is basically a sham. A *yogi* gradually surmounting the steps of *Kriyāyogasādhana* attains this *Brahma*-knowledge and becomes a *Brahma-jñānī* (*Brahma*-knowledgeable).

Cakrá — Lit. wheel. Life is equivalent to a river. Just as a river has a constant flow of water, similarly life has constant flow of *Prâṇá*. Just as a river-current gushes down from the mountains, it's source forming whirlpools at different points in its's course, similarly *Prâṇá*-current gushing down from it's source, the *Sahasrâra cakrá* flows through the spinal cord and forms whirlpools at different locations of the body, these whirlpools are designated as *cakrás*. It's allegorical representation is the river Ganges emanating from Siva's head (i.e. Himalayas or the *Sahasrâra Cakrá*) and flowing down to earth i.e. *Mūlâdhāra cakrá*, being brought down by Bhagirath the body-chariot, which is a receptacle for enjoyment and suffering. *Prâṇá*-current originates from *Sahasrâra Cakrá* and flows till *Mūlâdhāra Cakrá* located at the back of the rectum. *Svâdhisṭhāna Cakrá* is located on the opposite side of the genitalia, *Maṇipūra Cakrá* opposite to the navel, *Anāhata Cakrá* at the back of the midpoint of thorax, *Viśuddha Cakrá* at the centre of the nape and *Ājñā Cakrá*, the occipital bone. These six *cákras* of the body-chariot geographically symbolise the six pilgrimages located along the course of the Ganges. The first pilgrimage is *Devaprayāg* (*Ājñā Cakrá*), second is Rishikesh (*Viśuddha Cakrá*), third Hardwar (*Anāhata Cakrá*), fourth Allahabad-Prayag (*Maṇipūra Cakrá*), fifth Varanasi (*Svâdhisṭhāna Cakrá*) and sixth Gangasagar (*Mūlâdhāra Cakrá*). For this reason Ganga is worshipped as a holy river. Thus from what has been explained *cakrá* is certainly not the anatomical nervous plexus for it depicts a particular point where whirlpools are formed during the flow of *Prâṇá*-current and is not a bundled mass.

Candrá — Lit. moon. It's yogic significance is the soul-moon. When a *yogi* continually practising *Kriyāyogasādhana* is rapt in it he can envision the Soul-Moon in his *Kúṭastha*. The resplendence is immense and powerful like *koti candrá* — resplendence of ten millon moons.

Chinnamastā — Another beheaded shape of goddess *Kālī*.

Dakshinā — Lit. tribute. Yogically it is the self paying tribute to the soul i.e. when the *yogi* is engaged in ardent *Kriyā* practice he loses consciousness of the self and is constantly engrossed in the soul thereby paying tribute to the soul.

Daṇḍa — Lit. time and staff. Yogically it infers that time holds no importance to a *yogi* as he is able to go beyond the state of time. Yogically staff denotes the staff of death which a *yogi* envisions in his *Kúṭastha*. He remains unapalled by it and endeavours to continue his rigorous *sādhana* practice so that he can transcend the state of death.

Dárśana — Lit. vision. Yogically it connotes the intra-vision which occurs to a *yogi*. For a *yogi* all sensory aspects transform into the extra-sensory, so through this intra-vision which is occasioned only after diligent arduous endeavours a *yogi* envisions the intensely powerful soul-effulgence, is expiated of his sins and attains clairvoyance. *Dṛishṭi* literally infers sight. Yogically this intra-perception is possible only to an elevated *yogi*.

Dātā — Lit. the bestower. Yogically the bestower is the *yogi* himself because if he is conscientious and ardent in his efforts at *Kriyā* practice, surely the Absolute, the One with Whom he aspires to attain mergence ultimately bestows graces on him, as he is oriented solely on the soul. As a result the *yogi* himself becomes his own bestower.

Devadatta — See *Prâṇá vāyú*.

Devādidevá — Lit. the Primordial One. He is referred to as *Mahādevá*. A *yogi* practising ardent *Kriyāyoga* can elevate himself to envision *Mahādevá* in his *Kúṭastha*. Later he himself can attain the state of *Mahādevá*.

Devatā — Lit. god. Yogically it does not infer the gods worshipped grossly for a *yogi* practising *Kriyāyogasādhana* is metamorphosed into a god because he worships the universal *Prâṇá* and is conversant about the soul-essence.

Dhan — Lit. wealth. Yogically it is the yogic wealth — spiritual power which transcends all material wealth as this spiritual wealth contributes to the elevation of a *yogi* enabling him to attain mergence with the Absolute. A *yogi* conscientiously practising *Kriyāyogasādhana* can surely gain access to the sublime yogic wealth or spiritual power in gradation till he achieves emancipation.

Dhananṇjaya — See *Prâṇá vāyú.*

Dhanuka — Lit. bow. Yogically it represents the bowlike body. For a *yogi* the body is bowlike because he can execute the arrowlike breathing motion — internal *Prâṇâyāma* which is the most principal part of *Kriyā* practice, as excellent *Prâṇâyāma* entails stilling of the kineticism and ultimate mergence with the Absolute. Without the human body this cannot be executed.

Dhāraṇā — Lit. idea, opinion. Yogically it connotes the sixth stage of eightfold *yóga*. On practising *Kriyā*, visualisations occur to a *yogi* and these visualisations enable him to gain a concept of the soul. See *samādhi*.

Dharma — Lit. religion or disposition. Yogically the One Who bears the total creation i.e. *Prâṇá*. Therefore *Prâṇá* is *dhárma*. This *Prâṇá* is universal, therefore *dhárma* is only one. Disposition of an individual is dependant on the sensory faculties but a *yogi* endeavours to transcend the sensory factor because worshipping *Prâṇá* his disposition assumes a Pranaic quality i.e. then the *yogi* goes beyond the vices and the sensory dispositions.

Dhvani — Lit. sound. Yogically it depicts the internal sounds which are intrinsically audible through regular conscientious *Kriyā*-practice. This occurs when the *yogi* attains partial stillness within. Not being attracted to external sounds, he can concentrate on the various dulcet internal sounds and remain engrossed in it. These internal sounds are incomparable to the gross external sounds no matter how melodious they are.

Dhyāna — Lit. meditation. The seventh penultimate stage of eightfold *yóga*. After succeeding the severely exact six previous stages of *yóga* discipline, *dhyāna* occurs. Therefore *dhyāna* and meditation cannot and should not be allied. The latest fad is meditation and through this, instant self-awakenings are arrived at. Unfortunately all this is a hoax for the term *dhyāna* has been distorted enough. It implies a complete engrossment or absorption with the inner consciousness which is effected through transcendental vision and thus is of a transcendental nature. Hence *dhyāna* signifies *Ātmadhyāna* or *antardhyāna* i.e. soul-absorption or absorption in the Inherent-Intrinsic respectively. Meditation is the continuous flow of thoughts towards one object. Therefore obviously this purports that *dhyāna* and meditation cannot be the same as thoughts emanate from the mind, the master of the ten sensory faculties. *Dhyāna* being the penultimate stage of eightfold *yóga*, all the sensory faculties including the mind have attained statice and in this step the *yogi* prepares himself for the final stage of Absolute Union (*samādhi*). See *samādhi*.

***Dṛishti* —** See *dárśana*.

***Durgā* —** Lit. the ten-handed goddess. Yogically it infers the one who resides in the *durg* — fort. Body is the fort. *Prâṇá* dwells within the body-fort, therefore *Prâṇá* is *Durgā*, the One Who annihilates all sorts of kineticism, the root of all sorrows. Ten hands symbolise action. There are ten sensory faculties — five organs of function and five of perception. The faculties of perception are sight, sound, smell, taste, touch. The five organs of function alongwith their faculties are tongue — speech; hand — action; anus — excretion; foot — motion; reproductive organs — reproduction.

***Dvāpárayuga* —** See *yuga*.

***Dvārakā* —** See *ājñācakrá*.

***Erādā* —** Lit. wish. Yogically it signifies that wish evolves from the mind, mind from dynamic *Prâṇá*, therefore both evolve from kinetic state of *Prâṇá*. When there is no kinetic *Prâṇá*, mind and desires are also absent. A *yogi* endeavours to transcend the non-vibratory state and reach the static state. When wish or desires are absent, sorrow and happiness are also absent.

***Gagan* —** See *āsmān*.

***Gaṇapati* —** See *Gaṇeśa*.

***Gắṇapatya* —** See *Śaiva*.

***Gaṇeśa* —** Lit. the elephant-headed god, son of *Pārvatī* and *Śivá*. *Vyāsa* dictated *Vedas* to *Gaṇeśa* who penned it down. He is the deity granting success. His other names are *Gaṇapati* and *Vināyak*. Worshippers of this deity are termed as *Gáṇapatyas*. Yogic interpretation ọf *Gaṇeśa* is that his trunk indicates long ardent endeavours of *Prâṇâyāma*. By continual austere *Prâṇâyāma* practice internal air stores up in the abdomen granting it an appearance of bloatedness. This is why *Gaṇeśa* sports a paunch. When a *yogi* arrives at this state he achieves the state of attainment i.e. emancipation. The mount of *Gaṇeśa* is the rat whose gnawing disposition makes it a destructive agent for it gnaws without cause, thus is harmful. Similarly when a *yogi* is about to attain salvation his inner sensory faculties or externally any evil-minded person can bring harm to him without any reason. Like *Gaṇeśa*, all gods and godddesses of Hindu mythology symbolise the different esoteric aspects of *yóga*.

Gaṅgā — Lit. the holy river of *Bhārata* (India). English interpretation is Ganges flowing from the Himalayas to the Bay of Bengal. Yogic significance is the *Iḍā nāḍī* flowing through the left nostril. It is also the *candrá nāḍī* (moon nerve) i.e. the source of lunar energy in the body. This infers that Bhagirath has brought the *Gaṅgā* from the head of *Śivá*. This denotes that *Prâṇá* is static on the head. From the static state, *Prâṇá* descended till *Mūlâdhāra* by deriving kineticism. Bhagirath implies the body. (See Gl. *cakrá*).

Gārhastya — See *āśrama*.

Gāyatrí — The principal Vedic hymn, therefore the mother of the *Vedas*. Yogic connotation is, breath is *Gāyatrí*.

Ghar — Lit. room.Yogic connotation is the Immortal Abode. *Sthir ghar* denotes non-vibratory Abode. *Amar ghar* = Immortal Abode. *Ajar ghar* = Ageless Abode; *Agam ghar* = Inaccessible Abode. By practising *Kriyā-yoga*, a *yogi* can reach all the Abodes sequentially. All the Abodes are the states of a *yogi*, which he experiences.

Ghaṭ — Lit. pot. Yogic interpretation is the body container. *Sarvaghaṭ* infers bodies of all living creatures.

Ghatākāś — See *āsmān*.

Gītā — The Divine *śāstrā* of *Bhārata* (India), a portion of *Mahábhārata*, through which *Bhagavān* Krishna spiritually directs Arjuna, representative of humanity on the battlefield, by sitting on the chariot, on the various chapters of *yoga* to attain God.

The *Mahábhārata* and *Gītā* are not separate. They constitute the principle and technique of *yógasādhana*. As a result they are regarded as sublime spiritual texts en masse. For this reason it is not any historical narrative or epic poem. Therefore the concept of *yógasādhana* has been allegorically represented in these two spiritual texts. The essential requisite for *yógasādhana* practice is the indomitable spirit of a hero, therefore Arjuna has been portrayed as the great hero. He symbolizes what a *Kriyābān* should be in the true aspect. The battle waged between the two warring parties *Kauravas* and *Pāṇḍavas* have been described in these two texts. *Kauravas* signify propensity towards material attachment. This propensity perpetually impels man towards materialism. *Pāṇḍavas* signify material detachment and impel all towards detachment. These texts expatiate the manner by which man can ward off material attachment and proceed towards the path of material detachment. For this reason *Bhagavān* (God) presented Himself towards material detachment, lent succour to the heroic *yogi* and eventually material detachment triumphed. To proceed in the path of material detachment one has to become a *yogi*, so *Bhagavān* imparted counsel to Arjuna to become a *yogi* sitting on the chariot. A *yogi* never executes massacre on the warring force through the medium of gross gory battles and *Bhagavān* can never advise to establish peace through the medium of mass slaughter, (it does not conform to His rules and discipline) this would then tantamount to imputing a fault to Him. But imputing a fault to Him is never possible.

Hence the yogic connotation of both these texts is as follows :—

The chariot on which *Bhagavān* Krishna being seated counsels Arjuna is the body-chariot. The *Kűṭastha* within this body is Krishna. Thus Krishna is seated at the forefront of the chariot, as He prevails in *Kűṭastha* in the forehead. In the midportion of the body i.e. at the navel *samānά* air is located, which is referred to as the heat-essence (the seat of hunger and digestion) hence Arjuna. For this reason Arjuna is the fire progeny. He sits in the middle of the chariot. *Yudhisthira* is progeny of *dhárma* (righteousness) or else the space essence, he represents the still intellect in the battle. *Bhīma* is progeny of air, in other words the air essence of *Anāhata Cakrá* hence *Prâṇávāyu*; *Nakula* is progeny of water, water essesne of *Svâdhisṭhāna Cakrá* hence blood. Finally *Sahadev* represents the earth essence existent in *Mūlâdhāra Cakrá*, hence flesh. These five *Prâṇás*, five airs and five essences infer the five *Pāṇḍavas*. Therefore the five *Pāṇḍavas* conjoinedly accepted dynamic *Prâṇá* in the form of *Draupadi* as their wife. The word *Draupadi* implies a pair of feet. The dynamic *Prâṇá* manifests through the medium of *Iḍā* and *Piṅgalá* and travels in the path from *Mūlâdhāra Cakrá* to *Viśuddha Cakrá*. So the spouse of dynamic *Prâṇá* is the five essences only. *Dhṛitarāshṭra* of the *Kaurava* camp symbolises the egotistical blind mind and *Duryadhana* represents the evil mind. *Kauravas* connote performance of all actions with the expectation of results and *Pāṇḍu* indicates the five elements of the macrocosm hence of the microcosm. *Sanjay* denotes clairvoyance of the still mind.

The word '*Bhārata*' (India) has threefold applications. The name of this nation is '*Bhārata*'; the spiritual scripture is named *Mahābhārata* and Arjuna has been ascribed the name '*Bhārata*'. Thus the threefold applications of *Bhārata* are — as a nation; as a *śāstrá* and *yogi* respectively. (See *Bhārata*).

Gītā comprises eighteen chapters, the *Mahábhārata* battle was waged for eighteen days and in that battle eighteen divisions of army troops were killed. This pattern of division existed in ancient India. The number eighteen has been given top priority in all respects here. First let us consider what the eighteen divisions were. It comprised 1,09,350 foot soldiers, 65,610 cavalrymen, 21,870 fighters on elephant back and 21,870 charioteers. In other words 2,18,700 troops = 1 pattern of the eighteen segments of army troops x 18 = 39,36,600 = 18 divisions of army troops. Thus from this it can be deduced that 18 is a predominant number. Each of the numbers mentioned above add up to 18. 18 is divisible by 3, the product being 6. Let us now dwell on the yogic significance of the number 18. The Rajayoga of *Gītā* and *Kriyāyoga* of *Pātañjala Yogasūtrá* constitute the same *sādhana*. In both respects internal *Prâṇâyāma* only is the sublime *dharma* (*Prâṇâyāmaḥ Mahádhárma*). The esotericism of this internal *Prâṇâyāma* is known exclusively to a *yogi*. One *Prâṇâyāma* entails travel through six *cakrás* in the upward motion and travel through these 6 cakras again in the downward motion. So 6+6=12. In this manner after practising several *Prâṇâyāmas* when the *Prâṇá* air is stilled then a *yogi* taking recourse to 6 *cakrás* proceeds upwards to *Kūṭastha* and attaining permanent statice there, he achieves salvation. So 6+6+6=18. It is for this reason that the number 18 is so predominant in *Gītā* and *Mahábhārata*.

Now let us study why the numbers 6 and 3 have been given so much importance. The 3 attributes of *Sattva, Rájas* and *Tamas* and the continuous flow of *Prâṇá* vibration within the body in the path of the 3 nerves of *Iḍā, Piṅgalá* and *Sushumná* explain this. *Bhagavān* has advised Arjuna to achieve the state beyond the 3 attributes. To achieve this state it is imperative to practise internal *Prâṇâyāma* (*apâne yuhavati Prâṇâḥpâneapânaḥ tathāpare*).

This *Prâṇâyāma* has to be practised by overcoming the *Iḍā* and *Piṅgalá* in the path of *Sushumná* through the 6 *cakrás*, which can be obtained from a *yogigurú*. It is because of this, 3+6 has been ascribed importance.

Hence *Gītā* and *Mahábhārata* are not epic poems, they are scriptures. Had they been epic poems, time or period would have found mention in them, but this is absent. Instead treading on the heels of *Mahábhārata* at a later date many places in *Bhārata* have been named, because the map of undivided *Bhārata* and the human shape with two outstretched arms are akin to each other. (See *Bhārata*). The present generation has deviated from eternal *yógasādhana* and due to the religious decadence of *Káliyuga* now, it has gained obsolescence. Thus *Bhārata* is a spiritual country since aeons.

Gó — Lit. cow. Yogic interpretation is the tongue (*jihvā*). *Jihvā* or tongue again does not bear the apparent significance for a *yogi*, for he strives to attain the *khecari* state. *Lol jihvā* is the lolling tongue of goddess *Kālī*. Regular practice of *Tālavya*, an exercise of the tongue which elongates it, enabling attainment of the *khecari* state. Hence the lolling tongue of goddess *Kālī* is a symbol of *khecari*.

When a *yogi* practises K*armayoga* he raises his tongue and places it in the palatal cavity. When it reaches and fixes in the palatal cavity, it is the *khecari* state. This practice is the consumption of beef (g*ó*) to a *yogi*. After continual practice he can constantly remain in this state and spontaneously become reticent. This *khecari* state is the first step to enable him to reach his original still state.

Gopi — Lit. the devotees of *Bhagavān* Krishna. His female devotees were named as *gopinis*. Yogic connotation is, the practisants of *Kriyāyoga* in solitude.

Gurú — Lit the Master. Spiritual Preceptor. Spiritual connotation is one who leads from darkness to light i.e. from ignorance to true knowledge which is spiritual knowledge. Lit. meaning of *Gurúcaran* is the Lotus Feet of *Gurú*. Yogic significance is realization of *Prâṇá* through *Kriyā* practice. (See *Sadgurú*).

Gurúprasād — See *prasād*.

Haṉsá — Lit. swan. A swan's disposition is to sift milk from water, when two of these fluids are mixed together. In the *Ṛig Veda* the swan sifts *soma* from water. It's yogic interpretation is the internal breathing motion which causes statice. A living being in his present state is dynamic, thus his breathing is external. But once he executes internal *Prâṇâyāma* and continues this practice he spontaneously grows engrossed in the still state. This is *Haṉsákriyā*. Practising *Haṉsákriyā* one can achieve the state of *Paramahaṉsá* which is akin to a swan's disposition because he no longer dwells in the dynamic state of aberration, the cycle of births-deaths have ceased for him, he becomes supratemporal for he can then sift the spiritual essence from the gross, murky material world.

Hari — A name of *Víshṇu*. It's yogic interpretation is the one who seizes material attachment.

Harinām — Lit. repetitive superficial chanting of *Hari's* name. Yogic significance is the intrinsic chanting that is practice of internal *Prâṇâyāma*.

Haripada — Lit. the Lotus Feet of *Hari*. Yogic connotation is attaining the state of *Hari* through austere regular *Kriyāyoga* practice.

Haṭhayoga — Lit. a name for one of the several *yógas*. This *yóga* leads towards realization through rigorous discipline. Physical exercise is a part of *haṭhayoga*. *Haṭhayoga* is the other name for *karmayoga*. *Ha* = *Piṅgalá*, the flow of heat energy, *ṭha*= *Iḍā*, the flow of cool energy, *yóga* = union. *Haṭhayoga* implies the union at *Sushunmá* by superseding the *Iḍā* and *Piṅgalá*, after which realization dawns.

Hṛiday — Lit. a central, vital, essential part of the seat of life or the soul. Yogic significance is that the central, vital essential part or the seat of *Prâná* is *Kūṭastha*. *Kūṭastha* is the borderline between the still state and the dynamic state. *Hṛiddese* is the place of *Kūṭastha*.

Hṛiddese — See *hṛiday*.

Iḍā — The external flow of *Prâṇá*-air through the left nostril. This flow is the lunar energy effecting cool essence. This flow is also termed to be the *Támas* attribute which symbolizes the sensory faculties and impels man to remain in the non-original dynamic state.

Indriya — Lit. the sensory faculties. There are three divisions— the sense of perception, the sense of action and the inner sense. The quintuple senses of perception are — sight, hearing, touch, taste, smell; the quintuple senses of action are speech, performance, mobility, excretion, reproduction. Mind is the controller of these ten sensory faculties. The inner sense is fourfold — (*mánas*) mind, intellect, ego, subtle mind.

Īśvará/Bhagavān — See page NB after foreword.

Jagadīśvará — See *Jagannāth*.

Jagannāth — Lit. idol of God in the temple at Puri, Orissa. Scriptural inference is Master and Protector of the universe, *Víshṇu*. *Víshṇu* connotes pervasion. The yogic significance is the *Prâṇá*-pervaded universe, hence *Prâṇá* is the Master and Protector, therefore *Prâṇá* only is *Jagannāth*. *Prâṇá* also is *Jagadīśvará*, *Vísvanāth*, Universal Protector.

Jāgeṅge — Lit. readvent. (See foreword). God has assured in the *Gītā* that He will mark His Readvent at the transition of each *yuga* (see *yuga*) when there is a religious decadence.

Jápa — Lit. counting of beads (rosary). Yogic significance is the internal *Prâṇâ-yāma*.

Jihvå — See *gó*.

Jīva — See *jīvana*.

Jīvana — Lit. life. It's yogic significance is the dependant essence on which life continues i.e. *Jīvātmâ* or dynamic *Prâṇá*. *Jīvātmâ* is the vibrated state of *Prâṇá* indwelling in a living being and this *Jīvātmá* induces him to perform actions which compels him to fall into bondage. *Jīva* is the enhanced dynamic state of *Jīvātmâ* indwelling in the embodied self which maintains the vortex of actions and precipitates him into bondage. *Jīvana*, *Jīvātmâ* and *Jīva* all the three states are within the ambit of 10% to 100,000 *Prâṇá* vibrations. (See *Prâṇá* for details).

Jīvatma — See *jīvana*.

Jñāna — Soul-knowledge or *Brahma*-knowledge accruing from perpetual engrossment in the *ātmâ* or soul. This is the true knowledge which is exclusively spiritual and does not denote any material knowledge. Through attainment of this knowledge release from the continuum of births-deaths is achieved. This knowledge showers enlightenment on what the fundamental principle of human life should be. Through this soul-knowledge a *yogi* can supersede his present existence and merge in it. This union of the present self with soul-knowledge is termed as *Jñānayoga*.

Jñānayoga — See *Jñāna*.

Jyoti — See *Ātmasūrya*.

Kāl — Lit. time or period. It's spiritual connotation denotes otherwise. When a *yogi* ardently and regularly practising *Kriyāyoga* attains statice he becomes an epitome of stillness. The momentum of time loses it's impact over him. Time can then hold no sway over him. Because then he embodies the concept of *kālākāl* or timelessness. He then attains supratemporality (*Mahākāl*). For him then time is neither auspicious nor inauspicious (*akāl*). *Akālmṛityú* or untimely death loses it's significance to a *yogi* for two reasons. Firstly because he is supratemporal, secondly at the apex of *yóga*, he learns the art of dying thereby overcomes life's greatest fear i.e. the fear of death, thus a *yogi* then becomes master of both time and death. *Akālmṛityú* does not exist thus it does not connote the original significance. *Mṛityú* generally connotes death. But when a *yogi* arriving at *sādhanā's* pinnacle stills all his dynamism then his heartbeat which is so essential for a human being to subsist, also ceases. He then goes beyond the birth-death cycle; this is the real death. So having mastered the art of dying or death, *mṛityú* cannot affect him. A *yogi* can embrace death whenever he desires. It is not an external agent for him but a very natural phenomenon not pertaining to time.

Kālācnād — See Krishna.

Kālākāl — See *kāl*.

Kālī — Lit. a female deity. Another manifestation of goddess *Durgā*. She killed the demon named *Raktabīj* which represents human desires. These desires detract man from following the spiritual path. Yogically She is the Primordial Female Energy. She is the kinetic state of *Prâṇá* from whom creation emanates. Common man considers worldly knowledge to be actual knowledge, for this reason *Kālī* has been depicted as black because in her state of first manifestation, worldly knowledge did not evolve amidst creation.

Her lolling tongue is symbolical of *khecari mudra* of a *yogi*. The falchion in Her left hand symbolises the annihilation of ignorance of a *yogi* and entry into the realm of knowledge. Practising ardent *Kriyā* a *yogi* attains soul-realization, then he achieves omniscience. The 108 garland of demon heads indicate the 108 bestial proclivities in man. These devilish propensities have evolved from the kinetic state of *Prâṇá* within man and deter him from remaining materially detached. But when *Prâṇá* is still, the activities of these devilish propensities cease, this cessation of activity is symptomatic of destruction. Therefore *Kālī* has been depicted with the falchion severing the 108 demons. This severance of ignorance is necessary, for a *yogi* is purified and attains soul-knowledge.

The feet of *Kālī* indicate *Īḍā* and *Piṅgalá* breathing motion. When these feet become one it indicates a *yogi*'s breathing motion to continue in *Sushumná*. Again a *yogi's* perpetual diligent endeavours entitle him to go above *Sushumná* and merge in the Absolute void. At this moment the feet of *Kālī* evanesce to a *yogi*.

Kālī is represented as having one leg on *Śivá*'s chest and the other on His thigh —this purports her dual nature. Leg on *Śivá*'s chest connotes stillness and leg on His thighs connotes dynamism for this is the region of maximum dynamism. *Kālī* atop *Śivá* also symbolizes the union of kineticism with stillness. It refers to the reversion into stillness from maximum dynamism, conversely also the commencement of dynamism retrogressing from stillness.

Káliyuga — See *yuga*.

Kalpa-Bṛiksha Nāl — The cornucopian tree. Cornucopia infers the horn of plenty symbolizing the overflowing bounty. The legendary significance is that anyone going near this tree has his wishes fulfilled. The yogic interpretation is that a *yogi* does not require to take recourse to this gross wish-yielding tree because if he practises austere *yógasādhana*, he envisions the *Kū́ṭastha* eye and automatically then if he wishes anything, his wishes are fulfilled. Body is the tree and it's main support or origin is *Kū́ṭastha*. For a *yogi* of high stature who has achieved settlement in *Kū́ṭastha*, material desire and aspirations of course hold no place for him, nevertheless any dormant desires if at all possessed by him is spontaneously fulfilled. He does not have to strive for this be it material or spiritual for it is the result of his austere endeavours in *yógasādhana*.

Karmayoga — See *Kriyāyoga.*

Kartikeya — Lit. son of *Śivá.* When *Śivá* and *Parvatī* were in coitus, the gods appeared. *Śivá* stood up, in the process His semen fell to the ground but this semen was redirected by the earth essence to the fire essence and *Kartikeyā* was born. The yogic significance of this is as follows:- *Śivá* connotes still *Prâṇá* and *Parvatī* dynamic *Prâṇá.* When dynamic *Prâṇá* evolving from still *Prâṇá* is in union with the latter, there is a prominence of the space essence (appearance of the gods). Semen falling to the ground is the essence of creation. At the time of union *Śivá* reverted to *Viśuddha cakrá*, space essence or the appearance of the gods. This is the apparent segregation of the still and dynamic *Prâṇá.* Breath originates from *Kūṭastha* dot, falls upon *Mūlâdhāra cakrá* (the earth essence). and bounces back to *Maṇipūra cakra* (the fire essence). From here dynamism is scattered throughout the body — this is the sustenance of the body. This body is the bow and breath the arrow. *Kartikeyā* wields a bow and arrow in his hands. By executing internal *Prâṇâyāma* (i.e. shooting of arrows) within this bowlike body, a *yogi* endeavours to annihilate dynamism and proceed towards stillness. Hence *Kartikeyā* is the epitome of warriorhood, this denotes him to be an aspirant *yogi* who is diligent. Therefore all *yogis* should strive to be akin to him in this respect for only then can they revert to their original still state. The mount of *Kartikeyā* is the peacock. The peacock possesses a tail with eyelike marking. This eye of the peacock's tail is resemblant to the *Kūṭastha* eye. Like *Kartikeyā*, all gods and goddesses of Hindu mythology symbolise the different esoteric aspects of *yóga.*

Kāsi — See *triśul.*

Kaurava — See Krishna and *Gītā.*

Kevala Kumbhaka — See *Kumbhaka.*

Khodā — See *Āllāh.*

Koṭi Candrá— See *candrá.*

Kṛikara — See *Prâṇá vāyú.*

Krishna — Lit. black, darkness. God Himself appeared in the Form of Krishna at the end of *Dvāpárayuga* (3228 B.C.). He was the son of *Vāsudeva* and *Devakī*. His wife *Rukminī* was Princess of Vidarbha state. *Rādhā* was His principal consort. She was an embodiment of total surrender and true devotion to Krishna after having attained realization that Krishna was Absolute *Brahma. Bhagavān* Krishna is famed to have several other consorts. Sage Sandipani was *Gurú* of *Bhagavān* Krishna. In the legendary battle waged at Kurukshetra between *Pāṇḍavas* and *Kauravas* cited in *Mahábhārata* He sided the *Pāṇḍavas* and was the charioteer of

Arjuna's chariot. His counsel to Arjuna during this battle is the Holy scripture *Śrīmad Bhagavad Gītā* authored by *Vyāsadeva*. While resting on the branch of a tree, a hunter mistook His Lotus Feet to be a bird and shot an arrow at it. On this plea *Bhagavān* Krishna caused a cessation to His Mortal Existence.

Yogic connotations are as follows :—

Black or darkness is the second circle of the *Kūṭastha*-Eye. It is called *Kālācnād*, the dark Soul-moon which the *yogi* envisions. Krishna infers *Purāṇá*-Krishna, implying the Primordial Krishna or Primordial Being. He is the source of this universe. He is also *Prâṇá*-Krishna (still state). Still *Prâṇá* inheres in every individual. *Vāsudeva* denotes soul and *Devakī* body. *Rukminī* is the state of *Lakshmī*. *Rādhā* symbolises dynamic *Prâṇá*. The universe is borne by dynamic *Prâṇá*. Dynamic *Prâṇá* evolves from still *Prâṇá* so both are inextricable and complementary to each other. Love of dynamic *Prâṇá* and still *Prâṇá* is the Divine Love of *Rādhā*-Krishna. The conjoined image of *Rādhā* and Krishna is the uniting of dynamic *Prâṇá* in still *Prâṇá* — the sublime union (see *Vṛindāvana*). Several other consorts infer the irresistible attraction dynamic *Prâṇá* bears towards still *Prâṇá* because dynamic *Prâṇá* has evolved from still *Prâṇá*. Dynamic *Prâṇá* here purports the comprehensive female energy.

Sandipanī originates from *Sandipan*. *Sandipan* signifies the heat essence situated at the navel. Through the heat essence a *yogi* performs *Prâṇâyāma*. Though Krishna is *Bhagavān*, He practises *Prâṇâyāma* through this heat-essence in accordance with His Own discipline. *Sandipanī* is not any particular person but the *Gurú* essence. Krishna had to abide by His Own discipline of having a *Gurú* to reveal to mankind that a *Gurú* is always necessary for entering the spiritual path.

Krishna Himself is the heat-essence. *Arjuna* is the son of the heat essence. Therefore a spiritual rapport existed between Krishna and *Arjuna*. Hence Krishna selected *Arjuna* amongst the five *Pāṇḍava* brothers to impart spiritual counsel. *Arjuna* was also fortunate to receive the grace from his *Gurú*, Krishna of having the universal visualisation of the resplendence of thousand suns akin to the intense effugence of the Soul-Sun at *Kūṭastha*.

Kurukshetra war is the war between material attachment (*Kauravas*) and material detachment (*Pāṇḍavas*) which is incessantly continuing in all living beings. See *Mahābhārat* and *Gītā*. Chariot is the body-chariot. Krishna's counsel to disciple is the *Gurú*'s counsel to disciple as to how he should proceed in the *sādhana*-battle. *Arjuna* represents heroism and fortitude each aspirant *yogi* should posseess. *Gītā* is the *yóga*-scripture (see *yóga*). *Vyāsadeva* is the state of an all-knowing *yogi*. Hunter epitomises cruelty. Each individual possesses cruelty in some measure or the other. Vibration of *Prâṇá* prevails till the last portion of the body i.e. the feet. Arrow was shot at the feet inferring the commencement of the withdrawal of dynamism from this part of the body proceeding upwards through *Prâṇâyāma* (the arrow-like breath) and ultimately gaining stillness at *Kűṭastha*. Bird represents the *Prâṇá* bird. A bird's disposition is to fly with the help of it's wings. Again when it perches on the ground it folds it's wings. This connotes that it's travel is limited within the five elements from earth to sky. The wings of the *Prâṇá*-bird are *Iḍā* and *Piṅgalá* — the inhalation-exhalation process of every living being. This external breathing process confines all to material attachment. Cessation of mortal existence signifies cessation of *Prâṇá*-dynamism and mergence with the Absolute still *Prâṇá*.

Literally the term 'Krishna' is an appellation (a noun) but yogically it is a verb. As a verb the term 'Krishna' connotes that a *yogi* has to cultivate his body-field for annihilating dynamism and attaining stillness.

Kriyābān — See *Kriyāyoga* and *Gītā* .

Kriyânvita — See *Kriyāyoga*.

Kriyār Parābasthā — Transcendental state of *Kriyā*. *Kriyā* denotes soul-action which is the only action by which salvation is attained. *Parābasthā* or transcendental state is the state which surpasses this soul-action. Then the *yogi* performs all superficial actions spontaneously and can travel everywhere by remaining in *Kűṭastha* and above i.e. he is in constant communion with the soul. This is *parampad* or the ultimate supreme state. All actions occur as it should occur, but a *yogi* is not in any of these actions because he abides in a state of detachment. None can discern this state excepting he himself. This state is beyond the state of *samādhi*. Hence this state transcends the barriers of the mind, intellect and senses, so it is a state of static and eternal peace. Remaining here, the *yogi* becomes boundless. It is the Absolute state. This term has been coined by Yogiraj Himself as this prerogative lies with Him only.

Kriyāyoga — *Kriyā* infers action, *yóga* union. Hence *Kriyāyoga* or *Kriyāyoga-sādhana* is the action i.e. the process or technique by which union with the Absolute is achieved. This is an exclusively afferent science which can be solely derived from the *Gurú*. Thus *Kriyāyoga* and *Karmayoga* imply the same as *karma* also signifies *Prâṇákarma* or *Ātmasādhana* hence *Prâṇásādhana* (*Prâṇá* or *Ātmâ* both connote the soul) process. This pertains to that which inheres or is intrinsic i.e. the soul, it is also referred to as *Ātmasādhana*, *Prâṇásādhana*, *Prâṇákarma*, *Prâṇá-kriyā* thus soul action or soul-practice. Total engrossment in this afferent practice entails the accruement of *Ātmasādhana* i.e. soul-*dhárma* which is eternal hence universal and does not pertain to any particular sect or creed. Man and the total creation is entirely soul-dependant.

Kriyāyoga is the supreme spiritual science for barring it nothing else in this world can cease *Prâṇá*-dynamism to 0%. A human being is invested with this *Prâṇá*-dynamism after being born and for this he has to traverse millions of births.

Therefore each and every human being can and should practise this soul *dhárma* (*Ātmasādhana*) or *Prâṇákriyā* and fulfil his human existence i.e. ultimately merge with Absolute *Brahma*. The one who practises this *sādhana* (*Kriyāyoga*) is a *Kriyābān* or *Kriyânvita*.

Kumbhaka— On being born *Prâṇá* attains dynamism. This dynamism gradually reverts to stillness through the *yogic* process of *pūraka* (internal inhalation) and *recaka* (internal exhalation). On continual practice of *recaka* and *pūraka* there is a spontaneous cessation of breath which the *yogi* enjoys. This cessation of breath is *kumbhaka* and because of it's spontaneity is termed to be *kévala kumbhaka*. This *kévala kumbhaka* state is the step towards the attainment of stillness.

Kuṇḍalini — The latent energy of *Mūlâdhāra cakrá* is coiled akin to the serpentine coil. The *Prâṇá* energy originating from the *Sahasrâra Cakrá* bounces on the *Mūlâdhāra Cakrá*. This descent towards *Mūlâdhāra* gives birth to kineticism. Through the yogic process *Prâṇá* energy or the newly attained *Prâṇá* dynamism is uplifted from *Mūlâdhāra cakrá* towards the *Sahasrâra cakrá* through *Sushumná*. This energy is *Kuṇḍalini śakti* or *Ādyāśakti* thus the Primordial Female Energy because this is the seat of maximum vibrations by which the universal law of generation and creation is maintained.

Kūrma — See *Prâṇá vāyú*.

Kurukshetra — Lit. a place near Delhi, India where the legendary battle of *Mahābhārata* between *Pāṇḍavas* and *Kauravas* were waged. It's yogic interpretation is the body field. In this body itself the *yogi* wages a battle between material attachment and material detachment. His purpose is to annihilate the propensities of material attachment which is abetted by *Prâṇá* dynamism. Thus this body-field is the region through which the *yogi* can reach stillness by warding off dynamism. (See also Krishna).

Kūṭastha — See *Ājñācakrá*.

Lakshmī — Lit. goddess of wealth and prosperity, wife of *Víshnu*. Yogic interpretation is when a *yogi* practising *yógasādhana* attains the exalted state he achieves the *Lakshmī* state i.e. he is not devoid of anything. His entirety is borne by the Soul-God. Mount of *Lakshmī* is the owl. It is a nocturnal bird. Since it's habits are nocturnal it symbolises the darker attributes of life (*Támas* attribute). Similarly if a man achieves immense wealth he is oriented towards material pursuits. Like *Lakshmī*, all gods and goddesses of Hindu mythology symbolise the different esoteric aspects of *yóga*.

Layayoga — *Laya* connotes mergence and *yóga* union. By practising austere *Kriyāyoga* and mounting the gradual steps of *Kriyā*, achieving the relative levels of realisation, one reaches the transcendental state of *Kriyā*. The basic purpose of *Kriyā* practice is to achieve union with the Absolute. Only if union with the Absolute in this manner is achieved, salvation occurs. This is *layayoga*, the mergence or absolute union and human life is fulfilled if it undergoes *layayoga*. No *yogi* can return back to his living-being state after attaining *layayoga*. The present living-being state is kinetic, *Kriyā* practice annihilates *Prâṇá*-dynamism and facilitates the living-being state to become static and attain mergence. *Layayoga* is the ultimate step of *Kriyāyóga*.

Liṅga — Lit. the male organ of generation; the phallus of *Śivá*. *Śivá* is worshipped in the form of a stone or marble column which generally rises out of a *yóni*. *Yóni* is the female organ of generation.

Yogic interpretation is that *Śiváliṅga* or *Śiváliṅgam* symbolises the generative power of nature. When *yoni* unites with *liṅga*, it becomes a symbol of divine procreative energy. *Yóni* is the source or origin, place of birth, fountain. *Liṅga* is the mind, *yoni* is *Kűṭastha*. The cumulative symbol of this is the form of *Śiváliṅga*. Kinetic mind attains statice by practising *yógasādhana*, this still mind is placed on *Kűṭastha-Yóni*, the repository or resting-place. Everything evolves from *Kűṭastha-Yóni*. When the *liṅga*-mind settles in *Kűṭastha-Yóni* the *yogi* arrives at a beatific state — a state of supreme ecstasy and infinite bliss. This surpasses the gross coital ecstasy.

Shape of the *yóni* is a triangle, similar triangle is noticed in *Kűṭastha* through the medium of *Ómkāra Kriyā*. A dot or the seed of the universe (*Brahmāṇu*) is noticed in *Kűṭastha*. Entrance by the phallic mind in the *Kűṭastha-Yóni* gives rise to the tranquil state which is *Bhagavān* (God). *Kűṭastha* is the place of impregnation and later the dot (*Prâṇá* -soul) expands in the form of the body. Gross wombs or *yónis* are separable but *Kűṭastha-Yóni* or *Brahma* is inseparable because He is the Supreme place of Origin thus both the Mother and Father.

Mahābhārata — See *Gītā*.

Mahādevá — See *Devādideva*.

Mahākal — See *Kāl.*

Mahāpurusha — *Mahā* = Supreme, *Púrusha* = Primordial Male Energy. When a *yogi* merges with the Absolute Void *Brahma* then he himself becomes great. This type of *yogi* then metamorphoses into a *Mahāpurusha.*

Mahāsāmadhi — See *samādhi.*

Mahāśaya — Lit. a term for paying respect. Yogically speaking this is an elevated state of a *yogi.* When he transcends desires perpetually remaining in *Kriyā's* transcendental state he is in a state of bliss. He is also termed a *Mahātmā* or *Mahātman* (high-souled) then. He is high-souled because now he loses the necessity for spiritual desires also — that of salvation. This type of exalted *yogi* is scarce to find as austere endeavours only enable him to reach such a glorious state.

Mahātmā or Mahātman — See *Mahāśaya.*

Mánas — Mind, the principal or eleventh sense. On being born one attains 1,00,000 vibrations but in the original state his mind is still and static. Due to the kinetic mind he suffers the pangs of bondage and mortal afflictions for which he himself is responsible as his mind controls him to be materially attached. *Yógasādhana* provides the scientific technique of stilling the kinetic mind in gradual degrees so that the individual can revert to his original still state and attain emancipation, the principal objective of human life.

Mandir — Lit. temple. A building where in a particular place (sanctum sanctorum) idols or images of gods or goddesses are installed for worship. Yogic connotation is that the temple as a whole is symbolic of the body. The particular place where images are installed symbolises *Kūṭastha.* General people are not conversant about the real worship through *yóga.* They visit the temple for performing external worship. This is superficial, but a *yogi* knows the real-worship — *Prâṇá*-worship. *Prâṇá* is the principal idol within this body-temple. Still *Prâṇá* is God. When a man on being born attains 1,00,000 vibrations he achieves dynamism and is buffeted by material attachments. An aspirant *yogi* grows disappointed and craves for reverting to the original still state. So ardently practising *Prâṇá*-worship within his body-temple on a regular basis he propitiates his *Prâṇá*-deity and arrives at the sanctum-sanctorum within his temple. So propitiating *Prâṇá* entails universal propitiation. This is *Kūṭastha* or repository because here the *yogi* is free from all material attachments and reverts to his *Prâṇá*-god, the still state. Hence *Kūṭastha* is the holiest place of the body-temple.

Maṇipūra Cakrá — See *cakrá.*

Mántra — Lit. repeated phrase or formula obtained from *Gurú* for practising meditation. Yogic significance is the deliverance of the mind. In other words the deliverer of the mind is *Kriyā*. So *Kriyā* is *mántra*. When kinetic mind attains stillness through constant *Prâṇâyāmâ* practice, this state is termed *mántra*. The *mūlmántra* (principal deliverance) is the *Ómkāra*. This body; the infinitude beyond the corporeal frame and the dot within this infinitude; is *Ómkāra* in totality.

Mánu — First lawgiver of mankind and progenitor of the human race. There are 14 *mánus*. The present world is governed by the seventh *mánu Vaibasvata* in accordance with the cyclical pattern of the *yuga*. Yogically *mánu* signifies the vibratory mind and this mind manifests itself as the imperishable *yógasādhana* which each individual in the world has to practise when they are evolved enough to obtain it.

Māyā — Illusion. The one who is bound by the discipline of Nature, non-enlightenment, attachment, material cravings, ignorance and considers these to be the positive factors of life is stated to be in illusion. Illusion evolves from the dynamic *Prâṇá*. It is absent in static *Prâṇá*.

Moksha — See *nirvāṇa, piyās*.

Mṛityú — See *kāl*.

Mumukshu — The one who seeks salvation or release from earthly bondage or mortal affictions.

Mūlâdhāra cakrá — See *cakrá*.

Nāga — See *Prâṇá vāyú*.

Nārāyaṇá — Another appellation of *Víshṇu*. Yogically *nār* infers water, *ayaṇá* abode i.e. the one who infinitely abides upon water. Water is formless. When a *yogi* after prolonged *Kriyāyógasādhana* arrives at *Kúṭastha* and settles in Amorphous Void *Brahma*, this state of a *yogi* is termed as *Nārāyaṇá*.

Nirākār — See *rūpá*.

Nirvāṇa — Lit. to be extinguished. Yogic significance is *nir* = cessation, *vāṇa* = breath. In other words it is the cessation of breath producing salvation. The scientific technique of *yógasādhana* can only impart *nirvāṇa* that is going beyond the birth-death cycle. All of us execute actions good or bad which inevitably has a consequence. Good actions harbour good results, bad actions bad. This is the principle of cause and effect or yogically the law of *karma*. But a *yogi* practising *Prâṇákarma* goes beyond this law of *karma*. This is an exalted state of a *yogi* because only fervent austere endeavours enable him to attain complete emancipation (*moksha*). No matter how much one is pious or diligent in regular prayers or performs good actions, attaining *moksha* or *nirvāṇa* is impossible because he prays or performs good actions with his kinetic mind but a *yogi* does not pray in the stipulated sense. His prayer is *Prâṇákarma* (inherent-intrinsic action) through which he causes a cessation of the external breathing motion hence all the dynamism which is superficial and ultimately merges in the Absolute still state from which there is no return.

Nishkām — Lit. dispassionate. Work performed withoout possessing the motive for ulterior gain. Yogically it infers the state when a *yogi* grows apathetical or stoic towards the material world and spiritual domain for he knows, only *Prâṇákarma* lacks desires and aspirations because it continues (internal breathing process) whether attention is paid towards it or not. Thus the *yogi* practising incessant *Prâṇá* action goes beyond desires and aspirations. This is a time when he practises *yógasādhana* without the motive for attaining salvation. This is the pre-transcendental state of *Kriyā*. This is the state when there is a cessation of total desires, because in the next stage he will be remaining affixed in *Kűṭastha*, a place sans the sensory provocations.

Niyama — Lit. regulation of life, religious observance. Yogically it connotes discipline. It is the second step of eightfold *yóga*. After undergoing the discipline of self-control (*yama*) the *yogi* becomes attuned to the concept of disciplining himself to regularly and conscientiously sit in *āsana*(the 3rd step) for ardent *Kriyāyoga* practice each day at an appointed hour. See also *samādhi*.

Ómkāra — Lit. *mántra*. The symbol *Ómkāra* (ॐ) has three divisions (ও) is the body and the parenthesislike sign attached to the alphabet '্' indicates the senses.The second division 'ঁ',the crescent moon denotes infinity.Third division is the dot signifying the first manifestation of void *Brahma*.

When a *yogi* regularly practises prolonged *Kriyāyoga* he goes beyond body-consciousness and the sensory faculties.After this when he enhances his *yóga* practice he absorbs and settles in the crescent moon(*Kűṭastha*).At this time he is enveloped with the tranquil radiance of million moons and envisions this. But on progressing further through austere *yógasādhana* he goes beyond the intense effulgence of the Soul Moon and settles in the dot, Void *Brahma*. Later he overcomes the dot. This purports he has attained mergence in the infinitude or Void *Brahma*.

While practising *Kriyā* the *yogi* can hear *Ómkāra* or *Praṇáva dhvani* or sound from within which is a deep *oum*. When this holy sound evolves from within, the last syllable keeps on ringing in the bass pitch then it declines, again recurs with the deep rich sound. It never stops. This occurs to a *yogi* when the *Prâṇá*-vibration arrives at a declension. It is a mellifluous sound effecting peace and serenity within. This whole process is *Ómkāra Kriyā*.

Through *Ómkāra Kriyā* a *yogi* travels within his body.The rotatory motion (*ārati*) by the priest is symbolical of the circular movement a *yogi* undertakes within his body-temple.The deity is fanned either by a peacock feather (representing the *Kūṭastha*-Eye) or a fly-whisk or an ordinary hand-fan.This fanning indicates the serene and calm state a *yogi* arrives at after practising austere *sādhana*.

Lighting of the five lamps indicate the five *Prâṇás*.The fire of the lamps denote the pervasion of body-heat. During *ārati* different external musical instruments like the conch-shell, tabor, drum, dish of bell-metal etc. are all used symbolising the ten intra-sounds a *yogi* hears while practising *Ómkāra Kriyā*. The use of incense sticks and flowers during *ārati* infer the internal fragrance and internal beauty respectively a *yogi* perceives within. When a *yogi* is rapt with intra-sounds, intra-fragrance, intra-beauty; external sounds, fragrances or beauty bear no importance to him. Thus all these external rituals are a symbol of the internal ritual a *yogi* performs within his body.

Pañcabadrī — See *Pañcadevatā*.

Pañcadevatā — Lit. the five deities of *Ganeśa, Sūrya, Víshṇu, Śivá, Durgā*. Visualisation occurs to a *yogi* on his practising continual *Kriyā*. As he progresses in his *sādhana* he envisions *Pañcanan* or the pentaheaded *Śiva* Who is the Primordial One. Here we note that the number five is an auspicious and cardinal number in *yóga* because it indicates the *pañcasrota* which is the segregation of the principal *Prâṇá* into five divisions of *Prâṇá, Apâná, Vyāna, Samāná and Udāna*. These five *Prâṇás* flow in quintuple flows throughout the body nurturing it. The source or origin of each of the five divisions of the *Prâṇá* flow is the *pañcabadrī* which indicates the five places of pilgrimage literally located in the Himalayan region. The source or origin of *pañcabadri* is *Pañcānan* because from Him the five divisions evolve. For a *yogi* his body-temple is the pilgrimage centre because he performs the so-called gross ablutions within his body. *Kriyā* practice entails bathing in the *Prâṇá*-flow which absolves him of all transgressions.

Pañcānan — See *Pañcadevatā*.

Pañcasrota — See *Pañcadevatā*.

Pāṇḍava — See *Gītā* and *Krishna*.

Paṇḍitá — Lit. erudite. Yogic interpretation is, a *yogi* practising regular prolonged *sādhana* arrives at the *paṇḍitá* state or the equanimous state. This signifies that on arrival at the state; good or evil, birth or death hold no importance for him. Both are equal to him. He grows stoical and is the true erudite.

Pani — Lit. water. *Yóga* concept is ambrosia or *somdhārā* which exudes from *Sahasrâra*. This occurs only to an elevated *yogi* while he is engrossed in the *cakrá* or in transcendental state of *Kriyā*. He can taste the sweetness of this nectarine water in his palate for from here it drops to the tongue. This drink is incomparable to any drink in the world and a *yogi's* rapt state during this exudation transports him into the realm of heady ecstatic bliss. He drinks this nectarine water causing the blissful state, this is *santoshāmṛita pān*. Thus by drinking this, a *yogi* attains immortality.

Parambrahma — See *Brāhma*.

Parampad — See *Kriyār parābasthā*.

Prakṛiti — See *Purāṇá Púrusha*.

Parampúrusha — See *Púroshôttama*.

Prâṇákarma — See *Kriyāyoga*.

Prâṇá Krishna — See *Krishna*.

Praṇáva/Praṇáva Dhvani — See *Ómkāra*.

Patañjala — A sage, *rishi*. He set forth the *yóga* philosophy. His *yógasutras* or *yóga* scriptures detailing the different facts and intricacies of *yóga* are of immense importance for the study and practice of *yóga*.

Piṅgalá — The external flow of *Prâṇá*-air through the right nostril. This is the solar energy effecting the heat essence. It is also the *Rájas* attribute which denotes the dual force impelling man to remain in the vacillating state. This attribute promotes the endeavour to perform either type of action.

Piyās — Lit. thirst. Yogic interpretation is the spiritual thirst for salvation. Just as thirst is quenched when one drinks a glass of water; for this the person has to make an effort to obtain it, similarly attainment of salvation or *moksha* is not easy. By simply crying for it or repeating the word '*moksha*' salvation is impossible. Only through the yogic process of stilling the kineticism of the body and mind and ultimately losing all material attachment uniting with the Absolute Supreme Brahma, salvation is possible. Thus the endeavour for quenching spiritual thirst is imperative.

Prabhú — Lit. Master, Controller. Yogically it denotes the same. *Yóga* explains through science and rationality how a *yogi* can become master of himself. Austere ardent *yóga* endeavours result in the upliftment of the *yogi* who then attains mergence with the Supreme Being — becoming one he becomes master of his own self.

Prâṇá — The prevailing concept that *Prâṇá* is the life force, life giving force, breathing, breath, breath of life is a misconstrued one. Life-force connotes breath but breath is not *Prâṇá*. It is the external mainfestation of *Prâṇá*. *Prâṇá* is the kinetic state of the soul. He originates from *Brahma* or *Ātmâ*, the total creation has evolved from *Prâṇá*. He is the essential mainstay for the universe. Still *Prâṇá* is *Brahma* or *Ātmâ*, when this still *Prâṇá* attains vibration it metamorphoses into the dynamic *Prâṇá*. How this still-like *Prâṇá* or still *Prâṇá* becomes vibrated and again reverts to stillness has been explained by the sketch below:-

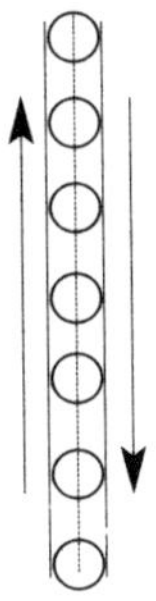

Sahasrâra (beyond essences)	100% static *Brahma*.
Ājñā or Kūṭastha (beyond essences)	0 (1,2,3,4,5 .... 9).
Viśuddha (space essence)	10 vibrated state x 10
Anāhata (air essence)	100 vibrated state x 10.
Maṇipūra (heat essence)	1000 vibrated state x 10.
Svâdhisṭhāna (water essence)	10,000 vibrated state x 10.
Mūlâdhāra (earth essence)	100,000 vibrated state.

Thus this sketch imports how 1% of still *Brahma* or still *Prâṇá* attaining dynamism the whole creation was created and a living being continued living in sound health till 100,000 vibrations persisted. When the body becomes indisposed, vibration decreases in accordance with the level of indisposition. At the time of death a living being reverts to 10 vibration but can never go beyond it. Therefore it signifies that death is reversion from *Prâṇá*'s 100,000 vibrations to 10 vibration and birth is gradual return from 10 dynamism to 100,000 dynamism. This is the span of birth-death. Therefore if a living being can supersede *Prâṇá's* 10 dynamism, he can merge with his place of origin, *Brahma* or still *Prâṇá*. The technique of causing dynamic *Prâṇá* cessation is *Kriyā-yoga*. It is the supreme spiritual science. No science has yet been invented in this world which can reach a living being's present dynamic state to zero dynamism.

Thus this purports that a living being deviating from his root, *Brahma* or still *Prâṇá* gradually retrogresses. To expatiate this a chronological arrangement of retrogression and progression is detailed. See *Bhagavān*. After reaching the abysmal depth of retrogression, progression is inevitable.

Hence the scriptures rightly testify.

"*Prâṇá* Himself is God (*Bhagavān*), He is *Víshṇu*, the Progenitor. *Prâṇá* is the Cosmic Bearer, the Omneity, Pervader."

Pranām/Prenām — Lit. obeisance either by touching the space between the eyebrows with folded hands or by lying prostrate and touching the feet. Yogic inference also is obeisance but not the gross one. Yogically the place between the eyebrows is *Kúṭastha* or the Third Eye where the *yogi* endeavours to constantly affix himself. This ardent endeavour to an exalted *yogi* results in the dynamic self paying obeisance to the still self spontaneouslly and effortlessly.

Prâṇá vāyú — The body comprises 49 airs of which 5 are vital and 5 subsdidary, each with different functions. *Prâṇá-vāyú* is the principal air of the 10 airs. It originates from dynamic *Prâṇá*. The remaining 48 airs evolve from *Prâṇá-vāyú*. It pervades the whole thoracic region upwards till the sensory faculties of eyes, ears, mouth, nose. All these sensory facilities are the play of the 49 airs within our body. *Prâṇá-vāyú* is the most dominant air because it is this air only which ceases the function of the body in the end and departs. The second vital air is *apâná* which is located in the region spanning the genitalia to the thorax. it's function is to regulate the excretory process by causing digested food particles to descend and create pressure on the bladder for micturition and colon for excretion of faeces. *Vyāna* air circulates throughout the body and a slight tilt in it's balance causes disease. *Udāna* air travels between the region of thorax and pharynx. If it attains imbalance then the vital organs of the body is affected with disease. *Samāná* air is located in the navel region and it's function is to maintain the body mass in position. The next 5 airs are subsidiary airs. *Nāga* air causes the action of belching; *Kūrma* air controls the function of batting of eyelids; *Kṛikara* air regulates the function of sneezing; *Devadatta* air produces yawn when the body is depleted with oxygen and *Dhanaṃjaya* air occasions the grave internal *Prâṇâyāma* sound.

Prâṇâyāma — Lit. the breathing exercise. The *Prâṇâyāma* in vogue now stipulates pressing of the nostrils and executing it. This *Prâṇâyāma* is external hence superficial because *Iḍā* and *Piṇgalá* are in motion. *Prâṇâyāma* in *yóga* is the technique by which the stilling of dynamism is effected. It is the fourth step of *yóga*. This is the internal action of *Prâṇá* and *Apâná* airs. It is only through this internal *Prâṇâyāma* that emancipation or salvation which is reversion to the original still state from which there is no return, can be attained. In the *Sanātána* (eternal) scriptures *Prâṇâyāma* has been stipulated to be *Mahādhárma* or supreme *Dhárma*. It can be only obtained from *yogi Gurú*. See *samādhi*.

Prasād — Lit. infers food which is initially offered to any deity and later distributed amongst devotees and others as the blessings showered by that deity. It also connotes *Gurúprasād.* i.e. the Divine grace or benediction of *Gurú*. Everyone aspires for this but in actuality the grace of the *Gurú* should never be asked for, because anyone acting in accordance with his instructions will duly be rewarded with it. When a *yogi* diligently practises *Kriyā* he derives *ātmaprasād* himself without the help of any extraneities and revels in it. By this soul's grace (*ātma-prasād*) he can realise the soul essence, hence attain external bliss. Therefore essentially speaking, *prasād* is that which generates spontaneously within a *yogi* and he being at peace with himself can engender eternal peace and love.

Pratyāhāra — Lit. withdrawal or retraction. It is the fifth step of eightfold *yóga*. Yogically it infers withdrawal of the mind from all sensory objects i.e. material detachment. When a *yogi* continues regular practice of prolonged *yóga*-action, there is a gradual stilling effect in him as then there is a declension of material proclivities in him. This new-found stillness deters him from all material attachment. The *yogi* now grows apathetical to all grossness. See *samādhi.*

Prem — Lit. love. Love can connote affection of mother towards child, child's craving for his mother love between or among friends, people, animals, plants etc. But all this love is gross love because it emanates from the mind, the principal sense. Yogic connotation of love is different. It infers soul-love. Barring *Kriyāyoga* this type of love cannot evolve. Continual ardent devoted practice of *Prâṇá*-action causes a development of attraction towards the Supreme Infinite Soul. The Infinite Soul is an incarnate of love, fountain-head of love, is imbued with love, effects a pervasion of love and symbolises boundlessness of love. The *yogi* comprehends this at an elevated stage of his *sādhana* practice and then the gradual development of attraction results in falling in love with the Supreme Being, for then he himself becomes pervaded with love and constantly communes with the Infinite Soul. The total universe grows to be a non-entity for him, the *yogi* methodically performs all gross actions but is constantly affixed and united with the Infinite Soul.

Pūraka — See *kumbhaka.*

Purāṇá Krishna — See Krishna.

Púrusha — See *Purāṇá Púrusha*.

Pūjā — Lit. worship. Yogically it denotes the worship of the Inherent-Intrinsic. A *yogi* does not observe any gross ritual or ceremony because he performs all of them within his body-temple. He believes in one God — the all pervasive *Prâṇá* Who is Master and Controller of the microcosm and macrocosm. *Prâṇásādhana* or *Kriyāyogasādhana* process or technique is the yogic ritual or ceremony through which purification of the body essence occurs, because regular *yóga* practice showers all the factors which promote goodness hence purification. Thus a *yogi* achieves the actual worship or *pūjā*. External worship is the symbol of this.

Purāṇá Púrusha — The Primordial Being. He is also referred to as *Ādi Púrusha* or *Ādideva* i.e. the origin and *Akshar Púrusha* or *akshar* — the Imperishable Being or the Indestructible Being. He is the source and Fountain Head of the macrocosm. The totality has evolved from Him and eventually will merge in Him and become *Purāṇá Púrusha*. Similarly *Ādi Purāná Kishuṇ* connotes the origin, Primordial *Kṛishṇa*. Man on being born attains dynamism but after traversing several millions of births he undergoes purification to receive *Kriyāyoga* from his *Gurú* and practise it, then at the most after three subsequent births his kineticism being stilled he can achieve mergence in the Primordial Being. *Púrusha* literally denotes the male individual but in actuality it is the Primordial Male Energy, the Master, Controller, the Supreme, the One. He exists from the beginning, therefore He is the root, the fundamental and *Prakṛiti* the Primordial Female Energy develops from Him, for the sole purpose to maintain the continuum of creation. Therefore He is the only *Púrusha* and the rest are generically the female species though classified as masculine and feminine genders. Constant and ardent practice of *Kriyāyogasādhana* entails the visualisation of *Aṅgusṭha Purāṇá Púrusha*. This is the thumbesque Being. When a *yogi* engrosses himself in *sādhana* he can visualise the diminutive form of his own self akin to the size of a thumb in his *Kūṭastha* Who is the Primordial Being. Hence, He is *Aṅgusṭha Pramāṇa Púrusha*.

Puróhita — Lit. priest. Yogic connotation is *pur*=body, *hita*=welfare. Therefore the one who executes welfare remaining within the body is *puróhita*. This *puróhita* is none else other than *Prâṇá*. This *Prâṇá* is omnipresent and univocal. This *Prâṇá* only is the master of all actions. *Yóga*-action denotes stilling of dynamic *Prâṇá* and reverting to the original still state. Good and evil evolve from dynamic *Prâṇá*. If a human takes recourse to dynamic *Prâṇá* then all evils will evanesce for him. Still *Prâṇá* has to be attained through dynamic *Prâṇá*. Therefore dynamic *Prâṇá* performs worship of still *Prâṇá* to attain mergence in Him. This is the welfare it executes for through this mergence only a human's life is fulfilled. It is now only that he attains salvation. Therefore dynamic *Prâṇá* is the priest or *puróhita*.

Púroshôttama — The Supreme Being. Exalted stage of *yógasādhana* entails envisionment of *Púroshôttama* or *Parampuúrusha*. He is self-nascent, eternal, amorphous, perpetually inhering within Himself. *Púroshôttama* visualization for a *yogi* is the bountiest reward for him as after this, attainment of mergence thereby salvation remains for him to be attained.

Rādhā — See *Krishna* and *Vṛindāvana*.

Rājāyoga — The term "*Rāja*" connotes the principal and *yóga*, the union, thus the principal technique by which union with the Absolute is attained is *Rājayoga*. *Rājayoga* and *Kriyāyoga* are the same. *Gītā* speaks of *Rājayoga* and *Patañjala Yógasūtra* of *Kriyāyoga*.

Rāma — Lit. incarnation of *Víshṇu*. *Rāma* was the eldest son of Dasarath, king of Ayodhya and Kaikeyi. The history of *Rāma* is narrated by sage *Vālmiki* in *Rāmāyaṇa* which is one of the oldest epic poems in Sanskrit. *Rāmāyaṇa* celebrates the life and exploits of *Rāma*. It speaks of *Rāma's* wife *Sītā*'s abduction by the tenheaded demon king *Rāvaṇa*. With the help of *Hanumān* and the monkey kingdom *Rāma* conquered *Rāvaṇa* and rescued *Sītā*.

The yogic interpretation of *Rāma* is as follows:-

a (अ) + a (अ) = *ā* (आ)

R + a = Ra hence *Rā*

(र Ra + अ) = hence रा (*Rā*)

Ra (र) in Sanskrit connotes carnal desire, vibration, heat etc.

a (अ) in Sanskrit infers the negative essence, in other words,

Rā (रा) denotes the state where carnal desires, vibration, heat are absent.

Ma (म) in Sanskrit infers *Brahmā*, *Víshṇu*, *Mahêśvara*, i.e. the self essence or *Īśvará* (God). Hence *Prâṇá* signifies the state where on arriving one can go beyond carnal desires, vibration, heat and attain the state of *Brahmā*, *Víshṇu*, *Mahêśvara* or *Īsvara* i.e. still *Prâṇá*. *Ayaṇa* (अयन) in Sanskrit implies the path of *sādhana*, shelter, support, haven or resting place. Thus *Rāmayaṇa* connotes *Rāma* plus *ayaṇa* = *Rāmayaṇa*. In other words, the *ātmasādhana* path through which progress being made the shelter of the still *Prâṇá* is achieved; where on arriving at the end of the long sojourn in the path of *ātmasādhana* a resting place is found and the true prop or succour is achieved; in other words attainment of soul-knowledge entails the state of going beyond the eternal birth-death cycle and attaining the state of salvation.

Rāmāyaṇa lit. infers chanting *Rāma's* name, but yogically *Rāma* is not a name, it is the *ātmâ* in other words *Rāmanām* infers chanting of *Ātmâ* or *Ātmâ* worship,which is the practice of *Kriyāyogasādhana* — such constant ardent practice entails the practitioner to envision *Rāmadvār* — i.e. the gate of *Rāma*, which is *Kūṭastha*. This is a much desired and important visualisation of a *yogi* for after envisioning *Kūṭastha*, a *yogi* gradually achieves mergence in *Kūṭastha* then he derives the essence of *Ātmârāma* (Soul-*Rāma*).

Rāmadvār — See *Rāma*.

Rāmanām — See *Rāma*.

Rāmāyaṇa — See *Rāma*.

Recaka — See *Kumbhaka*.

Ṛishi — Lit. the one who is the embodiment of knowledge, truth, austerity in *sādhana* practice and the one who gleans the spiritual essence through spiritual counsel. He is also author of the scriptures. Yogically it infers the *yogi* in whom the culmination of knowledge, truth, austerity in *sādhana* and gleaning of the spiritual essence is complete. Thus the *yogi* who has attained settlement in *Kūṭastha* is a *ṛishi*.

Rudrá — Lit. *Śivá*. *Rudrá* is the dynamic state of *Śivá*. This dynamic state maintains the total creation including the body. When a *yogi* practises austere *Kriyāyoga* he is able to stop his dynamism and this is the symbol of *Rudrá* or destruction. *Rudrá* causes dissolution of the universe. Dissolution denotes annihilation of dynamism and reversion to stillness. To a *yogi* dissolution is certainly not a terrifying factor for a *yogi's* main objective is to revert to his original still state. Actually destruction connotes annihilation of dynamism.

Rūpá — Lit. connotes form, beauty, etc. A *yogi* as he advances in his *sādhana* practice visualisation of several forms and of beauty occurs. One such visualisation of the advanced stage is *Svetrūpá* or *Svetvarṇa* — the white form or colour. White is not a colour. Therefore it is colourless hence neutral. Thus this refers to the visualisation of the Absolute Being. So when the Primordial Being appears before a *yogi* in the White Form, He is referred to as *Svetpúrusha* — White Being. A *yogi* is also blessed with the visualisation of *anantarūpá* — i.e. endless forms. In other words this implies the Form of the Omniform i.e. the Primordial Being once again. All forms are *aparūpá*. The gross interpretation of *aparūpá* is incomparably beautiful. This signifies that all forms are fundamentally amorphous (*nirākār*). This all pervasive amorophousness is the inherent beauty, without inherent beauty external beauty cannot exist.

Sadgurú — '*Sad*' infers truth, the soul; '*gurú*' the Master that is the one who leads from darkness (ignorance) to light (knowledge) i.e. the Master who is established in truth. He is also referred to as *Śrīgurú*—*Śrī* connotes beauty, glory, splendour, repleteness. Hence whose Inherent-Intrinsic is pervaded with Soul-Effulgence and replete with beauty, glory, splendour, truth; is the *Śrīgurú* or *Sadgurú*. (See *Gurú*).

Sādhaka — A religious seeker who practises *jápa*, chanting, worship, repetition of the *mántras*, pilgrimages etc.

Sādhana or Sādhanā — Lit. quest and practice of spiritual discipline. Yogically it is the practice through which soul-realisation is attained, mergence with the Absolute hence salvation effected.

Sahajákarmá — Lit. easy action. Yogically a living being obtains breathing motion at birth. This breathing is the external motion but it's converse internal motion exists in all living beings though they are unaware of this inherent motion of *Prâṇá* vibration. *Kriyāyoga* is based on the internal flow which spontaneously occurs within all human beings. One has to abide by this innate action (which inheres in all living beings since birth) to attain the still state. This innate action is *Sahajákarma* which can be obtained from a *yogi gurú*.

Sahajá Samādhi — See *samādhi*.

Sahasrâra Cakrá — See *cakrá*.

Sahasrâṇśu — See *Ātmasūrya*.

Śaiva — In accordance with the respective *yuga* discipline *Sanātána Dhárma* has been quintuply arranged namely *Śaiva, Śākta, Vaishṇava, Sāurya* and *Gáṇapatya* :-

Śaiva — Those who worship *Śivá, Mahādevá, Mahêśa, Mahêśvara* etc. the Primordial Male Energy which is the static still state of universal *Prâṇá*, are *Śaivas*.

Śākta — Those who worship *Śakti, Kālī, Durgā* etc; the Primordial Female Energy which is the kinetic state of universal *Prâṇá*, are *Śāktas*.

Vaishṇavá—Those who worship *Víshṇu*, the Primordial Male Energy, static state of universal *Prâṇá* are *Vaishṇavás* or *Vaishnavites*.

Saúrya — Those who worship the Soul-Sun, the first manifestation of the still void non-dual state of universal *Prâṇá* are *Saúryas*. In actuality, the worship of the gross sun is executed but it is temporary and not omnipresent. It evolves from the Soul-Sun.

Gáṇapatya —Those who worship *Gaṇeśa*, the state of universal *Prâṇá* who grants success, are *Gáṇapatyas*.

Śākta — See *Śaiva*.

Samādhi — Lit. eighth and final stage of eightfold *yóga* — *yáma, niyama, āsaná,* *prâṇâyāma, pratyāhāra, dhāraṇā, dhyāna, samādhi*. Yogically by practising austere *samādhi* one has to surmount each step and proceed, *samādhi* will arrive at the final stage. In the *samādhi* state there is a cessation of body-consciousness, mind and sensory faculties. It is now that the state of *sahajá samādhi* arrives. Advancing deeper *savikalpa samādhi* occurs. Then also soul-visualisation is existent. Delving further deeper in the recesses of *yóga*, a *yogi* arrives at *nirvikalpa samādhi* or *mahásamādhi* which is *Kriyā's* transcendental state. In this state the *yogi* merges with the Absolute. Common man opines that in the state of *mahásamādhi*, one does not return but this is an erroneous concept. Even after merging with the Absolute to effect human welfare a *yogi* does return but does not digress from this state.

Samāná — See *Prâṇá vāyú*.

Śāmbhavī Mudrā — Related to *Śambhú* or *Śivá*. Sometimes the posture of *Śivá* in *padmâsana* is noticed. His eyes are half-opened raised upwards fixed in intra-vision between the eyebrows. He is in the *khecari* state. A *yogi* practising *Kriyāyoga* assumes this posture and a co-ordination of the eye position, *khecari* and *padmâsana* is *śāmbhavī mudrā*.

Sāṃkhyayoga — Lit. a *yóga* philosophy propounded by *Kapila*. It is based on matter and soul which relates to numbers. This philosophy expounds the theory that matter is transitory whereas soul is permanent. Yogically a living being lives depending on the number of breaths inhaled and exhaled within 24 hours amounting to 21,600 times. This is the external flow of *Prâṇâ*-vibration. When a human being is in the vibratory state of *Prâṇâ*, he distinguishes between *Púrusha* and *Prakriti* — thus habits in the dual state. By practising austere *Kriyāyoga-sādhan*a when a *yogi* overcomes the external flow of breathing and engrosses within then he settles in the static state of *Prâṇâ*. This state of *Prâṇâ* is the original state of soul, then the attachment of the mind towards *Púrusha* and *Prakriti* is withdrawn, because he then realises that his existence depends on the numeral essence of the breathing motion, so he strives to go beyond it. Thus he proceeds through numbers and then supersedes it because now the mind which executed the counting has ceased, therefore who will execute the counting? He is now established in non-duality. This infers the practice of dethorning by a thorn itself. This is the concept of *sāṃkhyayoga*.

Saṃnyāsa — See *saṃnyāsin*.

Saṃnyāsin — Lit. one who has renounced the domestic existence and habits in *maṭhas, missions, āśramas* and monasteries sporting the saffron coloured garb, this gross renunciation is referred to as *saṃnyāsa*. *Saṃnyāsa* is the fourth stage of the fourfold life. In actuality renunciation of the domestic existence and assuming the saffron coloured garb does not infer *saṃnyāsa* or a *saṃnyāsin* because though he abandons his family existence, his daily needs of food, clothing, shelter, medicines etc. cannot be abandoned by him and these necessities are provided by the householders. Conversely householders are not dependent on *saṃnyāsins*. Yogically *saṃnyāsa* is the intrinsic complete renunciation for a *yogi* perpetually remains engrossed in the soul. A *yogi* is the actual *saṃnyāsin* as he is beyond the sensory faculties and material attachment. *Yogi* only is the one who performs all actions without being into it; he eats, sleeps, drinks, performs all other actions being non-attached to them as they occur in accordance with his habits. It is the withdrawn mind now which is centred on the soul in constant communion with the Absolute.

Thus this inherent-intrinsic renunciation is the true *saṃnyāsin* state irrespective of whether the renunciate maintains a domestic existence or whether he does not remain within the ambit of domestic existence. Moreover the superficial transformation of attire is irrelevant to the true *saṃnyāsin*. The present day concept of *saṃnyāsin* has suffered a retrogression from the scriptual precepts since last 1200 years approximately.

Saṃsāra — Lit. a wandering through; the endless cycle of deaths and rebirths to which life in the material world is bound. Yogically it connotes the dynamic state of *Prâṇá*-motion. Due to this a man continues to traverse the cycle of births and deaths. Till *Prâṇá*-vibration exists this cycle will continue. Thus a *yogi* endeavours to cease the *Prâṇá*-vibration and reach the still state of *Prâṇá*, the Absolute.

Sanātána — Eternal. *Sanātána Dhárma* is the eternally flowing religion which was never born nor will ever die. It has not been established by any particular person or created at any particular time. It is the *dhárma* of the universe inhering the total creation. It's base is *yóga*.

Sanātána Bhārata — See *Bhārata*.

Santoshāmṛita pān — See *pāni*.

Sarasvatī — Lit. goddess of wisdom, knowledge and speech. Wife of *Brahmā*. She holds a *viṇā* (heptachord) in her hands. Her mount is the swan. Her complextion is white. *Sarasvatī* is also a tributary of the holy Ganges. It's yogic connotation is that a *yogi* engaged in austere *yógasādhana* practice reaches the exalted state of wisdom or knowledge—both spiritual (soul-knowledge) and material. Speech indicates dynamism. Hence on attaining birth *Prâṇâ* enters into 1,00,000 vibrations. *Viṇā* symbolises the internal breathing motion. Hand or *pāṇi* symbolises action and for a *yogi*, *Kriyāyogasādhana* is the true action. She is also referred to as *Vināpāṇi*. Disposition of a swan is to sift milk from water. Thus a *yogi's* disposition should be akin to it for ardent *yóga* practice enables him to sift the spiritual essence from the gross murky material world. White connotes neutrality because it is devoid of any hue. Yogically it denotes the infinite void hence the Supreme Being. An ardent *yogi* who is constantly in communion with the Absolute (soul) ultimately merges himself in Him. Like *Sarasvatī* all gods and goddesses of Hindu mythology symbolise the different esoteric aspects of *yóga*.

Śāstrá — Lit. scripture. Yogically *śā*=breath, *astrá*=weapon, i.e internal *Prâṇâyāma*. Through this internal *Prâṇâyāma* the kineticism of the body and mind is annihilated. By practising this internal *Prâṇâyāma* austerely the *munis* and *ṛishis* have attained settlement of the still state and abiding in this state they were pervaded by soul-knowledge and composed the scriptures. Therefore the essence of the scriptures is latent with this soul-knowledge. Soul is eternal hence soul-knowledge scriptures are eternal.

Satyáyuga — See *yuga*.

Saúrya — See *Śaiva* and *Ātmasūrya*.

Savikalpa samādhi — See *samādhi*.

Sthir ghar — See *ghar*.

Sudarśaná cakrá — Lit. a circular weapon of *Víshṇu* or Krishna. By that weapon Krishna killed many evil characters. *Su*=beautiful, *darśaná*=appearance, in other words a beautiful appearance. When a *yogi* by practising austere *sādhana* settles in radiant *Kūṭastha*, he then envisions a disc. The extent of the power of the disc is co-related with the extent of his engrossment and then all the evil within him are annihilated. This is possible by the potentiality of the disc. Krishna is *Kūṭastha*.

Śūnyá — See *āsmān*.

Sūraj — See *Ātmasūrya*.

Sūrya — See *Ātmasūrya*.

Sushumná — This is the flow of *Prâṇá*-air between *Iḍā* and *Piṅgalá*. One should strive to remain in this flow for this path facilitates the progress to stillness hence spiritual orientation occurs. It is also termed to be the *sattva* attribute which infers virtuosity. One abiding in this attribute always thinks and acts good, is far removed from the turbulent dynamism of life and constantly endeavours to remain good by which the origin, still state can be achieved.

Svadhárma — *Svadhárma* is one's own inherent *dhárma* pervading the total creation. It pertains to the soul and since soul is omnipresent everyone has the right to know it. (See footnote pg 156).

Svádhishṭhāna — See *cakrá.*

Svetpúrusha — See *rūpá.*

Svetrūpá or Svetvarṇa — See *rūpá.*

Tántra — Lit. the estoteric spiritual discipline by which *Ṡakti*, *Kālī*, *Durgā* the Absolute Female Energy is worshipped. Through this *Kuṇḍalini* is awakened and the two principles of *Ṡivá* and *Ṡakti* united. Yogically that which nurtures the body is *tántra*. There are 49 airs within the body and this constant flow of airs within each nerve nurtures the body, so this air flow is *tántra.*

Trétāyuga — See *yuga.*

Triṡul — Lit. trident of *Ṡivá*. It is commonly observed that *sādhus* sport an iron trident. Yogically it is the symbol of *Iḍā*, *Piṅgalá* and *Sushumná*, the three flows of breathing motion or *sattva*, *rájas* and *támas*, the three attributes. These three flows unite in *Kūṭastha* which yogically is *Kāṡhi*, the Abode of *Ṡivá*. *Yogis* likewise causing a cessation of the three flows go beyond the three attributes and achieve settlement at *Kūṭastha*, in other words the *Kāṡhi* abode or Abode of *Ṡivá*. It is now that stillness akin to *Ṡivá* is attained.

Udāna — See *Prâṇá vāyú.*

Upavāsa — Lit. observing a fast. It is noticed that on religious occasions people fast to purify themselves. Yogically *upa* infers proximity, *vāsa* infers abode. A *yogi* by executing austere *Kriyāyogasādhana* ardently, ultimately settles in *Kūṭastha* abode. This is a holy region so a *yogi* automatically attains purification. He does not have to aspire for superficial purification. Hence habiting in proximity to the *Kūṭastha* abode or in *Kūṭastha* is termed as *upavāsa.*

Vaishṇavá — See *Ṡaiva.*

Vānaprastha — See *āṡramas.*

Vāyú — Lit. air. Yogically *Prâṇá* air. *Prâṇá* air is divided into 49 airs. These *Prâṇá* airs maintain the body. *Prâṇá* mainfesting in the body in the form of air and vibration maintains the body. The *yogi* ceasing this vibration of air merges with the Absolute stillness. If the kinetic air flow is disturbed for any reason disease occurs. If this kinetic air by the internal *yogic* process is stilled there is an absence of afflictions.

Veda — Lit. the four fundamental *Sanātaná Dhárma* (eternal religion) scriptures of divine origin. They are ageless and immortal. The four *Vedas* are *Ṛig Veda, Yajur Veda, Sama Veda* and *Atharva Veda*. Yogically it connotes soul-knowledge, *Brahma*-knowledge. Soul-knowledge originates from static state of *Prâṇá*. Therefore it transcends the birth-death cycle. Practice of *Kriyā* is chanting of the *Vedas*. The original *Vedas* (*Kriyā*) was one. Later *Vyāsadeva* split *Veda* (*Kriyā*) into four steps due to the degradation of the human intellect. At a much later date Yogiraj split *Kriyā* into six steps due to further degeneration of the human intellect. This splitting of cardinal instrinsic *Kriyā* into six steps acts as a precursor to the division of the *Vedas* into six parts at the appointed time.

Vedānta — Lit. end of *Vedas*. Yogically it infers the end of knowledge, soul-knowledge, *Brahma*-knowledge. A *yogi* practising austere *Kriyāyogasādhana* after mounting the various steps of *sādhana* one by one, ultimately attains the steps of knowledge, realisation, action. It is a state of complete cessation and is the state of non-duality because it is the state of mergence.

Vīṇā — See *Sarasvatī*.

Viṇāyak — See *Gaṇeśa*.

Vishādayoga — Lit. a melancholic or disillusioned state. It is the first chapter of *Gītā*. Yogically it connotes the onset of apathy and detachment in a man's life. In accordance with the gradual evolution in the life cycle of man, a period arrives when man realises he has experienced the joys and sorrows of the world enough, it is now that he spontaneously hankers to dissociate himself from these earthly attachments which are farcical and orient himself towards soul or God. Therefore this is the awakening of soul-consciousness.

Víshṇu — See *Jagannātha*.

Viśuddha Cakrá — See *cakrá*.

Vísvakarmā — Lit a deity. He is the artisan of the kingdom of deities. Generally the industrial people worship him as their principal deity because factories are production centres where all types of goods are designed for consumer and industrial use. *Vísva* infers the universe, *karma* infers action. Yogically kinetic *Prâṇá* pervades the universe and maintains it. Thus kinetic *Prâṇá* is designer of both the macrocosm and microcosm. Action evolves from kinetic *Prâṇá*. In still *Prâṇá* there is no action. Thus kinetic *Prâṇá* is *Vísvakarmā*. This kinetic *Prâṇá* is the designer of the universe because kinetic *Prâṇá* crafted this beautiful universe.

Víśvāsa — Lit. faith, belief. The present faith or belief originates from the kinetic mind. Yogic interpretation is that faith or belief is never possible sans *Kriyā* practice for then it becomes an emotional phenomenon. *Vi*=negation, *śvāsa*=breath i.e. negation of dynamism. Ardent *Kriyā* practice entails a *yogi* to attain stillness —i.e. taking recourse to dynamic *Prâṇá* he travels to still *Prâṇá*. It is now that his external breathing motion hence dynamism is extirpated. Only then will true faith or belief, dawn; this is devotion. Faith or belief acquired thus is never vacillating and is perpetually unflinching. This unflinching faith or belief results in non-transitory love for the Omnipresent *Prâṇá* or soul.

Vraja — See *Vṛindāvana*.

Vṛindāvana — Lit. a holy place near Mathura also referred to as *Vrajá*. It is famed as the holy place where *Bhagavān* Krishna executed His Divine Abstruse Causations with *Rādhā*, His principal consort and other consorts (*gopinis*). It is a place of pilgrimage. Thousands of devotees pay respect to this holy spot. Yogically it connotes the play between still *Prâṇá* (Krishna) and dynamic *Prâṇá* (*Rādhā*) within the body which is *Vṛindāvana*. (See Krishna). Dynamic *Prâṇá* is perpetually attracted to still *Prâṇá* and still *Prâṇá* brings dynamic *Prâṇá* into it's fold. Dynamic *Prâṇá* strives to attain stillness, so it hankers for still *Prâṇá*. In actuality a man is originally still but on being born attains 1,00,000 vibrations, but eventually he has to revert to his original stillness, merge with the Absolute and attain salvation. For achieving the still state, endeavours have to be made through dynamic *Prâṇá*. Therefore still *Prâṇá*krishna cavorting with His consorts (dynamic-*Prâṇá*), is a symbol of this.

Vyāna — See *Prâṇá vāyú*.

Vyāsadeva — See Krishna.

Yajñá — Lit. oblation through fire. A *yogi* undergoes the stilling process through austere *Kriyāyoga* practice and strives to revert to the original still state. To achieve this he has to proceed through the medium of dynamic *Prâṇá* to arrive at still *Prâṇá*. He executes this through the fire of the heat essence located at the navel (*Maṇipūra cakrá*). Thus this procedure is the oblation of the dynamic *Prâṇá* to the still *Prâṇá*. for when the *yogi* attains still *Prâṇá, dynamic Prâṇá* responsible for all vices has lost it's entity. This is the true oblation or *ātmayajñá*, soul-oblation.

Yáma — Lit. first step of eightfold *yóga* that is cultivation of self-restraint from sensory aspects; the second literal interpretation is death. Death is an inevitable phenomenon of creation, common man is appalled by it, but a *yogi* aspiring to merge with the Absolute, making diligent endeavours in *sādhana* reaches the state of death then he develops a state of fearlessness hence is in a position to embrace death at any given moment, for he only can go beyond the state of death. Common man fears to experience *yáma-yantraṇā* i.e. the pain experienced at the moment of death, but a *yogi* can supersede this by the yogic technique. See *samādhi*.

Yáma-yantraṇā — See *yáma*.

Yóga — Lit. union. Yogically it connotes the process by which dynamic *Prâṇá* reverts to still *Prâṇá*, in other words dynamic *Prâṇá* achieves union with the Absolute. Here it does not constitute the physical exercise—*yóga*. A practitioner of internal *yóga* is a *yogi*. The principles of spiritual *yóga* is expatiated in the *yóga* scriptures (*yógaśāstra*) authored by *munis*, *ṛishis* and *yogis*. A *yogi* is engaged in arduous diligent practice of *yóga* — this is *yóga* action (*yógakarma*) or *yóga* practice. A *yogi* who is perpetually engrossed in the principles of spiritual *yóga* is stated to be abiding by the *yóga*-religion (*yógadhárma*), which is not a gross religious practice but an inherent-intrinsic practice.

Yógadhárma — See *yóga*.

Yógakarma — See *yóga*.

Yógaśāstra — See *yóga*.

Yógeśvara — See Page N.B.

Yogiraj — See page N.B.

Yóni — See *liṅga*.

Yuga — Lit. age, era. There are four ages *Satyáyuga* (golden age), *Trétāyuga* (silver age), *Dvāpárayuga* (copper age) and *Káliyuga* (iron age). Yogically it connotes the four ages also within the human i.e. *Satyáyuga* infers remaining in *Kriyā's* trancendental state, *Trétāyuga* infers engrossment in *Kriyā*, *Dvāpárayuga* signifies the ecstasy derived due to *Kriyā* practice, *Kaliyuga* implies disinterest in and non-practice of *Kriyā*. This purports the gradual declension of *Kriyā*-orientation in accordance with the gradual change of eras.